Human–Computer Interaction Series

Editors-in-Chief

Desney Tan
Microsoft Research, Redmond, WA, USA

Jean Vanderdonckt
Louvain School of Management, Université catholique de Louvain,
Louvain-La-Neuve, Belgium

The Human—Computer Interaction Series, launched in 2004, publishes books that advance the science and technology of developing systems which are effective and satisfying for people in a wide variety of contexts. Titles focus on theoretical perspectives (such as formal approaches drawn from a variety of behavioural sciences), practical approaches (such as techniques for effectively integrating user needs in system development), and social issues (such as the determinants of utility, usability and acceptability).

HCI is a multidisciplinary field and focuses on the human aspects in the development of computer technology. As technology becomes increasingly more pervasive the need to take a human-centred approach in the design and development of computer-based systems becomes ever more important.

Titles published within the Human–Computer Interaction Series are included in Thomson Reuters' Book Citation Index, The DBLP Computer Science Bibliography and The HCI Bibliography.

More information about this series at http://www.springer.com/series/6033

Tilman Dingler · Evangelos Niforatos
Editors

Technology-Augmented Perception and Cognition

 Springer

Editors
Tilman Dingler
University of Melbourne
Melbourne, VIC, Australia

Evangelos Niforatos
Delft University of Technology
Delft, the Netherlands

ISSN 1571-5035   ISSN 2524-4477   (electronic)
Human–Computer Interaction Series
ISBN 978-3-030-30459-1   ISBN 978-3-030-30457-7   (eBook)
https://doi.org/10.1007/978-3-030-30457-7

Preface

This edited volume is the culmination of the WAHM series: the Workshops on Ubiquitous Technologies for Augmenting the Human Mind, which were held over the course of four years across multiple conference venues, including Ubicomp'14 in Seattle, Ubicomp'15 in Osaka, MobileHCI'15 in Copenhagen, Ubicomp'16 in Heidelberg, and Ubicomp'17 in Maui. Over these years, this workshop series brought together researchers, designers, and practitioners at the intersection of technology and psychology. Crucial to the founding of it was the EU project *RECALL* funded by the Future and Emerging Technologies (FET) programme within the 7th Framework Programme for Research of the European Commission, under FET grant number: 612933. In RECALL, four partner universities (University of Lancaster, University of Essex, Universitá della Svizzera italiana, and University of Stuttgart) set out to redefine the notion of memory augmentation through ubiquitous technologies. By combining technological interventions with basic research questions in memory psychology, this 3-year research project (November 2013–October 2016) focused on investigating and enhancing the way people use technology to remember and to externalize memory. Both editors of this volume completed their Ph.D. in this project, which now lives on in a global community of researchers working on Technology-Augmented Perception and Cognition.

Byron Bay, Australia   Tilman Dingler
Delft, the Netherlands   Evangelos Niforatos

Acknowledgements We stand on the shoulders of giants some of which have contributed to this volume.

Contents

From Toolmakers to Cyborgs 1
Tilman Dingler, Evangelos Niforatos, and Albrecht Schmidt

Cognitive Enhancements and Learning

The Effect of Neurofeedback Training in CAVE-VR for Enhancing Working Memory 11
Floriana Accoto, Athanasios Vourvopoulos, Afonso Gonçalves,
Teresa Bucho, Gina Caetano, Patrícia Figueiredo, Lucio De Paolis,
and Sergi Bermudez i Badia

Memory Augmentation Through Lifelogging: Opportunities and Challenges 47
Tilman Dingler, Passant El Agroudy, Rufat Rzayev, Lars Lischke,
Tonja Machulla, and Albrecht Schmidt

Technology-Mediated Memory Impairment 71
Sarah Clinch, Cathleen Cortis Mack, Geoff Ward, and Madeleine Steeds

Designing Task Resumption Cues for Interruptions in Mobile Learning Scenarios 125
Christina Schneegass and Fiona Draxler

Sensory Enhancements

Insertables: Beyond Cyborgs and Augmentation to Convenience and Amenity 185
Kayla J. Heffernan, Frank Vetere, and Shanton Chang

Augmented Senses: Evaluating Sensory Enhancement Applications 229
Francisco Kiss and Romina Poguntke

Reflections

Privacy and Security in Augmentation Technologies 257
Mohamed Khamis and Florian Alt

Summary and Outlook 281
Evangelos Niforatos and Tilman Dingler

Editors and Contributors

About the Editors

Tilman Dingler is a Lecturer in the School of Computing and Information Systems at the University of Melbourne. He studied Media Computer Science in Munich, Web Science in San Francisco, and received a Ph.D. in Computer Science from the University of Stuttgart, Germany, in 2016. Tilman is an Associate Editor for the PACM on Interactive, Mobile, Wearable and Ubiquitous Technologies (IMWUT) and serves as Associate Chair for CHI among others. He is the co-founder of the SIGCHI Melbourne Local Chapter. Tilman's research focuses on cognition-aware systems and technologies that support users' information processing capabilities. e-mail: tilman.dingler@unimelb.edu.au

Evangelos Niforatos is an Assistant Professor in Human-AI Interaction at the Faculty of Industrial Design Engineering (IDE), TU Delft, the Netherlands. He received a PhD in Informatics from Universitá della Svizzera italiana (USI), Switzerland in April 2018. He then joined North Inc. (now Google) in Canada as an HCI Research Scientist and Project Lead in the Advanced R&D department. At North Inc., he was part of the team that designed, developed, and successfully launched Focals, the first socially acceptable smart glasses that closely resemble a typical pair of glasses. As a postdoctoral researcher at NTNU in Norway, his research focused on designing and developing "neuroadaptive systems"—systems that augment human perception and cognition. Ultimately, he is interested in building technologies that extend the human capacities. e-mail: e.niforatos@tudelft.nl

Contributors

Floriana Accoto University of Salento, Lecce, Italy

Passant El Agroudy University of Stuttgart, Stuttgart, Germany

Florian Alt Bundeswehr University, Neubiberg, Germany

Sergi Bermudez i Badia Universidade da Madeira, Funchal, Portugal

Teresa Bucho Instituto Superior Técnico, Lisbon, Portugal

Gina Caetano Universidade de Lisboa, Lisbon, Portugal

Shanton Chang University of Melbourne, Melbourne, Australia

Sarah Clinch The University of Manchester, Manchester, UK

Cathleen Cortis Mack The University of Essex, Colchester, UK

Lucio De Paolis University of Salento, Lecce, Italy

Tilman Dingler University of Melbourne, Melbourne, Australia

Fiona Draxler LMU Munich, Munich, Germany

Patrícia Figueiredo Instituto Superior Técnico, Lisbon, Portugal

Afonso Gonçalves Universidade da Madeira, Funchal, Portugal

Kayla J. Heffernan University of Melbourne, Melbourne, Australia

Mohamed Khamis University of Glasgow, Glasgow, UK

Francisco Kiss University of Stuttgart, Stuttgart, Germany

Lars Lischke Vrije Universiteit Amsterdam, Amsterdam, Netherlands

Tonja Machulla University of Munich, Munich, Germany

Evangelos Niforatos Delft University of Technology, Delft, the Netherlands

Romina Poguntke University of Stuttgart, Stuttgart, Germany

Rufat Rzayev University of Regensburg, Regensburg, Germany

Albrecht Schmidt LMU Munich, Munich, Germany

Christina Schneegass LMU Munich, Munich, Germany

Madeleine Steeds The University of Manchester, Manchester, UK

Frank Vetere University of Melbourne, Melbourne, Australia

Athanasios Vourvopoulos Instituto Superior Técnico, Lisbon, Portugal

Geoff Ward The University of Essex, Colchester, UK

From Toolmakers to Cyborgs

Tilman Dingler, Evangelos Niforatos, and Albrecht Schmidt

Abstract Humans have an ingenious ability to shape the environment we live in. Twenty thousand years ago, this started with simple shelters and has now advanced to manipulation on a planetary scale. Human abilities are tightly linked to the tools and technologies we have at hand. Nearly nothing that surrounds us in a modern world can be created without sophisticated tools. The clothes we wear, the vehicles we use, the buildings we live and work in, and communication we rely on are only feasible due to tools and technologies humans have invented. Human evolution is inevitably linked to the tools we use. Our ability to survive and procreate goes together with technological advances. Early on, tools made survival easier and freed time for humans to advance their knowledge and create even better tools. Evolution and tool use are linked. Tools and technologies have long complemented and extended our physical abilities: from pre-historic spearheads to steam-propelled ploughs and high-tech prosthetics. We have come a long way. Human abilities have increased through technology; we can talk to people on the other side of the world, travel at the speed of sound, and lift loads that are many times our own weight. This past wave of innovation was mainly focused on our ability to act in and manipulate the **physical** world. With more recent technological advancements, however, the extension of our **perceptual** and **cognitive** qualities has increasingly taken shape.

T. Dingler (✉)
University of Melbourne, Melbourne, Australia
e-mail: tilman.dingler@unimelb.edu.au

E. Niforatos
Delft University of Technology, Delft, the Netherlands
e-mail: e.niforatos@tudelft.nl

A. Schmidt
LMU Munich, Munich, Germany
e-mail: albrecht.schmidt@um.ifi.lmu.de

© Springer Nature Switzerland AG 2021
T. Dingler and E. Niforatos (eds.), *Technology-Augmented Perception and Cognition*,
Human–Computer Interaction Series, https://doi.org/10.1007/978-3-030-30457-7_1

1 Introduction

Over thousands of years, humans have created tools to aid their cognitive and perceptual abilities. Writing-starting with cuneiform, one of the earliest systems of writing
used by Sumerians in ancient Mesopotamia-and book printing have provided humans
with a virtually unlimited and lasting memory. The development of optical lenses
granted humankind insights into the micro- and macrocosms extending our perception and literally changing how we see the world.

For a human only 10,000 years ago, the achievements of today, the increased
physical abilities and the augmented perception and cognition would appear truly
magical. It would seem that people achieved god-like powers. And as history has
shown these additional powers can be used to make the world a better place, but also
to bring massive destruction.

Digital technologies are the next step in empowering humans. Digital technologies
and their interlinking with the physical world change human abilities at an unprecedented scale. Sensors, actuators, networking, and processing—often summarized as
ubiquitous computing—is redefining what humans can do. In this book, we aim to
capture and share research that explores this massive change ahead. Much of the
vision is still at a conceptual or prototypical stage, but we believe they give a glance
into what will become feasible in the next 50 years. Enhancing our ability to capture
information, to store and share it, to retrieve (or remember) it, and to act on it, is at
the core of many ideas. We believe that the next 50 years will see a multitude of technologies that will increase, augment, and amplify our cognitive abilities, including
memory and perception to a level that seems still magical, God-like, at the present
day.

Besides technological advancements, the economic framework changes. Automation (from the industrial revolution onwards) massively changed the cost structure
in manufacturing. Replacing manual labour by machines and automation, that happened in agriculture and production, will in the next decade fundamentally change
white-collar work.

Information, software, and systems that build on artificial intelligence exhibit cost
structures that are entirely different from physical goods. There is a massive start-up
cost to create the initial version, but scaling it to millions or even billions can be done
at marginal cost. One implication of this is that only things that scale (globally) are
likely to work well economically.

Connecting the physical and the digital–the Internet of Things–ties the digital
and physical world closer together. We can create environments that support us and
respond to us. If such environments are well designed, we may not be consciously
aware of the help we are receiving. It will appear natural that there is always a chair
when we feel like sitting down, that there is always a coffee on the table, even before
thinking about it. Creating such an environment is technically challenging, but for
us, the question of what world this creates and who can decide about the features of
that world is even more challenging. Hence, we find it essential for us—and probably

for humankind—to not delay the discussion of what kind of future of an augmented world we want us to create.

Already with current technologies available, ranging from automated driving cars to global-scale social media, we see the massive impact they have on our lives and society. We also see that enhancements, augmentations, and amplifications will become a part of our body. Already now, pacemakers, artificial joints, prostheses, and exoskeletons are moving closer to our body and have become part of us. So far, they are mainly used to replace and enhance 'broken' body parts, but it is apparent that there is a drive to use them as an enhancement, even if the body parts are intact, but 'inferior'.

We are already cyborgs–both in a physical and cognitive sense. *"Technology as the external organs of the body"* (Marshall McLuhan). Technology can provide already now superhuman powers. In this volume, we have collected examples that reflect on the trajectory towards augmenting human abilities in various ways. It integrates current research efforts, results, and visions from the fields of computer science, neuroscience, and psychology. It gives a glimpse into the state-of-the-art and future applications of how technologies assist and augment human perception and cognition by using applications and explorations straight out of various research labs.

2   Cognitive Enhancements in Memory and Learning

Simulating our environment allows us to experiment with reality itself. VR is a powerful tool to control aspects of our environment that we would not be able to manipulate in the real world. Therefore, we can use it as a tool to study the specific circumstances in which people perceive, process, and make sense of the world. We can dream up and design any condition that may become ubiquitous in the future. What if we were aware of our own brain activities? Could this help us understand our productive states better? Could we induce flow—the sought state of stimulation and challenge in balance—when needed? This volume starts out with a chapter investigating these technologies. By combining EEG signals and VR outputs, can we become more self-aware of our bodies and minds? What if we knew about our brain activities at the moment? Accoto and colleagues take us on a journey of using visual and auditory stimuli in VR to give us a glimpse into our own brain's workings. Such new ways of personal insights allow us to associate mental states with brain activation patterns to purposefully steer ourselves into productive states of mind: flow states on demand. Vivid learning environments in VR may become the future of education as we can design our surroundings to optimally support and motivate learners, help them keep their concentration while alleviating boredom.

Leonardo Da Vinci is often quoted as one of the most universal geniuses of all times. With his studies in arts, he became immortal as a sculptor, painter, architect, and inventor. His contribution to science cover anatomy, meteorology, geology, botany, as well as philosophy. His curiosity and perennial hunger for knowledge make him the prodigy of the polymath envied across centuries. A versatile mind, along with a perfect memory, is a dream that has become ever more prevalent with our knowledge society. Lifelogging technologies, in their essence, help us document our lives by recording our activities and experiences to the point where a comprehensive lifelog complements and augments our innate memory. Not only does the vision of lifelogs encompass a searchable fundus of memories, but also the summary of our experiences. Digital recordings selected and summarized by algorithms create snippets of our lives that can help us strengthen those neural connections and improve our vivid memory. In Chap. 3, we dive into the use of lifelogs and the challenges of lifelogging technologies with respect to social norms and perceptual limitations. Dingler and colleagues built a series of prototypes that allowed them to investigate aspects, such as the positioning of on-body cameras, the implicit and explicit collection of lifelogging data, the effectiveness of lifelogging reviews, the automation of summary creation, and the effective navigation of multimedia lifelogs. This chapter highlights the potential of these technologies to augment human memory and discusses the obstacles of bringing memory prosthetics into the mainstream.

If we leave it up to algorithms, however, to strengthen certain aspects of our experiences, what happens with those that do not make it into said summaries? When we start filtering our memories, how much control do we have in selecting the filter itself? Photo collections, for example, are poor snapshots compared to the richness of the lived experience no matter how sophisticated the recording or all-encompassing the blend of modalities. Socrates himself insisted that with the adoption of writing, we risk the destruction of memory and the weakening of the mind. Lucky for us, his disciples disagreed and wrote down his words, which were passed down generations. But what are today's risks of our lives' recordings and reliance on technological gadgets to help our memory out?

Clinch and her colleagues go to the bottom of such risks by looking at the unintended consequences of our reliance on technology to be readily available and all-knowing. When was the last time you, dear reader, memorized a phone number of a friend or family member? Was there ever such a time? If so, we bet it was before the first smartphone made it into your pocket. What about your spatial memory and your first GPS navigation device? Does our reliance on technology increase or inhibit the capabilities of our memory?

Chapter 4 ventures into these questions by looking at technologies and their abilities to inhibit or distort our memory at three stages: the encoding of memories, their rehearsal, and retrieval. When we use memory prostheses, such as lifelogs, what happens to those memories that do not make it into our picture summaries? Those that are not actively strengthened through the process of rehearsal. Can memories be attenuated through selection and filters? Can technologies go as far as to implant false memories?

They certainly help us strengthening our memory when it comes to learning tasks. Especially mobile devices and the plethora of available apps allow us to fill gaps between our daily activities with short learning sessions, be they watching a course video on *Khanacademy*, solving a Math puzzle on *WolframAlpha* or rehearsing foreign language vocabulary using *Duolingo*. But with ubiquity and mobility come challenges to the undivided attention often required for complex learning tasks.

Mobile learners are inherently susceptible to interruptions, either from their surrounding environment (navigating on the sidewalk), from the device (in the form of incoming calls or notifications) or users themselves (through rising thoughts, feelings, and urges). In Chap. 5, Schneegass and Draxler investigate the nature of such interruptions and review strategies to guide users back to their task at hand. The resulting design space is an insightful guide for mobile app designers to augment mobile learning experiences with cognitive support and entice users to resume their learning where they left off.

This first part of the book is, therefore, all focused on memory and learning and the connection and interplay with technologies. Because cognitive performance plays such an important role in our knowledge society, the support and advancement of cognitive functions is a very active field of research and the subject of commercial endeavours. Gradually, we have seen an increasing variety of devices to capture and replay experiences, tools to support our memory and learning, as well as productivity tools that help us focus in a world of near-constant digital stimulation.

The second part of this book will look at how some of that stimulation itself has been changing. Technology inherently changes the way we look at the world: physically, through the invention of optical lenses, and perceptually through the information available at our fingertips. But while most incoming information is limited to one or more of our five sensory modalities, technology has the potential to enhance existing and even create new perceptual channels.

3 Sensory Enhancements

The idea of '*cyborgs*', who share organic and biomechatronic body parts, has inspired science fiction writers for centuries. In 1839, the poet Edgar Allan Poe published the short story "The Man that was used up" about a war veteran whom he described as made up of so many prostheses that he had to be assembled piece-by-piece. The fascination of partly human and partly machine inspires *transhumanists* to this day. With the goal of augmenting their bodies beyond '*human norms*' they seek to extend their senses, mental, and physical abilities. As prostheses become more sophisticated and equipped with technologies, such as predictive movement and haptic feedback, usage of bodily extensions is increasingly moving away from medical cases and hobbyists' explorations to early adopters, i.e., individuals who insert devices inside their bodies to enhance or gain new capabilities.

The second part of the book starts with a look at such people and their communities around their quest of becoming '*cybors*' of sort. Heffernan et al. explore motivations behind so-called *insertables* and their application beyond medical purposes. For some, these technologies are a mere convenience (e.g., opening doors using an implanted RFID chip) while for others they play such a central role that they become part of their identity. Magnets, chips, or LEDs are inserted for the purpose of artistic expression, presenting flashy gimmicks, and being at the forefront of blending with a world where technology dominates huge parts of daily life. No longer limited to 'cyber-punks' and 'transhumanists', such technology enthusiasts see an inherent benefit or convenience of living with technology inside their body. Some even report about the thrill of gaining new senses: by placing magnets inside their bodies they are able to literally feel electromagnetic fields.

For those for whom the idea of sliding microchips under the skin seems less appealing, there are other options for upgrading the senses. In Chap. 7, Kiss and Poguntke present a range of technologies aimed at giving users superhuman senses by piggybacking on existing modalities. What if we could feel the tingle of an imminent rain shower? Or listen in on specific conversations across a busy conference hall? What about a new sense of direction when the waters get murky, and star navigation during a swim is less of an option? This chapter dives into a review of the human sensing condition and explores the possibilities of augmenting the way we perceive the world around us. Making the invisible visible, the silent sound, and the abstract vibrate.

As technology weaves itself ever deeper into our lives, under our skin, influences our attention, and augments our senses, careful examination of its capabilities, risks, and benefits is warranted. Clinch et al. bring up the threats of human hacking, of viruses targeting the technical components we increasingly tend to rely on. The need for secure augmentations is becoming a crucial priority. If we digitize our senses and cognitive processes, what kind of privacy intrusions do we potentially expose ourselves to? In Chap. 8, Khamis and Alt present a privacy framework as a result of retrospection on the technologies discussed throughout this book. Privacy, security, and safety concerns need to guide designers' thinking throughout the entire design process rather than being added post-hoc. As we extend our bodily senses and capabilities by interfacing with technologies on an increasingly deeper level, security holes may compromise far more than locations and credit history. With new powers come new responsibilities.

This volume integrates current research and implications of technologies that augment human perception and cognition. Experts in the field explore how modern technologies both extend and disrupt the way we sense, learn and recall information in the emerging era of human cognitive augmentation. We hope this selection of cutting-edge research projects will inspire the reader, foster an understanding of and boost appetite for the exciting realm of human augmentations. We have come thus far as a species; now it's time to take the next step.

Tilman Dingler Tilman is a Lecturer in the School of Computing and Information Systems at the University of Melbourne. He studied Media Computer Science in Munich, Web Science in San Francisco, and received a Ph.D. in Computer Science from the University of Stuttgart, Germany, in 2016. Tilman is an Associate Editor for the PACM on Interactive, Mobile, Wearable, and Ubiquitous Technologies (IMWUT) and serves as Associate Chair for CHI among others. He is the co-founder of the SIGCHI Melbourne Local Chapter. Tilman's research focuses on cognition-aware systems and technologies that support users' information processing capabilities

Evangelos Niforatos is an Assistant Professor in Human-AI Interaction at the Faculty of Industrial Design Engineering (IDE), TU Delft, the Netherlands. He received a PhD in Informatics from Universitá della Svizzera italiana (USI), Switzerland in April 2018. He then joined North Inc. (now Google) in Canada as an HCI Research Scientist and Project Lead in the Advanced R&D department. At North Inc., he was part of the team that designed, developed, and successfully launched Focals, the first socially acceptable smart glasses that closely resemble a typical pair of glasses. As a postdoctoral researcher at NTNU in Norway, his research focused on designing and developing "neuroadaptive systems"—systems that augment human perception and cognition. Ultimately, he is interested in building technologies that extend the human capacities.

Albrecht Schmidt is a computer science professor at the Ludwig-Maximilians-Universität München in Germany. He studied in Ulm and Manchester and received a Ph.D. from the Lancaster University. In his research, he focuses on amplifying the human mind and he is excited about improving cognition and perception through information technology. In 2018, he was elected to the ACM CHI Academy. Besides his academic work, he co-founded ThingOS, where he is the Chief Scientist.

Cognitive Enhancements and Learning

The Effect of Neurofeedback Training in CAVE-VR for Enhancing Working Memory

Floriana Accoto, Athanasios Vourvopoulos, Afonso Gonçalves, Teresa Bucho, Gina Caetano, Patrícia Figueiredo, Lucio De Paolis, and Sergi Bermudez i Badia

Abstract In recent years, increasing evidence of the positive impact of Virtual Reality (VR) on neurofeedback training has emerged. The immersive properties of VR training scenarios have been shown to facilitate neurofeedback learning while leading to cognitive enhancements such as increased working memory performance. However, in the design of an immersive VR environment, there are several covariates that can influence the level of immersion. To date, the specific factors which contribute to the improvement of neurofeedback performance have not yet been clarified. This research aims to investigate the effects of vividness in a Cave automatic virtual environment (CAVE-VR) on neurofeedback training outcome, and to assess the effect on working memory performance. To achieve this, we recruited 21 participants, exposed to neurofeedback training inside a CAVE-VR environment. Participants were divided

F. Accoto (✉) · L. De Paolis
University of Salento, Lecce, Italy
e-mail: floriana.accoto@studenti.unisalento.it

L. De Paolis
e-mail: lucio.depaolis@unisalento.it

A. Vourvopoulos (✉) · T. Bucho · P. Figueiredo
Instituto Superior Técnico, Lisbon, Portugal
e-mail: athanasios.vourvopoulos@tecnico.ulisboa.pt

T. Bucho
e-mail: teresa.bucho@gmail.com

P. Figueiredo
e-mail: patricia.figueiredo@tecnico.ulisboa.pt

A. Gonçalves · S. B. Badia
Universidade da Madeira, Funchal, Portugal
e-mail: afonso.goncalves@m-iti.org

S. B. Badia
e-mail: sergi.bermudez.badia@gmail.com

G. Caetano
Universidade de Lisboa, Lisbon, Portugal
e-mail: caetanogina@gmail.com

11

into three experimental groups, each of which received feedback in a different neurofeedback training scenario with increasing level of vividness (i.e., low, medium,
high) while also assessing the effect of neurofeedback on working memory performance. Current findings show that highly vivid feedback in CAVE-VR results
in increased neurofeedback performance. In addition, highly vivid training scenarios had a positive effect on user's motivation, concentration, and reduced boredom.
Finally, current results corroborate the efficacy of the neurofeedback enhancement
protocol in CAVE-VR for improving working memory performance.

1 Introduction

Technology has undoubtedly impacted our cognition and the way our mental actions
like attention, problem-solving, and working memory is formed (Dingler et al. 2016).
One way of improving behavior and cognition is by controlling certain brain signals
in a closed feedback loop called neurofeedback (Enriquez-Geppert et al. 2013; Huster and Herrmann 2017; Zoefel et al. 2011). Neurofeedback is a form of biofeedback
that self-regulates brain activity, with the aim of improving mental states or processes (Gruzelier 2014). During neurofeedback training, the user receives real-time
feedback of one's own electrical brain activity acquired through electroencephalo-
graphic (EEG) signals. Specific components of the EEG signal (or EEG bands)
are extracted in real-time from the user and presented via visual or auditory feedback. This enables the user to consciously perceive their own brain activity, which
is otherwise impossible since there are no somatic receptors to register the electrical
brain activity as measured by the EEG. Consequently, the user forms associations
between specific mental states and desired brain activation patterns (Kober et al.
2017). It has been shown that voluntary modulation of specific EEG bands leads
to improvements in behavior and cognition (Gruzelier 2014). Moreover, studies of
working memory training have shown that specifically designed mental exercises
(i.e., cognitive training paradigms) could be used to enhance cognitive performance
(Morrison and Chein 2011). Working memory refers to the ability of the brain to
provide temporary storage and manipulation of information, necessary for cognitive
tasks such as language, learning, and reasoning (Baddeley 1992). Although neurofeedback has demonstrated benefits in many aspects, a critical issue in neurofeedback
studies is that not all subjects showed satisfactory learning ability to regulate electrical brain activity (Wan et al. 2014): about 15–30% of neurofeedback users cannot
attain control over their brain signals (Kober et al. 2017). There are different attempts
to explain this phenomenon (Kober et al. 2013), but the specific reason why some
people cannot control their own brain signals remains largely elusive. Nevertheless,
there are some prior studies providing evidence for psychological aspects influenc-
ing neurofeedback performance. For instance, motivation of the user turned out to
play an important role (Kleih et al. 2010). It should also be considered that to obtain
cognitive or behavioral improvements, a large number of repeated neurofeedback
training sessions are mandatory, and this can induce fatigue to the user. Furthermore,

neurofeedback practice requires users to stay focused and concentrated on the neurofeedback task over a long training period (Kober et al. 2016). In this context, the feedback design might play a crucial role. Traditional feedback modalities use auditory (e.g., a tone changes its volume or pitch in dependence on the brain activity level) and/or two-dimensional (2D) visual (e.g., simple bars or circles increase/decrease in size in dependence on the brain activity level) stimuli. Such relatively monotonous feedback methods might not attract users to focus on them (Yan et al. 2008), leading to decreased motivation, interest, concentration, and finally to a lower neurofeedback performance and success rate (Kleih et al. 2010). Hence, an increasing number of recent neurofeedback studies have utilized Virtual Reality (VR) in their feedback design (Kober et al. 2017). In spite of that, still little is known about the effectiveness of VR-based neurofeedback training and the effect it might have on working memory performance. To date, studies on this topic mainly focused on the effects of dimensionality (comparing traditional 2D vs. 3D VR-based feedback), and results suggest that neurofeedback training is more effective with immersive virtual environments when compared with traditional 2D feedback modalities (Kober et al. 2016). Moreover, concerning the effect of vividness on neurofeedback training performance, the literature suggests that the immersive properties of virtual environments are effective in cognitive training (Cho et al. 2002). To address current limitations. The objective of this study is twofold. First, to investigate the effect of vividness in VR in terms of neurofeedback performance and subjective user experience, and second, to assess the effect of upper-Alpha neurofeedback training on working memory performance. To achieve this, we designed three virtual environments, with different level of vividness in a CAVE-VR environment. Participants were divided into three groups and underwent five neurofeedback training sessions. Each group was exposed to feedback in a different virtual environment during the neurofeedback procedure. An upper-Alpha neurofeedback protocol was used, in which participants learned to increase their brain activity in the upper-Alpha frequency band voluntarily. Alpha band training is one of the most commonly used protocols since upper-Alpha has consistently been shown to be correlated with cognitive performance (Zoefel et al. 2011). Hence, to promote interpretability of neurofeedback study results, a similar protocol was selected.

2 Background

Here we give a brief background on brain electrical activity referred to as brain oscillations, using electroencephalography (EEG) and the way it is utilized in neurofeedback. Moreover, we present the importance of immersion and vividness in neurofeedback through the use of Virtual Reality (VR). Finally, we present the impact of neurofeedback training in working memory.

2.1 *EEG and Brain Waves*

The root of neurofeedback and the related field of electroencephalography can be traced back to Hans Berger, a German psychiatrist who recorded the first human electroencephalogram (EEG) in 1924 (Berger 1933). EEG is a noninvasive recording method to measure the electrical activity of the brain. The human brain contains billions of neurons that generate electrical impulses to communicate with one another (neural firing). By placing electrodes on the scalp, this electrical activity can be detected and recorded, and the resulting output is known as the electroencephalogram. More specifically, the EEG results from the synchronous firing of a specific type of neurons in the cortex, known as pyramidal neurons (Teplan 2002). This synchronous electrical activity is referred to as brain oscillations or brain waves. In general, a raw EEG recording is comprised of a collection of neural oscillations in several frequencies. After the raw brainwave signal is recorded in digital format, it can be transformed into brainwave data, by extracting information about the extent of specific frequency bands that are contributing to the overall power of a waveform. These patterns of electrical activity are split into different brain waves based on their frequencies, that represent how fast the waves oscillate, as measured by the number of waves per second or Hertz (Hz). With EEG, researchers had the opportunity of identifying the relationship between brain oscillations and different mental or behavioral states. Berger himself was the first to describe a predominant emerging rhythm of the human brain. This rhythm increased in power between 7.8 and 13 Hz when subjects had their eyes closed and decreased when subjects opened their eyes. He also verified how this phenomenon was reproduced in response to other sensory stimuli, which made him conclude that those waves should represent fundamental activity at the cortical level (Teplan 2002). In present days, these brain waves are referred to as "Alpha waves", also known as "Berger waves". Since then, the scientific community has found a wider variety of different brain waves associated with different subjective phenomena. Brain waves are traditionally classified into Delta (<4 Hz), Theta (4–8 Hz), Alpha (8–12 Hz), Beta (13–40 Hz), and Gamma (>40 Hz) (Ros et al. 2014). The designation of the range of Hz covered by these frequency bands is somewhat arbitrary and not always consistent in the literature. Moreover, these frequency components have subsets. For example, the sensorimotor rhythm (SMR) frequency band (13–15 Hz) is related to motor tasks (even during movement imagination) and entitled as low Beta (Marzbani et al. 2016). The Alpha rhythm is usually divided into two subsets: lower Alpha in the range of 8–10 Hz and upper-Alpha in the range of 10–12 Hz (Marzbani et al. 2016). It is important to note that all of the traditional frequency bands are always present across the scalp, but which is the most prevalent depends on the task being undertaken by the individual and the scalp location in question. In general, the more prevalent the higher frequency bands are, the more alert the individual is thought to be. So, Delta waves tend to dominate the EEG when the individual is asleep, Theta when the individual is drowsy, Alpha when the individual is relaxed but alert, Beta when the individual is alert and concentrating, and Gamma when the individual is trying to solve problems (Marzbani et al. 2016). However, this association between EEG rhythms and activation state is a convenient simplification, because each frequency band may reflect many diverse functional states of neural communication and may be generated through different processes (Gruzelier and Egner 2005).

2.2   Neurofeedback Training

Neurofeedback is part of a broader group of biofeedback applications, all of which have the goal of facilitating the self-regulation of physiological functions with the purpose of normalizing them in clinical populations or optimizing them in healthy subjects. Biofeedback is an operant conditioning procedure in which participants learn to gain self-control over physiological functions (e.g., muscle activity, respiration, heart rate) that usually are not consciously perceived or controlled (Heinrich et al. 2007). Operant conditioning is a method of learning that occurs through rewards and punishments for behavior. Through operant conditioning, an individual makes an association between a given behavior and a consequence: positive consequences increase the likelihood of the behavior, whereas negative consequences decrease it (Huster and Herrmann 2017). In the 1960's Joseph Kamiya, today considered the father of neurofeedback, was the first to verify whether operant conditioning methods could be used to induce direct changes in the EEG (Peper and Shaffer 2010). He conducted experiments in order to investigate if subjects had the ability to distinguish, in a subjective way, which kind of waves were being generated by their brain. In these first studies, subjects were asked to keep their eyes closed and periodically prompted to report whether they were producing dominant Alpha waves or not. Participants were also told whether they were responding correctly, and they exhibited an increased ability to associate the subjective experience with the presence of Alpha EEG oscillations. They also demonstrated their ability to produce Alpha oscillations on demand, effectively bringing EEG parameters under operant control. Joseph Kamiya was the first researcher to demonstrate the human's ability to control one's own Alpha waves. Since then, many studies have been conducted that confirm the effectiveness of neurofeedback in self-control of the brain activity (Hanslmayr et al. 2005; Heinrich et al. 2007; Zoefel et al. 2011). Researchers developed several protocols, which entail the upregulation or suppression of the amplitude of specific brain waves. This ability of consciously controlling brain activity through neurofeedback is of great importance and can be used in at least two ways: (1) as a therapeutic tool to normalize neurological patients' deviating brain activity, in order to influence symptoms; (2) as so-called peak-performance training to enhance cognitive performance in healthy participants (Huster and Herrmann 2017).

2.3 Neurofeedback Training Efficacy

Undoubtedly, controlling brain activity is an ability that can be learned. There is ample literature from the last fifty years providing evidence of the effectiveness of neurofeedback. However, individuals differ in their ability to learn how to regulate brain activity by neurofeedback. Little is known of how these individual differences arise and what enables one person to learn better or faster than the other. These differences may exist in internal and external factors. Learner internal characteristics that determine the success of neurofeedback training have become the focus of attention recently (Huster and Herrmann 2017). Learner specific aspects such as positive mood states (Subramaniam and Vinogradov 2013), motivation (Kleih and Kübler 2013; Kleih et al. 2010), focus of control (Witte et al. 2013), all turned out as being relevant for the prediction of individual learning success. Evidence also suggests that the morphology of brain areas generating EEG features used for neurofeedback training may be associated with training success (Halder et al. 2013). Variability in external factors can be found by comparing the design of training protocols between studies. To date, there is no consensus on the parameters that should lead to an effective neurofeedback protocol (Enriquez-Geppert et al. 2013). The duration of sessions applied in different studies can vary within a range of 30–60 min. The number of neurofeedback sessions can differ from 5 (Escolano et al. 2011; Zoefel et al. 2011) to more than 40 (Lofthouse et al. 2012). Spacing of sessions over time also differs, but most studies involve two or three sessions a week. Even training frequency bands vary in width and range among studies. Sometimes several frequencies are trained simultaneously, such as Alpha enhancement paired with Theta inhibition training, while other researchers argue that training a single frequency is more effective. Furthermore, researchers can employ a variety of forms of feedback, some using visual feedback such as dynamic shapes and others use auditory feedback or a combination of both. Late research on the impact of the type of feedback showed that auditory feedback may be as effective as the more commonly used visual feedback (Bucho et al. 2019).

All the aspects mentioned above may affect the efficacy of the training. There is increasing awareness that the effects of changing such parameters should be explored further, in order to define an effective neurofeedback protocol. In particular, researchers recently started to focus on the effects that feedback design can have on neurofeedback training. Traditional feedback modalities, often using two-dimensional objects, can be relatively monotonous and not encourage users to focus on them. Since mood, motivation, and interest are relevant aspects for successful neurofeedback learning, it is crucial that the feedback is engaging and attractive. For this reason, an increasing number of recent neurofeedback studies use Virtual Reality based feedback designs (Kober et al. 2017; Vourvopoulos and Bermúdez i Badia 2016), showing that VR is more effective than traditional modalities. We will describe the results of these studies in the next section.

2.4 Neurofeedback Training in Working Memory

As mentioned previously, the term working memory refers to the temporary storage and manipulation of the information necessary for complex cognitive tasks (Baddeley 1992). The definition of working memory evolved from the concept of short-term memory and it is often confused with it. The difference lies in the fact that working memory requires the simultaneous maintenance and manipulation of information, while short-term memory refers to the temporary storage of information only, without the attention component of working memory. Although they are conceptually different, the use of the terms short-term memory and working memory in literature is not always strict and there is evidence for a large or even complete overlap between the two constructs (Aben et al. 2012).

Different studies proved the hypothesis that neurofeedback training in the upper-Alpha sub-band (10–12 Hz) can lead to memory performance enhancement. Hanslmayr et al. (2005) showed that only those subjects who were able to increase their upper-Alpha power performed better on mental rotations after neurofeedback training, showing that training success (extent of neurofeedback training-induced increase in upper-Alpha power) was positively correlated with the improvement in cognitive performance (Hanslmayr et al. 2005). Similarly, the impact of upper-Alpha neurofeedback training on cognitive abilities was assessed by Zoefel et al. (2011). The expectation of an enhancement of cognitive performance was confirmed when their study participants in the neurofeedback training group obtained an increase in the upper-Alpha activity and the increase in performance of mental rotations (rotation of mental representations of objects) was significantly larger for the neurofeedback training group than for the control group. Since mental rotation is an ability that involves working memory (Prime and Jolicoeur 2009), these results suggest that upper-Alpha neurofeedback has a positive effect on working memory. The specific effect of upper-Alpha neurofeedback training on working memory was further investigated by Escolano et al. (2011). Their experiment consisted of five neurofeedback sessions, during which participants learned to increase their upper-Alpha amplitude as described in previous sections. Results show that participants in the neurofeedback group obtained an increase in the upper-Alpha activity, as well as a significant enhancement in memory performance compared to the control group. In 2012, Nan et al. (2015), proposed the use of Alpha neurofeedback to improve short-term memory performance. In this case, the neurofeedback protocol established the training of brain activity in the whole Alpha (not only upper-Alpha) band. Short-term memory was evaluated by a digit span test. The experimental results showed that the participants were able to learn to increase the amplitude in the Alpha band during 20 sessions of neurofeedback training and short-term memory performance was significantly enhanced by neurofeedback training. More importantly, further analysis revealed that the improvement of short-term memory was positively correlated with the increase of the amplitude only in the upper-Alpha sub-band. Hsueh et al. (2016) showed that subjects had a progressive significant increase in the Alpha amplitude following neurofeedback training, where the accuracies of both working and episodic memories were significantly improved in a large proportion of participants, particularly for those with remarkable Alpha amplitude increases. In this case, the neurofeedback training was not limited to the upper-Alpha sub-band, but on the whole Alpha band. Nonetheless, results are consistent with prior studies.

2.5 Immersion and Vividness in Virtual Reality

Virtual Reality (VR) is defined as "a medium composed of interactive computer simulations that sense the participant's position and actions and replace or augment the feedback to one or more senses, giving the feeling of being mentally immersed or present in the simulation (a virtual world)" (Sherman and Craig 2002). A concept frequently mentioned in VR is "immersion", which is defined as the perception of being physically present in a nonphysical world. This perception is created by means of images, sounds or other stimuli that surround the user, providing a very absorbing environment. A VR system is immersive when the simulated world is perceptually convincing, it looks authentic and real, and the user has the feeling of "being there" (Freina et al. 2015). For example, immersive VR has been utilized for therapeutic purposes, such as stroke rehabilitation (Vourvopoulos 2019b), investigating ethical decision-making by enacting moral dilemmas (Niforatos et al. 2020), remote learning and virtual tourism by "placing" one in a virtual classroom (Bailenson et al. 2008) or at a virtual location (Marchiori et al. 2017), respectively. Even if immersion seems to be a crucial element, VR can also be non-immersive when it "places the user in a 3D environment that can be directly manipulated, but it does so with a conventional graphics workstation using a monitor, a keyboard, and a mouse" (Robertson et al. 1993). Immersion is the measurable feature of VR technology that could make a user feel present in a virtual environment. Slater and Wilbur (1997) have laid out a series of definitions for immersion that will be used in this work. Immersion is what technology delivers from an objective measure and describes the extent to which users can feel part of the environment. The more a system conveys view that preserve fidelity in relation to their corresponding real-world sensory modalities, the more immersive it is. Finally, immersion requires that there is a match between the participant's proprioceptive feedback about body movements—the sense of the relative position of one's own body and movement—and the information vividly generated on the displays with the richness, information content, resolution, and quality of the displays. Vividness is related to the resolution, photo-realism, and visual fidelity of the virtual scenario (Slater and Wilbur 1997). We are particularly interested in studying vividness because of its heavy reliance on visual stimuli. Since virtual environments are mainly graphical interfaces, humans heavily rely on their visual sensory system to perceive their surroundings. Hence, modifications to the scene vividness should result in significant effects. For example, Slater and Wilbur (1997, use shadows as a way of vividness manipulation. It has been shown that the scenes where shadows and reflections are present are perceived as more realistic (Slater et al. 2009). Wang and Doube (2011) considered image roughness and shadow softness as perceivable characteristics of realism. It has been shown that images appear more realistic when the surfaces of their objects are perceived to be rough. Conversely, they appear less realistic when the surfaces of their objects appear smooth. Moreover, images in which objects project hard shadows under the illumination of strong, directional light are perceived as less "real" than images in which soft shadows are projected under normal diffused illumination. Further, Toczek (2016), used a texture resolution approach, populating high and Low vividness conditions with objects of varying pixel resolution. Finally, VR settings with increased vividness could help in forming better VR memories with increased performance in recall tasks (Marchiori et al. 2018).

2.6 Neurofeedback in Virtual Reality

Immersive VR is considered to be more effective concerning the acquisition of several abilities and has a positive impact on human performance, compared to non-VR approaches (Vourvopoulos and Bermúdez i Badia 2016; Zimmons and Panter 2003). VR can simulate aspects of everyday life, helping to transfer the learned skills to the real world. For this reason, neurofeedback researchers started to investigate the hypothesis that virtual reality feedback causes an improvement in neurofeedback learning performance in many applications, such as motor recovery and movement re-learning (Hubbard et al. 2017; Vourvopoulos and Bermúdez i Badia 2016). Berger et al. (2018) used neurofeedback to train subjects to increase their level of Alpha amplitude. After five neurofeedback training sessions, they found out that learning slopes were higher in participants who received feedback in the 3D virtual environment, while the training of the 2D group was unsuccessful. On the other hand, Kober et al. (Kober et al. 2016), compared 2D versus 3D feedback with no significant differences. However, regarding user experience, they found that motivation and challenges were higher in the 3D group. In another study by Gruzelier et al. (Gruzelier et al. 2010), the lighting level and the audience noise in the virtual environment changed according to the EEG activity. Two levels of immersion were examined. In one, the auditorium was rendered on a conventional computer screen. This was compared with a CAVE-like system, a more immersive medium, where the seated participant was surrounded by the same theater auditorium projected seamlessly on the surrounding walls. EEG analysis revealed that the presence enhancing properties of the more immersive CAVE-like system context had benefits: neurofeedback learning was facilitated (participants learned faster) in the CAVE rendition of the theatrical space versus the computer screen, even though the same auditorium was depicted. Prior studies make comparisons between different types of feedback on different plans, sometimes comparing the same VR content in different settings (e.g., screen vs. CAVE, or screen vs. head-mounted display), sometimes comparing VR contents with traditional non-VR feedback. Even if the VR modalities used in these studies are heterogeneous, in every comparison, the most immersive feedback resulted in more effective training. Specifically, being immersed in a virtual room was better than looking at 2D objects on a screen; visualizing virtual contents with a head-mounted display or in a CAVE was better than a computer screen. Overall, the immersive properties of VR bring advantages in neurofeedback training, either in facilitating neurofeedback learning or increasing motivation and interest.

3   Study

In this study, our target is to investigate the effects of vividness in VR on neurofeedback training outcome and to assess the effect on working memory performance. In order to achieve this, we designed a study by incorporating EEG data acquisition for real-time neurofeedback in a virtual environment delivered through a Cave Automatic Virtual Environment (CAVE).

3.1   Participants

Twenty-one participants (15 male and 6 female), ranging in age from 20 to 42 years old ($M = 28$, $SD = 5.2$), took part in the experiment. Participants were recruited based on their motivation to participate among students and staff at the Madeira Interactive Technologies Institute (M-ITI), Funchal, Portugal. Inclusion criteria for participation in the study included the following: (i) be over 18 years old; (ii) can understand English; (iii) and have no past of brain injuries and no neurological disorders. Finally, all participants signed an informed consent. Participants were quasi-randomly (by order of enrollment in the study) assigned to the three experimental groups. Each group consisted of 7 participants (5 male and 2 female).

3.2   Experimental Conditions

This experiment used three experimental groups based on levels of vividness in VR: Low, Medium, and High. Vividness is associated with the resolution and fidelity simulated within a particular modality. High vividness scenarios were designed to be the "most realistic" while the Low vividness scenarios were designed to be the "least realistic". These differences were made evident by changing the geometric complexity of the elements in the environment and using textures, shadows, and reflections (Table 1).

The virtual environments were developed using the Unity game engine (Unity Technologies, San Francisco, CA). We reproduced three versions of the same living room at different levels of vividness. In the Low vividness level, we used simple geometric shapes (i.e., cube, cylinder, sphere) to reproduce objects. Each additional vividness level was created incrementally from the previous one, by implementing

Table 1 Differences in the level of vividness

	Low vividness	Medium vividness	High vividness
Geometric complexity	Low geometric complexity	Higher geometric complexity	High geometric complexity
Textures	Smooth surfaces	Limited textures	High-resolution textures
Shadows/reflections	No shadows/reflections	No shadows/reflections	Soft shadows/reflections

new details, modifying textures and shadows, and using more elaborate 3D models (see Fig. 1).

3.3   VR CAVE

For delivering the VR feedback, a CAVE was used. The NeuroRehabLab CAVE has a configuration of three orthogonal walls and a floor (Fig. 2). It uses a Kinect v2 sensor for tracking, thus enabling motion parallax effects and body interaction through the KAVE plugin, developed for the integration of Unity applications with CAVE systems (Gonçalves and Bermúdez 2018). The feedback consisted of an object changing color. We chose this type of feedback because it is often used in literature for upper-Alpha neurofeedback training (Escolano et al. 2011; Hanslmayr et al. 2005; Zoefel et al. 2011). In the Low vividness environment, the object was a cylinder while in the other two environments it was the light from a lamp.

The color scheme ranged from a highly saturated red to a highly saturated blue. The color changed according to the upper-Alpha ratio. Red and blue values indicated the upper-Alpha ratio above or below the THRESHOLD value. Respectively; the full saturated red corresponded to an upper-Alpha ratio greater than or equal to the MAX value; the full saturated blue corresponded to an upper-Alpha ratio less than or equal to the MIN value; the closer the upper-Alpha ratio was to the THRESHOLD, the whiter the color became (Fig. 3).

3.4   EEG Acquisition

For EEG acquisition, the Enobio 8 (Neuroelectrics, Barcelona, Spain) system was used. Enobio, is a wearable, wireless EEG sensor with 8 EEG channels and a triaxial accelerometer, for the recording and visualization of 24-bit EEG data at 500 Hz. The spatial distribution of the electrodes followed the 10–20 system over the locations F3, F4, C3, Cz, C4, Pz, O1, O2 (as shown in Fig. 4). Enobio connects via Bluetooth to the Neuroelectrics Instrument Controller (NIC) software, for visualizing real-time EEG

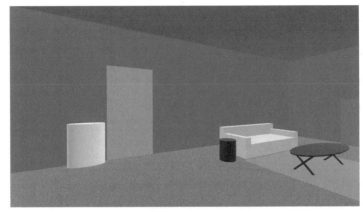

(a) Low vividness.

(b) Medium vividness.

(c) High vividness.

Fig. 1 VR feedback level of vividness. **a** Low vividness: Low geometric complexity, Smooth surfaces, No shadows/reflections; **b** Medium vividness: Higher geometric complexity, Limited object textures, No shadows/reflections; **c** High vividness: High geometric complexity, High-resolution textures, Soft shadows/reflections

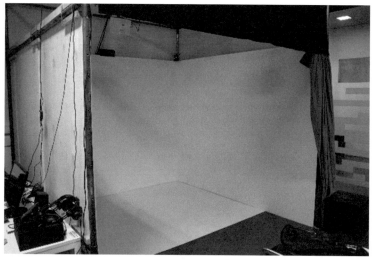
(a) NeuroRehabLab CAVE outline.

(b) participant using real-time NF to control the VR feedback.

Fig. 2 **a** NeuroRehabLab CAVE outline, **b** participant using real-time neurofeedback to control the VR feedback (lamp light) inside the CAVE

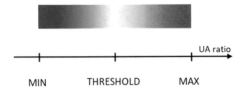

Fig. 3 Color scheme. The color changed from blue to red according to the upper-Alpha (UA) ratio. A highly saturated red corresponded to a high upper-Alpha relative amplitude. Participants' task was to make the color as red as possible, in order to increase their upper-Alpha relative amplitude

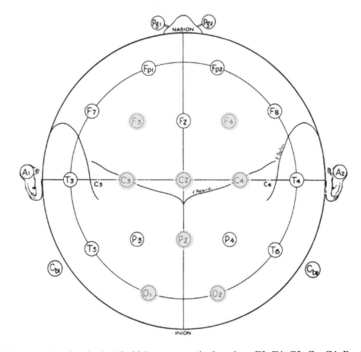

Fig. 4 Electrode location in the 10–20 layout over the locations F3, F4, C3, Cz, C4, Pz, O1, O2

while streaming the data via the Lab Streaming Layer (LSL) protocol[1] to a dedicated computer. LSL was used to send raw data to the OpenVibe platform (Renard et al. 2010) for real-time EEG processing before sending it to the application used for the VR feedback.

---

[1] https://github.com/sccn/labstreaminglayer/.

3.5 EEG Feedback Parameter

We adopted an upper-Alpha enhancement protocol, with the objective of increasing the amplitude of the brain activity in the upper-Alpha frequency band (10–12 Hz). The absolute EEG amplitude has large inter-individual differences owing to influences of many factors (such as anatomical and neurophysiological properties of the brain, cranial bone structure, and electrode signal quality) (Nan et al. 2015). Furthermore, additional confounding factors across sessions could result from changes in the time of day (Aeschbach et al. 2001; Vourvopoulos et al. 2017), mood or spontaneous cognitive activity (Laufs et al. 2003). Simple ratios between EEG band amplitudes are commonly used in neurofeedback protocols as relative measures are less sensitive to differences from these uncontrolled factors that modulate EEG amplitudes (Nan et al. 2015). Hence, in order to ensure comparability across participants and sessions, we used the upper-Alpha relative amplitude as a feedback parameter. The upper-Alpha relative amplitude was defined to the analyzed frequency band (upper-Alpha: 10–12 Hz) amplitude relative to the EEG band amplitude from 4 to 30 Hz (Nan et al. 2012; Wan et al. 2014). For brevity, we will refer to the upper-Alpha relative amplitude as an upper-Alpha ratio.

$$UA_{relative\,amplitude} = \frac{UA(10-12\text{Hz})_{amplitude}}{EEG(4-30\text{Hz})_{amplitude}} \tag{1}$$

3.6 Experimental Design

3.6.1 Protocol

Participants received neurofeedback training session on five consecutive days (except weekend days), from Day 1 to Day 5. On Day 1, before the start of the neurofeedback training, participants signed an informed consent form and provided some basic demographic information (i.e., age, gender). Then they performed three working memory tests (Pre-tests): the digit span test and N-back tests (in the 2-back and 3-back versions). After that, they started the neurofeedback training session. The same neurofeedback procedure was repeated from Day 1–5, and after every session, the participant filled out a set of questionnaires to assess some subjective user variables. On Day 5, after the end of the neurofeedback session, each participant completed an additional neurofeedback session (Transfer session) and repeated the same working memory tests performed on Day 1 (Post-tests). The transfer session consisted in the same neurofeedback training of the previous sessions, but with a different type of feedback (Fig. 5).

During the neurofeedback session, participants were placed in the CAVE, seated on a chair. The CAVE was in a dark and quiet room. The experimenter helped the participants to wear the EEG device and headphones for sound isolation. The preparation

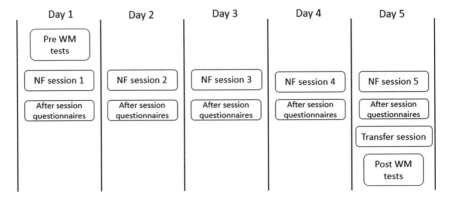

Fig. 5 Overview of the experimental procedure

of the recording equipment took from five to ten minutes, during which the quality of the recorded signals and the contacts between skin and electrodes were checked. Participants were instructed not to move their head during the neurofeedback session to avoid interference with the signal acquisition.

3.6.2 Procedure

Each session was composed of three blocks: a resting Baseline block and two neurofeedback Training blocks. The Baseline block consisted of a 5-min recording in a resting state where subjects were instructed to stay relaxed and look at the object in front of them. During the Baseline recording, they did not receive feedback about their brain activity (i.e., the color of the object was fixed to white, didn't change). Moreover, the Baseline stage before training was used as a familiarization stage to ensure each participant had enough time to explore in the virtual environment.

Next, two Training blocks followed Baseline, with each block lasting 5 min, with a 2 min break in-between (Fig. 6). During the Training blocks, participants tried to modulate their brain activity in the desired direction. They were instructed to make the color as red as possible. No other instruction or suggestion about strategies was given since effective mental strategies vary among individuals (Nan et al. 2012). Moreover, they were not allowed to keep their eyes closed, because Alpha activity naturally increases with eyes closed.

3.7 Subjective Measures

Besides assessing the effect of vividness on neurofeedback learning, we measured the effect it could have on a subjective measure of presence. First, we used the

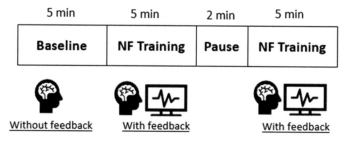

Fig. 6 Neurofeedback session structure

Slater-Usoh-Steed (SUS) questionnaire, that aims at measuring presence in immersive virtual environments (Slater et al. 1994). SUS questionnaire was composed of 5 questions, each on a 1–7 scale where the higher score indicates greater presence. The overall score was computed as the mean value from responses to the five questions.

In addition, we used a component of the Intrinsic Motivation Inventory (IMI) in order to measure the perceived competence. Participants answered 6 questions, rating on a scale from 1 to 7 how much they felt competent during the task. The overall score was the mean of the rating of each question.

Finally, we assessed the perceived workload for every session with the NASA Task Load Index (TLX) (Hart and Staveland 1988). NASA-TLX gives a subjective estimate of workload considering the six factors of Mental Demand, Temporal Demand, Physical Demand, Performance, Effort, and Frustration. Each factor is rated in a scale with 20 points (1 = very low, 20 = very high). The original version of the NASA-TLX requires a weighting process of the six sub-scales in order to obtain the overall score of the questionnaire. We used one of the most common modifications of the NASA-TLX, the Raw TLX, in which the overall task load index is obtained by averaging the rating of each subscale.

3.8 Working Memory Measures

Two commonly used tests for working memory assessment are the Digit Span test and the N-back test (Ma et al. 2017). For this, we used Presentation[2] (Neurobehavioral Systems Inc.), a software application for psychological and neurobehavioral experiments, to run a Digit Span test and two N-back tests, respectively, in the 2-back and 3-back versions (see Table 2).

---

[2]http://www.neurobs.com/.

Table 2 Working memory performance metrics

WM Test	Metric	Definition
Digit span	Forward DS	Length of the longest sequence participants can repeat back in the correct order on at least 50% of trials
	Backward DS	Length of the longest sequence participants can remember correctly in backward order on at least 50% of trials
2-back	Target accuracy (2-back)	Percentage of correctly identified Targets in the 2-back task
	Distractor accuracy (2-back)	Percentage of correctly identified Distractors in the 2-back task
3-back	Target accuracy (3-back)	Percentage of correctly identified Targets in the 3-back task
	Distractor accuracy (3-back)	Percentage of correctly identified Distractors in the 3-back task

3.8.1   Digit Span Test

The Digit Span (DS) is a test consisting of two tasks: a forward and a backward task. In the forward task, participants listen to a sequence of numbers and are required to recall back the sequence correctly. The length of the sequences increases every two trials (i.e., there are two trials of length 3, then two trials of length 4, and so on). The forward digit span is defined as the length of the longest sequence the participant can repeat back in correct order on at least one of the two trials. The test ends when the person fails to recall both the sequences of a given length correctly. The same holds for the backward task, except for the fact that the participants listen to the sequence of numbers and must recall it back in the reverse order. Thus, the backward digit span is the length of the longest sequence the participant can remember correctly in backward order. We considered both the measure forward DS and backward DS, although the backward DS is regarded to be more related to working memory, while the forward DS is to attention (Choi et al. 2014).

3.8.2   N-Back Task

In the N-back task, subjects are presented with a stream of stimuli one-by-one. In our case, participants visualized a sequence of letters (Fig. 7). The task is to decide for each item whether it matches the one presented N items before. An item that matches the one presented N steps before is called Target, otherwise, it is a Distractor. When a Target item was recognized, participants had to report it (by clicking the mouse button); while Distractor items should be ignored. We measured performance in the

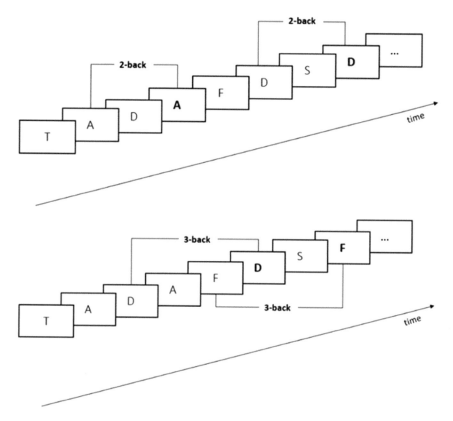

Fig. 7 Examples of 2-back and 3-back tasks. The highlighted letters are Target items, the remaining are Distractors

N-back test considering both the accuracy of the subject in identifying Target items and the accuracy in identifying Distractor items (i.e., the percentage of correctly identified Targets/Distractors).

We have tested two levels of difficulty: 2-back and 3-back (in which subjects must find a match with the item presented 2 and 3 steps before, respectively). Thus, we had four metrics of N-back performance:

1. Target accuracy in 2-back
2. Distractor accuracy in 2-back
3. Target accuracy in 3-back
4. Distractor accuracy in 3-back

3.9 Data Analysis

3.9.1 Average UA Relative Amplitude Compared to Baseline

To quantify the changes in the upper-Alpha ratio within a session, we subtracted the average upper-Alpha ratio during the resting baseline from the average upper-Alpha ratio during the training session. This means that any resulting positive value represents enhancement above baseline and any negative value represents falling below the baseline.

For every participant, we computed the average change of the upper-Alpha (UA) relative amplitude (L_1)

$$L_1 = \frac{\sum_{i=1}^{N_{sess}} (mean(UA_{ratio\,training_i}) - mean(UA_{ratio\,baseline_i}))}{N_{sess}} \tag{2}$$

where N_{sess} was the total number of NF sessions, i.e., 5 in our case.

3.9.2 Percentage of Time Above the Threshold

For every session, we considered the percentage of time during which the upper-Alpha ratio was above the threshold, where the threshold was the median value of the upper-Alpha ratio during the corresponding pre-training resting baseline. For every participant, we computed the average percentage of time above threshold (L_2)

$$L_2 = \frac{\sum_{i=1}^{N_{sess}} \%\,time\,above\,threshold_i}{N_{sess}} \tag{3}$$

In order to check how the two measures (upper-Alpha relative amplitude and percentage of time) changed across sessions, we defined the following across sessions learning indices L_3 and L_4, which presented the learning ability across the whole training process and indicated accumulative training effects.

3.9.3 Average UA Relative Amplitude Compared to Baseline

For every training session, we considered the upper-Alpha ratio (or UA ratio) increase from baseline. This means that we subtracted the average upper-Alpha ratio during the resting baseline from the average upper-Alpha ratio during the training session like we did when computing L_1

$$UA_{ratio\,increase_i} = mean(UA_{ratio\,training_i}) - mean(UA_{ratio\,baseline_i}) \tag{4}$$

Then, for every participant, we computed L_3 as the linear regression slope of that value over the 5 sessions.

3.9.4 Percentage of Time Above the Threshold

For every session, we considered the percentage of time during which the upper-Alpha ratio was above the threshold, where the threshold was the median value of the upper-Alpha ratio during the corresponding pre-training resting baseline. Then, for every participant, we computed L_4 as the linear regression slope of that value over the 5 sessions.

3.9.5 Neurofeedback Transfer

The transfer session served to assess if the ability to control the upper-Alpha rhythm, acquired during the neurofeedback training in a particular modality, could generalize to other types of feedback. In the ideal situation, a proper neurofeedback training should translate into good performance during the Transfer session.

Performance during the Transfer session was measured using the same metrics described before: the upper-Alpha relative amplitude compared to baseline, and the percentage of time the upper-Alpha ratio is above baseline.

4 Results

Here we present the impact of vividness of feedback in neurofeedback performance in terms of learning, presence, and how is upper-Alpha activity related to working memory.

4.1 Is Vividness of Feedback Affecting Neurofeedback Performance?

4.1.1 Vividness

By comparing the average upper-Alpha relative amplitude (L_1 index), we observe a tendency for participants in higher vividness groups to have a higher L_1 value (Fig. 8a).

Low vividness group has a median value below 0, meaning that participants did not manage to increase the upper-Alpha relative amplitude successfully. Medium vividness group and High vividness group have a positive median value, thus the partici-

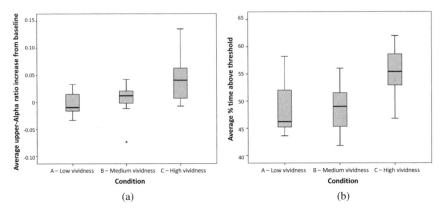

Fig. 8 Effect of vividness in neurofeedback performance. **a** Average upper-Alpha ratio increase from baseline, **b** average percentage of time above threshold

pants managed to modulate the upper-Alpha relative amplitude in the desired direction, with High vividness group performing better than Medium vividness group.

Participants in higher vividness groups tended to better modulate the upper-Alpha relative amplitude in the desired direction compared to lower vividness groups. However, a Kruskal-Wallis H test showed that there was not a statistically significant difference in the upper-Alpha ratio increase between the different groups, $H(2) = 4.839$, $p > 0.05$, although close to significance ($p = 0.089$).

The same tendency is also observed in the percentage of time above the threshold (L_2 index) for participants in higher vividness (Fig. 8b).

During a training session, participants in the High vividness group managed to modulate their upper-Alpha relative amplitude above the threshold level for a longer time than participants in the Medium vividness group. And the same holds for the Medium vividness group compared to Low vividness.

A Kruskal-Wallis H test showed that there was not a statistically significant difference in the percentage of time above the threshold between the different groups, $H(2) = 5.705$, $p > 0.05$.

Concerning the L_3 index–corresponding to the linear regression slope of the upper-Alpha ratio increase over the five training sessions–the median value is negative for all the groups, suggesting there was not an overall increase of upper-Alpha ratio across sessions. Finally, the Kruskal-Wallis test found no significant difference in the regression slope between groups, $H(2) = 2.494$, $p > 0.05$.

The L_4 index–corresponding to the linear regression slope of the percent time above threshold–has also a negative median value for all the groups, suggesting there was not an increase in the percentage of time above threshold across sessions. A Kruskal-Wallis test showed that there was not a statistically significant difference in the L_4 value between the different groups, $H(2) = 1.955$, $p > 0.05$.

4.1.2 Correlation Between Learning Indices

A correlation analysis between the four learning indices was performed, using the Spearman's rank correlation coefficient. We found a statistically significant positive relationship between L_1 and L_2 ($r = 0.93$, $p < 0.01$, $N = 21$) and between L_3 and L_4 ($r = 0.94$, $p < 0.01$, $N = 21$). L_1 and L_2 measure the change of upper-Alpha relative amplitude and percentage of time above threshold respectively, within a session. While L_3 and L_4 measure the change of upper-Alpha amplitude and percentage of time across sessions. Hence, the results indicate a strong correlation between the two metrics of upper-Alpha, the relative amplitude and percentage of time above threshold. Similarly, an increase in the upper-Alpha amplitude across sessions corresponds to an increase in the percentage of time across sessions. Moreover, a negative correlation between L_1 and L_3 was found, even though not statistically significant ($r = -0.38$, $p = 0.09$, $N = 21$). This relationship suggests that participants who performed better within a session, achieving a higher increase of upper-Alpha ratio with respect to the baseline level, tended to show a lower increase of upper-Alpha ratio across sessions. Conversely, participants who showed low upper-Alpha ratio increase within a session attained a high upper-Alpha ratio increase across sessions.

4.2 Neurofeedback Learning over Time

Concerning neurofeedback training performance, we analyzed the upper-Alpha relative amplitude increase during the transfer session from the baseline level and the percentage of time above the threshold.

4.2.1 Upper-Alpha Relative Amplitude Increase from Baseline

Figure 9a depicts the increase in the upper-Alpha relative amplitude during the transfer session per group. Only for Medium vividness, the median value is above 0, suggesting that during the transfer session participants successfully modulated the upper-Alpha ratio above the baseline level.

A Kruskal-Wallis test showed no statistically significant difference between groups, $H(2) = 0.475$, $p > 0.05$.

4.2.2 Percentage of Time Above Upper-Alpha Threshold

The graphical depiction (box plot) of the percentage of time the upper-Alpha ratio was above the baseline level during the transfer session per group, can be found in Fig. 9b.

Results are comparable between groups and a Kruskal-Wallis test showed no statistically significant difference, $H(2) = 0.282$, $p > 0.05$.

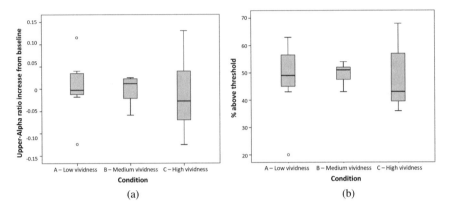

Fig. 9 Neurofeedback learning over time. **a** Upper-Alpha ratio increase from baseline during the neurofeedback Transfer session. **b** percentage of time above threshold during the neurofeedback transfer session

4.3 How Does Vividness Affect Presence?

In terms of presence, participants in the Low vividness group reported the lowest SUS score, but no statistically significant difference was found between groups, $H(2) = 4.954$, $p > 0.05$ (Fig. 10).

Regarding motivation, from current results, we can identify an increasing trend, with participants in higher vividness groups reporting to feel more motivated during neurofeedback training (Fig. 11a). However, a Kruskal-Wallis test showed no statistically significant difference between groups, $H(2) = 3.680$, $p > 0.05$.

Fig. 10 SUS questionnaire score between all three conditions

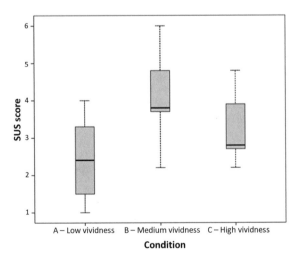

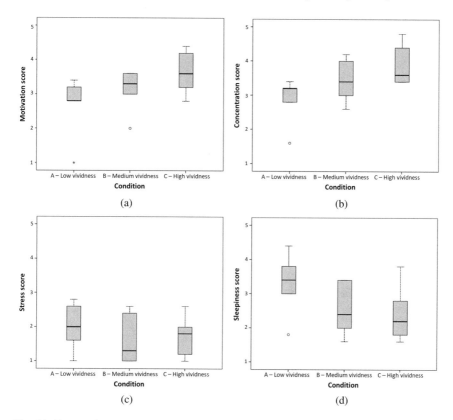

Fig. 11 Post-session survey results. **a** Motivation score per condition, **b** concentration score, **c** stress score, **d** sleepiness score

In terms of concentration, as for motivation, participants in higher vividness groups tended to feel more concentrated during neurofeedback training with respect to lower vividness groups (Fig. 11b), although a Kruskal-Wallis test showed no statistically significant difference between groups, $H(2) = 5.637, p > 0.05$.

Moreover, participants reported low-stress scores with no statistically significant difference found between groups, $H(2) = 1.085, p > 0.05$ (Fig. 11c).

For sleepiness, we observe a pattern between the groups with participants in Low vividness group feeling drowsier during neurofeedback training sessions (Fig. 11d). A Kruskal-Wallis test showed no statistically significant difference between groups, $H(2) = 2.397, p > 0.05$.

In terms of perceived competence, there is no major differences between groups, with no statistically significant difference between groups, $H(2) = 0.831, p > 0.05$ (Fig. 12).

Finally, in terms of perceived workload, as reported through NASA-TLX, we observe a tendency to increase in higher vividness compared to lower vividness

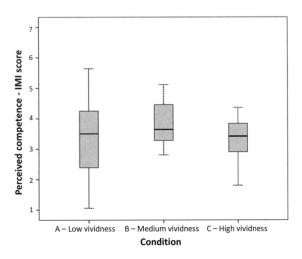

Fig. 12 IMI Perceived competence score

groups (Fig. 13). However, no statistically significant difference was found in the TLX score between groups, $H(2) = 2.753$, $p > 0.05$.

4.4 Is Upper-Alpha Activity Related to Working Memory?

The Digit Span test results showed that the forward Digit span slightly increased in the post-test, while the backward Digit span stayed at the same level (median increase equal to 0). Moreover, a Spearman's rank correlation between forward and backward Digit Span increase and the indices of neurofeedback learning showed no

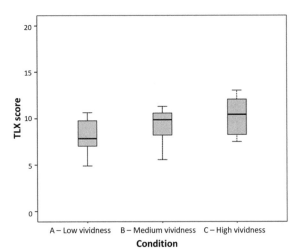

Fig. 13 TLX perceived workload score

statistically significant relationship (Fig. 14). In the N-back test, results showed that only the Target accuracy in the 2-back and the Distractor accuracy in the 3-back slightly increased from the pre to the post-test (Fig. 15).

A Spearman's rank correlation between the indices of neurofeedback learning and the performance measures in the N-back test revealed a statistically significant relationship between the Distractor accuracy increase in the 3-back test and the neurofeedback learning index L_3 ($r = 0.641$, $p < 0.01$) and the neurofeedback learning index L_4 ($r = 0.639$, $p < 0.01$) as well (Table 3). This relationship suggests that, when the upper-Alpha ratio or the percentage of time above threshold increased across the neurofeedback sessions, it corresponded to an enhancement in the Distractor accuracy in the 3-back test.

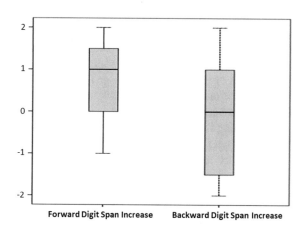

Fig. 14 Differences in Digit Span increase from pre to post-test

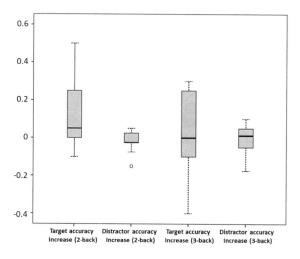

Fig. 15 2-back and 3-back test results

Table 3 Relationship between the indices of neurofeedback and performance measured

	Target accuracy increase (2-back)	Distractor accuracy increase (2-back)	Target accuracy increase (3-back)	Distractor accuracy increase (3-back)
L3—Slope UA ratio increase from baseline	−0.315	0.244	0.054	0.641*
L4—Slope % time above threshold	−0.374	0.111	0.027	0.639*

*Significant correlations ($p < 0.05$)

5 Discussion

In the present study, we manipulated the vividness level of the virtual environment used for providing neurofeedback training. Our aim was to assess the effect of different levels of vividness on presence levels during neurofeedback training as well as on the neurofeedback training outcome. Furthermore, we evaluated the effect of upper-Alpha neurofeedback training on working memory performance.

Concerning the effect of vividness on neurofeedback training performance, the literature suggests that the immersive properties of virtual environments facilitate neurofeedback learning. We hypothesized that a more vivid (thus more immersive) virtual environment would imply better neurofeedback performance. In terms of neurofeedback performance, we measured it using two metrics: the increase of upper-Alpha relative amplitude with respect to the baseline level and the percentage of time the participants spent above the baseline threshold. These two metrics were shown to be strongly positively correlated. From current results, it emerges that participants in higher vividness groups tended to perform better within a neurofeedback session, in terms of both performance metrics than participants in lower vividness groups. Specifically, participants in the High vividness group attained better neurofeedback performance within a training session compared to participants in Medium vividness; the same holds, in turn, for participants in the Medium vividness group, who showed an improved neurofeedback training performance compared to the Low vividness group. Statistical analysis showed that the difference between groups was only marginally significant, with a p-value slightly above 0.05. However, given the small sample size ($N = 7$ for each group), it is consistent with a positive effect of vividness on neurofeedback training, in accordance with our hypothesis. It is important to notice that participants in Low vividness group failed to attain control on their upper-Alpha relative amplitude, showing no increase in the upper-Alpha ratio with respect to the baseline level. We would have expected that every group was able to modulate the upper-Alpha ratio in the desired direction, with an advantage for the higher vividness groups. An explanation could be that the Low vividness virtual environment itself hampered participants in acquiring the upper-Alpha self-regulation skill—it was monotonous and boring—thus not engaging compared to the higher vividness virtual environments. This could have made participants tired and reduced their dedication to the neurofeedback task (Berger and Davelaar 2018). This seems to confirm the importance of vividness and the advantage of a highly vivid virtual environment.

While evidence of neurofeedback learning within a session was found, there was no improvement in neurofeedback performance across sessions (neither in upper-Alpha amplitude increase nor in time spent above threshold). This could be due to the length of the training period. Our training schedule consisted of five neurofeedback session, each composed of two 5-min training blocks, for a total of 50 min of neurofeedback training. Studies in which significant upper-Alpha learning across sessions was found used a neurofeedback procedure with longer sessions (25 min) (Escolano et al. 2011; Zoefel et al. 2011) and/or with a higher number of sessions (about 10) (Hsueh et al. 2016; Kober et al. 2016), resulting in at least double the neurofeedback training time than in our experiment. Furthermore, it has been shown that significant neurofeedback changes across sessions are usually found when comparing between the first and the later sessions, with no significant differences identified for the intermediate sessions. This suggests that, in the early stage of the neurofeedback training, changes across sessions cannot be detected. This is in agreement with our study, where a relatively short (50 min overall) neurofeedback training might be the reason why an enhancement of neurofeedback performance across sessions was not found. Furthermore, we noticed a negative relationship between the performance measure within a session (ability to up-regulate the upper-Alpha relative amplitude in a session) and across sessions (ability to enhance the upper-Alpha relative amplitude across sessions). This indicates that participants who showed a low increase of upper-Alpha ratio within a session tended to enhance neurofeedback performance across sessions. Finally, yet importantly, no significant difference was found in neurofeedback performance during the neurofeedback Transfer session between groups. The transfer session aimed to assess how the ability acquired during the neurofeedback training generalizes to another type of feedback. Since results were comparable between groups, we can argue that the vividness of the training scenario had no effect on neurofeedback transferability.

From self-reported measures, it is shown that the vividness of the virtual environment had no statistically significant effect on subjective presence response, as measured with the SUS questionnaire. Even though not significant, we could notice that presence levels tended to be higher for Medium and High vividness groups compared to Low. This is in-line with findings in the literature (Slater et al. 1994; Usoh et al. 2000), and seems to confirm that subjective presence response increases with higher levels of immersion. The fact that the greater difference was found between low and medium vividness levels, but not between medium and high, could be explained by the greater transitions of textures and geometric complexity. Specifically, in low-medium transition, there was a jump from no textures to limited object textures and from simple geometric shapes to complex 3D models; while the high level was created by increasing the textures resolution and the complexity of 3D models. It appears that the transition from nothing to something (e.g., no texture vs. some textures) had a more profound effect on the way users perceive the environments and subjectively represent their sensation of presence. No statistically significant effect of vividness was found on the variables motivation, concentration, stress, and sleepiness. However, there was a clear trend in both motivation and concentration tended to increase with greater levels of vividness. Participants in higher vividness groups reported to feel more motivated and focused on the task during neurofeedback training compared to participants in lower vividness groups. Furthermore, the results relative to the sleepiness variable showed that participants in the Low vividness group tended to feel drowsier during neurofeedback training compared to participants in Medium and High vividness group. The Low vivid training scenario made participants feel bored and lose interest in the neurofeedback training. As previously hypothesized, this could explain the fact that participants in group A did not achieve successful results in upper-Alpha modulation. The analysis of perceived competence and workload data showed no statistically significant difference between groups. The results of perceived competence were comparable between groups, suggesting that the vividness of the training scenario did not affect the sense of mastery in executing the neurofeedback task. Although non-significant, there was an increasing trend in workload results, showing that the perceived workload increased with a greater level of vividness.

Regarding working memory, there is evidence in the literature that upper-Alpha enhancement training has the effect of improving working memory performance (Escolano et al. 2011; Laufs et al. 2003; Zoefel et al. 2011). The hypothesis that an increase in upper-Alpha activity is correlated with increasing working memory performance seemed to be confirmed by the findings of this study. In fact, a statistically significant correlation was found between the improvement of performance in a 3-back test and the enhancement of neurofeedback performance across neurofeedback training sessions. Specifically, it has been shown that an increase in the upper-Alpha ratio or in the percentage of time above threshold across neurofeedback sessions corresponded to an increase in the Distractor accuracy in the 3-back test.

6   Conclusions

The objectives of this study included first, the investigation of the effect of vividness in VR in terms of neurofeedback performance and subjective user experience, and second, the effect of upper-Alpha neurofeedback training on working memory performance.

From current results, we have been able to identify that vividness of feedback is affecting neurofeedback performance, showing in all performance metrics in the Medium and High vividness groups performed better than Low vividness. Moreover, highly vivid training scenarios had a positive effect on user's motivation, concentration, and reduced boredom. Nonetheless, we did not observe any learning effects across sessions for any of the groups. Finally, our results show that upper-Alpha neurofeedback training is an effective procedure to improve working memory performance, showing a positive correlation of upper-Alpha with working memory performance. This is also in-line with the findings of prior studies, indicating that also vivid VR feedback could possibly affect working memory training outcome.

7 Limitations and Future Work

Current limitations include the relatively small sample size per experimental group and also the short period of training time (5 sessions) per participant. There is evidence in the literature that a longer neurofeedback practice may be necessary to detect long-term effects. Therefore, the number of sessions in this study might not have been enough to show significant effects of vividness on neurofeedback transferability and on the improvement of neurofeedback performance across sessions. For future study, a prolonged neurofeedback training is necessary including a follow-up assessment for detecting the long-term effects. Importantly, future research should consider investigating further immersive factors for effects on neurofeedback performance and subjective response measures. Besides vividness, other variables such as extensiveness, proprioceptive matching, and inclusiveness could be examined, holding the potential for significant effects on neurofeedback outcomes. Finally, as wearable sensors become more ubiquitous in human-computer interaction, we aim to investigate further how we can gather unobtrusively ecologically-valid data in a CAVE-VR environment through the use of a wearable-EEG prototype in the shape of commercial smart glasses (Vourvopoulos et al. 2019a).

References

Aben B, Stapert S, Blokland A (2012) Front Psychol 3. ISSN1664-1078. https://doi.org/10.3389/fpsyg.2012.00301. https://www.ncbi.nlm.nih.gov/pmc/articles/PMC3425965/

Aeschbach D, Postolache TT, Sher L, Matthews JR, Jackson MA, Wehr TA (2001) Neuroscience 102(3), 493–502. ISSN 0306-4522. https://doi.org/10.1016/S0306-4522(00)00518-2. http://www.sciencedirect.com/science/article/pii/S0306452200005182

Baddeley A (1992) Science 255(5044), 556–559. ISSN 0036-8075. 1095–9203. https://doi.org/10.1126/science.1736359. http://science.sciencemag.org/content/255/5044/556

Bailenson JN, Yee N, Blascovich J, Beall AC, Lundblad N, Jin M (2008) J Learn Sci 17(1):102–141

Berger AM, Davelaar EJ (2018) Neuroscience 378:189–197. ISSN 0306–4522. https://doi.org/10.1016/j.neuroscience.2017.06.007. http://www.sciencedirect.com/science/article/pii/S0306452217304050

Berger H (1933) p 555. ISSN 1433-8491 (Electronic) 0940-1334 (Linking). https://doi.org/10.1007/bf01814320

Bucho T, Caetano G, Vourvopoulos A, Accoto F, Esteves I, Badia SBU, Rosa A CD, Figueiredo P (2019) Comparison of visual and auditory modalities for upper-alpha EEG-neurofeedback. Berlin, Germany. ISBN 978-1-5386-1311-5

Cho B-H, Ku J, Jang DP, Kim S, Lee YH, Kim IY, Lee JH, Kim SI (2002) Cyberpsychol Behav 5(2), 129–137. ISSN 1094-9313. https://doi.org/10.1089/109493102753770516. https://www.liebertpub.com/doi/abs/10.1089/109493102753770516

Choi HJ, Lee DY, Seo EH, Jo MK, Sohn BK, Choe YM, Byun MS, Kim JW, Kim SG, Yoon JC, Jhoo JH, Kim KW, Woo JI (2014) Psychiatry Invest 11(1), 39–43. ISSN 1738–3684. https://doi. org/10.4306/pi.2014.11.1.39. https://www.ncbi.nlm.nih.gov/pmc/articles/PMC3942550/

Dingler T, Agroudy PE, Le HV, Schmidt A, Niforatos E, Bexheti A, Langheinrich M (2016) IEEE MultiMedia 23(2):4–11 (2016). ISSN 1070–986X. https://doi.org/10.1109/MMUL.2016.31

Enriquez-Geppert S, Huster RJ, Herrmann CS (2013) Int J Psychophysiol 88(1), 1–16. ISSN 0167-8760. https://doi.org/10.1016/j.ijpsycho.2013.02.001. http://www.sciencedirect.com/science/ article/pii/S0167876013000330

Enriquez-Geppert S, Huster RJ, Herrmann CS (2017) Front Hum Eurosci 11. ISSN 1662–5161. https://doi.org/10.3389/fnhum.2017.00051. https://www.frontiersin.org/articles/10.3389/ fnhum.2017.00051/full

Escolano C, Aguilar M, Minguez J (2011) EEG-based upper alpha neurofeedback training improves working memory performance. In: 2011 annual international conference of the IEEE engineering in medicine and biology society, pp 2327–2330. https://doi.org/10.1109/IEMBS.2011.6090651

Freina L, Canessa A (2015) Immersive vs Desktop virtual reality in game based learning

Gonçalves A, Bermúdez S (2018) In: Proceedings of the ACM on Human-Computer Interaction, vol 2 (EICS):10:1–10:15. ISSN 2573-0142. https://doi.org/10.1145/3229092. http://doi.acm.org/10. 1145/3229092

Gruzelier J, Egner T (2005) Child Adolesc Psychiatr Clin N Am 14(1):83–104

Gruzelier J, Inoue A, Smart R, Steed A, Steffert T (2010) Neurosci Lett 480(2), 112–116. ISSN 0304-3940. https://doi.org/10.1016/j.neulet.2010.06.019. http://www.sciencedirect.com/ science/article/pii/S0304394010007524

Gruzelier JH (2014) Neurosci Biobehav Rev 44:124–141. ISSN 0149-7634. https://doi. org/10.1016/j.neubiorev.2013.09.015.   http://www.sciencedirect.com/science/article/pii/ S0149763413002248

Halder S, Varkuti B, Bogdan M, Kübler A, Rosenstiel W, Sitaram R, Birbaumer N (2013) Front Hum Neurosci 7. ISSN 1662-5161. https://doi.org/10.3389/fnhum.2013.00105. https://www.ncbi.nlm. nih.gov/pmc/articles/PMC3613602/

Hanslmayr S, Sauseng P, Doppelmayr M, Schabus M, Klimesch W (2005) Appl Psychophysiol Biofeedback 30(1), 1–10. ISSN 1573-3270. https://doi.org/10.1007/s10484-005-2169-8

Hart SG, Staveland LE (1988) Development of NASA-TLX (Task Load Index):results of empiri-cal and theoretical research. In: Hancock PA, Meshkati N (eds) Advances in psychology, vol 52 of human mental workload. North-Holland, pp 139–183. https://doi.org/10.1016/S0166-4115(08)62386-9. http://www.sciencedirect.com/science/article/pii/S0166411508623869

Heinrich H, Gevensleben H, Strehl U (2007) J Child Psychol Psychiatry 48(1), 3–16. ISSN 1469-7610. https://doi.org/10.1111/j.1469-7610.2006.01665.x. https://onlinelibrary.wiley.com/ doi/abs/10.1111/j.1469-7610.2006.01665.x

Hsueh J-J, Chen T-S, Chen J-J, Shaw F-Z (2016) Hum Brain Mapp, 37 (7):2662–2675. ISSN 1097-0193. https://doi.org/10.1002/hbm.23201

Hubbard R, Sipolins A, Zhou L (2017) Enhancing learning through virtual reality and neurofeed-back: a first step. In: Proceedings of the seventh international learning analytics & knowledge conference, LAK'17, New York, NY, USA. ACM, pp 398–403. ISBN 978-1-4503-4870-6. https:// doi.org/10.1145/3027385.3027390. http://doi.acm.org/10.1145/3027385.3027390

Kleih SC, Kübler A (2013) Front Hum Neurosci 7. ISSN 1662-5161. https://doi.org/10.3389/fnhum. 2013.00642. https://www.ncbi.nlm.nih.gov/pmc/articles/PMC3797970/

Kleih SC, Nijboer F, Halder S, Kübler A (2010) Clin Neurophysiol 121(7), 1023–1031. ISSN 1388-2457. https://doi.org/10.1016/j.clinph.2010.01.034. http://www.sciencedirect.com/ science/article/pii/S1388245710000775

Kober SE, Witte M, Ninaus M, Neuper C, Wood G (2013) Front Hum Neurosci 7. ISSN 1662-5161. https://doi.org/10.3389/fnhum.2013.00695. https://www.ncbi.nlm.nih.gov/pmc/articles/ PMC3798979/

Kober SE, Reichert JL, Schweiger D, Neuper C, Wood G (2016) Effects of a 3d virtual reality neurofeedback scenario on user experience and performance in stroke patients. In: Bottino R,

Jeuring J, Veltkamp RC (eds) Games and learning alliance, lecture notes in computer science. Springer International Publishing, pp 83–94. ISBN 978-3-319-50182-6

Kober SE, Reichert JL, Schweiger D, Neuper C, Wood G (2017). Does feedback design matter? a neurofeedback study comparing immersive virtual reality and traditional training screens in elderly. Int J Serious Game 4(3). https://doi.org/10.17083/ijsg.v4i3.167

Laufs H, Krakow K, Sterzer P, Eger E, Beyerle A, Salek-Haddadi A, Kleinschmidt A (2003) Proc Natl Acad Sci USA 100(19), 11053–11058. ISSN 0027-8424. https://doi.org/10.1073/pnas.1831638100. https://www.ncbi.nlm.nih.gov/pmc/articles/PMC196925/

Lofthouse N, Arnold LE, Hersch S, Hurt E, DeBeus R (2012) J Atten Disord 16(5), 351–372. ISSN 1087-0547. https://doi.org/10.1177/1087054711427530. https://doi.org/10.1177/1087054711427530

Ma L, Chang L, Chen X, Zhou R (2017) PLOS ONE 12(3):e0175047. ISSN 1932-6203. https://doi.org/10.1371/journal.pone.0175047. https://journals.plos.org/plosone/article?id=10.1371/journal.pone.0175047

Marchiori E, Niforatos E, Preto L (2017) Measuring the media effects of a tourism-related virtual reality experience using biophysical data. Information and Communication Technologies in Tourism 2017. Springer, Berlin, pp 203–215

Marchiori E, Niforatos E, Preto L (2018) Inf Technol Tour 18(1–4):133–155

Marzbani H, Marateb HR, Mansourian M (2016) Basic Clin Neurosci 7(2):143–158. ISSN 2008-126X. https://doi.org/10.15412/J.BCN.03070208. https://www.ncbi.nlm.nih.gov/pmc/articles/PMC4892319/

Morrison AB, Chein JM (2011) Psychon Bull Rev 18(1), 46–60. ISSN 1531-5320. https://doi.org/10.3758/s13423-010-0034-0. https://doi.org/10.3758/s13423-010-0034-0

Nan W, Rodrigues JP, Ma J, Qu X, Wan F, Mak P-I, Mak PU, Vai MI, Rosa A (2012) Int J Psychophysiol 86(1), 83–87. ISSN 0167-8760. https://doi.org/10.1016/j.ijpsycho.2012.07.182. http://www.sciencedirect.com/science/article/pii/S0167876012005478

Nan W, Wan F, Vai MI, Da Rosa AC (2015) Front Hum Neurosci 9. ISSN 1662-5161. https://doi.org/10.3389/fnhum.2015.00677. https://www.ncbi.nlm.nih.gov/pmc/articles/PMC4685657/

Niforatos E, Palma A, Gluszny R, Vourvopoulos A, Liarokapis F (2020) Would you do it?: enacting moral dilemmas in virtual reality for understanding ethical decision-making. In: Proceedings of the 2020 CHI conference on human factors in computing systems, pp 1–12

Peper E, Shaffer F (2010) Biofeedback 38(4):142–147

Prime DJ, Jolicoeur P (2009) J Cogn Neurosci 22(11):2437–2446. ISSN 0898-929X. https://doi.org/10.1162/jocn.2009.21337. https://www.mitpressjournals.org/doi/10.1162/jocn.2009.21337

Renard Y, Lotte F, Gibert G, Congedo M, Maby E, Delannoy V, Bertrand O, Lécuyer A (2010) Presence Teleoperators Virtual Environ 19(1):3553. ISSN 1054-7460. https://doi.org/10.1162/pres.19.1.35

Robertson GG, Card SK, Mackinlay JD (1993) Computer 26(2):81. ISSN 0018-9162. https://doi.org/10.1109/2.192002

Ros T, Baars BJ, Lanius RA, Vuilleumier P (2014) Front Hum Eurosci 8. ISSN 1662-5161. https://doi.org/10.3389/fnhum.2014.01008. https://www.ncbi.nlm.nih.gov/pmc/articles/PMC4270171/

Sherman WR, Craig AB (2002) Understanding virtual reality: interface, application, and design. Morgan Kaufmann Publishers Inc., San Francisco, CA, USA. ISBN 978-1-55860-353-0

Slater M, Wilbur S (1997) Presence Teleoperators Virt Environ 6(6), 603–616. ISSN 1054-7460. https://doi.org/10.1162/pres.1997.6.6.603. https://doi.org/10.1162/pres.1997.6.6.603

Slater M, Usoh M, Steed A (1994) Presence Teleoperators Virt Environ 3(2), 130–144. ISSN 1054-7460. https://doi.org/10.1162/pres.1994.3.2.130. https://doi.org/10.1162/pres.1994.3.2.130

Slater M, Khanna P, Mortensen J, Yu I (2009) IEEE Comput Graph Appl 29(3):0272–1716. ISSN 76-84

Subramaniam K, Vinogradov S (2013) Front Hum Neurosci 7. ISSN 1662-5161. https://doi.org/10.3389/fnhum.2013.00452. https://www.frontiersin.org/articles/10.3389/fnhum.2013.00452/full

Teplan M (2002) Meas Sci Rev 2(2):1–11

Toczek YG (2016) The influence of visual realism on the sense of presence in virtual environments. Thesis, 29 Sep 2016. https://research.tue.nl/en/studentTheses/the-influence-of-visual-realism-on-the-sense-of-presence-in-virtu

Usoh M, Catena E, Arman S, Slater M (2000) Presence Teleoperators Virt Environ 9(5), 497–503. ISSN 1054-7460. https://doi.org/10.1162/105474600566989. https://www.mitpressjournals.org/doi/10.1162/105474600566989

Vourvopoulos A, Bermúdez i Badia S (2016) J NeuroEng Rehabil 13(1):69. ISSN 1743-0003. https://doi.org/10.1186/s12984-016-0173-2

Vourvopoulos A, Niforatos E, Hlinka M, Škola F, Liarokapis F (2017) Investigating the effect of user profile during training for BCI-based games. In: 2017 9th international conference on virtual worlds and games for serious applications (VS-Games), pp 117–124. https://doi.org/10.1109/VS-GAMES.2017.8056579

Vourvopoulos A, Niforatos E, Giannakos M (2019a) Eeglass: an eeg-eyeware prototype for ubiquitous brain-computer interaction. In: Adjunct proceedings of the 2019 ACM international joint conference on pervasive and ubiquitous computing and proceedings of the 2019 ACM international symposium on wearable computers, pp 647–652

Vourvopoulos AT, Jorge C, Abreu R, Figueiredo P, Fernandes J-C, Bermúdez i Badia S (2019b) Front Hum Neurosci 13:244

Wan F, Nan W, Vai MI, Rosa A (2014) Front Hum Neurosci 8. ISSN 1662-5161. https://doi.org/10.3389/fnhum.2014.00500. https://www.frontiersin.org/articles/10.3389/fnhum.2014.00500/full

Wang N, Doube W (2011) How real is really? a perceptually motivated system for quantifying visual realism in digital images. In: 2011 international conference on multimedia and signal processing, vol 2, pp 141–149. https://doi.org/10.1109/CMSP.2011.172

Witte M, Kober SE, Ninaus M, Neuper C, Wood G (2013) Front Hum Neurosci 7. ISSN 1662-5161. https://doi.org/10.3389/fnhum.2013.00478. https://www.frontiersin.org/articles/10.3389/fnhum.2013.00478/full

Yan N, Wang J, Liu M, Zong L, Jiao Y, Yue J, Lv Y, Yang Q, Lan H, Liu Z (2008). ISSN 1609-0985. http://hub.hku.hk/handle/10722/175308

Zimmons P, Panter A (2003) The influence of rendering quality on presence and task performance in a virtual environment. In: IEEE virtual reality, 2003. Proceedings, pp 293–294. https://doi.org/10.1109/VR.2003.1191170.

Zoefel B, Huster RJ, Herrmann CS (2011) NeuroImage 54(2):1427–1431. ISSN 1053-8119. https://doi.org/10.1016/j.neuroimage.2010.08.078. http://www.sciencedirect.com/science/article/pii/S105381191001181X

Floriana Accoto holds an M.Sc. in Computer Engineering from the University of Salento, Lecce, Italy. Her master thesis was focused in assessing the effect of VR elements in Upper Alpha neurofeedback.

Athanasios Vourvopoulos is a Postdoctoral Researcher at the Institute for Systems and Robotics (ISR) of Instituto Superior Técnico, Lisbon, Portugal. He holds a Ph.D. in Computer Engineering and his research is focused on multimodal Human-Machine interaction using Brain-Computer Interfaces and Virtual Reality for neurorehabilitation.

Afonso Gonçalves is an aerospace engineer and informatics engineering Ph.D. candidate at the University of Madeira, in the field of Human-Machine Interaction. His research, at the NeuroRehabLab of Madeira Interactive Technologies Institute, is focused on the study of exergames to promote physical activity in the older age, and virtual reality.

Teresa Bucho completed her master studies in Biomedical Engineering in 2018 at Instituto Superior Técnico (Lisbon, Portugal). Soon after, she began her Ph.D. at the Netherlands Cancer Institute (Amsterdam, the Netherlands), focusing on the development and application of artificial intelligence in medical imaging.

Gina Caetano holds a Ph.D. from Aalto University, with a thesis on multisensory interaction and the human mirror neuron system. She is currently an invited professor and researcher at the University of Lisbon. Her research interests include the application of neuroimaging techniques in clinical and basic neuroscience.

Patrícia Figueiredo has a BSc in Physics Engineering from Instituto Superior Técnico, Universidade de Lisboa (IST), DPhil in Neuroimaging from the University of Oxford and Habilitation in Biomedical Engineering from IST. She is Assistant Professor at IST, and coordinator of the Biomedical Engineering Lab, Institute for Systems and Robotics Lisboa.

Lucio Tommaso de Paolis had a Degree in Electronic Engineering from the University of Pisa (Italy) and is the Director of the Augmented and Virtual Reality Laboratory (AVR Lab). His research interest concerns the applications of Virtual and Augmented Reality and the development of human-computer interfaces in medicine and education.

Sergi Bermudez I Badia is a Senior Researcher and member of the board of directors of the Madeira-ITI, Associate Professor at the University of Madeira, and President of the International Society for Virtual Rehabilitation. Graduated in telecommunications engineering from the UPC (Barcelona) and Ph.D. neuroinformatics from ETH (Zurich).

Memory Augmentation Through Lifelogging: Opportunities and Challenges

Tilman Dingler, Passant El Agroudy, Rufat Rzayev, Lars Lischke, Tonja Machulla, and Albrecht Schmidt

Abstract Perfect memory is a dream long sought and which has become especially prevalent in our knowledge society. While only a few are blessed with a photographic memory, most people compensate for the fallacies of their memory with the use of tools and tricks to organize information, schedule reminders and remember facts. Most aspects of our lives, however, leave behind some sort of data trail. We explicitly document our trips and experiences while our phones implicitly record our movements and messages. The sum of these recordings paints a holistic picture of our activities in a so-called lifelog. Lifelogging technologies have long been praised for extending our memory's capacity by allowing us to recall and browse our recorded experiences. But despite positive, well-documented effects on memory and well-being, lifelogging largely remains a niche activity with few commercially successful applications. Over recent years, we built a series of prototypes to investigate the challenges and opportunities of lifelogging technologies. We investigated the positioning of on-body cameras, the collection of implicit and explicit lifelogging data, requirements for effective lifelog reviews, automated summaries and ways to

T. Dingler (✉)
University of Melbourne, Melbourne, Australia
e-mail: tilman.dingler@unimelb.edu.au

P. E. Agroudy
University of Stuttgart, Stuttgart, Germany
e-mail: passant.el.agroudy@vis.uni-stuttgart.de

R. Rzayev
University of Regensburg, Regensburg, Germany
e-mail: rufat.rzayev@ur.de

L. Lischke
Vrije Universiteit Amsterdam, Amsterdam, Netherlands
e-mail: l.m.lischke@vu.nl

T. Machulla · A. Schmidt
University of Munich, Munich, Germany
e-mail: tonja.machulla@um.ifi.lmu.de

A. Schmidt
e-mail: albrecht.schmidt@um.ifi.lmu.de

© Springer Nature Switzerland AG 2021
T. Dingler and E. Niforatos (eds.), *Technology-Augmented Perception and Cognition*,
Human–Computer Interaction Series, https://doi.org/10.1007/978-3-030-30457-7_3

47

navigate multimedia lifelogs. In this chapter, we discuss the potential of these technologies to augment memory and the obstacles of bringing memory prosthetics to a
broad audience.

1 Introduction

Lifelogging has spurred considerable interest in both the academic community and
the commercial sector. Widely known self-experiments like the one undertaken in
Gordon Bell's project *Mylifebits* (Gemmell et al. 2002) and a broad range of consumer products, such as the *Autographer* or *Narrative Clip*, have spurred the quantified self-movement in recent years. Technologies have become available that make
lifelogging increasingly practical: Moore's law in processing power and memory
allows for smaller cameras, a variety of more comprehensive sensors, near-constant
recording and the necessary file storage. There is a certain consumer need for sharing
experiences as the success of social media platforms shows resulting in large collections of explicitly taken personal footage and meticulously crafted posts. But more
than that, most aspects of our lives have a digital component and, therefore, leave a
trail that can be picked up and transferred to a lifelog.

   Various research projects have produced empirical evidence for the positive effects
that reviewing lifelogs can have on memory (Hodges et al. 2006), self- and social
reflection (Fleck and Fitzpatrick 2009), and cognitive abilities (Silva et al. 2013).
Studies using Microsoft's SenseCam have shown that memory enhancements work
by documenting and reviewing daily activities (Hodges et al. 2006). To this day,
there is little use of lifelogging beyond academic labs, fitness tracker and a small
number of dedicated technology enthusiasts. Recent commercial endeavours such as
the Autographer—successor of Microsoft's SenseCam—were discontinued in 2016
and the Narrative Clip, a body-worn time-lapse camera, transferred operations, which
begs the question: is the value of memory augmentation not enough or are there other
problems with lifelogging that prevent widespread user adoption?

   In this chapter, we share our experiences and insights from a series of prototypes
we built over recent years and field studies we conducted focusing on user experiences
and technical challenges of lifelogging technologies in everyday life. Our work spans
investigations on where to attach cameras to achieve most memorable lifelog footage,
implicit collection of meta-information to augment lifelog data, and explorations of
lifelog summaries and reviewing techniques with the goal of fostering and supporting
memory. We identified a number of challenges such technologies face with regard
to technological hurdles, social settings, privacy issues and personal attitudes. Some
of these challenges start by recruiting participants for long-term studies where study
participation affects participants' social and work environment, and culminate in
challenges to data privacy and consequently memory security. In the course of this
chapter, we provide and discuss a list of technical and societal issues that need to be

addressed while moving memory augmentation through lifelogging from the lab to the real world and how some commercial products have already started to effectively incorporate memory-enhancing features.

2 Background

In his article 'As we may think', first published in 1945, Vannevar Bush (Bush 1979) pictured a device called 'Memex' that holds records, communications and media as a complement to people's memory, a smart office that remembers all work activities. But more than that, Bush envisioned a collective memory machine that would make knowledge more accessible and, thereby, lead society into a knowledge explosion. For decades, his Memex inspired researchers to implement this vision through a focus on comprehensive data collection, data processing, filtering, organization and presentation.

Among those inspired by Bush's vision were Gordon Bell and Jim Gemmel. They built a system they called *MyLifeBits*, a comprehensive lifelog containing records of all personally relevant information (Gemmell et al. 2006). With the goal of digitizing an entire lifetime, this lifelog was meant to capture and store any sensory experience, document and activity, including the radio and TV programme listened to, the paper and digital documents passed, the locations and websites visited, and the transactions made. Bell was the primary user of the system for several years, turning all his physical memorabilia into digital ones.

To capture real-world experiences, visual imagery needed to be recorded in a near-constant manner. Steve Mann (Mann 1997) proposed the use of wearable cameras as 'visual memory prosthetic'. Embedded in glass-like prototypes, they would allow for real-life image capturing with the goal of creating a personal photo/videographic memory prosthesis (Mann 1998). Microsoft subsequently built the *SenseCam*—later known as the *Autographer*—an on-body sensor-enhanced camera that automatically takes pictures in a determined interval (Hodges et al. 2006).

Hodges et al. (2006) used the *SenseCam* in a 12-month clinical trial with a patient suffering from amnesia for reviewing experiences that had been forgotten. The research with the *SenseCam* has since demonstrated the application of lifelogging for self- and social refection (Fleck and Fitzpatrick 2009; Harper et al. 2008), for monitoring health behaviours (O'Loughlin et al. 2013), and for supporting memory (Browne et al. 2011; Hodges et al. 2006). Sellen et al. (2007) conducted a study to investigate the effect of lifelogging photos on natural recall in daily life. They found that photos were successful cues aiding participants to remember past and connected events. They also helped participants 'know' about past events, such as where they had placed objects, even if they did not remember these objects themselves. Reviewing lifelogs has been shown to boost episodic, working and autobiographical memory (Silva et al. 2013). Further, Isaacs et al. (2013) showed that using electronic tools, in general, to reflect on past memories has positive effects on memory and increases overall well-being.

These research efforts have been accompanied by the development of a series of commercial products: wearable gadgets, as well as smartphone applications, helped spawning the so-called *quantified self-movement*. There is a great number of activity trackers available, such as *Fitbit* for recording steps and calories burned, biophysiological data recording (e.g. *Zephyr BioHarness*), image capturing (e.g. *Narrative Clip*) or the plentitude of sensors integrated in today's smartphones, watches and glasses, which allow for rich data collection. Many of these products and services provide proprietary interfaces to track their respective data and build a user community of sharing to foster motivational aspects for behaviour change. Prior work has addressed this challenge by collecting additional context data during image capture to derive an image's significance (Gurrin et al. 2005) and detect and recognize activities (Fathi et al. 2011a, b; Pirsiavash and Ramanan 2012).

Lifelogging technologies may just be the modern-day version of what Lamming et al. coined *memory prostheses* (Lamming et al. 1994). He and his colleagues envisioned a device similar to Bush's Memex, but with a clear focus on compensating for where our memory fails us. In a diary study, they identified three memory problems people encounter in everyday life: (1) retrospective problems, i.e. the trouble recalling memories or details from the past, (2) prospective problems, i.e remembering to carry out an intended action and (3) action slips, i.e. losing one's train of thought during an action. Hints to understanding the origins and consequences of these three problems can be found in the psychological literature on human memory.

3 Memory

Memory is the primary reference to our knowledge and experience. It interacts with our perception, cognition and emotions but is subject to a variety of distortions (Schacter 1999), such as a decay over time or misrepresentations of original memories. Larry Ryan Squire (Squire 1992) proposed a model of the brain where he categorized memory into two distinct parts: *implicit* and *explicit* or *declarative* memories, where implicit refers to motor skills which reflect in performance rather than through remembering (e.g. riding a bike or playing the guitar) and explicit refers to knowledge that we can describe and reflect on (e.g. knowing that eggs contain a high amount of protein). Endel Tulving further proposed the distinction in explicit memory between *episodic* and *semantic* memories (Tulving et al. 1972):

1. *Episodic memory*: Episodic memory concerns personal experiences. Information stored here relate to a particular context, such as a time and place. '*I remember the day when uncle David put the electric kettle on the gas stove and burned down the kitchen*' is a statement that resembles a personal memory, which can trigger associations to sensations, emotions and other personal associations. Retrieval of information stored in the episodic memory system can also affect and modify the memory system.

2. *Semantic memory*: Semantic memory refers to principles, such as the notes of a C major chord, and therefore holds abstract knowledge about the world independent of its context.

Information processing takes place in three stages: (1) receiving and encoding information through sensory systems, (2) storing that information in long-term memory and (3) retrieval of that information in the form of memories later on. Failure in one of these areas leads to what we call *forgetting*. Ebbinghaus (Ebbinghaus 2013) famously investigated the nature of forgetting. Hence, the memory of information declines exponentially if no attempt is made to retain it. To prevent a rather rapid decline, repetitions need to be spaced out in a way that the information is encountered just when it is about to be forgotten (Nakata 2008). Emotions and other associations can strengthen the memory of information and therefore prolong the process of forgetting.

Various techniques have been proposed to prevent forgetting, most of which are focused on memory retrieval. A popular learning technique lies in applying *mnemonics*, i.e. catchy words, puns or rhymes to aid information retention and retrieval. They work by creating mental associations between new information and the existing knowledge network. Most schooling systems rely on *spacing effects*, i.e. the repetition of information over time and thereby strengthen the mental associations. Optimal spacing is timed in accordance with Ebbinghaus' forgetting curve so that information is re-encountered just when it is about to be forgotten. Dempster (2020) ran experiments around foreign language vocabulary learning and found that words were better retained when learning sessions were spaced apart than when they were presented in direct succession. One spacing method was particularly popularized: the so-called Leitner-style schedule is based on the principle of spaced repetition and often applied in flashcard applications (Godwin-Jones 2010). Learning applications and educational software are often based on a variance of this type of schedule.

So if repetition leads to better memory, the question is whether we can retain our experiences through sessions of active recall and reflection? Like going through an old photo album, could we strengthen our everyday memory by recording and reviewing our daily experiences? This is where lifelogging comes in.

4   Lifelogging

Lifelogging entails the recording of multimedia cues from everyday life spanning photos, audio, videos, activities and even bio-signals. Over the past few decades, continuous advances in wearable capture devices, miniaturization and extension of data storage, and ubiquitous connectivity have fueled the enthusiasm of lifeloggers. Lifelogging has especially been embraced by the quantified-self movement: a group of people dedicated to recording, measuring and tracking most aspects of lives. The resulting recordings are subsequently used not only to track and optimize various aspects of people's lives but also for creating a comprehensive collection of experiences, which can be searched and revisited. Czerwinski et al. (2006) envisioned such a set of personal data to change how these recordings were used for reflection and reminiscence. They would allow us to go back and search our digital memory space and help us locate long-lost objects, recognize forgotten faces, resurface misplaced documents and review recent meeting minutes. We could share our experiences with each other in unprecedented detail and reminisce in our memories together. Sellen et al. (2010) paint a more nuanced picture of an 'obsession' to capture everything. They distinguish between *total capture*, a holistic recording of any type of data available, and *situation-specific capture*, i.e. rich data capture in very specific domains and situations, such as lecture recordings. Sellen and colleagues focus on the potential benefits of such vast recordings for memory, which they label 'the five Rs': recollecting, reminiscing, retrieving, reflecting and remembering. Particularly, they highlight the potential of revisiting lifelogs for emotional well-being but question whether current lifelogging technologies do, in fact, provide any of the often claimed benefits.

Numerous technologies have been developed in the past decades to capture multimedia lifelog data. Wearable cameras like Google Glass, SenseCam and the Narrative Clip, provide lifelogs close to a first-person perspective. Cameras installed in the environment complement that perspective by providing third-person-view lifelogs. The footage is either captured continuously or triggered by specific conditions, at fixed time intervals or whenever a particular event is detected. Capture technologies have so far been commercial niche applications. For example, the Narrative Clip wearable camera was sold for around $150 USD and captured ca. 1700 photos per day. Complementary, tech companies offer software solutions to manage the resulting massive datasets. *Google Photos*, for example, automatically organizes pictures into albums and video clips, and tags people, dates and locations. Another application, the *1-Second-Everyday App*, encourages users to capture only memorable, representative 1-second clips of[1] their days and creates a video from them.

Lifelogging technology seeks to be effortless, i.e. characterized by a passive and unobtrusive collection of data. Explicit data sources, such as diary entries and camera photos, may very well find their way into lifelogs, but the idea is to complement such explicit recordings with implicitly collected data sources to capture a holistic snapshot of the human experience. Recent advances in near-continuous recording devices, vastly available storage capacity and clever algorithms to organize and index the resulting information have lead to a number of commercial offerings. But despite their availability and affordable prices, user adoption has mostly been confined to niche user groups, such as extreme sports and the adoption of first-person cameras (GoPro), and failed to achieve mass-market penetration. Wearable cameras like the SenseCam and the Narrative Clip struggled to maintain a profitable business model, often resulting in termination of their product lines. Google Glass, having failed the social acceptability test, has been pushed to niche applications in augmented reality, mainly supporting field workers.

---

[1] http://1se.co/.

With the proliferation of capture technologies, high-bandwidth networking and cheap cloud storage, we see the most prevalent challenge to wide adoption of lifelogging in the application layer. Over recent years, we have developed a number of lifelog applications and conducted a range of user studies to elicit and address these challenges with a special focus on (1) memory capture and (2) memory support through lifelogging technologies.

5 Capture

In recent years, a range of wearable cameras has come out of research as well as industry labs. Not only do they differ in their technical specifications, but also in their intended on-body positions.

5.1 Camera Positions and Media Types

While the Autographer, SenseCam and NarrativeClip are all chest-worn devices, Google Glass and other cameras integrated into glass frames provide more of a first-person view. In a 2015 study, we assessed the positioning and media type of lifelogging cameras with regard to their utility for memory lifelogs (Wolf et al. 2015). By comparing lifelogging footage taken from the chest and head location (Fig. 1), we were interested in which perspective tended to yield better quality images and meaningful snapshots. We also compared full video capture versus the still images most lifelogging cameras provide. The assessment was done in two ways: (1) purely quantitative evaluation of the feasibility to automatically extract and process information captured, such as image quality (i.e. sharpness) and the application of vision algorithms, such as face recognition and (2) from the user's perceived quality, i.e. the expressiveness, level of occlusion and perceived image properties.

In the study, we had 30 participants wear two cameras recording video with 30 frames per second. The OctaCam HDC-700 is a pair of glasses with a $1280 \times 720px$ camera integrated into its nose bridge. Study participants were wearing two camera glasses at the same time, one in its regular nose position and the other one mounted to the chest using a chest-band. The study comprised three different situations challenging lifelog capturing in various ways during (1) attending a meeting, (2) walking and (3) having a meal in company.

To assess such footage with regard to its value for memory-enhancing applications, we split the experiment into two parts: a recording session on one day followed by a review session on a subsequent day. Across 30 participants, we recorded a total of 545 min (272.5 per camera) of footage, i.e. 18.2 min per participant. For the review session, we processed the previously recorded footage using software we developed that cut the videos into chunks of 30 seconds. The software also produced the video stills by using the first frame of each 30-second clip as a snapshot. Participants were

Fig. 1 While head-worn cameras tend to capture more faces due to the first-person perspective, chest-worn cameras are less subject to motion blur and, therefore, provide more stable footage

shown each still image or 30-second video clip, after which they filled in four Likert-style rating scales about the perceived image quality, including camera perspective, image sharpness, occlusion and perceived value as a memory cue. In this way, we collected 1744 ratings, 872 for each camera position and each media type.

Comparing chest versus head perspective, the subjective image quality was often dependent on the task. During meals, for example, hands often occluded the chest-worn camera, and hence this footage was rated less useful than footage taken from the head perspective. Also, motion blur was a prominent problem for stills taken from the chest perspective due to movements of hands and arms. Comparing video with still images, video taken by the head-worn camera lead to better recall results due to the proximity to the first-person perspective. Overall, the perceived quality of head-worn camera footage was preferred to lifelogging data recorded from a chest-mount with regard to perspective, occlusion artefacts, camera motion blur (due to occluding objects) and situational recall value.

We then processed the videos and still images using OpenCV to assess which perspective and media type have a better potential for automatic feature extraction. Research in autobiographical memory has shown that persons, activities and places make important memory cues for recalling past events (Robinson 1976). Gurrin et al. (2005) have shown to make use of metadata, including date, time and location for organizing lifelog data in a way that allows users to search their photo archives. Subsequently, machine learning can be applied to perform activity recognition. Consequently, we examined the captured footage in its feasibility to be processed by visual algorithms, such as motion blur and face recognition. Our software, therefore, extracted image properties, such as video sharpness, features, such as hands and faces, and scenes by segmenting fore- and background.

Footage captured by the chest-worn camera was generally more stable and contained less motion blur allowing feature detection to perform better than footage from the head-worn camera. Interestingly, this is the opposite finding from the subjective ratings of participants who found occluding hand motions to often blur the overall scene. The head-worn camera, however, captured significantly more faces leading to higher facial detection rates. The video media type also captured significantly more faces compared to the stills.

Hence, our study results indicate that video footage captured by head-worn cameras provides a generally richer base for memory cues as opposed to chest-worn lifelogging devices. It seems there is a trade-off between the relative unobtrusiveness of chest-worn devices and their utility. As a result, when comparing lifelogging footage to memories from a first-person perspective, they tend to disappoint. Google Glass made a famous attempt at integrating a head-worn camera into a consumer product. The product, however, failed on a consumer level partly due to reasons of social acceptance, i.e. people rejected cameras at eye level in everyday situations (Wolf et al. 2014). In niche communities, such as extreme sports, however, such cameras have had more commercial success: Popular accessories for the GoPro camera include the head, helmet and bite mount, all of which allow users to capture footage hands-free from a first-person point-of-view. Such technology serves the need for explicitly capturing experiences. For near-constant lifelogging, however, cameras lack the unobtrusiveness and social acceptance necessary to allow mainstream adoption. Implicit collection of metadata can complement footage that is relatively sparse to provide a more holistic lifelog. This is especially true for ordinary workdays where experiences may blend into each other rather than containing extraordinary experiences that stand out on their own.

5.2 Implicit Capture Triggers

Information workers perform the bulk of their daily activities on desktop computers and increasingly also on mobile devices. Thereby, they implicitly leave a digital trail that can be used to reconstruct their workday. Such work lifelogs allow for performance assessments, but can also convey a feeling of productivity and invite for reflection. While the browser history, for example, can be used to keep track of sites visited and articles read, creating activity summaries based on this record alone does not allow the full reconstruction of a day's work. Recording and archiving screenshots, on the other hand, give a more holistic image of people's daily activities (Gemmell et al. 2002). In an in-the-wild study, we used eye tracking in combination with screen capture data to build automated summaries of people's daily work (Dingler et al. 2016a). We tracked eye movements to detect reading activities under the assumption that active information gain is worth revisiting.

In a field study with 12 participants, we deployed a *Tobii EyeX* eye tracker along with a software that took screenshots of users' desktop screens. We compared three triggers for logging desktop activity: (1) at a fixed time interval of 2 min as a baseline, (2) whenever the user's eye focus switched between open windows and (3) when a reading activity was detected based on idiosyncratic eye movement patterns. We logged participants' activities over 3 days, each day with a different trigger. At the end of each day, the software presented a screenshot summary for participants to review their day's activities and rate the summary's utility, accuracy and effect on recall.

Triggering implicit data collection in the form of snapping screenshots of desktop activities reduced the sheer amount of images captured compared to a fixed time interval capture and increased the relevance of the daily automated summary. Reading-based triggers lead to only 5% of the image volume of a fixed, 2-minute interval. Interestingly, despite differing overall image volume in our three conditions, there was no statistically significant difference in the time participants spent with each summary. In large-volume image summaries, participants seemed to speed up the review process and spent less time with each screenshot, whereas less overall screenshots lead to participants spending more time reviewing materials that seemed to be more relevant. This lingering on relevant records allowed participants to engage in reflection, which has been shown to support long-term memory (Isaacs et al. 2013). Consequently, content captured by means of detecting reading was perceived as more relevant and allowed the daily reviews to summarize a day's activities in a more concise manner.

Lifelog capture does, therefore, not necessarily need to be a constant stream of records. Implicitly collected activity information and metadata can be used as either a trigger to capture a certain moment or to tag specific moments for later retrieval and relevance ratings. By filtering the memorable and memory-worthy moments in comprehensive lifelogging datasets, meaningful summaries can then be put together to review experiences and information with the intention to strengthen long-term memory retention. Through the ubiquity of smartphones and their sensors, meta- and contextual data can be further implicitly collected in a near-constant manner. Consequently, we were interested in whether daily summaries could also be created based on such implicit data troves.

5.3   Implicit Lifelog Collection

Reflecting on previous experiences has been shown to support episodic memory (Li et al. 2011). Collecting personal data manually, however, is challenging: it demands time and dedication while people usually lack holistic awareness about their own activities (Wilson and Dunn 2004), which makes it hard to spot patterns in their behaviours (Li et al. 2010). Near-continuous lifelog collection, therefore, needs to be complemented by implicit data recordings, which Li et al. (2011) proposed to support reflection.

Given the ubiquity of smartphones and the multitude of sensors they contain, we created an Android application that implicitly collects personal and contextual data streams with the goal of creating daily summaries (Rzayev et al. 2018). The app collects, stores and visually displays data summaries prompting users to reflect on them. It taps into various data streams, including the user's communication data,

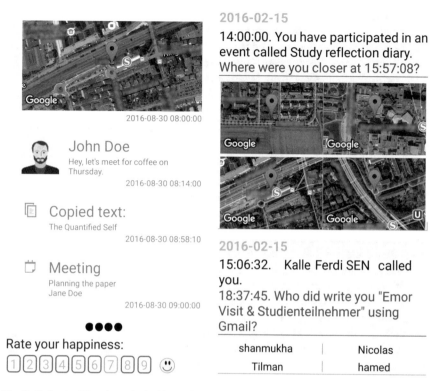

Fig. 2 *ReflectiveDiary* is an Android app that creates automated summaries (left) from implicitly collected data and invites users to reflect on past events through quizzes (right)

sleep and movement behaviour, visited places, weather information on these places, calendar events and smartphone clipboard data. Once a summary is available, the app triggers a notification inviting users to reflect on the data collected over the course of the previous day in chronological order (see Fig. 2).

We conducted a field study in-the-wild to assess the utility of the app by comparing the recognition rate of implicitly collected data that was explicitly reflected on and such that was not reflected on. Recognition was measured by a quiz, which we built into the app. The quiz was generated from the data collected for each day. Over the course of 16 days, 11 participants installed and ran the app on their phones. During the first 8 days, the app collected the data streams and prompted participants to reflect on the implicitly collected data once every 2 days. During the second 8 days of the study, participants took a quiz once a day that was generated using the data from the previous 8 days of data collection. After each quiz, participants rated the usefulness of the collected data streams on a 7-point Likert-style rating scale. At the end of the 16-day study, participants provided general feedback about the application in a debriefing.

Our study results showed that reflections on implicitly recorded personal and contextual data lead to better memory recognition. Participants scored higher in the quizzes based on data they had reflected on. In terms of which data items made for useful memory cues, participants found information about calls and calendar entries most useful. Participants valued the advantages of implicit data collection as time-saving and indicated that communication data, especially received messages, to be useful memory cues. These findings show that implicitly collected personal data can be used to create but also augment lifelog reviews as an effective way to foster episodic memory.

6 Summaries and Reviews

The difference between a photo album and an image lifelog is the sheer amount of image data collected and the selection process of which photo should be taken and archived. Essentially, lifelogging technologies, such as the Narrative Clip record by default, may apply some post hoc filtering, i.e. throw away pictures that are particularly blurry or homogeneous due to the lens having been covered. Photo albums are traditionally manually curated whereas given the size of lifelogs an automatic selection method is required. Google Photos has made tremendous progress in recent years thanks to the utilization of machine learning techniques to automatically detect locations, objects and faces to tag and cluster images into photo summaries and videos. In 2016, we presented a set of guidelines to inform automated video summaries made from Narrative Clip images (Le et al. 2016). The goal was to investigate what needs to go into automated video summaries that invite for reflection and impact episodic memory. In a user study with 16 participants, we elicited characteristics of meaningful summaries and their effects on cognitive load, user experience, memory and recall.

In this study, participants recorded their everyday lives using the Narrative Clip and joined a series of workshops, in which we elicited the key features for lifelogging summaries to support the review of past events. Each participant wore the Narrative Clip for 5 days, after each of which we invited participants to join a workshop to review and discuss their recorded footage. We asked participants to browse through their images and group them to semantic clusters based on which participants then created manual video summaries while following the 'think-aloud' protocol. By closely observing the manual video creation process, we noticed that the resulting summaries were predominantly structured around the presence of people, places, objects and actions.

In subsequent workshop sessions, we then created summaries for our participants based on these observed characteristics. Participants then rated and discussed these videos, which helped us refine a set of guidelines to create lifelog summaries. These guidelines build the basis of a system we built for the creation of automated video summaries from lifelog data. Summaries should be between 2 and 3 minutes in duration and focus on the presence of people, places, objects and actions as well as be chronologically structured. Single images are to be displayed for 2–3 s. The aim of summaries is to provide scaffolding (e.g. chronology, context) to support the reconstruction of memories. When it comes to the representation of certain events, the proportion of these events in the summary does not necessarily need to reflect the actual duration of the experience. Prolonged activities, such as a commute to work, do not need to be prominently represented in a summary (as they would in a static time-lapse review) but rather compressed to a semantic unit and chronologically embedded into the narrative of the day. Such summaries serve a variety of purposes, including reminiscence, self-reflection, promotion of self-identity and social interaction/sharing (Le et al. 2016).

In our study, the video summaries we generated for participants based on these principles outperformed time-lapse reviews and manual browsing in terms of subjective assessments with regard to memory vividness, coherence, accessibility, time perspective, visual perspective, sharing, distancing and valence (Luttechi and Sutin's (Luchetti and Sutin 2016) memory experience questionnaire). Such summaries do not need to be limited to the pictures we take, but should rather incorporate multiple data sources as the original vision of Vannevar Bush outlines (Bush 1979). Particularly, data that can be implicitly gathered is of interest here as data collection that runs in the background does not interfere with daily activities. Insights from our study show that incorporating metadata is a desirable feature to augment the often predominantly visual content of lifelogging cameras.

6.1   Tools to Review Lifelog Footage

Reviewing captured lifelogging data remains challenging due to a large amount of recorded data. As we have seen, current design guidelines and video players do not adequately address the challenge of navigating through recorded content. In a related study, we proposed the use of information cues for accessing autobiographical memory also for the navigation through lifelogging data (Wolf et al. 2016). These information cues facilitate access to autobiographical memory by focusing on *what* happened, *who* was present, *when* and *where* the event happened (Barsalou 1988; Burt 1992; Wagenaar 1986). Not only single information cues but also the combination of cues can be used to access autobiographical memory (Wagenaar 1986). We, therefore, implemented five video players to review lifelogging data using different cues for navigation (see Fig. 3):

1. The video player using the **presence of people** as a cue for navigation shows all persons appearing in the recorded video as thumbnails next to the video stream. By selecting one person, the player plays all scenes, in which this person is present.
2. The player using the **location**, where the video was recorded as a navigation cue, presents the video in 10-second snippets on a tilted map. Thereby, a 2.5D view

Fig. 3 Interfaces of our video player: video player using the present persons as navigation cue (top left), the location (top centre), the recording time stamp (top right), a combination of the time stamp of the recording (bottom left) and the location as primary navigation cue (bottom right) along with other cues

is created, in which the user sees the video snippets above the map. During the review, users view one snippet after another and move across the map.

3. The player using the **recording time** as navigation cue looks similar to a regular video player. Instead of showing the time relative to the video length, this player uses the time stamp when the video was recorded.
4. The players use the combination of all cues and focus on the recording time.
5. The players use the combination of all cues and focus on the location.

In a lab study with 18 participants, we compared all five interfaces by measuring the time required to find a specific scene in the recorded video as well as the mental effort it takes to find that scene. For assessing the mental effort, we used the SMEQ scale (Zijlstra and Doorn 1985). Overall, participants had the shortest task-completion time when using the time-based interface. In the qualitative feedback, participants valued the location-based interface for providing easy access to scenes where they met other people, as the location was generally well remembered. Beyond the comparison of the interfaces using the different information cues, this work shows that providing multiple navigation techniques using various cues helps users to review specific situations in their lifelogging data.

7   Towards a Memory Prosthesis

In 1994, Lamming et al. (1994) presented the notion of creating a *memory prosthesis*. The need for such prostheses stems from the observation that people employ a range of sophisticated procedures to compensate for a memory that is prone to fail them. Organizing our homes, keeping todo lists and setting alarms are ways of acknowledging our fallible memory and taking steps to mitigate their fallout.

With more sophisticated tools and technologies, we become better equipped to complement our cognitive capabilities. What Lamming and colleagues coined the *'intimate computer'* has manifested itself in a combination of near-constant data recording devices, the availability of vast storage capacity, the connection through high-bandwidth networking, the development of efficient algorithms to index and surface information without the need to explicitly organize data, the use of machine learning techniques to tag information and detect situations and the timing of when to surface certain memory cues, and the ubiquity of screens and other modes of information delivery. The resulting combination is lifelogging technology that brings us closer to fixing at least two out of the three shortcomings that come with our memory, according to Lamming et al. (1994):

- **Retrospective memory**: The collection of comprehensive lifelogs creates a data trove that can be browsed, queried and used as a basis for experience summaries, reviews and reflection. This is where the majority of our studies were focused on. Findings have shown that reflection and reviewing of lifelog data strengthen recall and, therefore, episodic memory. The presentation of even partial information about an event has been shown to trigger memory and helps people remember more details about that same event (Cohen and Faulkner 1986). Lifelog capture, therefore, does not need to be all-encompassing but can take shape in a combination of explicit, implicit, more and less obtrusive recording techniques, which are sufficient to strengthen memory while providing a compromise with regard to potential privacy infringements.
- **Prospective memory**: To help people remember to follow through with planned actions, memory cues need to be well-timed and delivered. Multimedia lifelogs allow the collection and extraction of multimedia memory cues (Dingler et al. 2016b), which paired with clever algorithms (e.g. activity recognition and event detection) can be delivered in the right moment on any ubiquitous device (e.g. smartphone or watch). While alarms and todo lists will likely continue to support our prospective memory, increasingly proactive agents can learn from past behaviours and support us throughout the day. Context-aware notifications on smartphones, for examples, can remind us of a medication that is due to take, a traffic alert that reminds us to leave in time to get to the next appointment, a reminder that an article we intended to read fits into the time our commute to work takes (Dingler et al. 2018; Pielot et al. 2015) or a nudge that it's time to review a foreign language vocabulary before it is forgotten (Dingler et al. 2017).

By combining explicitly and implicitly collected data we can nowadays generate rich lifelogs, from which summaries, quizzes and reviews can be generated to help their users effectively commit their experiences to long-term memory. Designing memory augmentation solutions based on lifelogs is generally centred around two schools: the first relies on creating an external memory prosthetic allowing its users to query and browse recorded material. By utilizing state-of-the-art object and facial recognition, large image collections, for example, can be effectively searched.

Google Photos, an online image storage and management tool, allows users to select a particular face and retrieve all images in which this particular person appears. If a user was wearing a lifelog camera and engaged in near-constant data recording, such software could easily pinpoint the moment when that person was met for the first time. The same accounts for places visited or meals enjoyed. In these cases, however, we still depend on the lifelog data and the efficiency of the algorithms that help us surface relevant information.

The second school of memory augmentation through lifelogging aims at enhancing the human memory itself. It is based on processing, summarizing and presenting recorded material in a manner that allows its users to strengthen their innate associations and, therefore, memory itself. Users of technologies who improve memory in that way are capable of better recalling and, therefore, are more independent from the technology itself. Hence, even if the technology is removed, the skill (i.e. better memory) persists.

In our work, we seek to combine these two approaches by investigating near-constant capture and efficient retrieval methods but also focus on the way data summaries can be presented to strengthen memory itself and augment people's cognitive abilities. We envision memory prosthetics that act as a natural extension of our memory, allow us to browse and search our lifelog archives and help us boost our innate memory capacities (Dingler et al. 2016b).

8 Challenges and the Path Forward

In this last section, we will reflect on some of the challenges of deploying lifelogging technologies in-the-wild and the potential impact they may have on large-scale adoption. For most of our study participants, the notion of wearing an always-on camera was new to them. We observed a number of obstacles and listened to participants' concerns, which shed some light on why comprehensive lifelogging technology has not reached a mass audience as of now.

8.1 Camera Awareness

Sharing personal information has become commonplace with the rise of social media. A selfie cult has gained platforms, such as *Facebook* and *Instagram*, unprecedented user numbers. Images posted on these platforms, however, are explicitly taken and carefully crafted, which comes closer to a diary with selected entries than a comprehensive lifelog. Attempts have been made to bring always-on cameras to consumers in the form of commercial products, such as the Narrative Clip or the GoPro camera. Throughout our studies, we recorded common user sentiments with regard to the near-constant presence of cameras.

Some participants seemed to become quite used to the presence of recording devices throughout some of our studies describing the camera as '[an] external body part', 'another accessory like a mobile phone' and becoming 'part of a dress'. Some participants reported taking special care, in the beginning, to make sure the camera was not accidentally covered. The Narrative Clip is often attached to the wearer's shirt and subsequently covered by a jacket or overall. Eventually, most participants started getting used to the camera as part of their 'daily routine' as one participant stated: '[...] with the passing of time, I just forgot about it, and I did normal stuff as if the camera wasn't with me'. With the new-found familiarity, however, study participants have been shown to run the risk of forgetting about the camera altogether, which can become intrusive in private spaces, such as bedrooms and bathrooms (Clinch et al. 2016). '[A] couple of times I forgot to take it off while going to the toilet and I remembered only when I was back'. Accidental capture can be especially infringing on bystanders' privacy. At times, participants reported having been approached by other people inquiring what the camera is recording. At other times, work colleagues of our participants assumed the Narrative Clip to be a medical device or MP3 player due to its form factor. The Narrative Clip's colour influenced its perception: We handed out white- and orange-coloured devices. While the white camera seemed more inconspicuous, participants wearing the orange clip reported it to be more often the subject of conversations. Resounding feedback we received from participants taking the camera into their private life was about the importance of making it clear to the people in their surroundings—at work and in their homes—what it is that is being recorded at any time.

The mere presence of the camera, therefore, influenced participants' interactions with those around them ranging from 'funny faces [made] to the camera' to attempts to capture selfies. Participants also shared concerns they had especially in public spaces: 'sometimes the people [...] in a subway looked at me with a strange face, and they looked directly [at] the camera'. This sentiment is shared by numerous customer reviews for Google Glass and, therefore, presumed to be one of the major obstacles to its commercial success. The unease was not limited to public encounters, but included private conversations: 'If my friend sounds [serious], I take it off but put it on again later'.

When technology tracks their users' every step, individuals trigger non-deliberate events just by being in a certain location. The interaction with lifelogging technologies is not always clear from a user perspective, and mechanisms need to be researched and collectively agreed on by which we indicate the presence of and the consent to recordings. Near-constant image/video recording is, therefore, still confined to situations where wearing a camera is generally acceptable, such as sporting events or as dashboard cameras make their way into cars for potential liability litigations. Neither is there a need to capture everything as our studies have shown that implicitly collected data from alternative data sources can very well complement lifelog records for the purposes of memory augmentation.

8.2 Data Privacy and Security

Throughout our prototype deployments and user studies, we frequently faced questions about data security and privacy, including where the collected data was stored, who would get to see it and how long it was retained. The active debates in recent years triggered by unauthorized data access, such as through Cambridge Analytica, have increasingly raised awareness in the public eye. The introduction of the General Data Protection Regulation (GDPR) by lawmakers in the European Union is the first regulatory attempt to limit the unchecked collection and usage of data. Without doubt, these developments will also influence the debate around lifelogging technologies and the access to and ownership of a comprehensive personal data vault.

Many of our prototypes are designed to run unobtrusively in the background and capture a great deal of potentially sensitive information. This presented some major concerns with some participants of our studies and presented a serious obstacle to creating comprehensive lifelogs more generally. Software that captures desktop activities (Dingler et al. 2016a), for example, records a whole range of potentially sensitive private as well as professional information. Especially in a corporate context, such capture technology can be outright prohibited by corporate directives. In our studies, we have had multiple cases of participants having to drop out of our study as well as not being able to commence in the first place after realizing corporate policy violations through near-constant image capture.

The benefit of granting access to such a vast amount of information needs to outweigh the risks. In general, people are concerned about sharing their location information but the gains of using navigation services, such as *Google Maps*, make them compromise on their private data policy. Most of our prototypes, therefore, saved data to a physical, local storage unit without the need to transfer or process any of the data in some ominous cloud. The notion of '*Privacy by Design*' ensures that privacy and security are core issues that accompany the entire chain of the engineering process (Langheinrich 2001). With lifelogging technologies, we should make sure that sensitive information does not leave the user's reach but is processed mostly in-place. For more power- or data-intensive processing that exceeds local device resources, *homomorphic encryption* presents a viable option to securely encrypt data locally, transmit it to a remote server where it is anonymously processed and sent back without ever having been decrypted (Gentry and Boneh 2009). Users remain sole owners of their own data. But even though storing and processing personal data in this way may appear secure at the time, it does not guarantee the data's inviolability for any time to come. Risks need to be constantly reassessed as technology advances.

Another risk for data storage is its integrity, i.e. the potential for manipulation. If lifelogs help us boost our memory, could manipulation of data lead to manipulation of memory? The next chapter will go into more details on this, but we noticed in our studies that participants reviewing their own lifelogging data occasionally showed having doubts about surrounding details of events or their authenticity, especially when participants were not immediately able to recognize their own photos. One participant explained: 'some events just happen at a day when they usually don't happen. I looked at them, and I didn't recognize them'. Another proclaimed 'sometimes the pictures are so vague, so I am wondering where am I?'. Knowing that our memory is fallible, we may run the risk of trusting an 'objective' lifelog storage more than our very own memories. Data inconsistencies may consequently lead to doubting ourselves rather than the technology. If that is the case, the potential for manipulation bears the risk of considerable abuse of these technologies. Data integrity checks and security protocols need to be built into these technologies from capture to review mechanisms.

8.3 Applications

Navigating through and filtering lifelogging data is a challenging and time-consuming task. Only with adequate filtering techniques can users retrieve meaningful data and recall specific moments in time. We proposed the use of information cues, known from accessing the autobiographical memory to navigate through lifelogging videos (Wolf et al. 2016). We see comparable approaches in applications, such as *Google Photos*, which presents personal photos from a specific date or location. Future research should explore identifying meaningful moments in the lifelogging data by analyzing collected sensor data. Detecting relevant moments automatically has the potential to minimize the search time for specific data points and will enhance the possibilities for lifelogging in daily use.

In our studies, when participants browsed through larger lifelogs, they were often predominantly interested in reviewing positive experiences (Le et al. 2016) showing the potential of lifelogs to be used as a type of emotion regulation strategy that goes beyond mere reminiscing. And while participants generally did not want to have image capture always-on ('Not for the daily purposes, but for some important events'), a comprehensive lifelog that goes back a while bears the potential to relive and reminisce: 'by lifelogging, you see a younger version of you. It is like recalling your great past and trying to match that in your present as well'. In 2015, Facebook introduced 'On This Day', which shows users posts and tags from a particular date in the past. Integrated into the timeline, it provides a memory refresher and provides an emotional connection to people in their network.

Our studies have shown that lifelog reviews strengthen memory even if the information is collected implicitly (Le et al. 2016; Rzayev et al. 2018). Hence, users do not need to carry an always-on camera with them at all times but can combine data streams from different sources to take advantage of lifelogging technologies. Cloud storage solutions like *Google Photos* use machine learning to tag, filter and organize users' photos. Thanks to the GDPR, users have the right to request all data collected about them, which–in the case of, for example, Google–covers photos, locations, emails, search queries and a broad range of further data sources. With our households being equipped with more and more sensors and devices, the combined data of these personal collectors make for one large lifelog. While the ownership, accessibility and cross-service exchange of these data are still being legally negotiated, the vision of a comprehensive lifelog as formulated by Bush (1979) and Gemmel (2002) has become a de-facto reality. The utilization of this data treasure for augmenting memory is still a niche application at this point, but our research findings show positive reinforcements and memory strengthening as well as the potential for improved well-being through reflection. While memory augmentation features are sporadically added to existing services (e.g. Facebook's 'On This Day'), the application space of memory augmentation through lifelogs may soon become a reality few people will want to live without.

9 Conclusion

The prototypes presented in this chapter allowed us to explore the utility, challenges and opportunities of lifelogging technologies with respect to memory augmentation. In recent years, we investigated various aspects of lifelogging, including the capture of explicit footage and implicit data trails as well as their utility for memory-enhancing applications. Most applications and devices we use in everyday life create data that constitute some sort of lifelogging. The challenge is to channel and process this data into an effective memory prosthesis that produces summaries that can be reviewed to strengthen innate memories. Even the capture and presentation of partial information about an event can help people associate events and recall details that would be inaccessible without appropriate cues. Lifelog capture does not need to be all-encompassing but works if it combines explicit and implicit recording techniques to strengthen memory.

While we are closer than ever to Bush's envisioned Memex device (Bush 1979), the work described in this chapter focuses on applications to compensate for where our memory fails us. But the introduction of near-constant data capture comes with challenges to social norms and perceptual limitations. We see lifelogging features slowly seep into commercial tools and applications to make comprehensive data capture more palatable and enticing as a universal and perfect memory remains an ambitious human desire.

References

Barsalou LW (1988) Remembering reconsidered: ecological and traditional approaches to the study of memory, pp 193–243
Browne G, Berry E, Kapur N, Hodges S, Smyth G, Watson P, Wood K (2011) Memory 19(7):713–722. https://doi.org/10.1080/09658211.2011.614622
Burt CD (1992) Appl Cogn Psychol 6(5):389–404
Bush V (1979) ACM SIGPC Notes 1(4):36–44
Clinch S, Davies N, Mikusz M, Metzger P, Langheinrich M, Schmidt A, Ward G (2016) IEEE Pervasive Comput 15(1):58–67
Cohen G, Faulkner D (1986) Br J Dev Psychol 4(2):187–197

Czerwinski M, Gage DW, Gemmell J, Marshall CC, Pérez-Quiñones MA, Skeels MM, Catarci T (2006) Commun ACM 49(1):44–50

Dempster FN (1987) Effects of variable encoding and spaced presentations on vocabulary learning. J Edu Psych 79(2):162

Dingler T, Agroudy PE, Matheis G, Schmidt A (2016a) Reading-based screenshot summaries for supporting awareness of desktop activities. In: Proceedings of the 7th augmented human international conference 2016, pp 1–5

Dingler T, El Agroudy P, Le HV, Schmidt A, Niforatos E, Bexheti A, Langheinrich M (2016b) IEEE MultiMedia 23(2):4–11

Dingler T, Weber D, Pielot M, Cooper J, Chang C-C, Henze N (2017) Language learning on-the-go: Opportune moments and design of mobile microlearning sessions. In: Proceedings of the 19th international conference on human-computer interaction with mobile devices and services, MobileHCI'17. Association for Computing Machinery, New York, NY, USA. ISBN 9781450350754. https://doi.org/10.1145/3098279.3098565

Dingler T, Tag B, Lehrer S, Schmidt A (2018) Reading scheduler: proactive recommendations to help users cope with their daily reading volume. In: Proceedings of the 17th international conference on mobile and ubiquitous multimedia, MUM 2018. Association for Computing Machinery, New York, NY, USA, pp 239–244. ISBN 9781450365949. https://doi.org/10.1145/3282894.3282917

Ebbinghaus H (2013) Ann Neurosci 20(4):155

Fathi A, Farhadi A, Rehg JM (2011a) Understanding egocentric activities. In: 2011 IEEE international conference on computer vision (ICCV). IEEE, pp 407–414. https://doi.org/10.1109/ICCV.2011.6126269

Fathi A, Ren X, Rehg JM (2011b) Learning to recognize objects in egocentric activities. In 2011 IEEE conference on computer vision and pattern recognition (CVPR). IEEE, pp 3281–3288. https://doi.org/10.1109/CVPR.2011.5995444

Fleck R, Fitzpatrick G (2009) Int J Hum Comput Stud 67(12), 1024–1036. ISSN 1071-5819. https://doi.org/10.1016/j.ijhcs.2009.09.004. http://dx.doi.org/10.1016/j.ijhcs.2009.09.004

Gemmell J, Bel, G, Lueder R, Drucker S, Wong C (2002) Mylifebits: fulfilling the memex vision. In Proceedings of the tenth ACM international conference on multimedia. ACM, pp 235–238

Gemmell J, Bell G, Lueder R (2006) Commun ACM 49(1):88–95

Gentry C, Boneh D (2009) A fully homomorphic encryption scheme, vol 20. Stanford university Stanford

Godwin-Jones R (2010) Lang Learn Technol 14(2):4–11

Gurrin C, Jones GJF, Lee H, O'Hare N, Smeaton AF, Murphy N (2005) Mobile access to personal digital photograph archives. In Proceedings of the 7th international conference on human computer interaction with mobile devices & services, MobileHCI'05. ACM, New York, NY, USA, pp 311–314. ISBN 1-59593-089-2. https://doi.org/10.1145/1085777.1085842. http://doi.acm.org/10.1145/1085777.1085842

Harper R, Randall D, Smyth N, Evans C, Heledd L, Moore R (2008) The past is a different place: they do things differently there. In: Proceedings of the 7th ACM Conference on designing interactive systems, DIS'08. ACM, New York, NY, USA, pp 271–280. ISBN 978-1-60558-002-9. https://doi.org/10.1145/1394445.1394474. http://doi.acm.org/10.1145/1394445.1394474

Hodges S, Williams L, Berry E, Izadi S, Srinivasan J, Butler A, Smyth G, Kapur N, Wood K (2006) Sensecam: a retrospective memory aid. In: International conference on ubiquitous computing. Springer, Berlin, pp 177–193

Isaacs E, Konrad A, Walendowski A, Lennig T, Hollis V, Whittaker S (2013) Echoes from the past: how technology mediated reflection improves well-being. In: Proceedings of the SIGCHI conference on human factors in computing systems, CHI'13. Association for Computing Machinery, New York, NY, USA, pp 1071–1080. ISBN 9781450318990. https://doi.org/10.1145/2470654.2466137

Lamming M, Brown P, Carter K, Eldridge M, Flynn M, Louie G, Robinson P, Sellen A (1994) Comput J 37(3):153–163

Langheinrich M (2001) Privacy by designâATprinciples of privacy-aware ubiquitous systems. In: International conference on ubiquitous computing. Springer, Berlin, pp 273–291

Le HV, Clinch S, Sas C, Dingler T, Henze N, Davies N (2016) Impact of video summary viewing on episodic memory recall: design guidelines for video summarizations. In: Proceedings of the 2016 CHI conference on human factors in computing systems, pp 4793–4805

Li I, Forlizzi J, Dey A (2010) Know, thyself: monitoring and reflecting on facets of one's life. In CHI'10 extended abstracts on human factors in computing systems, CHI EA'10. Association for Computing Machinery, New York, NY, USA, pp 4489–4492. ISBN 9781605589305. https://doi.org/10.1145/1753846.1754181

Li I, Dey AK, Forlizzi J (2011) Understanding my data, myself: supporting self-reflection with ubicomp technologies. In: Proceedings of the 13th international conference on ubiquitous computing, UbiComp'11. Association for Computing Machinery, New York, NY, USA, pp 405–414. ISBN 9781450306300. https://doi.org/10.1145/2030112.2030166

Luchetti M, Sutin AR (2016) Memory 24(5):592–602

Mann S (1997) Computer 30(2):25–32

Mann S (1998) 'wearcam'(the wearable camera): personal imaging systems for long-term use in wearable tetherless computer-mediated reality and personal photo/videographic memory prosthesis. In: Second international symposium on wearable computers. Digest of Papers. IEEE, pp 124–131 (1998)

Nakata T (2008) ReCALL 20(1):3–20. https://doi.org/10.1017/S0958344008000219

O'Loughlin G, Cullen SJ, McGoldrick A, O'Connor S, Blain R, O'Malley S, Warrington GD (2013) Am J Preventive Med 44(3):297–301. https://doi.org/10.1016/j.amepre.2012.11.007

Pielot M, Dingler T, Pedro JS, Oliver N (2015) When attention is not scarce-detecting boredom from mobile phone usage. In: Proceedings of the 2015 ACM international joint conference on pervasive and ubiquitous computing, UbiComp'15. Association for Computing Machinery, New York, NY, USA, pp 825–836. ISBN 9781450335744. https://doi.org/10.1145/2750858.2804252

Pirsiavash H, Ramanan D (2012) Detecting activities of daily living in first-person camera views. In: 2012 IEEE conference on computer vision and pattern recognition (CVPR). IEEE, pp 2847–2854. https://doi.org/10.1109/CVPR.2012.6248010

Robinson JA (1976) Cogn Psychol 8(4):578–595

Rzayev R, Dingler T, Henze N (2018) Reflectivediary: fostering human memory through activity summaries created from implicit data collection. In: Proceedings of the 17th international conference on mobile and ubiquitous multimedia, MUM 2018. Association for Computing Machinery, New York, NY, USA, pp 285–291. ISBN 9781450365949. https://doi.org/10.1145/3282894.3282907

Schacter DL (1999) Am Psychol 54(3):182

Sellen AJ, Whittaker S (2010) Commun ACM 53(5):70–77

Sellen AJ, Fogg A, Aitken M, Hodges S, Rother C, Wood K (2007) Do life-logging technologies support memory for the past? An experimental study using sensecam. In: Proceedings of the SIGCHI conference on human factors in computing systems, CHI'07. Association for Computing Machinery, New York, NY, USA, pp 81–90. ISBN 9781595935939. https://doi.org/10.1145/1240624.1240636

Silva AR, Pinho S, Macedo LM, Moulin CJ (2013) Am J Preventive Medi 44(3):302–307. https://doi.org/10.1016/j.amepre.2012.11.005

Squire LR (1992) J Cogn Neurosci 4(3):232–243

Tulving E et al (1972) Organ Mem 1:381–403

Wagenaar WA (1986) Cogn Psychol 18(2):225–252

Wilson TD, Dunn EW (2004) Ann Rev Psychol 55

Wolf K, Schmidt A, Bexheti A, Langheinrich M (2014) IEEE Pervasive Comput 13(3):8–12

Wolf K, Abdelrahman Y, Schmid D, Dingler T, Schmidt A (2015) Effects of camera position and media type on lifelogging images. In: Proceedings of the 14th international conference on mobile and ubiquitous multimedia, MUM'15. Association for Computing Machinery, New York, NY, USA, pp 234–244. ISBN 9781450336055. https://doi.org/10.1145/2836041.2836065

Wolf K, Lischke L, Sas C, Schmidt A (2016) The value of information cues for lifelog video navigation. In: Proceedings of the 15th international conference on mobile and ubiquitous multimedia, MUM'16. Association for Computing Machinery, New York, NY, USA, pp 153–157. ISBN 9781450348607. https://doi.org/10.1145/3012709.3012712

Zijlstra FR, Van Doorn L (1985) The construction of a scale to measure subjective effort. Delft, Netherlands 43:124–139

Tilman Dingler Tilman is a Lecturer in the School of Computing and Information Systems at the University of Melbourne. He studied Media Computer Science in Munich, Web Science in San Francisco and received a PhD in Computer Science from the University of Stuttgart, Germany, in 2016. Tilman is an Associate Editor for the PACM on Interactive, Mobile, Wearable and Ubiquitous Technologies (IMWUT) and serves as Associate Chair for CHI among others. He is co-founder of the SIGCHI Melbourne Local Chapter. Tilman's research focuses on cognition-aware systems and technologies that support users' information-processing capabilities

Passant ElAgroudy is a researcher at the Visualizations and Interaction System Institute at the University of Stuttgart. Her work focuses on investigating memory degradations caused by ubiquitous systems and on creating memory prosthetics for memory augmentation. She contributed to several EU projects focusing on augmenting human capabilities such as RECALL and AMPLIFY.

Rufat Rzayev is an HCI researcher at the University of Regensburg, Germany. He has a background in computer science. While his primary research focuses on augmented and virtual reality, he is also interested in assistance-oriented tools to enhance human perception and memory.

Lars Lischke is Assistant Professor for human-computer interaction at the Vrije Universiteit Amsterdam. He worked as Postdoctoral Researcher at the Future Everyday Group at the Eindhoven University of Technology after which he had received his PhD under supervision of Albrecht Schmidt from the University of Stuttgart. His research focuses on enhancing information communication through interactive technology and on the interaction with large high-resolution displays.

Tonja-Katrin Machulla has a background in psychology, cognitive neuroscience and human-computer interaction. She is the Assistant Professor for 'Assistive Technologies' in the Department of Rehabilitation Sciences, TU Dortmund, Germany. Her research focuses on multisensory augmentations, particularly for elderly individuals and individuals with visual impairments.

Albrecht Schmidt is a Professor of Computer Science at the Ludwig-Maximilians-Universität München in Germany. He studied in Ulm and Manchester and received a PhD from the Lancaster University. In his research, he focuses on amplifying the human mind and he is excited about improving cognition and perception through information technology. In 2018, he was elected to the ACM CHI Academy. Besides his academic work he co-founded ThingOS, where he is Chief Scientist.

Technology-Mediated Memory Impairment

Sarah Clinch, Cathleen Cortis Mack, Geoff Ward, and Madeleine Steeds

Abstract The technology and tools that we develop have always been transformative, but the pace of change, particularly in the last few decades is undoubtedly altering humans in ways we don't understand. As researchers look to develop novel prosthetics and tools to enhance our memories and extend cognition, further consideration is needed to understand how technologies can help (or, indeed, hinder) our inherent abilities. In this chapter, we identify two distinct forms of cognitive risk associated with current and emerging technologies: memory inhibition and memory distortion. We describe how lifelogging, search engines, social media, satnavs and other developments are prompting us to retain less information for ourselves (inhibition), and present three specific examples of this phenomenon: the Google effect, photo-taking-impairment and alterations in spatial memory attributed to satnav use. We further consider cases in which technology actually increases the likelihood of errors in what and how we remember (distortion), including doctored evidence effects, creation of false memories for current or historical affairs ("fake news") and retrieval-induced forgetting. Finally, we provide an exploration of these cognitive vulnerabilities in the context of human memory augmentation, including the reporting of a mixed design experiment with 48 participants in which we demonstrate both retrieval-induced forgetting and false memory creation for real-world experiences.

S. Clinch (✉) · M. Steeds
The University of Manchester, Manchester, UK
e-mail: sarah.clinch@manchester.ac.uk

M. Steeds
e-mail: madeleine.steeds@manchester.ac.uk

C. Cortis Mack · G. Ward
The University of Essex, Colchester, UK
e-mail: ccorti@essex.ac.uk

G. Ward
e-mail: gdward@essex.ac.uk

© Springer Nature Switzerland AG 2021
T. Dingler and E. Niforatos (eds.), *Technology-Augmented Perception and Cognition*,
Human–Computer Interaction Series, https://doi.org/10.1007/978-3-030-30457-7_4

As the previous chapter described, developments in lifelogging, quantified-self, and similar technologies allow capture of a rich feed representing the human experience that can then be summarised and presented back to the user to help cue retrieval and strengthen connections between the neurons that form a memory trace. These can easily be used to support memory for experiences (episodic memory) but as the previous chapter explored, they also have value to help rehearse and consolidate other learnings, i.e., knowledge acquired through those experiences (semantic memory). However, lifelogging technologies are by no means the only ones enhancing our memories and cognitive abilities—we daily encounter a range of tools and technologies that enhance the quantity and quality of information available to us, reducing the burden on our own minds.

In a typical working day, I might use an electronic calendar to store and remind me of my upcoming appointments, a satellite navigation system to direct me to those appointments, and may consult email archives and instant messaging histories to reinstate context from previous discussion with the colleagues I am meeting. When back in my own office, I make heavy use of the Internet and other electronic resources for information on a wide range of topics. So prevalent is this final behaviour that the verb "to google", used to refer generally to the process of looking up information on the web, was added to the Oxford English and Merriam-Webster dictionaries in 2006. In a more social moment, services such as Facebook hold text and image representations of experiences going back over ten years, and features such as Facebook memories deliberately aim to encourage rehearsal, reminiscence and sharing of these experiences.

The use of technology and tools to enhance cognition is not new—current wireless and cloud technologies were preceded by physical storage (CDs, floppy disks), which in turn were predated by analogue media such as written notes, books and even cave paintings. For as long as a practice of externalising knowledge has existed, using such tools has prompted debate about their impact on remembering and forgetting. On the one hand, cognitive offloading has been argued to free up mental resources for other tasks including higher thinking. Proponents of this perspective note that Albert Einstein was unable to recall the speed of sound, reporting that the information was "readily available in a book". On the other hand, there is a fear that new technologies weaken our inherent capabilities by disrupting our natural processes (e.g., encouraging new, detrimental, patterns of thinking and attention).

Considering just this latter argument, it's possible to identify two distinct possible negative effects of technology (Fig. 1). In the first case, technologies may act as an *inhibitor*, somehow preventing normal cognitive processes from taking place. An example of this inhibitive effect can be seen in the common observation that individuals no longer commit telephone numbers to memory due to the ubiquitous presence of the mobile phone. In the second case, technologies may act as a *distortion*, altering the normal cognitive processes to introduce inaccuracies or errors. These effects are arguably more subtle but are still pervasive. An example of this distortive effect can be seen in the current focus on concerns around fake news, and the role of technology in shaping memory of significant societal events. Although the above examples suggest a difference in intent between inhibitive and distortive memory

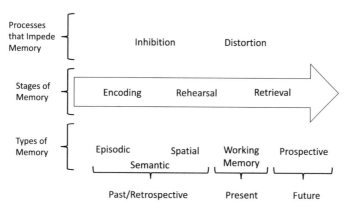

Fig. 1 A visual overview of core memory dimensions, and the potential for negative effects generated by technology use. Both Inhibition and Distortion effects can be seen, and these effects may occur at any one (or more) stages of memory formation across multiple types of memory. Note that whilst both type and stage of memory have temporal aspects, their timelines are independent

effects (i.e., that inhibition may occur accidentally whilst distortion is the result of deliberate adversarial action), this is an artificial distinction and later sections of the chapter will provide counter-examples.

In this chapter, we consider the potential for cognition aids to exploit vulnerabilities in our mental processes, reducing our ability to operate independently of technology. We explore both inhibitive and distortive effects on a variety of memory types. The remainder of the chapter is structured as follows. We begin by describing research that explores how technologies that are already commonplace might be impeding our ability and inclination to commit information to memory (inhibition). We reflect on new technologies emerging in this context and how encouraging similar cognitive offloading may impact encoding, rehearsal and retrieval of retrospective memories of all kinds. We then explore research that suggests that new technology might not only inhibit our natural human memories, but also actively distort it. Finally, we describe how leveraging known psychological phenomena might enable technologies to deliberately enhance or attenuate specific memories, and the potential for introducing false memories. Given these weaknesses, we identify a need for greater understanding when designing new systems to augment cognition and perception.

1 Inhibition: Technology that Encourages Us to Forget

The idea that The Internet and other technologies may be "making us stupid" has received considerable press attention. Writers such as Nicholas Carr (Carr 2008a) have produced numerous books and press articles that use personal observations to highlight how technology use appears to be eroding humans' capacity for focused attention, deep processing and extended reflection. However, amongst these anecdotal accounts and speculation, there is surprisingly little scientific evidence.

The reasons for this limited body of evidence can be attributed to a number of core challenges that arise when attempting to study the impact of technologies on cognition. Firstly, many of the devices and services at the centre of current debates about the role of technology on cognition are extremely pervasive. Whilst their ubiquitous nature renders them prime targets for study, it also presents difficulties in terms of enabling meaningful comparative studies between those who do, and those who do not, use the technologies. Although communities may exist in which a given technology has not yet reached high levels of penetration, those communities often differ in multiple ways from communities with high levels of that technology's use, making it difficult to identify causal relationships. Secondly, the cognitive effects attributed to technology are largely considered to be the product of long-term use, with typical arguments focusing on the cumulative effects of embedding technology into our everyday activities. Such longitudinal phenomena are impossible to replicate in the time-constrained setting of a laboratory experiment. Finally, the pace of innovation and breadth of technologies developed means that a considered study of every technology prior to its widespread adoption is inviable. Although law and policymakers could mandate a thorough evaluation of new devices and services, this would likely hamper innovation and limit the significant societal growth that has been associated with technology development to date. Furthermore, since many technologies fail to reach high levels of saturation (and accurate predictions of which technologies will succeed or fail are extremely challenging), an appropriately thorough study of every emerging technology would be undesirable.

In this section, we summarise current understanding on the potential inhibitive effects of technology on three specific areas of memory. Firstly, we consider semantic memory, and the impact that the large scale data storage, indexing, and the World Wide Web may have on our capacity to remember pieces of information. Secondly, we consider episodic memory, and the role of photos and lifelogging technologies in remembering our experiences and deriving knowledge from these experiences. Finally, we consider spatial memory, and the role of navigation technologies in supplanting the cognitive processes that help us remember how to traverse our physical environments.

1.1 The Google Effect

The first, and perhaps most well-known set of experiments to explore the impact of technology on our memories was conducted by Sparrow et al. in (2011).

Sparrow et al.'s first experiment focussed on the associations an individual makes when presented with a knowledge gap. Their method used a variant on the popular *Stroop test* (Stroop 1935) in which subjects are presented with words written in coloured text and asked to either name the word or colour presented. When primed to think about a topic related to the presented word, participants are slower to name

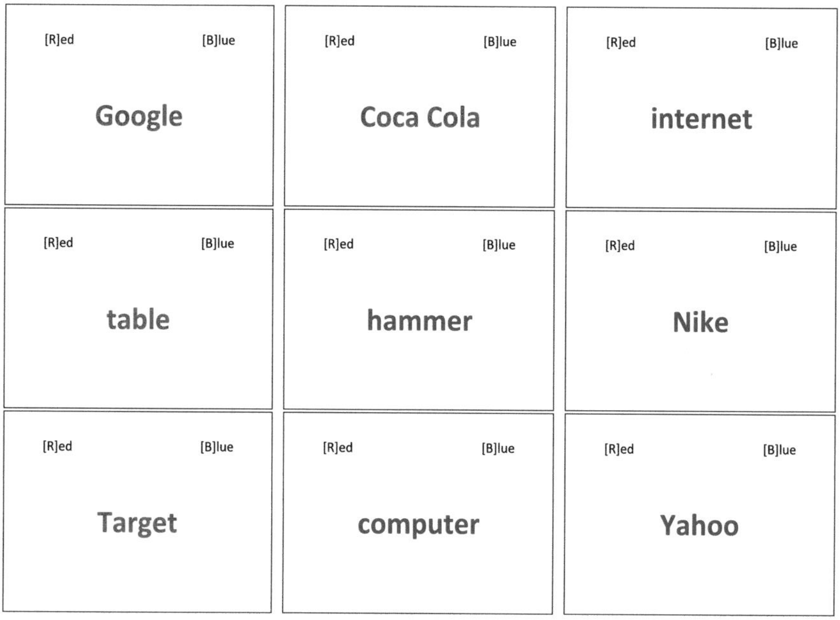

[R]ed [B]lue	[R]ed [B]lue	[R]ed [B]lue
Google	**Coca Cola**	**internet**
[R]ed [B]lue	[R]ed [B]lue	[R]ed [B]lue
table	**hammer**	**Nike**
[R]ed [B]lue	[R]ed [B]lue	[R]ed [B]lue
Target	**computer**	**Yahoo**

Fig. 2 Example stimuli used in Sparrow et al.'s (2011) Stroop test. Each of the pictured slides would be presented one at a time, and participants asked to indicate whether the text appeared in red or blue. Stimuli included computer and non-computer terms, both common and proper nouns (Sparrow et al. 2011)

the text colour because the word itself is more accessible and distracts attention from the colour naming task. In their experiment, Sparrow's participants were presented with a set of trivia questions and then asked to complete a Stroop test that involved a selection of computer (e.g., Google, Yahoo) and non-computer terms (Nike, Target). Participants completed two trivia quizzes, one hard and one easy, and each was followed by the Stroop task. Results showed that, after completing the trivia questions, participants took longer to name the colour of the ink in a Stroop task (i.e., larger effects) for computer terms (712 ms) than non-computer terms (591 ms), but that this effect was considerably greater when participants were asked the more difficult questions. This increase in response time is taken as evidence that answering trivia questions primes participants to think of computers and/or the Internet (Fig. 2).

These findings from Sparrow et al. provide some initial evidence that we have strong mental associations between recollection of knowledge and technology use. To explore these associations in more depth, (Storm et al. 2017) developed a method to establish the degree to which participants relied on the Internet when answering trivia questions. In their first experiment, Storm et al. presented forty participants with eight difficult trivia questions followed by eight easy questions. A further twenty participants answered only the easy questions. When answering the difficult questions, half the participants (20) were asked to answer the questions from memory and half were asked to answer the questions with the help of Google Search. When answering the eight easier trivia questions, all participants were given the option of using Google Search to find the answers. Storm et al. found that participants who were instructed to use the Internet to answer the first set of questions relied on the Internet (83%) more often whilst answering the second set of questions than those who had earlier relied on their memory (63%) and the baseline (65%). In a subsequent variation on this experiment, eighty participants were again asked to answer eight difficult trivia questions followed by eight easy questions, with the first questions either answered from memory ($n = 40$) or with the help of Google Search ($n = 40$). For the subsequent easier questions, participants in both conditions (memory vs. Google Search) were further divided into two sub-groups. Half the participants from each group were sat on a sofa on the opposite side of the room to a table and desktop computer, whilst for the other half the computer was replaced with a first-generation Apple iPod Touch. If they wished to use Google to help them answer one of the easy trivia questions, participants were required to leave the sofa and cross the room to use their allocated device; participants had to return to the sofa to receive the next question. Replicating results from the preceding study, participants who answered the difficult questions with the Internet also answered the easy questions with the Internet (62%) more often than those who had earlier used their memories (48%). Participants used the Internet less often when it was on the smaller device, but this did not interact with prior Internet use, showing that use of the Internet as an information source can influence the future use of the Internet as an information source even when using the Internet is made increasingly inconvenient. In their final experiment, Storm et al. explored how prior use of the Internet to access information might alter the speed with which participants decided whether or not to search the web in subsequent information retrieval. Forty participants answered ten difficult trivia questions followed by ten easy questions; again half of the participants were instructed to search for the difficult answers using the Internet whilst the others relied on their own memories. After a 5-minute distraction task, the ten relatively easy questions were presented to participants who were asked to answer each question as quickly and as accurately as possible. All participants were given the option of using Google Search to find the answers but were not required to do so. In line with results from the prior two experiments, those participants who had used Google for the preceding difficult trivia questions were significantly more likely to Google for the answers to these easier questions. Furthermore, participants who used the Internet to answer harder questions touched the keyboard or mouse significantly faster when Googling for the answers to easier questions, i.e., they took less time consulting their own memory before choosing to rely on Google.

Taken together these studies from Sparrow et al. and Storm et al. suggest that Internet use may be a common strategy for information access, even when that information would be readily recalled without the Internet. However, in light of these a key question remains unanswered—what is the impact of this strategy on cognition itself? It's possible that retrieving previously encountered information from technology is easier than bringing it to mind ourselves—if the technology were to fail, we might simply fall back on our own cognition. To understand how memory for information was impacted by potential computer use, Sparrow et al. (2011) conducted three further experiments. The studies explored participants' memory for trivia that they believed they would later have access to (analogous to information they could look up online) and for the locations at which that information could be found. In Experiment 2, Sparrow et al. presented four groups of participants with forty memorable trivia statements similar to those one might look up online and asked them to retype them into a computer. Half of their participants were informed that the computer would save the answers whilst the others half believed that the answers would be erased. Experiment 3 followed a similar format but used a within-subjects design in which all participants were told per-item that the trivia had been saved, erased or saved to a specific location (one of six folders with semantically similar names, e.g., "facts" and "data"). In subsequent tests of recall (Experiment 2) and recognition (Experiment 3), Sparrow et al. found that participants had a poorer memory for statements that they believed the computer had saved.

Participants in Experiment 3 were additionally asked whether the trivia statement in their recognition test had been saved or erased and if the statement had been saved to a folder, which folder it had been saved into. In response to this question, participants more accurately remembered what they had saved than erased (i.e., the opposite pattern to the trivia items themselves), but had poor recognition memory for the specific folder to which the statement had been reportedly saved. Hypothesising that using the computer to store the trivia enhances memory for the fact that the information could be accessed (rather than memory for the information itself), Sparrow et al. conducted one final experiment (Experiment 4) in which participants retyped the trivia statements and were notified for each that it had been saved to one of the six folders. Participants were next given two recall tasks—the first for the statements themselves: writing down as many of the statements as they could remember, and then second for the locations. In this second recall task, a prompt was given for each original trivia statement and participants were required to type the name of the folder in which the item had been saved. In line with the previous studies, results showed that participants were better able to remember where information was saved than they were to remember the statements themselves—participants around 2–3 times more likely to recall nothing at all, or just the folder name, than they were to recall the statement with or without the folder.

Sparrow et al.'s second and third experiments manipulated participants' availability expectations by explicitly notifying them that information would be saved or erased. Further exploration of the impact of availability expectations was conducted by Macias et al. (2015). In their study, Macias et al. presented 150 Amazon Mechanical Turk participants with twenty facts, half of which were considered to be "lookupable" (e.g., "The first major motion picture to star an African-American woman was ZouZou"), and half that were not (e.g., "Tamara Greene has the largest sticker collection of anyone in the elementary school."). Participants were shown the facts, one at a time for ten seconds each. A fill-in-the-blanks recall test followed the fact presentation, with one question relating to each of the previously presented facts (e.g., "The first major motion picture to star an African-American woman was _____"). Participants were instructed not to use any aids when completing the recall test, and compliance was verified with a lure question in which one of the lookupable fill-in-the-blank facts was replaced with a previously unseen fact (no participants correctly answered the lure question). Results showed that participants correctly recalled fewer of the lookupable facts (44.6%) than the nonlookupable facts (52.8%). Furthermore, when participants were divided based on a prior test of their ability to lookup information on the Internet, results indicated that those who demonstrated greater skill with looking facts up online performed better on the memory test overall and had an even stronger tendency to better remember nonlookupable facts. These findings are consistent with those from Sparrow et al., providing further evidence that individuals memory encoding is shaped by the perceived future availability of the target information.

1.2 Digital Photography and Episodic Memory

As the previous chapter recounted, technological advances make it increasingly possible to capture and then display digital records of our day-to-day lives. Worn lifelogging cameras and high-quality digital cameras on our readily accessible smartphones enable continuous capture of digital images of everyday events at little or no cost that we can view immediately, share directly or via social media. It is often the case that when we later review such images, the directly observable contents may cue additional information relating to the context (the time, the place, the company) in which the image was captured. This may include details such as: what we were thinking of at the time, what we were doing before or after the captured moment, as well as associations arising from the captured scene (I remember when person X bought that top, I remember that around the corner from this street scene there was the cafe where we once got coffee).

Recent studies in human memory have examined the mnemonic consequences of reviewing images to help relive our autobiographical experiences (Burt et al. 1995; Koutstaal et al. 1998, 1999). Whereas in the past we might have been reliant on written diary entries to act as cues to our autobiographical memories (Linton 1975; Wagenaar 1986, technological advances are radically changing the nature and scale of the external cues that can be used, such that it is now possible to capture, store and process multiple streams of near-continuous data, to be later used as cues to help retrieve associated episodic details (Bell and Gemmell 2007; Clinch et al. 2016; Davies et al. 2015; Dodge and Kitchin 2007; Gurrin et al. 2014; Harvey et al. 2016; Sellen and Whittaker 2010; Silva et al. 2018).

There is considerable evidence that use of wearable cameras, such as Sense-Cam Hodges et al. (2006), Hodges et al. (2011) can enhance later recall and recognition of both memory-impaired participants Allé et al. (2017), Kapur et al. (2002), Silva et al. (2013) and healthy younger participants (Sellen et al. 2007). However, as the previous section has indicated, memory augmentation devices that provide access to semantic knowledge may lead to subsequent decline in the degree of information accessible in our natural or "internal" memory. Recent studies suggest that this effect may not be constrained to semantic memory, but may also the impact memory for experiences captured in photographs (episodic memory).

One study showing a decline in memory following technology use is that of Henkel (2014), who examined whether photographing objects encountered on a museum tour impacted what was remembered about them. During two experiments, participants were supplied with a digital camera and led on a guided tour of an art museum. Participants were given a list of art objects (paintings, sculptures, pottery, tools, jewels, and mosaics) to visit and attend to during the tour; participants were instructed to pay attention and told that they would later be asked about the appearance of the objects. Participants read aloud the name of each object on their list and were led by the experimenter to view the object in the museum. The experimenter directed the participant to look at the object for a short period of time (around 30 s) and in some cases the participant was also asked to take a photograph. Each object on the list was visited in turn, with participants being guided through the museum by the experimenter. In experiment one, for half of the objects, Henkel's participants were directed to take photographs that clearly captured the whole object (the remaining objects were simply observed). In experiment two, Henkel's participants were asked to either take photographs that clearly captured the whole object (one-third of items), to photograph a specified detail within the object (one-third of items), or to simply observe the object (the remaining third).

The day after the museum tour, participants were issued with a memory test for objects seen at the museum. Memory tests across the two studies followed similar formats, with both including name and photograph recognition tests. If a participant indicated during the name recognition test that they had studied this object in the museum, then multiple-choice questions about details of the object were issued. In both studies, participants who took a photograph of the object as a whole showed a photo-taking-impairment effect: they remembered fewer objects, fewer details about the objects, and fewer object locations in the museum than if they instead only observed the objects and did not photograph them. However, participants who zoomed in to photograph a specific part of the object in experiment two did not demonstrate a photo-impairment effect. Their subsequent recognition and detail memory was not impaired, and, interestingly, memories for features that were not zoomed in on were just as strong as memory for features that were zoomed in on.

Barasch et al. (2014) also report a field study in which participants explored a local museum. Before entering one of the galleries, half the participants were instructed to "*take as many photos as possible*", the remaining participants were asked to "*view the exhibit as you normally would*". In both this field study, and two follow-on lab studies (both featuring a "virtual bus tour"), participants again demonstrated a memory-inhibiting effect from taking photographs. Although photography enhanced several subjective measures of experience, participants were actually less likely to correctly answer questions about what they had observed.

One theory explaining Henkel (2014) and Barasch et al.'s (2014) results is that by taking a photograph of the object, participants make a decision to "offload" the remembering of their experiences—the digital photograph serves as a readily accessible artefact (transactive memory partner—see Sect. 1.4) that negates the need to form a personal memory. The validity of this explanation was explored in a recent set of laboratory experiments by Soares and Storm (2018). In their two experiments, Soares and Storm had participants view a computer-based slideshow featuring representations of fifteen figurative paintings, the artwork's titles and artists. The artworks were divided into three counterbalanced blocks and participants were instructed how to attend to each block of images as follows:

(i) *Observe*—for this block, participants were instructed to look at the image and caption;

(ii) *Camera*—participants viewing this block of images were asked to take a photograph of the entire image and caption with the default smartphone camera app.

Instructions for the third block differed between Soares and Storm's two experiments, but in both cases the block represented a case in which participants would not have access to photographs after taking them.

(iii) *SnapChat* (experiment one only)—participants viewing this block of images were asked to take a photograph of the entire image and caption with ephemeral photo-messaging application Snapchat.

(iii) *Delete* (experiment two only)—participants viewing this block of images were asked to take a photograph of the entire image and caption with the default smartphone camera app, then were asked to immediately delete their photograph of the painting.

After a ten-minute delay, participants were presented with a multiple-choice memory test that asked about details within the viewed images. Contrary to the participants' expectations, immediately prior to the test, participants were informed that they would not have access to photographs taken in the camera app. Soares and Storm's results showed a photo-taking-impairment effect in both the Camera and SnapChat conditions of experiment one and in the Camera and Delete conditions of experiment two.

Tamir et al. (2018) also explored factors impacting the photo-taking-impairment effect. In two studies, participants undertook a self-guided tour of Stanford Memorial Church, a building with significant architectural interest, stained glass windows, mosaics, and other details. Participants were given a tour booklet and were randomly allocated to either tour the building without technology, or carrying an iPod touch to be used to take photographs; half of the iPod participants were additionally told that they would upload the pictures to their Facebook accounts upon completion of the tour. In one experiment, participants toured the church alone and in the other participants completed the tour in pairs. Immediately following the tour, a check was made that participants in the Facebook-sharing condition had posted at least two of their photographs to the website. Seven-to-ten days later, participants individually completed a surprise multiple-choice memory test for information featured in the tour brochure. Tamir et al. observed the same photo-taking-impairment effect on memory as the previously described experiments. In both studies by Tamir et al., use of the iPod to take photographs reduced the memory participants had for the tour, replicating the photo-taking-impairment effect of other experiments. However, no statistically significant differences were reported between those who took photographs to share with Facebook and those who simply took photographs to keep after the tour was completed. This suggests that despite its prevalence, social media sharing may not be an important factor in photo-taking impairments.

Taking photos may make people more familiar with an event rather than just feel like they are more familiar. Barasch et al. (2017) conducted a study investigating the effect of freely taking photos compared to not taking photos. In the first experiment of this study, participants went on a self-guided tour of two museum exhibits with an audio guide. The first exhibit was the one used in the memory task, whilst the second served as a distractor. Participants were either assigned to the camera (using their own devices) or no-camera group. After viewing the exhibits with the audio guide, participants were asked to answer questions about the exhibits in a recognition memory task which they had not been informed of at the beginning of the study. Some of the questions were about visual information and others were about the information from the audio guide. It was found that those in the camera group correctly answered more visual questions than the non-camera group and both groups performed similarly on the audio questions. The second experiment was similar to the first, however, it was conducted through Amazon mTurk as a computer task in order to try and better control for confounding variables. The results of this study also found that the camera group (who took photos by clicking a camera button on the screen) had better visual recognition of the paintings in a virtual gallery tour than the no-camera group. However, they also found that the no-camera group performed significantly better than the camera group at answering the questions related to the audio guide.

Barasch et al. suggest the findings from experiment 1 indicate that participants did not offload their memories to their devices and as such aimed to further investigate this by conducting a study where participants were told their photos would be saved or deleted. This was conducted using the same procedure from experiment 2 but participants were either in the no-camera group, the save group or the delete group. The findings supported the results of experiment two as participants with no phone performed better on the auditory recognition. Similarly the camera groups performed better on visual recognition regardless of whether they were told the photos would be saved or deleted. This supports their conclusions that participants are not using their devices to offload memory because if they were, the save group would have remembered less items than the delete group. Barasch et al. instead suggest that there are attentional processes underpinning the effect they have identified. To test this, in their final experiment they again used the procedure from experiment two, but added in a third condition where if the participants would have taken a photo in real life, they were to instead take a mental photograph. It was thought that if attentional processes were underlying the effects seen in the previous studies, taking a mental photograph would direct attention the same way taking a real photograph does, and as such should produce similar effects on memory.

The results supported the hypothesis, as both the camera group and the mental photograph group performed better on the visual recognition test than the no-camera group. For auditory information, the mental photograph group did not differ significantly from either of the other conditions but the no-camera group did correctly answer significantly more of the auditory questions than the camera group. Overall this suggests that utilising cameras does not necessarily lead to cognitive offloading. This contradicts the findings discussed earlier in this section. As such, more research may need to be conducted in this area.

In regards to lifelogging, a literature review by Jacquemard et al. (2014) highlighted the benefits and challenges associated with lifelog technologies. Whilst the challenges covered a range of issues including privacy and technological limitations, here we will focus on the challenges pertaining to memory. As well as highlighting the risk of individuals becoming reliant on lifelogs to remember for them, Jacquemard et al. suggested that the use of lifelogs could impact people's perceptions of the past. For example, when looking at a photo depicting a big decision, one might find with the benefit of hindsight that the decision made was the wrong one and thus this reminder may cause them to be harsher on themselves, or hold the past to standards they hold in the present. This would then have risks to the individuals sense of self, which memory plays a large role in forming.

Jacquemard et al. also highlight the content of memories may risk moving from episodic to semantic. As photographs capture concrete items rather then emotions or sensations, as the reliance on them grows, the semantic aspects of the photo may become more prominent and the personal components in turn may fade. Furthermore as lifelogging cameras tend to capture images automatically, the images captured may not always capture the important information, thus skewing memory towards features that are prominent but not necessarily useful.

Furthermore, whilst this chapter is highlighting the importance of memory and the risks of technology degrading memory, Jacquemard et al. suggest that forgetting is equally important to memory. As stated memory aids forming a sense of self and there are benefits to forgetting past opinions and experiences in this process. It is commonly said people should "forgive and forget" but if memories are digitally preserved, this may not be possible as the depiction of past hardships and slights will be preserved. This also has implications for those with mental health conditions. Lifelogs preserving events that trigger disorders such as post-traumatic stress disorder could be detrimental to health as if it was evoked in an unsafe way, the person may experience negative symptoms.

As such the question of how photographs may impact memory is not just restricted to the memory being degraded, but other negative consequences that may not be immediately intuitive or apparent. One final point to note is that whilst taking photographs has been largely demonstrated to prompt a memory impairment effect, several studies have shown that participants actually believe the opposite. Following the memory test in their paired-participant study, Soares and Storm (2018) asked participants *"What effect do you think taking a photo of an event has on your memory for it*". Likewise Barasch et al. (2014) asked participants to report their subjective memory—how well they thought they remembered the exhibition or bus tour. Both researchers found that taking photographs increased subjective memory perceptions despite significantly poorer performance in objective measures. This is consistent with current evidence that suggests that people are consciously using their cameras as memory aids. Finley, Naz and Goh (2018) report findings from a survey of 476 people which investigated how technology is used in everyday scenarios. Their findings suggest that 91% of individuals regularly carry a device capable of taking photos. When asked why they took photographs with these devices, just over half the participants gave answers pertaining to memory (i.e., related to documenting, remembering or preserving). Whilst 31% explicitly mentioned documenting friends, family or pets, 6% indicated they use photographs to store items that would be stored in semantic memory, such as passwords or where they parked. However, despite these intentions, participants estimated that the mean number of photographs they take a day was just 2.68, and only 14% of the participants mentioned reviewing the photographs they had taken at a later point.

1.3   Satellite Navigation and Spatial Memory

Memory for locations and space is critical in supporting many of our everyday activities, and societies have a rich history of developing techniques to support these processes.[1] Externalising these representations can act as a form of transactive memory, but the process of navigating using maps, signs or landmark descriptions is also a useful tool for developing an individual's *spatial memory*—the recollection and knowledge we have of our environment and our orientation in a space. For example, in a shopping mall, remembering where a specific shop is and how to get to it from the entrance of the mall draws on your spatial memory.

In modern society, it's increasingly rare to navigate anywhere without a technological aid. Dedicated satellite navigations devices (commonly referred to as a "satnav" or "GPS") are used for most automobile journeys and are capable of navigating almost anywhere. Communication applications allow the sharing of ones exact location with others, removing the need to describe locations with the landmarks and directions that might previously have been used for such exchanges (e.g., to facilitate a meet-up with friends). Further, personal devices such as smartphones now also typically include GPS tracking and navigation as standard, such that even pedestrian journeys are frequently subject to turn-by-turn navigation.[2] These tech-

---

[1]Some historians suggest that examples of local area mapping can be seen in pre-historic cave paintings and tusk carvings.

[2]Present systems tend to deliver navigation instructions over visual or audio channels, but recent innovation has taken the concept of steerable pedestrians still further by using haptics to deliver minimal directional information (e.g., vibration on the left side of the body to indicate that a left turn at the next junction), or even through use of electrical muscle stimulation to directly influence walking direction (Pfeiffer et al. 2015).

nological aids differ from their predecessors in a variety of ways, often delivering minimal information in a just-in-time manner and often with audio as the primary modality. What impact, then, are these aids having on our naturally occurring spatial memory?

Psychologists and neuroscientists have researched spatial memory in multiple species and as such, much is known about the mechanisms in the brain that underpin the process. Studies of spatial memory in rats in particular have contributed significantly to our understanding both of how spatial information is stored in the brain (Barnes 1988; O'Keefe and Speakman 1987), and of how environment itself impacts spatial memory (Nilsson et al. 1999). Medical imaging techniques such as MRI have also played a critical role in advancing knowledge of human spatial memory—perhaps most famously in London taxi drivers (Maguire et al. 2000). This oft-cited study by Maguire et al. found that the length of time a taxi driver had been licensed to work in London was evident in the visible structure of their brains. Specifically, areas of the brain that earlier research had indicated as being important for spatial memory were larger in individuals with more experience of driving professionally. Comparisons with non-taxi drivers of the same age (who did not show an increase) suggested that the practice of navigating spaces was resulting in a biological difference in the brains of the taxi drivers. However, as previously noted, way-finding has changed significantly in the twenty years since the publication of Maguire et al.'s findings and even taxi drivers make heavy use of navigation aids. Thus, more recent studies have set out to directly explore the impact of navigational aids on spatial knowledge and memory.

Ishikawa et al. (2008) asked participants to navigate six routes using either a GPS navigation system ($n = 22$), a paper map ($n = 23$) or direct experience ($n = 21$). In the direct experience, group participants were taught the route by an experimenter and then taken back to the start via a different route before navigating the taught route alone. Participants in the GPS and map groups were taken to the start of the route before being given their navigational aid and being asked to navigate to the end of the route. The maps had the start point and end point marked but no route, leaving participants to choose the route themselves. The results suggested that whilst all the groups reported a similar ability to navigate space (sense of direction), there were differences in their spatial understanding and knowledge. The GPS group was significantly worse at indicating the direction of the start point when they finished a route than the direct experience group, as well as drawing less accurate maps, suggesting worse spatial understanding. The map group was not significantly different to either of the groups for these measures suggesting that negative effects on spatial memory are specific to electronic navigational aids. However, participants in the GPS group also reported the task to be more difficult than those in the other conditions and only one participant in the the GPS group reported any prior experience with GPS (for reference, the popular brand TomTom had only released its first generation of satellite navigation devices in 2004). This unfamiliarity, combined with a relatively small screen size (4×5 cm) and a need to frequently attend to the screen in order to detect updates, may have decreased the group's attention to their environments contributing to the observed effects.

Ishikawa et al.'s observations of the GPS group suggest that increased cognitive load, divided attention, and a resulting reduction in engagement with the external environment could be an important factor in the formation of spatial memory. Similar findings have also been seen in more naturalistic studies. Leshed et al. (2008) travelled with participants, observing naturally occurring interactions between ten GPS users and their navigational aids; each journey was followed by a semi-structured interview. In line with the previously discussed findings from Ishikawa et al., observations of GPS navigation demonstrated that participants were able to successfully navigate with GPS. However, Leshed et al.'s findings suggested that users social and environmental interactions differed when using GPS compared to descriptions of past experience without GPS. Socially, drivers no longer required the passenger to navigate and thus drivers reported decreased interactions with their passengers (but in some cases drivers would talk to the GPS device itself). With regard to environmental engagement, Leshed et al. report that "the reduced need to feel oriented, keep track of locations, and maintain social interactions regarding navigation issues inhibit the process of experiencing the physical world by navigation through it" (Leshed et al. 2008, p. 6). Even having successfully navigated to a location with the aid of the GPS Leshed et al. observed cases in which their drivers were so disconnected from their environment that they struggled to locate their target point of interest in the real world.

More recently, Gardony et al. (2013) also found evidence for impaired spatial memory occurring as result of divided attention associated with use of technology-based navigational aids. In their study, participants were asked to navigate between landmarks in an immersive virtual environment on a desktop computer. Participants were guided using either a set of verbal instructions similar in construction to those issued by traditional turn-by-turn navigation systems, tonal instructions that used frequency and volume to represent direction and distance, or no instructions. Following the navigation task, participants were shown scenes from the virtual environment and asked to indicate which direction a landmark was relative to the perspective of the scene. Participants then drew a map of the environment they had explored. Results showed that whilst groups using navigation aids performed slightly better than the no instructions group at the actual navigation tasks, they performed significantly worse at the subsequent environmental recognition and mapping tasks. In a subsequent study, Gardony et al. (2015) attempted to directly examine the divided attention hypothesis, dividing participants into four groups corresponding to navigation-aid use (or not) with focussed versus divided attention. In this study, navigational aids impaired memory regardless of whether attention was divided but having no aid and focussed attention led to the best memory performance. Having no aid and divided attention led to similar performance to both conditions with aids. These studies suggest that technology may only be the tool that divides attention causing spatial memory impairments, rather than technology itself being the cause of memory degradation.

In parallel with this divided attention effect, others have hypothesised that the cognitive offloading that comes with GPS use may lead individuals to simply neglect to attempt to memorise spatial information. For example, in a set of semi-structured interviews with Barcelona taxi drivers, Girardin and Blat (2010) found that drivers reported a preference for GPS use over the traditional "Guia" (a book used to look up locations) because it was *faster and less cognitively demanding*. Even highly experienced drivers reported carrying a GPS device with them, even if not switched on, in the case they need it. By using GPS to reduce cognitive demand whilst navigating, other researchers have suggested that drivers might see a negative impact on spatial memory due to a "use it or lose it" effect (McKinlay 2016). In a direct attempt to combat these potential losses, Parush, Ahuvia and Erev (2007) conducted a study in which technology was used to increase demand on spatial processing. Participants were asked to locate an object within a virtual environment, either whilst having their position in the environment displayed continuously or having their location displayed to them for five seconds on request. Half of the participants in each group were also given quizzes about their orientation in the virtual world at random points in the study. Following these tasks, participants were shown a scene from the virtual environment and were asked to indicate the direction an object was located relative to the scene. This was a test of spatial knowledge, indicative of how well the participants could recall the space. Results showed that those with continuous access to a navigational aid were able to navigate the space more efficiently. However, participants who were subjected to the highest level of cognitive demand performed best in the test of spatial knowledge (i.e., those who took part in the quizzes and who only received navigation information on request). There was a significant main effect of being quizzed on orientation during the task, indicating that active engagement with location improves spatial memory. In their discussion of the results, Parush et al. suggest that users of navigational technology in the real world may be benefited by interventions that lead to increased engagement with the space around them, rather than full reliance on navigational aids. Preliminary work into designing navigational systems which promote learning has been found to be effective in virtual environments (Gramann et al. 2017; Oliver and Burnett 2008; Wen et al. 2014).

Together, these studies suggest that there is an observable difference in performance on spatial memory tasks for individuals whose navigation was supported by technology aids. However, neuro-imaging research also indicates a direct impact on brain structure. We previously noted the effect of navigation experience on brain regions associated with spatial memory (Maguire et al. 2000), with greater experience being associated with larger cortical structures for spatial memory. Given this existing knowledge, Fajnerová et al. (2018) set out to explore if these same brain regions would be reduced in size when navigational technology was used. They asked seventeen participants to wear smart glasses with an incorporated GPS guidance system and to use the system for their everyday navigation to unknown locations for at least three hours each week. A control group (sixteen participants) were asked to navigate to new places often during this period without using an aid. Comparisons of navigation performance in a virtual city before and after the three-month period showed little difference between the two groups. However, functional magnetic resonance imaging taken before and after the three-month period showed that some areas of the brain relating to spatial memory had changed over the intervention period. For the control group these areas had increased in size whilst in the experimental group, they had decreased. These findings reflect the findings of (Maguire et al. 2000) suggesting that whilst three months may not be sufficient use for navigational skills to be observably degraded by technology, neuroanatomical changes may already be in effect.

Finally, we note that spatial navigation and way-finding is not just an individual concern. Talking about and navigating space is a common social and cultural phenomenon with shared practices and knowledge. These collective memories (both of space itself and of the processes for navigating space) can be passed from person-to-person and between generations. For example, Aporta and Higgs (2005) report the impact of technology navigation aids on communities of Inuits, whose hunters traditionally navigate using naturally occurring environmental stimuli (wind patterns, geographic features, animal behaviour). With the advent of navigational technology, these skills are not being passed down and are at risk of being lost from the collective memory.

Overall then, it seems that there is an increasing body of evidence that spatial memory joins our semantic and episodic memory in being inhibited by technology use. Much like the previously described effects of the Internet and of digital cameras, the pace of change in navigation technologies makes it difficult to build a complete understanding. Further, as with many other technologies, evidence of negative impacts on memory are unlikely to dissuade individuals from using GPS devices. Speake (2015) investigated UK students' attitudes towards navigational technologies finding that smartphones were regularly used to navigate even familiar terrain and were positively regarded. In particular, use of navigation devices was associated with reports of feeling "confident"' and "happy", as opposed to feelings of being "afraid" and "angry" when the technology was absent. However, whilst technology users such as those in Speake's study indicate they feel more confident when they have navigational aids to help them, the devices are not always correct. Multiple news articles have reported times where people followed their GPS devices and found themselves in bodies of water (Daily Mail 2008; Toronto Sun 2016) or stranded (The Telegraph 2017; Times and Star 2019). Furthermore, should the device run out of battery or lose signal, individuals will need to rely on their own abilities to navigate to safety—however, if use of devices themselves reduce spatial abilities then this may be problematic. Attempts to provide navigational support whilst still engaging cognitive processes show some promise (Gramann et al. 2017; Oliver and Burnett 2008; Parush et al. 2007; Wen et al. 2014) but this is tricky balance to maintain.

1.4 Explaining Inhibition Effects

In this section, we've explored three examples of technology-based memory inhibition (affecting semantic, episodic and spatial memory, respectively). In their attempts to understand the causes of these phenomena, researchers in all three domains have typically converged on similar explanations. The most dominant explanation is the idea of *transactive memory*, one of several forms of *cognitive offloading*.

Cognitive offloading is described by Risko and Gilbert as "the use of physical action to alter the information processing requirements of a task in order to reduce cognitive demand" (2016, [p. 1]). In the context of memory, this could encompass a wide range of activities including tying a knot in one's handkerchief, writing an often-forgotten important date into one's calendar, or placing tomorrow's lunch by the door to act as a physical reminder to pick it up when leaving the house. As social beings, another common form of cognitive offloading relies on the use of others to remember information in our stead. The term transactive memory, coined by Daniel Wegner in the 1980s (Wegner et al. 1985), is used to refer to a knowledge bank that is distributed across individuals within a group. Each individual in the group stores some part of the overall knowledge plus a *metamemory*[3] consisting of other group members' expertise related to the topic (i.e., who to ask for the missing information).

Transactive memory takes advantage of the fact that people with a strong social connection come to know many things about the way each other's minds work. By leveraging the knowledge they have about each other's interests, expertise and abilities, each member of the group can selectively fail to attend to information that clearly falls within another member's interests. As long as the relationship remains intact, and the other members of the group accessible, this technique has the effect of extending an individual's memorial capacity and providing access to a greater volume of information. Furthermore, since members of a transactive memory system know each other's expertise and limitations, they can make judgments about the reliability and value of any information provided by others. Although the classic examples of transactive memory sit within families, friendships, romantic relationships and close working groups, Wegner (and others) have since gone on to identify technology such as note-taking and the Internet (Ward 2013; Wegner and Ward 2013) as potential transactive memory partners.

Whilst perhaps not a substitute for all of our transactive memory partnerships, the rise of smartphones, wireless internet, and search engines such as Google make for easy access to a wealth of semantic knowledge. When choosing a transactive memory partner, we typically make a judgement about the target's availability (*how likely is it that I will be able to retrieve information when I need it?*) and expertise (*how likely is it that the information retrieved will be correct?*). Technology devices and services typically score highly on both these attributes, making them attractive as potential members for a transactive memory system and potentially encouraging people to " replace their biological memory banks with digital forms of information storage" (Ward 2013, [p 344]). For this reason, transactive memory has been commonly used as an explanation for the Google effect and similar phenomenon (Ward 2013; Wegner and Ward 2013). For example, Wegner and Ward (2013) report that studies "suggest that we treat the Internet much as we would a human transactive

---

[3]Metamemory (Flavell 1971) is a term used to refer to our memory's "knowledge of its own knowledge" (Tulving and Madigan 2005), that is our awareness and monitoring of our own memory capabilities. Although often an unobtrusive feature of our memories, metamemory is critical when considering strategies for improving our memories (e.g., mnemonics) and may also come to the fore when realising that a vivid memory we strongly believe to be true cannot be correct (e.g., in many flashbulb memories).

memory partner. We offload memories to the 'cloud' just as readily as we would to a family member, friend or lover." (2013, [p 3]).

Although much of the evidence is consistent with a cognitive offloading explanation, some results challenge the completeness of this interpretation. For example, whilst results from both Soares and Storm (2018) and Tamir et al. (2018) replicate Henkel's initial observation of a negative effect on memory triggered by the taking of photographs (Henkel 2014), the results of Soares and Storm showed that the negative effects persisted even when participants knew that the data would be unavailable to them after capture (e.g., because they were taking them with an ephemeral photo application). This appears to contradict the suggestion that the memory impairment is the result of cognitive offloading. Soares and Storm propose two alternative hypotheses to explain their findings. Firstly, that some portion of the cognitive offloading that occurs is automatic and unconscious—participants have a learnt response that photography preserves information for later consumption, leading them to reduce the attention given for encoding even when they know that the photographs will be deleted. Secondly, that the act of taking a photograph actually prompts participants to develop an artificial sense of familiarity or *fluency* with the objects, leading them to think that they had already encoded the objects into their (human) memory and reducing the likelihood of them investing further time committing the objects to memory.

Support for the role of fluency has been found by Wilson and Westerman who conducted a series of experiments looking at the role of photographs being present at retrieval (Wilson and Westerman 2018). They found that participants were more likely to believe they had seen a word if it was presented with a related photo, but this effect did not occur if the photo was unrelated. The final experiment in this series asked participants to look at visuals which the experimenter said subliminally contained words (in reality it was just visual noise). Participants were then shown words and asked to indicate which of those words were strongly related to a word from the encoding. It was found that words presented with a picture were more likely to be judged as related. In contrast the experiment before this one found that the presence of photos did not affect which words participants said occurred during the visual noise. This indicates that it was the associations being elicited in the test of the final experiment which led to the fluency promoted by photographs having an effect. This suggests an overall connection between images and eliciting senses of familiarity. More on the role of images can be seen in Sect. 2.1.

In addition to these hypotheses, it's also possible that the camera simply acts as a distraction or cue to disengage (*attentional disengagement*); in a laboratory study reported by Tamir et al. (2018) a distraction task similar to a participants' memory capture task produced an even larger memory impairment than just the capture task itself. The attentional-disengagement hypothesis ties in with one final psychological concept that has also been linked to technology's inhibitive effects on memory. The *levels of processing* model for memory argues that deeper engagement with a stimuli will result in the formation of a stronger, longer lasting memory trace (Craik and Lockhart 1972). Craik and Lockhart (1972) propose that stimuli may be processed either at a superficial or shallow level (focussing, for example, on qualities such as how an item appears or sounds) or at a deeper level (e.g., extracting meaning). Stimuli that have been processed more deeply are considered to form stronger and more durable memory traces, whilst those processed shallowly will have weaker traces resulting in memories that are harder to recall.

Like theories of transactive memory, a levels of processing explanation of technology-based memory inhibition focuses on the process of memory encoding. However, the two differ significantly. Transactive memory theories suggest that individuals make a decision to entrust information with the technology device rather than expend redundant effort in recalling it themselves. By contrast, a levels of processing approach would instead suggest that use of the technology is causing us to engage less deeply with the original stimuli. Considering specifically the photo-impairment example, when people take photos they disengage from the moment to handle the task of capturing the object or experience, thus leading them to encode it less deeply or elaborately than they would have otherwise. Studies that fail to observe photo impairment when the images are captured passively with lifelogging cameras provide some evidence in support of both levels of processing and attentional disengagement. For example, recent work by Niforatos et al. (2017), replicated the photo-taking impairment effect, but only when participants manually took photos, investigating also the effect of limited photo-taking (Niforatos et al. 2014); the effect was not observed when photos were taken automatically by a wearable camera. Other studies have also indicated feelings of disengagement prompted by the experience of taking photographs. Mols et al. (2015), for example, found that when asked to use various methods to document a trip, participants reported feeling more disengaged from the experience when taking photos relative to other recording strategies. Such disengagement could prompt participants to perform shallower encoding processes and make them more likely to miss or fail to encode visual details into memory—not only during the photo-taking experience itself, but also, perhaps, when participants continue to process and consolidate the experience into memory after photo-taking is complete.

2 Distortion: Technology that Manipulates What We Remember

Augmentation technologies often focus on overcoming the *capacity* limits of human memory—allowing the encoding, storage and access to information that exceeds our natural perceptual, attention, storage and retrieval capabilities. This focus belies an underlying assumption that capacity is the primary limit on human abilities. However, psychologists have repeatedly demonstrated the susceptibility of humans to memory distortions—means and methods by which we can be convinced to report exposure to facts or events that we have not experienced, or to to fail to report those that were experienced.

Some of the earliest observations of memory distortions were made by Frederick Bartlett in his 1932 book *Remembering* (Bartlett 1932). In one classic example, Bartlett told British participants a North American folk tale and later asked them to retell it from memory. He noted that participants' retellings often omitted or modified unfamiliar elements, bringing the stories more in line with their own cultural experiences. Bartlett proposed that remembering was a process of *reconstructing* the past based on our existing knowledge structures and expectations (schemata). Other psychological research conducted around the same time demonstrated the influence of contextual language on the recall of visual images (Carmichael et al. 1932). Images were presented to participants, with a verbal comment that likened the image to one of two labels (e.g., the same image might be described either as resembling a crescent moon or the letter C). When later asked to reproduce the figures from memory, the most common errors saw participants adapt their reproduction to be a closer visual representation of the reference object named by the experimenter. Other studies have also demonstrated that false memories for words can be triggered by prior exposure to related items (Deese 1959); for example, presentation of a word list including words such as *sharp, haystack* and *thread* might lead participants to falsely recall the strongly related (but not presented) word *needle*.

Later research (in the 1970s) demonstrated memory distortion for more familiar information and events. Rather than using abstract figures or word lists, these studies used narratives and video as the initial stimulus. For example, presentation of text such as "*John was trying to fix the birdhouse. He was pounding the nail when his father came out to watch him and help him do the work.*" would lead participants to incorrectly state that they had seen text that referred to John using a hammer to fix the birdhouse (Johnson et al. 1973). Likewise, Elizabeth Loftus' research into eyewitness testimony demonstrated additions and inaccuracies for events seen in a video clip. In the studies by Loftus and Palmer, the phrasing of questions issued to participants frequently led them to report details not present in the original video. In several of their studies participants were shown a series video clips showing traffic collisions (Loftus and Palmer 1974). After each clip, one group participants were asked "*About how fast were the cars going when they smashed into each other?*", whilst others were asked a similar question in which the words *smashed into* were replaced with an alternative phrasing (e.g., *hit, contacted*). Use of the word *smashed* in the original question prompted participants to estimate that the cars were travelling with greater speed, but also to mistakenly respond "yes" to a question about whether they had seen broken glass in the video clip.

In this section, we explore the potential of augmentation technologies to distort human memory. Such distortions could simply be an unintentional by-product of cognitive enhancement, but researchers have already raised concerns that these innate cognitive vulnerabilities might pose a security risk allowing malicious parties to deliberately manipulate memory. We begin by exploring the phenomenon of false memories and the role technology can play in generating these. We then continue by looking at the targeted attenuation of memories through retrieval-induced forgetting, and the resulting potential for image selection algorithms to deliberately shape what is remembered and forgotten in episodic memory review.

2.1 False Memory

The examples above demonstrate the potential for false details (the presence of a hammer, or broken glass) to be added to fundamentally "true" memories. However, as arguably the most well-known researcher in the space of false memory, Loftus has also demonstrated the potential to generate completely false memories in her participants (Loftus and Pickrell 1995). In her "lost in the mall" experiment, short narratives describing three real childhood events[4] were presented to participants, also included was a fourth narrative, generated by the researchers, that described a fictitious occasion on which the participant was reported to have become lost in a shopping mall. Participants were first asked to extend the written narratives with any details they could remember and were later followed up with two interviews in which they again asked to describe the events as they remembered them. Over the course of these interactions, 25% of participants claimed to have some memory of the false event.

The studies described so far have all used narratives and researcher questioning to generate either fictitious details or completely false memories. However, as technology becomes increasingly dominant in maintaining our personal histories, it becomes important to understand if similar distortions can be created through the use of digital technologies. In particular, to what extent can memory be shaped by a *doctored evidence effect* (Nash et al. 2009a) in which artefacts are created or manipulated to generate false beliefs? For example, can manipulations of our digital photographs lead us to alter our memories of the events they represent? Does inserting new events into our online calendars, and/or altering locations in our GPS traces, prompt us to alter our recollection of how we spent time? Can record of emails read or sent, lead us to believe that we have seen messages from others that were in fact never received?

False memory creation through digital calendars, satnav traces or email is yet to be explored. The issue of digitally manipulated photographs has received more attention, perhaps as a result of a growing awareness of the ease with which convincing photographs can be produced.

2.1.1 Doctored Evidence and Episodic Memory

In 2002, Wade et al. (2002) adapted the methodology used in Loftus' "lost in the mall" studies to examine if digitally manipulated photographs could also be used to generate false childhood memories. Twenty participants were each shown four printed photographs, each depicting a childhood event; three were real photographs supplied by a relative, and the fourth was a doctored image showing the participant and one or more family members on a hot air balloon ride. Over the course of 7–16 days and three interviews, participants were asked to recall the events depicted in each of the four photographs, providing as much detail as they could. By the end of the third interview, 50% of participants claimed to have some memory of

---

[4]Narratives of real events were provided by family members.

the false event. A similar experiment by Garry and Wade (2005) also demonstrated that a substantial portion of participants presented with doctored images showing the fictitious childhood hot air balloon ride later claimed to be able to remember something about the event. However, in their experiment participants presented with a false narrative of the event rather than a photo were more likely to adopt the false memory (80% of participants did so) than those presented with the photograph and no narrative (50% of participants). Similar rates of false memory adoption (47%) for the childhood hot air balloon photographs were also reported in experiments by Strange (2005) and by Hessen-Kayfitz and Scoboria (2012). However in their experiments, presenting participants with a photograph that only showed the hot air balloon, and did not show the participant and their family members riding in the basket, reduced the propensity for false memories by around half (to 19% and 24% respectively). These experiments suggest that the inclusion of personal details may add some credibility to the false event. However Hessen-Kayfitz and Scoboria also note that including additional unfamiliar detail in the photographs (e.g., a lighthouse) appears to cancel out the effect of the personal detail (false memory rate in this condition was 26%).

Whilst it's evident that digital multimedia may be leveraged to convince us of fictitious long-forgotten childhood events, this may be an unlikely time-period to target for lifelogging platforms and similar memory augmentation tools in the near future. After all, for such an attack to be viable, these devices would need to have access to a lifetime of personal images. Whilst this may not be so far away, the largest (and most reviewed) collections of images relate to more recent experiences.

A series of experiments exploring the potential of digitally manipulated multimedia to distort memory of recently completed mundane actions were conducted by Nash et al. (2009b; 2009a). Three experiments followed the same overall structure and were each composed of three sessions. In session one (*the event phase*), participants echoed a series of simple actions performed by a researcher (e.g., browse a book, wave goodbye, make binoculars with your hands). Activities were video recorded. In session two (*the suggestion phase*), participants watched back the the video for a subset of performed activities, together with some new "false" actions that had not been performed. To allow participants to review false actions, Nash et al. created a set of doctored videos by splicing together new footage of the researcher completing unseen actions and existing video of the participant observing performed actions. In session three (*the memory test*), participants were asked about a large number of completed and new actions and were asked how strongly they *believed* that they had completed the action and their *memory* for doing so.

During their first two experiments, Nash et al. sought to tease apart the effects of two different processes previously used by researchers to generate false memories (Nash et al. 2009b). In the majority of the false image studies described so far, participants were both supplied with a photograph (the false evidence) and also asked to think back to or imagine the event. For these two experiments, participants in the suggestion phase first watched a subset of the action videos and were then asked to spend time imagining completing an (overlapping) set of actions. Since actions in the suggestion phase of these experiments were reviewed either (a) in a video clip, (b) through imagination or (c) both of these, the experimenters were able to separate the impact of the two processes. In both experiments, participants from all three conditions demonstrated a clear false memory effect in which unperformed actions reviewed in the suggestion session were scored more highly for both belief and memory than similar unreviewed unperformed actions. Results also showed that presentation of the false video clip and imagination were equally effective at creating memory distortions. Whilst combining false media with imagination produced the strongest false memory effect, in both experiments *the doctored media alone was sufficient to cause significant belief and memory distortions*.

In their third experiment, Nash et al. looked to understand which features of their doctored videos were most critical to false memory formation (Nash et al. 2009a). In this experiment, participants were assigned to one of three conditions that determined the format of the videos shown:

(1) videos showed the researcher performing the action and the participant observing,
(2) videos showed the researcher performing the action with a mask applied to left half of the image to cover any image of the participant,
(3) videos showed a stranger performing the action with a mask applied to left half of the image.

During the memory test, participants in all three conditions demonstrated a false memory effect, scoring viewed but unperformed actions more highly for both belief and memory than similar un-viewed and unperformed actions. However, participants who had viewed themselves in the (doctored) videos of unperformed actions were significantly more likely to score those actions more highly than similar un-viewed and unperformed actions.

These three experiments by Nash et al. demonstrate the potential of doctored media to elicit false memories for recent events. However, it could be argued that the impact of generating a false memory for such trivial actions is highly limited—perhaps the non-existent implications of having completed the actions meant participants were inclined to capitulate to the perspective provided by the doctored evidence. In a further two experiments, Nash and Wade again asked participants to engage in a video-recorded task and then presented them with doctored videos to prompt false memories (Nash and Wade 2009). Unlike the previous experiments, the doctored videos in these studies showed participants engaging a potentially undesirable behaviour—cheating in a gambling task. Participants were supplied with two piles of fake money, one to gamble with and one that represented the bank. They were then asked to play a computer-based multiple-choice general knowledge game. Following correct answers, a green tick appeared on the computer screen with instructions to take money from the bank. Likewise, if their answer was incorrect, a red cross appeared with instructions to return money to the bank. When participants returned for a second session later in the day, the experimenter falsely accused the participant of cheating and told them that as a result they had invalidated not only their own data but also that of another participant. In their first experiment, participants were accused of inappropriately taking money from the bank in response to a single incorrect answer; in the second, participants were accused of taking money on three separate occasions. As part of the accusations, participants were either shown faked video evidence or were simply told that incriminating video evidence existed.

To establish if participants had adopted false memories of the cheating events, participants were twice asked to sign a handwritten confession. Participants were told that by signing the confession they were accepting that they would not received payment for participation. Participants were then sat outside in the waiting room where a confederate initiated a conversation about the events. In both experiments 87% percent of participants signed the confession after a single request to do so. Following a second request, the remaining 13% of participants in experiment one signed the confession; in experiment two, half of the remaining participants signed the confession on the second request. Participants were equally likely to sign the confession if they were told that video evidence existed than if they saw the doctored video. During discussion with the confederate, 83% of participants in the first experiment and 73% of those in experiment two fully or partially internalised the cheating episode (that is, they made statements indicating that they believed they could have, or definitely had, cheated). Seven percent of participants in experiment one and 10% in experiment two hypothesised about how the cheating might have occurred, and a further 3% (experiment one)—7% (experiment two) fully confabulated details about how the cheating had occurred. Results indicated that seeing doctored video made participants significantly more likely to internalise the cheating episode than simply being told that incriminating video existed, suggesting that they doctored media prompted participants to genuinely accept the false cheating event as a real memory.

Applications of the doctored evidence effect go far beyond simply convincing users of historic or recent events—human memory plays a key role in self-identity (Neimeyer and Metzler 1994; Wigoder 2001; Wilson and Ross 2003) and future behaviour (Biondolillo and Pillemer 2015; Kuwabara and Pillemer 2010; Pezdek and Salim 2011). One key utilisation identified by Clinch et al. (2019) and Davies et al. (2015) is the use of episodic memories and experiences of brands to drive future purchases, i.e., to deliver personalised (and potentially unconscious) advertising. In such scenarios, users might simply be reminded of previous positive experiences of a product. However, in a more sinister approach, advertisers could pay to (a) have negative experiences of their product targeted for *attenuation* (see Sect. 2.2), or (b) to alter positive memories for competitor products, replacing the alternative brand with their own product. As a demonstration of how this latter scenario might be realised, we can consider an exploratory study by Hellenthal et al. (2016) who invited participants into the laboratory under the premise of contributing to a consumer research study. Each participant was first asked to score six differently branded items from within twelve different food categories, indicating how much they liked the brands and whether they would be likely to purchase each one. Participants were then supplied with half the brands (three) from each category and asked to compile a "personal brand lifestyle basket" containing the one brand per category that they liked the best. After all brands had been selected, participants were asked to pose with their "basket" and a photograph was taken. Seven days later, participants returned to the lab and were presented with a doctored version of their photograph. These photographs were a manipulation of the original image that replaced four of the originally chosen items with one of the two competitor brands that the participant had not selected. Participants viewed their doctored image and were given a short questionnaire to complete for each brand in the image. The following day, participants returned to the lab for one final session in which they were given a surprise recognition test for their original basket choices. Surprisingly, the majority of substituted non-chosen and less-liked brands were falsely attributed to the original basket—in 70% of cases participants stated that they had chosen these as their preferred brand when this was not the case. Furthermore, for approximately 80% of these false brand memories, participants agreed with a statement that they could vividly remember choosing the brand for their basket.

A study by Nightingale, Wade and Watson investigated how well participants could identify whether or not an image had been manipulated (Nightingale et al. 2017). In their first experiment, participants ($n = 707$) were shown 10 images. Participants were asked to indicate whether they thought the image had been altered. If so, they were asked to indicate where the image had been altered. The image was split into 9 sections and the participants indicated which region contained the alterations. Participants identified that photos had not been edited 72% of the time and correctly identified when an image had been edited 60% of the time, showing that whilst participants performed at a rate greater than chance, participants were notably worse at correctly identifying manipulated images compared to original images. Regarding locating the alterations, participants correctly identified the manipulation 45% of the time. Generally the more implausible the manipulation was, the more frequently it was identified. The exception to this was manipulations to shadows which were identified to a similar level as plausible manipulations such as air-brushing. Nightingale et al. further analysed the correlation between the level of correct judgements and the difference between the original photo and manipulated photo. This analysis suggested that the greater the difference between the original and manipulation, the more frequently the manipulation was located.

The second experiment aimed to investigate whether manipulations could be located even if they did not originally believe the photo was manipulated. The procedure was the same as in Experiment 1 except for (a) all participants ($n = 659$) being asked to locate manipulations regardless of if they believed they were there or not, (b) the image was split into 12 sections rather than 9 and (c) a new set of photos were used. Participants correctly identified 58% of the original images and 65% of the manipulated photos. Nightingale et al. suggest the drop in correctly identifying the original was potentially caused by participants being asked to look for where the image was manipulated for all photos. For the most extreme manipulations, over 80% of manipulations were detected and located, however, for airbrush manipulations (considered a plausible change), this number was between 10 and 20%. However for another plausible change, "add/sub", the proportion of manipulations correctly identified was just under 70%. As such, the researchers suggest individuals' abilities to identify manipulations may relate to the size of the change rather than the plausibility of the change. The analysis of the difference between the original photo and manipulated photo, and the proportion correctly located supports that larger changes were easier to detect, regardless of whether they were considered plausible or not. The overall results of this study suggest that people are not good at detecting whether images have been manipulated. In particular if the manipulation has been done in a subtle way, changing minimal features, the manipulation is likely to go unnoticed. Taken with the knowledge from memory research, we can see that it is easy to trick people into believing a photograph is real, and thus create false memories.

Finally, we note that digital manipulation of images and video may not, in fact, be needed. Evidence suggests that true photographs of our experiences could be leveraged by malicious parties to help contextualise and convince us of false memories. In these cases, true images might be combined with other manipulated data (e.g., GPS traces, calendar data, email) to add validity to these false traces (Brown and Marsh 2008). In a study using childhood memories, Lindsay et al. (2004) provided participants with narratives of three events alleged to have taken place during their primary school years. Two narratives recounted true events and provided by a parent, the third was a pseudo-event that had been personalised to include the name and gender of the participant's first grade teacher. Half the participants were supplied only with the written narrative, the other half were additionally issued with a copy of their school class photo for the year in which the narrated event was said to have taken place. Over two sessions, participants recounted their memories for the events presented in the narratives.

At the end of session two, 22.7% of participants presented with the narrative alone were considered (by two independent judges reviewing transcripts of their reports) to have a false memory for the pseudo-event, increasing to 65.2% for participants who were also supplied with the photo. Participants in the photo condition also self-rated their memories more highly on scales reflecting the degree to which they felt they were remembering and reliving the event, and the degree of confidence they had in their memories. Similar results were seen in experiments by Henkel and Carbuto (2008) and Henkel (2011). Henkel's experiments followed the same overall format as the "action" experiments of Nash et al., but in this case the selected mundane actions each produced a completion artefact (i.e., an opened nut for the action "*crack the walnut*"). Showing photographs depicting the completion artefact (and not the participant) still increased the likelihood that participants would mistakenly claim they had performed the action in the event phase. Henkel's results also indicated that a longer time interval between the suggest and test phase increases rates of false memory, as does a greater number of exposures to the lure photographs. This substantial increase in propensity for false memories for participants supplied with a temporally or semantically related photograph suggests that simply by providing related, valid evidence, one could increase the likelihood with which users accepted a false memory as truth.

Together, the studies described in this section have significant implications for memory augmentation technologies that use visual multimedia (images, video). Whilst the psychologists conducting the experiments were of the belief that "*most of us will never be confronted with images of ourselves doing things we have never done, or in places we have never been.*" (2005, [p. 4]), memory augmentation systems that capture, archive and visualise imagery of our experiences certainly provide the means to do so. We therefore suggest that, as posited by Clinch et al. (2019) and Davies et al. (2015), there is significant potential for memory augmentation systems to be valid targets for deliberate malicious activity. In particular, the findings of these false memory studies suggest that by doctoring an individual's multimedia, attacks on (or within) memory augmentation technology may: (i) support the creation of false memories for both historic (e.g., childhood) and recent events; (ii) support the creation of false memories for both mundane and unusual (potentially even implausible) events; (iii) support the creation of potentially harmful or incriminating false memories, (iv) manipulate details associated with existing "true" memories leading to altered beliefs and behaviour, and (v) support the manipulation of memory in both children and adults. Furthermore, these effects are robustly demonstrated through the use of relatively simplistic, non-interactive media. As memory technologies evolve to allow more seamless and interactive review, it's highly likely that these will in turn increase the potential for generating even larger false memory effects (Schlosser 2006).

Strategies for mitigating the cognitive effects of doctored evidence attacks conducted through memory augmentation may be possible. At an individual level, a user struggling to recall any details of an event presented by memory augmentation might simply choose to discuss the event with friends and family. Indeed, in a survey reported by Wade and Garry, 81% of participants needing to verify an uncertain memory presented to them by researchers reported that they would use discussion with family members as their primary or secondary strategy for verification (Wade and Garry 2005). Furthermore, evidence suggests that this strategy could prove highly effective—in a study by French et al. and reported by Strange et al. (2005) discussing a fictional childhood hot air balloon ride with a sibling reduced the likelihood of participants maintaining their initial false memory of the event. However, verification of every memory presented by future augmentation systems is impractical and negates the utility of such a device. This strategy would therefore require participants to have sufficient skepticism of a specific event that they consider there to be value in verifying with others. Furthermore, this strategy is only likely to be effective for a subset of memory types; those that relate to shared events that are memorable and distinctive enough for others to have confidence in their own recollections. Finally, this strategy assumes that any attack on an individuals' memory is conducted in isolation. That is, that the memory augmentation system doesn't simply attempt to implant the same shared false event into all parties memories simultaneously.

A second strategy for mitigating doctored evidence attacks on memory augmentation might simply be to increase public awareness of potential attacks and the risks they pose. The recent negative press associated with "spying" smart home devices provides an illustration of one likely manifestation of such an awareness campaign. Likewise, the EU Cookie law provides another—devices could be forced to issue warnings notifying users that it is possible for images and video to be distorted, and that distortions have been shown to lead to false memories. However, surveys issued to participants in several of the aforementioned doctored media studies indicate that people already have high levels of awareness of the potential for image manipulation. Furthermore, in Nash et al.'s study of false actions (Nash et al. 2009b), presentation of an explicit warning that both images and videos could be doctored did not significantly alter their propensity to false memories.

2.1.2 Fake News and Semantic Memory

The previous section provides clear evidence that the presence of doctored information can lead to the distortion of episodic memories, leading us to falsely recall events that never happened to us, and that digital capture, curation and presentation of memories provides new opportunities for introducing these distortions. However, episodic memories are not unique in their vulnerability to distortion. Misinformation by trusted sources may not be a new phenomenon, but in the last decade the term "fake news" has become part of the general population's everyday vocabulary.[5] One driving factor has been the influence of social media, with around two-thirds of American adults (68%) reporting that they source at least some of their news through social media (Shearer and Matsa 2018), online platforms with significant potential to create shared (but incorrect) understandings of significant events (Spinney 2017). In this section, we consider how our memory for information might be altered through exposure to false information, even when we know that information to be incorrect at the time of presentation. We focus on fake news as a contemporary example with demonstrable impact on individuals and society.

Memory for television, radio, web and print news (that has not been deliberately falsified) has been explored in considerable depth Booth (1970); David (1998); Findahl and Höijer (1985); Graber (1990); Gunter (1979); Lang et al. (2005); Newhagen (1998); Tannenbaum (1954), allowing researchers to build an understanding of factors that impact the memorability of a news item and its details. For example, there is considerable evidence that we have better recall for news items that: (i) are presented more frequently (Booth 1970) and are longer (Booth 1970; Lang et al. 2005), (ii) that appear first or last in their presentation medium Booth (1970), Gunter (1979), Tannenbaum (1954), (iii) that are supported by visual media David (1998), Graber (1990), Gunter (1979), Newhagen (1998), and (iv) relate to subjects that we are more familiar with (Findahl and Höijer 1985). To what extent then, do these findings carry over to fake news? Can these effects be leveraged to increase the chance of recalling false information? In this section, we focus principally on evidence relating to (iii) and (iv)—i.e., the role of visual media and subject familiarity/interest. However, there is also substantial evidence for an "illusory truth" effect in which simply repeating pieces of false information creates a belief that the information is more true.

Having discussed in some depth the role of imagery in creating false episodic memories, it is perhaps not too surprising that they also have a significant role to play in semantic memory. Firstly, the very presence of a photograph appears to help convince people that the information presented alongside the image is true (Fenn

---

[5]The 2016 US elections are often credited with the term's increased parlance Gill (2019); Pangrazio (2018). Reflecting its swift rise to prominence, the following year (2017) "fake news" was named as the Collins Dictionary word of the year.

et al. 2019; Newman et al. 2012, 2015). For example, in experiments by Newman et al. (2012), statements saying either "this famous person is alive" or "this famous person is dead" were more likely to be judged by participants to be true when the name of the target celebrity was presented together with a photograph. Likewise, short statements of general knowledge were also more likely to be judged as true if presented with a related, but non-probative photo (i.e., an image that could not directly validate or invalidate the claim). Perhaps counter-intuitively, this inclination to trust visual imagery appears to persist even for untrusted news sources (i.e., images published in a tabloid newspaper are considered more trustworthy than the newspaper itself (Kelly and Nace 1994) and when participants are well-briefed regarding the potential for digital tools to be used to manipulate images (Kelly and Nace 1994).

A subsequent set of experiments by Fenn et al. (2019) looked specifically at this "photo truthiness" effect in the context of social media platforms (a common distribution mechanism for fake news). Participants ($n = 164$) were shown a prototype social media application "Fact-O-Matic" that presented ninety-six general knowledge statements some of which were text-only and some that were presented with a non-probative image. Participants were asked to indicate if they thought the statement was true or false, and whether they would like and/or share it (two common interactions on social media). In line with the findings from Newman et al., results indicated that people did tend to judge statements as true when they were shown with an image, although this effect was stronger for true statements than for false ones. Participants were also more likely to like and share statements accompanied by images, and this effect was stronger for false statements than true statements.

A further set of experiments from Newman et al. (2015) suggest that the selection of images itself is important in creating a photo truthiness effect—photos that related closely to the text led participants to judge the text to be factually correct whilst photos that were unrelated led participants to judge the text to be factually incorrect. Moreover, these effects only occurred for a within-subjects (Experiments 1, 2, 3, and 4) or mixed design (Experiments 5 and 6); when participants saw only facts with relevant images, *or* those without images, *or* those with irrelevant images (Experiments 7 and 8), then they were no more likely to rate the facts as true or false when compared to those in other conditions.

Moving beyond judgements of truthfulness, Strange et al. (2011) demonstrate that the addition of a photograph to fake news headlines led participants to indicate that they had a personal memory of the events occurring. Strange et al. showed ninety-eight participants news headlines relating to events of global significance that had occurred over the last few years. Of the forty headlines shown, thirty-eight related true events (e.g., *"Bin Laden Offers Truce to Europe, not US"*[6]) and two were fictitious (e.g., *"Blair under fire for botched Baghdad rescue attempt; won't step down."*). Ten of the news headlines were selected for analysis including eight randomly chosen true facts and the two fake news headlines. Headlines were then presented either with or without a related photograph, and participants were asked to indicate whether they remembered the event, knew of it, or neither. It was found that people were more

---

[6]https://www.theguardian.com/world/2004/apr/15/alqaida.usa.

likely to indicate they remembered false events when they were accompanied by a photograph than when presented alone.

Taken together, these experiments by Fenn et al. (2019), Newman et al. (2012, 2015), and Strange et al. (2011) indicate that both considerations of truthfulness *and memory* for fake news (and other semantic information) can be enhanced through the presence of relevant imagery and that adding an image to false facts could make them more likely to propagate than true information. The presence of photos also seems to shape the exact details that we recall from a news story, suggesting that selection of images can lead us to "read between the lines" (Henkel 2012) and embellish the original story with facts that were not presented. For example, Garry et al. (2007) presented participants with a natural disaster news story that described damage to property arising from a hurricane in Mexico together with an image of one afflicted town taken either before or after the hurricane. In a surprise memory test, it was found that those who saw the "after" picture were more likely to incorrectly indicate that the article had described severe personal injuries (persons in hospital or missing presumed dead) than those who saw the "before" image. In another series of experiments, Henkel (2012) also found evidence that photographs that supported inferred but absent details from short stories led to confident recollections of those inferred details. She further found that inferences made by reading the article could lead to a false recollection for an accompanying photograph (i.e., remembering a confirmatory photograph when in fact a photograph had not been present or when the photograph had failed to support the inferences made).

Taking careful selection of supporting images one step further, researchers have also investigated the effects of *doctored* photographs on memories for recent news-worthy events. Sacchi et al. (2007) showed Italian participants photographs of two events—the Tiananmen Square protest (1989) and the protest against the Iraq war in Rome (2003)—in each case, participants were shown either a real image of the event, or one that had been edited. In the case of the Tiananmen square protest the manipulated image added large crowds, whilst in the case of the Rome image the manipulations removed banners proclaiming peace and added masked figures to suggest violent activity. Participants were then asked questions about the believability of the photos, their attitude towards the events, and their recollection of what had occurred during the events. Results indicated that manipulations made to the image directly influenced the way that participants remembered the related public events, leading a subset of those who saw the doctored images to remember that many people had been close to the tanks as the military entered into Tiananmen Square, and that the Rome protests had resulted in injuries, damage to property and even deaths. Whilst participants in both conditions rated the events equally historically significant, participants who saw the doctored images of the Rome protest perceived the event more negatively than those who saw the original image.

Similar results were found in a series of three experiments by Nash (2018), who also added a third condition in which the doctored image was accompanied by a text disclaimer that stated that the doctored image had been "Photoshopped". Experiments used images of the 2011 British Royal Wedding and the London 2012 Olympic torch relay and original, positive images were modified to add a protesting crowd and riot police. Results showed that although UK participants reportedly remembered the events well, those who viewed the doctored images were more likely to report that the event had drawn a larger number of protestors than those who viewed the original images (Experiments 1, 2 and 3). This effect was seen even if the doctored image was shown with a disclaimer (Experiment 1) and when the quality of the doctored image made the manipulation evident (Experiments 2 and 3). Effects were also seen across all three experiments for other critical questions (e.g., how much control the police had, how smoothly the event went, and degree of public support for the event).

Findings from Sacchi et al. (2007) and from Nash (2018) provide evidence that doctored evidence effects apply in the context of recent news events (semantic memory) as well as the previously described cases of episodic memory (Garry and Gerrie 2005). Doctored images can be convincing (and will likely only get better)—it's unsurprising therefore that individuals are often poor at identifying both when a photograph has been altered and the specific manipulations that have been made (Nightingale et al. 2017). However, results from Sacchi et al. and Nash (together with those from Kelly and Nace (1994)) seem to indicate that even if individuals were able to identify when changes had been made, this would not be sufficient to mitigate the effects of these false images on memory for the associated events. Even when individuals are presented with strong evidence that a story is untrustworthy, memory distortion still occurs.

It seems that knowledge of potential manipulation is insufficient to protect against distortions of memory prompted by fake news articles supported by photographic evidence. Perhaps though, good knowledge or interest in the topic itself might be more effective? In their studies of illusory truth, Fazio et al. observed that the effect persists even for obviously implausible facts (e.g., "*The Earth is a perfect square.*") (Fazio et al. 2019) and when participants actually know information that directly contradicts the presented fact (Fazio et al. 2015). Looking specifically at false memories for news, O'Connell and Greene (2017) asked 489 participants to rate seven topics for self-reported expertise and rank those same topics for degree of personal interest. Participants were then presented with eight news stories from the last three years. Each story consisted of a brief narrative together with a supporting photograph and participants were shown four stories relating to the topic they had ranked as most interesting and four relating to the topic they had ranked as least interesting. In each set of four, one story was false but potentially similar to real events. Participants were then asked to indicate if they remembered the event taking place as described in the article, if they remembered the event differently to how the article reported it, or if they didn't remember it at all. Results showed that participants were significantly more likely to recall both true and fake news stories when they related to their high-interest topic than their low-interest topic. Almost 25% of participants indicated that they remembered the fictional news event for their high-interest topic compared to 10% with a memory for the faked low-interest event. These effects occurred *even when the participant's level of knowledge on a topic was controlled for.*

O'Connell and Greene's results suggest that existing knowledge may have little protective impact against false memories prompted by fake news. Further, a personal interest in a new topic increases the risk of adopting memories for falsely reported items. However, much of the concern around fake news has been around politically or socially charged news topics rather than those of simple personal interest (i.e., on news about political scandal, gun control or reproductive rights rather than soccer, film or pop music). One study examining the influence of such topics on false memory formation was conducted by Murphy et al. (2019) in the run-up to the 2018 Irish abortion referendum. During the week preceding the referendum, 3,140 participants completed an online survey featuring six news stories that related to campaign events, four of the stories described true events whilst two reported false events that had not occurred. Each news story took the form of a short summary paragraph together with an unaltered photograph, and the number of true and false stories was balanced in terms of their support for each referendum outcome. For each news story, participants were asked whether they remembered the event, whether they remembered where they had heard about the event, and how they felt about the event at the time. After viewing all six events, participants were notified that they may have been shown one or more fake news stories and were asked to indicate which, if any, of the stories they believed to be false. 48% of participants reported remembering at least one of the two fabricated events, with a further 15% reporting that they "don't remember this but I believe it happened". Qualitative data provided further descriptions of the reported memories suggesting that some participants had formed rich and detailed memories for the false events. Further, the majority of those reporting a false memory did not change their mind even when told that one or more of the events may have been fabricated. Looking specifically at the role of existing beliefs on memory formation, Murphy et al. found that although the percentage of true stories remembered by "yes" and "no" voters[7] was comparable overall, participants were significantly more likely to report a memory for the false story that aligned with their intended voting direction.

Overall, the research reviewed here suggests that semantic memories are as vulnerable as episodic memories when presented with doctored evidence. However whilst in the previous subsection we noted that (at present) there's little likelihood of encountering falsified evidence for personal events that did not occur, the same cannot be said for semantic information; disinformation and misinformation are already highly prevalent, particularly in the form of so-called "fake news" articles. The very cognitive processes that help us to retain accurate knowledge are largely indifferent to truthfulness, meaning that memory processes for false semantic information directly compete with those for true information (Marsh et al. 2016). Further, it's relatively easy to increase the perceived truthfulness of false semantic information through repetition (Fazio et al. 2015, 2019) or the inclusion of a related image (Fenn et al. 2019; Newman et al. 2012, 2015) and neither the plausibility of the story, nor clear disclaimers that indicate image manipulation, nor even direct contradictory knowledge reduce these effects (Fazio et al. 2015, 2019; Nash 2018).

---

[7]Of the 3, 140 participants, 2,342 self-reported an intention to vote *yes*, 379 intended to vote *no*, and 147 were unsure how they would vote. The remaining participants did not plan to vote ($n = 128$) or declined to indicate their voting preference ($n = 144$).

In line with known confirmation biases, there's evidence that our existing perceptions regarding the topic of the news story itself plays a role in memory—both true *and false* memories are more likely when the topic is one of personal interest or importance Murphy et al. (2019); O'Connell and Greene (2017). Recent discussions around social media "filter bubbles", together with an increased propensity for news sourcing through social media combine to provide a clear mechanism for sharing false news that fits people's interests. Further, whilst the research summarised in this section is concerned with the memories held by an individual, recent commentary has highlighted the role of false information in collective memory Liv and Greenbaum (2020), Spinney (2017). These collective memories form the basis of a social group's understanding of historical events, justifying their beliefs and future actions. Thus, both "filter bubbles" and the collective memories they facilitate can have significant impact in terms of fostering polarisation and social division, prompting research that sets out to prevent the negative effects of fake news (Dijs 2019). Recent evidence suggests that whilst contradictory knowledge alone is not sufficient to prevent information consumers from accepting oft-repeated fake news as truth, the combination of existing contradictory knowledge *and an explicit prompt to focus on the accuracy of the false information* may help address an "illusory truth" effect. Others have suggested a responsibility for online platforms to detect and remove false news. Although valuable, efforts to detect false news pose considerable challenge and often involve some element of human input. Further, these also fail to deal with the problem of false information to which individuals have already been exposed. However, in a future world with technology-based memory augmentations, there's a novel opportunity to retrospectively leverage information about the inaccuracy of information—if information to which a user has previously consumed is discovered to be false then the system could potentially make use of its rehearsal strategies to inhibit memory for the false knowledge.[8] One such strategy might be built upon the cognitive phenomenon known as retrieval-induced forgetting.

2.2 Retrieval-Induced Forgetting

Both Sect. 1.2 and the previous chapter have recounted how cameras can be used to capture memory cues, which can assist in the later recall of specific details from earlier episodic events. One convenient means of reviewing these images is the end-of-day review (e.g., Finley, Brewer and Benjamin 2011), which has been used in the majority of SenseCam studies Hodges et al. (2006, 2011)). During a summary review, a subset of images (perhaps like a "highlights reel") are represented for review, and in the case of memory-impaired participants, the images are sometimes discussed with the help of a loved one. Recently, Cinel et al. (2018) have examined whether such reviews might expose users to an unforeseen cognitive vulnerability, the psychological phenomenon known as retrieval-induced forgetting (e.g., Anderson

---

[8]Although this in turn, raises ethical concerns.

et al. 1994). Put simply, through the use of technological review, participants may inadvertently cause the forgetting of related events that were not reviewed.

The idea of retrieval-induced forgetting is best illustrated with an experimental example. Cinel et al. (2018) took participants on a guided tour of a university campus in which they visited eight different campus locations (e.g., the Sports Centre, the Library, the Lake, etc). In each location they were shown six different to-be-remembered objects, which were introduced along with an associated comment (many of which had been invented for the purpose of the experiment). For example, when visiting the Library, the experimenter might point out a printer in the Library and say "Library–Printer: This is the most used printer in the library"; or when visiting the Lake, they may say "Lake–Bench: There are 72 identical benches on campus". After completing the tour, half the participants performed a cued-recall review of half of the objects from half of the locations (e.g., Library-Pr? [Can you name the objects and retrieve the associated comment?]). Following a delay, all the participants were then tested on all the to-be-remembered objects. Participants remembered the objects that were practiced, referred to as **RP+** items, at a significantly higher rate (0.798) than they recalled items from the non-practiced categories, referred to as **NRP** items (0.597). This difference in recall served as the baseline. However, as anticipated by Cinel et al., the recall of the unpracticed objects from the practiced locations, referred to as **RP-**, was attenuated: recall of these items (0.529) was at a significantly lower rate than the baseline items.

In a second experiment, Cinel et al. sought to offer the participants more control over the items that they had to remember. In the morning study phase, the participants were given two hours to perform a scavenger hunt, in which they were requested to find six objects of their choice on campus that fitted with each of eight experimenter-provided categories. These categories were either conceptual (e.g., "something electrical," "something living," "something made of metal," "something edible") or perceptual (e.g., "something orange," "something with stripes," "something soft," "something circular"). Each participant was equipped with a Samsung Galaxy SIII Mini smartphone, and the images were captured using the My Good Old Kodak Android application (Niforatos et al. 2017) that had been installed. This application had been set to deliver sets of camera rolls, each of six shots. The participants could always see the number of shots that were remaining on the roll (e.g., 2/6) on the viewfinder. Critically, in this application, the digital photos that were taken were stored in a locked and hidden folder such that the participants were not able to review the captured images on their camera roll. In addition, whenever an object was found and an image captured, the participant was instructed to record an interesting or memorable fact or associated comment (using the voice recorder of the smartphone) as to why they had selected that particular item. Once all the objects had been found, the participants returned the smartphone to the experimenter and took a lunch break. In an afternoon testing session, the participants were presented with half of the participant-selected objects from half of the categories. For each presented stimulus, participants saw the category name (e.g., "something orange"), the participant-selected object, and they were asked to try to retrieve their associated comment. In a later final test phase, Cinel et al. again found that specific items that had been practiced (0.798) were recalled significantly better than baseline items (0.658), which in turn were recalled significantly better than the unpracticed items that were from practiced categories (0.513). That is, Cinel et al. had again found that reviewing a subset of the studied material had significantly enhanced the later recall of the practiced items but had also significantly attenuated the later recall of the related but unpracticed items.

2.3   Cognitive Vulnerabilities Inherent in Memory Augmentation

The experiments by Cinel et al. (2018) demonstrated that a technologically generated end-of-day review had the potential to augment human memory: it could enhance later accessibility to the reviewed highlights of our day (as one would hope and expect), but may additionally inhibit access to related events that were not themselves cued. This reduction in accessibility may be entirely unwanted and unexpected, but could also be a phenomenon that could be exploited for good or bad reasons. For example, we might want to intentionally try to reduce accessibility to events that are unwanted, unhelpful or intrusive; potentially this could be achieved by engaging in retrieval practice of related events. However, we might unintentionally reduce accessibility to events either through ignorance of the phenomenon, or worse still, through the intentional attenuation by an external party.

For example, a laboratory-based study by Parker and Dagnall (2009) has shown the positive and negative effects on memory following the processing of adverts. In their study, Parker and Dagnall used a procedure similar to that used by Anderson et al. (1994). In a study phase, participants studied 6 brand names from each of 10 product categories (e.g., Cars-Volvo, Cars-Vauxhall; Crisps-Pringles, Crisps-Doritos). They then received retrieval practice on half the brands from half the categories. Thus, half the cars but none of the crisps may be practiced (e.g., Cars-Vo? may have been practiced but not Cars-Va?, Crisps-Pr?, Crisps-Do?). Parker and Dagnall found that later recall of the items that had received retrieval practice were best recalled (0.75), significantly higher than the recall of brands from product categories that had received no retrieval practice (0.52). However, the recall of unpracticed items that were related to those that were practiced (0.35) had been significantly reduced. Thus, advertising not only significantly increased accessibility to the advertised products (as one might expect), but had also decreased accessibility to its unpracticed competitors.

A laboratory-based study by Storm et al. into retrieval-induced forgetting has also shown that accessibility to a target item can be impaired even when retrieval practice involved cueing for a related but impossible cue (Storm et al. 2006). In their study, Storm et al. presented participants with 24 category-exemplar pairs to study (3 exemplars from 8 categories (e.g., metals-brass, fruit-orange, metals-nickel, metals-silver, fruit-pineapple, fruit-lemon). Two of the 8 categories were tested with initial letter cues for items that had not been presented but which could reasonably generate an unpresented category exemplar (e.g., metals-Al? [Aluminium], metals-Ir? [Iron], metals-Ni? [Nickel]) whereas a further two categories were tested with an initial letter that resulted in an "impossible cue" such that no items could (readily) be generated to the cue (e.g., fruit-Lu?). Storm et al. found retrieval-induced forgetting in both types of cues: retrieval-induced forgetting occurred when the cues during the retrieval practice phase could be used to generate unpresented list items and retrieval-induced forgetting even occurred when retrieval practice could not hope to be successful—by using impossible cues. These effects were still observable after 1 week. This study is potentially important in that it suggests that accessibility to a target item can be attenuated merely by attempting to retrieve an (unpresented or fake) item from a related category. The implication is that targeted attenuation of an event in memory could be attempted by the incorporation of an image from a related category into the set of items receiving retrieval practice.

Recently, we set about examining how vulnerable memory augmentation devices might be to these phenomena. Suppose that one used lifelogging technology to help augment one's human memory by reviewing an end-of-day highlights package consisting of a subset of images from experienced events. Following Cinel et al. (2018), we might expect that the mnemonic consequences would be to enhance the accessibility to those reviewed events and to attenuate the accessibility to related but unpresented events. But suppose that the end-of-day review contained material that the participant had in fact not experienced. Suppose false memory events became incorporated into the highlights package through technological failure or inaccuracy, through known third-party advertising or sponsorship (Parker and Dagnal 2009), or maybe through an uninvited malicious third-party. Would these non-experienced events (like those of Storm et al. 2006) additionally attenuate experienced events?

3   A Retrieval-Induced Forgetting Experiment Including False Events

The aim of this experiment was to identify whether providing inaccurate information during retrieval practice would hinder accessibility to memories of related encountered events. We adapted the scavenger hunt methodology used by Cinel et al. (2018) that was described in the previous subsection. In the Study Phase, a total of 48 participants were each given a list of nine categories (e.g., "something orange", "something with stripes"), and for each category they were asked to find and take a picture of eight different exemplars around the university campus. The photographs were captured using the My Good Old Kodak application (Niforatos et al. 2017) installed on an Android smartphone that was provided by the experimenter for this purpose. When the participants captured an image of an item, they were asked to say out loud an associated comment about the item, and this was recorded via the smartphone's audio microphone.

Upon completion of the campus scavenger hunt, each participant's images were downloaded and used for retrieval practice in a later session. In the retrieval practice phase, participants saw six practice items from six of the nine categories (36 items from the 54 total items) and these were each presented three times in a different random order. We manipulated the accuracy of the reviewed images by examining recall in two groups of participants: the Extreme manipulation group and the Nuanced manipulation group (see Procedure, Sect. 3.1).

Afterwards, the participants' memory of the to-be-remembered objects from each category was tested with a test of category-cued recall. This was followed by a short questionnaire to assess participants' awareness of the inaccurate information in each category, as well as its impact on their trust in technology. Finally, participants performed a forced-choice recognition test, whereby participants were required to choose the eight photos they had previously captured out of a total sixteen photos (8 targets, 8 foils) for each category.

3.1   Method

Participants. A total number of 48 students from the University of Essex, participated in this experiment in exchange for course credit or £20.[9]

Ethics. The study was given ethical approval from the Research Ethics Committee at the University of Essex.

Design. The study adopted a mixed design. The between-subjects variable was the level of accuracy in the retrieval practice, with two levels (*Extreme group* and *Nuanced group*). There were two-within-subjects independent variables: level of accuracy in the retrieval practice stage (with three levels: *No Review, Accurate, Inaccurate* for the Extreme group and *No Review, Mostly Accurate* and *Mostly Inaccurate* for the Nuanced group) and retrieval practice status (with three levels: *Nrp, Rp+* and *Rp-*). The main dependent variables were the proportion of items that were correctly recalled in the category-cued free recall memory test.

Stimuli and Apparatus. There were nine experimental categories [Table 1]. Exemplars for each category were selected by participants. For each category, a set of eight foils were selected from images captured in a prior study that had used the same photo capturing protocol and prompts. Participants were equipped with a Samsung Galaxy SIII Mini smartphone and used the My Good Old Kodak Android application (Niforatos et al. 2017) to capture the images. The smartphones' inbuilt microphone and voice recorder applications were used to record participants' comments. The experiment and instructions in the retrieval practice and test phase were presented using the SuperCard 4.7 application on an Apple Macintosh computer. Participants' verbal responses during retrieval practice were recorded with Audacity 2.0.5.

Procedure. The experiment was divided into two sessions. The first session, including the study phase, was completed in the morning. A second session took

---

[9]Approximately 25 USD or €22.

Table 1 The nine experimental categories used. Exemplars for each category were selected by participants	Experimental categories
	Something electrical
	Something made of metal
	Something orange
	Something with stripes
	Something living
	Something soft
	Something circular
	Something edible
	Something with writing

place in the laboratory in the afternoon of the same day. The gap between the end of the first session and the beginning of the second session was at least three hours.

In the first session, participants were given a smartphone and shown how to use the smartphone's voice recorder and the My Good Old Kodak application. This application was set to deliver camera rolls of eight photographs with the number of shots that were remaining on the roll (e.g., 2/8) visible on the viewfinder. The participants were also given a printed list with nine experimenter-selected categories (listed in a different random order for each participant). The participants were instructed to take photographs of eight different items that matched each of the nine categories. For each captured item, participants were instructed to record an interesting or memorable fact or comment using the phone's voice recorder app. Participants were told that the fact could be anything that they associated with the item, or some peculiar details about it or its context, but must not simply be a statement about the identity of the item. Participants were told that these facts would need to be retrieved in the afternoon session. Participants were also instructed to follow the order of the categories on the printed list and to take all eight photos within a category before moving on to another category. They were given two and a half hours to complete the first session, and photographs could be captured anywhere on the University of Essex campus. Once the first session was completed, the captured photographs and voice recordings were downloaded from the phone and all photos were checked to ensure that they matched their respective category.

In the second session, participants began with the retrieval practice phase. During retrieval practice, they were told that they would see a number of their images and that their task was to say aloud what the item in the photo was together with the interesting or memorable fact that they had previously associated with it. In the Extreme manipulation group, the nine categories were randomly assigned into three conditions: (1) three Extremely Accurate categories, where participants were shown six of their own items from these categories; (2) three Extremely Inaccurate categories, where participants were shown six false memory foils from three categories; and (3) three No Review categories, in which no items were practiced. In the Nuanced manipulation group, the nine categories were also randomly assigned into three conditions: (1) three Mostly Accurate categories, where participants were shown four of their own items and two related foils; (2) three Mostly Inaccurate categories, where participants were shown two of their own items and four related foils; and (3) three No Review categories in which no items were practiced. We told all the participants that one aim of the experiment was to test different algorithms that created cues to enhance human memory and we warned them that they might see some photos which may not be their own and that if that happens they were to simply continue with the task.

After the retrieval practice phase, participants were given a filler task, previously used by Cinel et al. (2018). In this task, participants were presented with the names of eight different countries ("France", "Italy", "Spain", "China", "USA", "Russia", "Germany" and "Egypt"). For each country, they were given one minute to write down as many things that they might do or see if they went there on holiday. Upon completion of the filler task, participants entered first in a test of recall and then a test of recognition.

In the Recall Test Phase participants were shown the names of each of the nine experimental categories, and they were given thirty seconds (per category) to write down as many of the items that they had captured during the scavenger hunt. Categories were presented in a random order that differed from the order used during prior stages of the experiment. Once they were finished, the experimenter took away their response sheets, so as not to affect the final two tasks. Participants then completed a short questionnaire, whereby for each of the nine experimental categories they were asked to answer the following four questions:

1. How many items (out of 8) do you think you have recalled in the recall phase? (Stage 3)
2. How many of your photos (out of 8) did you see during the practice phase? (Stage 1)
3. On a scale of 1 (not at all accurate) to 7 (extremely accurate), how accurate did you find the information presented during the practice phase? (Stage 1), and
4. On a scale of 0–100, how much would you trust the algorithm used to provide images to enhance your memory during the practice phase? (Stage 1)

In the Recognition Test Phase, participants were presented with an array of sixteen photos (the eight photos they captured plus eight false memory foils) for each of the nine experimental categories. For each category, they were asked to select the eight photos that they had captured during the scavenger hunt by clicking the corresponding checkboxes.

Finally, participants were asked to complete a cross-referencing task that allowed the researcher to correctly score output from the Recall Test Phase. For each category, the participant was shown the same array of sixteen photos used in the Recognition Test Phase. They were asked to cross-reference the items on display to the recalled items they had written down in the memory test sheet for that specific category. The experimenter then scored the memory test in the presence of the participant.

3.2 Results

Recall Test Accuracy. The main findings from the recall test can be seen in Table 2. An overall 2 (group: Extreme, Nuanced) x 3 (retrieval practice status: Rp+, Nrp, Rp-) mixed analysis of variance (ANOVA) showed a significant main effect of retrieval practice status, $F(2,92) = 96.96$, $MSE = 0.011$, $\eta_p^2 = 0.678$, $p < 0.001$, a non-significant main effect of group, $F(1,46) = 2.31$, $MSE = 0.045$, $\eta_p^2 = 0.048$, $p = 0.135$, and a non-significant interaction, $F(2,92) = 1.00$, $MSE = 0.011$, $\eta_p^2 = 0.021$, $p = 0.371$. Post-hoc Bonferroni tests showed that overall, items that received retrieval practice ($M = 0.669$) were recalled significantly better ($p < 0.001$) than those items from unpracticed categories ($M = 0.455$), showing clear retrieval practice effects. More crucially, items from reviewed categories that did not themselves receive retrieval practice ($M = 0.389$) were recalled significantly less often ($p = 0.004$) than those items from unpracticed categories ($M = 0.455$), showing retrieval-induced forgetting. Upon first analysis, therefore, one might conclude that the effects of retrieval practice and retrieval-induced forgetting do not depend upon the accuracy of the practiced items, with the effects just as strong with Extreme and Nuanced cues.

However, a more subtle pattern is found when one examines the data more closely. To do this we conducted separate analyses for each of the conditions in each of the two groups. In the Extreme group, we conducted an ANOVA on the recall from the categories that received extremely accurate retrieval practice. This revealed a significant main effect of retrieval practice status, $F(2,46) = 69.98$, $MSE = 0.013$, $\eta_p^2 = 0.753$, $p < 0.001$. Post-hoc Bonferroni tests showed that items that received Extremely accurate retrieval practice ($M = 0.665$) were recalled significantly better ($p < 0.001$) than those items from unpracticed categories ($M = 0.437$), which in turn were recalled better ($p < 0.001$) than items from reviewed categories that did not themselves receive retrieval practice ($M = 0.230$). An additional paired t-test found that there was not a significant difference between the recall from the unpracticed categories (M = 0.437) with the recall from the unpracticed items that were from categories that had received extremely inaccurate items ($M = 0.413$), $t(23) = 1.75$, $p = 0.090$. Thus, retrieval practice effects occurred with all practiced information, but significant retrieval-induced forgetting occurred only when authentic items were practiced.

Considering next the recall in the Nuanced group, a 2 (condition: Mostly accurate, mostly inaccurate) x 2 retrieval practice status (Rp+, Rp-) ANOVA revealed a significant main effect of retrieval practice status, $F(1,23) = 70.53$, $MSE = 0.020$, $\eta_p^2 = 0.754$, $p < 0.001$, a non-significant effect of condition, $F(1,23) = 0.28$, $MSE = 0.022$, $\eta_p^2 = 0.012$, $p = 0.602$, and a non-significant interaction, $F(1,23) = 0.28$, $MSE = 0.020$, $\eta_p^2 < 0.001$, $p = 0.995$. This analysis shows that there was little difference between the mostly accurate and the mostly inaccurate conditions in the Nuanced group. The similarities between the conditions were confirmed by additional paired t tests. Those items that received Mostly accurate retrieval practice ($M = 0.708$) were recalled significantly better than those items from unpracticed categories ($M = 0.473$), $t(23) = 6.53$, $p < 0.001$, but the unpracticed categories

Table 2 The mean proportion of correctly recalled exemplars for all three levels of the retrieval practice status for Experiment 1. Column $Rp+$ summarises results for practiced items from practiced categories, NRp for items from unpracticed categories, and $Rp-$ for unpracticed items from practiced categories. Values in brackets represent the standard error of the mean

	Rp+		Nrp		Rp-	
Extreme group	**0.625**	**(0.032)**	**0.436**	**(0.034)**	**0.371**	**(0.028)**
Accurate	0.625	(0.032)			0.229	(0.037)
Inaccurate					0.406	
No review			0.436	(0.034)		
Nuanced group	**0.713**	**(0.029)**	**0.472**	**(0.031)**	**0.407**	**(0.027)**
Mostly accurate	0.708	(0.031)			0.396	(0.039)
Mostly inaccurate	0.722	(0.043)			0.414	
No review			0.472	(0.031)		(0.028)

did not differ significantly from the unpracticed related items from the practiced categories, ($M = 0.395$), $t(23) = 1.98$, $p = 0.060$. Similarly, paired t tests comparing Mostly inaccurate retrieval practice ($M = 0.722$) were recalled significantly better than those items from unpracticed categories ($M = 0.473$), $t(23) = 5.90$, $p < 0.001$, but the unpracticed categories did not differ significantly from the unpracticed items from the mostly inaccurate practiced categories, ($M = 0.413$), $t(23) = 1.75$, $p = 0.090$.

In conclusion, we found clear and consistent retrieval practice effects: recall of the practiced items was always significantly higher than the unpracticed items from the same categories and from non-practiced control categories from retrieval practice. However, there is mixed evidence supporting retrieval-induced forgetting when related but inaccurate information is presented as a cue. On the overall ANOVA, there were clear effects of retrieval-induced forgetting across the entire experiment, and there was no interaction between the groups. However, when different subsets of the data were analysed separately, the degree of retrieval-induced forgetting was affected by the accuracy of the retrieval practice material. Statistically significant retrieval-induced forgetting ($p < 0.001$) was observed when six of the eight category members received practice in the extremely accurate conditions. However, statistically significant levels of retrieval-induced forgetting were not observed in the mostly accurate ($p = 0.060$), the mostly inaccurate ($p = 0.090$), and the extremely inaccurate ($p = 0.090$) conditions, when four, two and zero of the eight authentic items were practiced, respectively.

Questionnaire scores. Table 3 shows the mean ratings for each of the four questionnaire items. The first question examined participants ability to judge how well they remembered items from each of the categories. They had just performed the

Table 3 The mean scores of the responses given in the four questionnaire questions. Values in brackets represent the standard error of the mean

	Question 1 (out of 8)		Question 2 (out of 8)		Question 3 (7pt scale)		Question 4 (100pt scale)	
Extreme group	**3.72**	**(1.63)**	**1.90**	**(2.12)**	**3.86**	**(1.79)**	**49.9**	**(28.0)**
Accurate	4.19	(1.41)	3.42	(1.50)	4.57	(1.50)	59.4	(23.5)
Inaccurate	3.63	(1.69)	1.11	(1.81)	3.65	(1.79)	45.1	(29.3)
No review	3.35	(1.66)	1.17	(2.13)	3.36	(1.83)	45.3	(28.4)
Nuanced group	**3.85**	**(1.81)**	**1.77**	**(1.71)**	**3.76**	**(1.64)**	**43.5**	**(25.8)**
Mostly accurate	4.29	(1.67)	2.74	(1.48)	4.33	(1.37)	49.2	(23.3)
Mostly inaccurate	3.97	(1.62)	1.97	(1.39)	3.74	(1.58)	44.2	(25.9)
No review	3.79	(1.96)	0.61	(1.51)	3.22	(1.76)	37.1	(26.5)

category-cued free recall test, but could they remember how well they had done. Consistent with the participants retaining some memory for how well they had done, there was a significant positive correlation between the participants' responses to Question 1 and their recall test scores, ($r = 0.382$, $p = 0.007$).

However, as the results of Question 2 show, the participants were not so good at remembering how many of their own items they had seen in the retrieval practice phase. In general, the participants were sensitive to the number of authentic images they had been presented within the retrieval practice phase, but they tended to make underestimations. Across conditions where participants had been presented with six, four and two of their own authentic images, they estimated they had seen a mean of 3.42, 2.74 and 1.97, respectively. However, they also over-estimated the number of items they had seen in categories in which zero of their own items had been represented. Participants thought that a mean of 1.11 of their own captured images had been represented to them in the Extremely Inaccurate retrieval practice condition (where they had in fact seen none of their own photos). Although this may reflect source monitoring errors (participants misattributing the source of the externally sourced images as their own), it could also reflect general failure in memory, since non-zero numbers of participant's own images were estimated to be represented to the No Review categories (1.17 and 0.61, for the Extreme and Nuanced groups, respectively), even though these categories received no practice items of any kind during retrieval practice.

When answering Question 3, participants rated the accuracy of the images with which they had been provided. Within each group, they correctly identified that more accurate conditions were more accurate than the less accurate conditions, but the scores for the Mostly Inaccurate and Extremely inaccurate conditions were rated as more accurate than the No Review conditions. This could reflect uncertainty about how to review the accuracy of a condition for which no items had been presented, or it could be argued that participants rate more generously something that was presented (however inaccurate) compared to when nothing was presented.

Finally, participants' trust ratings were fairly low. The completely accurate categories of the Extreme Group was given a mean trust rating of only 59.4% whereas

Table 4 Recognition Memory performance. Mean probabilities of accepting an image as one's own. Column $Rp+$ summarises results for practiced targets from practiced categories and $Rp-$ for unpracticed targets from practiced categories. Column *Baseline NRp* summarises results for targets/foils from unpracticed categories

	Baseline NRP	Highly accurate		Less accurate	
Targets	Not seen	RP+	RP-	RP+	RP-
Extreme group	0.990	0.993	0.958		0.958
Nuanced group	0.984	0.979	0.969	0.986	0.972
Foils	Not seen	Seen in RP	Unseen in RP	Seen in RP	Unseen in RP
Extreme group	0.010		0.016	0.046	0.028
Nuanced group	0.016	0.042	0.021	0.031	0.017

the completely inaccurate categories of the Extreme Group received a trust rating of 45.1%, comparable to the ratings in the Nuanced group, and marginally higher than the trust for No Review conditions.

Recognition Test scores. Table 4 shows the probabilities of accepting an image as the participant's own for the participant's own captured images (targets) and the non-target foils. Overall, recognition probabilities were very high, but the incorporation of images of false memory events into the retrieval practice schedules increased the probabilities of accepting a false memory image as one's own.

Let us first consider, the baseline accuracy for those categories that did not receive any retrieval practice. The participants' ability to recognise their own eight captured photos images (from equal numbers of unseen foils) was very good: participants in the Extreme group accurately recognised 99.0% of their images, and participants in the Nuanced group accurately recognised 98.4% of their images.

Let us next consider, the recognition in the highly accurate categories. Participants in the Extremely accurate condition of the Extreme group were very accurate at recognising the six images seen in the retrieval practice phase (99.3%), but accuracy for the two unreviewed images in these categories fell significantly below baseline to 95.8%, $t(23) = 2.16$, $p < 0.050$. By contrast, participants in the Mostly accurate condition of the Nuanced group were also highly accurate at recognising the four images seen in the retrieval practice phase (97.9%), but accuracy for the four unreviewed images in these categories did not fall significantly below baseline to 96.9%.

Let us finally consider, the recognition in the less accurate categories. Participants in the Extremely Inaccurate categories of the Extreme group (who were presented at retrieval practice with none their own images) performed significantly less accurately (95.8%, $t(23) = 3.00$, $p < 0.001$) than baseline, whilst participants in the mostly inaccurate categories of the Nuanced group (who were presented at retrieval practice with only two of their own images) performed non-significantly less accurately for both their own images seen (97.9%) and their images that were not presented at retrieval practice (96.9%).

The complementary analyses are for participants' falsely recognising images that were not their own. Although the baseline rates are low for participants judging external images as their own for items from non-practiced categories (1.0% and 1.6% for the Extreme and Nuanced Groups, respectively), participants were more willing to accept an image as their own if it had been previously presented in the retrieval practice phase. Thus, items that had been seen in the retrieval practice phase were recognised significantly more often as their own (4.6% of occasions, $t(23) = 3.27$, $p < 0.010$) in the Extremely Inaccurate condition of the Extreme group. There were non-significant increases of 4.2% and 3.1% of occasions in the Mostly Accurate and Mostly Inaccurate conditions of the Nuanced group respectively. These findings show that if external false memory images are added to the retrieval practice phase (by technological error or otherwise) then there is an enhanced probability that they will be falsely recognised as their own.

Recall of foils. Since each participant had an individualised set of 72 different photos, the recall test was scored at the end of the experiment, in the presence of the participant. It was exceedingly rare for participants to identify a non-presented foil as one of the items that they had tried to recall in the No Retrieval Practice categories (0.69%). However, participants did incorrectly attribute foil items to their written down recalls when many foils were presented during retrieval practice. Thus 4.62% of the six foils presented per category in the Extremely Inaccurate condition of the Extreme group, which was significantly more than baseline, $t(2.50$, $p < 0.050)$. Additionally, participants attributed marginally more of the four foils (2.08%) presented per category in the Mostly Inaccurate condition of the Nuanced group, ($t(23) = 1.88$, $p = 0.070$).

3.3   Discussion

The aim of the experiment was to identify whether providing inaccurate information during the retrieval practice phase would hinder accessibility to memories of related encountered events. There were four main findings from this experiment. First, consistent with Cinel et al. (2018), we were able to show clear and consistent retrieval practice effects (the recall advantage for reviewed images). These recall advantages occurred for all conditions in both groups. Second, we found that there was indeed an overall reduction in the recall of unreviewed images that came from categories in which other items had been reviewed, suggesting that there were retrieval-induced forgetting effects even when the reviewed categories contained inaccurate images in the retrieval practice phase. When we analysed the data in more detail, by examining recall in separate analyses for each group and condition, we found the clearest evidence of retrieval-induced forgetting in the Extremely accurate conditions of the Extreme group in which only entirely accurate images were included in the retrieval practice phase. This finding is consistent with that observed by Cinel et al. (2018), who always used accurate images during retrieval practice. In the other conditions, we found that although there were always numerical reductions in the retrieval-induced forgetting conditions, these did not meet thresholds for statistical significance ($p <= 0.05$). Third, we found evidence that when inaccurate information was incorporated into the retrieval practice schedules, these items could show an increased likelihood of being recognised as one of the participants' own photos in a later test and were also sometimes more likely to be identified as being one of the images that the participants had recalled. Although these absolute increases were modest (e.g., from 1 to 4.6%), the relative increases were clearly of a substantial magnitude. Finally, the results of our questionnaire suggest that participants were only partially sensitive to the different manipulations that had been performed during the retrieval practice schedule: in categories where they had been presented some of their own photos, they tended to underestimate the numbers of their own images they had been represented with during retrieval practice; but for categories where they had been presented with none of their own photos, they tended to over-estimate the numbers of their own photos with which they had been represented.

In summary, technological advancements in providing an end-of-day review may expose the user to the twin cognitive vulnerabilities of false memory (Sect. 2.1) and retrieval-induced forgetting (Sect. 2.2). That is, as hypothesised in Sect. 2.3, memory augmentation devices might not only enhance later recall of reviewed events, but might also result in technology-mediated impairments in memory caused by retrieval-induced forgetting of related but unreviewed events that were similar to those in the end-of-day review, and false memory, if inaccurate information is allowed to enter the end-of-day review.

4 Concluding Remarks

Humans have long used technologies to extend aspects of their memory. Examples, from the historic to modern, include cave painting, the written word, photographs, PDAs, the World Wide Web and smartphones. However, for as long as such technologies have existed, there have been critics insisting that these augmentations will make humans lazy, leading them to use the technology instead of their brains. Further, as the pace of change has increased, so too has the degree of concern about how technology may be irreversibly shaping our cognition (e.g., Carr 2008a, 2008b).

As described in other chapters within this volume, recent developments in passive sensing, storage, machine learning, and in wearable actuators and displays have led researchers to express new visions for cognitive prosthetics including human memory augmentation. The reach of these envisioned systems go far beyond existing tools, fostering a symbiotic relationship in which cognition is transparently enhanced and extended (Schmidt 2017). Such technologies have obvious benefits, improving recall whilst simultaneously freeing up cognitive resource to be allocated to other tasks. However, these systems also introduce a new point of failure—individuals dependent on a technology may become dysfunctional when it is removed. In the best case, individuals revert to their natural state, losing any "superhuman" abilities enabled by the technology. In the worst case, the systems have irreversibly altered cognition, leading to poorer performance if the technology becomes absent than if it had never been present.

In this chapter, we've explored evidence regarding the potential negative impacts of technology on cognition, summarising current understanding and signposting how these effects may be exhibited in a future where memory augmentations and cognitive prosthetics become commonplace. In particular, we identify two distinct forms of cognitive risk associated with current and emerging technologies: memory inhibition and memory distortion. In the case of the former, technologies somehow interfere with the normal cognitive processes, often at the encoding stage of memory formation. In so doing, the technology exhibits an inhibitive effect such that information is recalled more poorly with the technology than without. In the latter case, technologies act as a distortion, altering normal cognitive processes to introduce inaccuracies or errors. In so doing, they provide novel opportunities to manipulate memory.

In Sects. 1 and 2 we've summarised much of the prior work, exploring how many of the current dominant technologies appear to exhibit inhibition and distortion effects, respectively. The technologies triggering these effects vary significantly in form, including internet search engines, digital cameras, satellite navigation and online news platforms. Further, they have been demonstrated to impact multiple different types of memory including retrospective memory (both semantic and episodic) and spatial memory,[10] and on our own awareness of our memory's function and limitations (metamemory). However, given the ubiquity of computing devices in our everyday activities, and the prevalence of claims that such devices are "making us stupid", we argue that the body of understanding is still highly limited. Furthermore, as technology begins to deliberately target cognition, there is a growing need for a critical evaluation that focuses on unintended side effects.

Research is needed to explore interactions between cognition and technology for two distinct cases: (1) augmentation systems that are primarily benevolent in nature, but that pose a risk to cognitive function, and (2) augmentation systems that deliberately seek to leverage cognitive vulnerabilities, manipulating what is remembered or forgotten. In Sect. 3 we contribute towards the second of these cases, conducting an experiment to identify whether providing inaccurate information during retrieval practice would hinder accessibility to memories of related encountered events. During a two-part experiment, 48 participants were initially asked to capture photographs and an audio fact snippet as part of a scavenger hunt activity. During the second session, participants engaged first in a retrieval practice session in which they viewed a subset of their photographs together with a selection of memory foils (i.e., images they had not photographed themselves but that met the original scavenger hunt category description). Following a short distraction period, the participants then engaged in a recognition test in which they were presented with all of their own photographs and an equal number of memory foils—participants were asked to select the eight photos

---

[10]Studies exploring the impact of smartphones on cognition have also shown effects on working memory (e.g., Ward et al. 2017).

that they had captured during the scavenger hunt. Finally, participants completed a questionnaire about their experiences. Consistent with prior work (e.g., Cinel et al. 2018), this experiment demonstrated both retrieval practice and retrieval-induced forgetting. However, we also found evidence that when inaccurate information (memory foils) were incorporated into the retrieval practice schedules, these items could show an increased likelihood of being recognised as one of the participants' own photos in a later test. Concerningly, the results of our questionnaire suggested that participants had limited awareness of manipulations made during the retrieval practice schedule, suggesting that technology could not only alter our memories, but could do so without us becoming cognisant.

The idea of cognitive vulnerabilities as a security concern for human memory was first proposed by Davies et al. (2015), with the suggestion that real-time monitoring, similar to current anti-virus software, might be a necessary addition to augmentation technologies. Such monitoring could, for example, build on the findings of studies reported in this chapter, to look for suspicious patterns of behaviour consistent with known psychological phenomena. However, realising such an intervention is still a considerably way off. Our prior work (Clinch et al. 2019) has explored the concept in more detail, identifying a need to first further develop our knowledge of cognitive vulnerabilities in human memory such that one could plausibly specify a set of "virus definitions". Conducting research in this area could be considered akin to the "white hat" hacking of the cyber-security domain—researchers would attempt to use technology to "break into" our cognition, detecting vulnerabilities before malicious parties discover and exploit them. However, as seen in many of the studies reported in Sect. 2, conducting research in this space raises considerable ethical concerns with deception of human participants as a given (Clinch et al. 2019). Furthermore, as in traditional cyber-security research, uncovering risks without solutions could lead to a window of opportunity for malicious parties. Given that a cognitive anti-virus is essentially a design fiction at present, this could create significant risks for our memories and minds. However, such risks are potentially unavoidable—current studies already demonstrate the potential for distortion effects and it's only a matter of time before parties deliberately seek to exploit these (e.g., to provide a competitive advantage when advertising a product).

Acknowledgements The authors' own research reported in this chapter was partially funded through the Future and Emerging Technologies (FET) programme within the 7th Framework Programme for Research of the European Commission, under FET grant number: 612933 (RECALL), and by the UK EPSRC under grant number EP/N028228/1 (PACTMAN).

References

Allé MC, Manning L, Potheegadoo J, Coutelle R, Danion J-M, Berna F (2017) Wearable cameras are useful tools to investigate and remediate autobiographical memory impairment: a systematic PRISMA review. Neuropsychol Rev 27(1):81–99

Anderson MC, Bjork RA, Bjork EL (1994) Remembering can cause forgetting: retrieval dynamics in long-term memory. J Exp Psychol: Learn Mem Cogn 20(5):1063–1087

Aporta C, Higgs E, Hakken D, Palmer L, Palmer M, Rundstrom R, Pfaffenberger B, Wenzel G, Widlok T, Aporta C et al (2005) Satellite culture: global positioning systems, Inuit wayfinding, and the need for a new account of technology. Current Anthropol 46(5):729–753

Barasch A, Diehl K, Zauberman G (2014) When happiness shared is happiness halved: how taking photos to share with others affects experiences and memories. ACR North American Advances

Barasch A, Diehl K, Silverman J, Zauberman G (2017) Photographic memory: the effects of volitional photo taking on memory for visual and auditory aspects of an experience. Psychol Sci 28(8):1056–1066

Barnes CA (1988) Spatial learning and memory processes: the search for their neurobiological mechanisms in the rat. Trends Neurosci 11(4):163–169 (1988)

Bartlett FC (1932) Remembering: a study in experimental and social psychology. Cambridge University, Cambridge

Bell G, Gemmell J (2007) A digital life. Sci Am 296(3):58–65

Biondolillo MJ, Pillemer DB (2015) Using memories to motivate future behaviour: an experimental exercise intervention. Memory 23(3):390–402

Booth A (1970) The recall of news items. Publ Opin Quart 34(4):604–610

Brown AS, Marsh EJ (2008) Recognition without identification, erroneous familiarity, and Deja Vu. Psychon Bull Rev 15(1):186–190

Burt CD, Mitchell DA, Raggatt PT, Jones CA, Cowan TM (1995) Towards augmented human memory: retrieval-induced forgetting and retrieval practice in an interactive, end-of-day review. Appl Cogn Psychol 9(1):61–74

Carmichael L, Hogan H, Walter A (1932) An experimental study of the effect of language on the reproduction of visually perceived form. J Exp Psychol 15(1):73

Carr N (2008a). The Atlantic Monthly (2008a). https://www.theatlantic.com/magazine/archive/2008/07/is-google-making-us-stupid/306868/

Carr N (2008b) The Shallows: what the Internet is doing to our brains. WW Norton, New York, NY

Cinel C, Cortis Mack C, Ward G (2018) Towards augmented human memory: retrieval-induced forgetting and retrieval practice in an interactive, end-of-day review. J Expe Psychol: Gen 147(5):632–661

Clinch S, Davies N, Mikusz M, Metzger P, Langheinrich M, Schmidt A, Ward G (2016) Collecting shared experiences through lifelogging: lessons learned. IEEE Pervasive Comput 15(1):58–67

Clinch S, Alghamdi O, Steeds M (2019) Technology-induced human memory degradation. In: CHI4EVIL: creative speculation on the negative effects of HCI research. Workshop at ACM CHI 2019

Craik FI, Lockhart RS (1972) Levels of processing: a framework for memory research. J Verbal Learn Verbal Behav 11(6):671–684

Daily Mail (2008) Pictured: the white van man who followed his sat-nav too closely and ended up in the middle of a lake. https://www.dailymail.co.uk/news/article-1080412/Pictured-The-white-van-man-followed-sat-nav-closely-ended-middle-lake.html

David P (1998) News concreteness and visual-verbal association: do news pictures narrow the recall gap between concrete and abstract news? Human Commun Res 25(2):180–201

Davies N, Friday A, Clinch S, Sas C, Langheinrich M, Ward G, Schmidt A (2015) Security and privacy implications of pervasive memory augmentation. IEEE Pervasive Comput 14(1):44–53

Deese J (1959) On the prediction of occurrence of particular verbal intrusions in immediate recall. J Exp Psychol 58(1):17

Dijs R (2019) It is all fake news! but what exactly is "fake news"?: an explorative study on the definitions of "fake news" and why news consumers perceive a news article as "fake news". Master's thesis, University of Twente

Dodge M, Kitchin R (2007) 'Outlines of a world coming into existence': pervasive computing and the ethics of forgetting. Environ Plan B: Plan Des 34(3):431–445

Fajnerová I, Greguš D, Hlinka J, Nekovárová T, Škoch A, Zítka T, Romportl J, Žácková E, Horácek J (2018) Could prolonged usage of gps navigation implemented in augmented reality smart glasses affect hippocampal functional connectivity? https://doi.org/10.1155/2018/2716134

Fazio LK, Brashier NM, Payne BK, Marsh EJ (2015) Knowledge does not protect against illusory truth. J Exp Psychol: Gen 144(5):993

Fazio LK, Rand DG, Pennycook G (2019) Repetition increases perceived truth equally for plausible and implausible statements. Psychon Bull Rev 26(5):1705–1710

Fenn E, Ramsay N, Kantner J, Pezdek K, Abed E (2019) Nonprobative photos increase truth, like, and share judgments in a simulated social media environment. J Appl Res Mem Cogn 8(2):131–138

Findahl O, Höijer B (1985) Some characteristics of news memory and comprehension. J Broadcast Electron Media 29:379–396

Finley JR, Brewer WF, Benjamin AS (2011) The effects of end-of-day picture review and a sensor-based picture capture procedure on autobiographical memory using SenseCam. Memory 19(7):796–807

Finley JR, Naaz F, Goh FW (2018) Memory and technology: how we use information in the brain and the world. Springer

Flavell JH (1971) First discussant's comments: what is memory development the development of? Hum Dev 14(4):272–278

Gardony AL, Brunyé TT, Mahoney CR, Taylor HA (2013) How navigational aids impair spatial memory: evidence for divided attention. Spat Cogn Comput 13(4):319–350

Gardony AL, Brunyé TT, Taylor HA (2015) Navigational aids and spatial memory impairment: the role of divided attention. Spat Cogn Comput 15(4):246–284

Garry M, Gerrie MP (2005) When photographs create false memories. Curr Dir Psychol Sci 14(6):321–325

Garry M, Wade KA (2005) Actually, a picture is worth less than 45 words: narratives produce more false memories than photographs do. Psychonom Bull Rev 12(2):359–366

Garry M, Strange D, Bernstein DM, Kinzett T (2007) Photographs can distort memory for the news. Appl Cogn Psychol: Off J Soc Appl Res Mem Cogn 21(8):995–1004

Gill G (2019) Fake news and informing science. Inf Sci: Int J Emerg Transdiscipl 22:115–136

Girardin F, Blat J (2010) The co-evolution of taxi drivers and their in-car navigation systems. Pervasive Mobile Comput 6(4):424–434

Graber DA (1990) Seeing is remembering: How visuals contribute to learning from television news. J Commun 40(3):134–155

Gramann K, Hoepner P, Karrer-Gauss K (2017) Modified navigation instructions for spatial navigation assistance systems lead to incidental spatial learning. Front Psychol 8:193

Gunter B (1979) Recall of brief television news items: effects of presentation mode, picture content and serial position. J Educ Telev Other Media 5(2):57–61

Gurrin C, Smeaton AF, Doherty AR et al (2014) LifeLogging: personal big data. Found Trends®. Inf Ret 8(1):1–125

Harvey M, Langheinrich M, Ward G (2016) Remembering through lifelogging: a survey of human memory augmentation. Pervasive Mobile Comput 27:14–26

Hellenthal MV, Howe ML, Knott LM (2016) It must be my favourite brand: using retroactive brand replacements in doctored photographs to influence brand preferences. Appl Cogn Psychol 30(6):863–870

Henkel LA (2011) Photograph-induced memory errors: when photographs make people claim they have done things they have not. Appl Cognit Psychol 25(1):78–86

Henkel LA (2012) Seeing photos makes us read between the lines: the influence of photos on memory for inferences. Quart J Exp Psychol 65(4):773–795

Henkel LA (2014) Point-and-shoot memories: the influence of taking photos on memory for a museum tour. Psychol Sci, 25(2), 396–402, (2014). ISSN 0956–7976:1467–9280. https://doi.org/10.1177/0956797613504438. http://journals.sagepub.com/doi/10.1177/0956797613504438

Henkel LA, Carbuto M (2008) Remembering what we did: how source misattributions arise from verbalization, mental imagery, and pictures. Appl Mem 213–234

Hessen-Kayfitz JK, Scoboria A (2012) False memory is in the details: photographic details differentially predict memory formation. Appl Cogn Psychol 26(3):333–341

Hodges S, Williams L, Berry E, Izadi S, Srinivasan J, Butler A, Smyth G, Kapur N, Wood K (2006) Sensecam: a retrospective memory aid. In: International conference on ubiquitous computing. Springer, pp 177–193

Hodges S, Berry E, Wood K (2011) SenseCam: a wearable camera that stimulates and rehabilitates autobiographical memory. Memory 19(7):685–696

Ishikawa T, Fujiwara H, Imai O, Okabe A (2008) Wayfinding with a GPS-based mobile navigation system: a comparison with maps and direct experience. J Environ Psychol 28(1):74–82

Jacquemard T, Novitzky P, O'Brolcháin F, Smeaton AF, Gordijn B (2014) Challenges and opportunities of lifelog technologies: a literature review and critical analysis. Sci Eng Ethics 20(2):379–409

Johnson MK, Bransford JD, Solomon SK (1973) J Exp Psychol 98(1):203

Kapur N, Glisky E, Wilson BA (2002) External memory aids and computers in memory rehabilitation. In: Baddeley A, Kopelman M, Wilson B (eds) The handbook of memory disorders. Wiley, pp 757–784

Kelly JE, Nace D (1994) Digital imaging & believing photos. Vis Commun Quart 1(1):4–18

Koutstaal W, Schacter DL, Johnson MK, Angell KE, Gross MS (1998) Post-event review in older and younger adults: Improving memory accessibility of complex everyday events. Psychol Aging 13(2):277–296

Koutstaal W, Schacter DL, Johnson MK, Galluccio L (1999) Facilitation and impairment of event memory produced by photograph review. Mem Cogn 27(3):478–493

Kuwabara KJ, Pillemer DB (2010) Memories of past episodes shape current intentions and decisions. Memory 18(4):365–374

Lang A, Shin M, Bradley SD, Wang Z, Lee S, Potter D (2005) Wait! Don't turn that dial! More excitement to come! The effects of story length and production pacing in local television news on channel changing behavior and information processing in a free choice environment. J J Broadcast Electron Media 49(1):3–22

Leshed G, Velden T, Rieger O, Kot B, Sengers P (2008) In-car GPS navigation: engagement with and disengagement from the environment. In: Proceedings of the SIGCHI conference on human factors in computing systems. ACM, pp 1675–1684

Lindsay DS, Hagen L, Read JD, Wade KA, Garry M (2004) True photographs and false memories. Psychol Sci 15(3):149–154

Linton M (1975) Memory for real-world events. In: Norman DA, Rumelhart, DE (eds) exploration in cognition. pp 376–404

Liv N, Greenbaum D (2020) Deep fakes and memory malleability: false memories in the service of fake news. AJOB Neurosci 11(2):96–104

Loftus EF, Palmer JC (1974) Reconstruction of automobile destruction: an example of the interaction between language and memory. J Verbal Learn Verbal Behav 13(5):585–589

Loftus EF, Pickrell JE (1995) The formation of false memories. Psychiatr Ann 25(12):720–725

Maguire EA, Gadian DG, Johnsrude IS, Good CD, Ashburner J, Frackowiak RS, Frith CD (2000) Navigation-related structural change in the hippocampi of taxi drivers. Proc Nat Acad Sci 97(8):4398–4403

Marsh EJ, Cantor AD, Brashier NM (2016) Believing that humans swallow spiders in their sleep: False beliefs as side effects of the processes that support accurate knowledge. In: Psychology of learning and motivation, vol 64. Elsevier, pp 93–132

McKinlay R (2016) Technology: Use or lose our navigation skills 531(7596):573. https://www.nature.com/news/technology-use-or-lose-our-navigation-skills-1.19632

Mols I, Broekhuijsen M, van den Hoven E, Markopoulos P, Eggen B (2015) Do we ruin the moment? exploring the design of novel capturing technologies. In: Proceedings of the annual meeting of the Australian special interest group for computer human interaction. ACM, pp 653–661

Murphy G, Loftus EF, Grady RH, Levine LJ, Greene CM (2019) False memories for fake news during Ireland's abortion referendum. Psychol Sci 30(10):1449–1459

Nash RA (2018) Changing beliefs about past public events with believable and unbelievable doctored photographs. Memory 26(4):439–450

Nash RA, Wade KA (2009) Innocent but proven guilty: eliciting internalized false confessions using doctored-video evidence. Appl Cogn Psychol: Off J Soc Appl Res Mem Cogn 23(5):624–637

Nash RA, Wade KA, Brewer RJ (2009a) Why do doctored images distort memory? Conscious Cogn 18(3):773–780

Nash RA, Wade KA, Lindsay DS (2009b) Digitally manipulating memory: effects of doctored videos and imagination in distorting beliefs and memories. Mem Cogn 37(4):414–424

Neimeyer GJ, Metzler AE (1994) Personal identity and autobiographical. In: The remembering self: construction and accuracy in the self-narrative, vol 6

Newhagen JE (1998) TV news images that induce anger, fear, and disgust: effects on approach-avoidance and memory. J Broadcast Electron Media 42(2):265–276

Newman EJ, Garry M, Bernstein DM, Kantner J, Lindsay DS (2012) Nonprobative photographs (or words) inflate truthiness. Psychon Bull Rev 19(5):969–974

Newman EJ, Garry M, Unkelbach C, Bernstein DM, Lindsay DS, Nash RA (2015) Truthiness and falsiness of trivia claims depend on judgmental contexts. J Exp Psychol: Learn Mem Cogn 41(5):1337

Niforatos E, Langheinrich M, Bexheti A (2014) My good old Kodak: understanding the impact of having only 24 pictures to take. In: Proceedings of the 2014 ACM international joint conference on pervasive and ubiquitous computing: Adjunct Publication, pp 1355–1360. ACM, (2014)

Niforatos E, Cinel C, Cortis Mack C, Langheinrich M, Ward G (2017) Can less be more?: Contrasting limited, unlimited, and automatic picture capture for augmenting memory recall. In: Proceedings of the ACM on interactive, mobile, wearable and ubiquitous technol, vol 1(2), pp 1–21. https://doi.org/10.1145/3090086

Nightingale SJ, Wade KA, Watson DG (2017) Can people identify original and manipulated photos of real-world scenes? Cogn Res: Princ Implic 2(1):30

Nilsson M, Perfilieva E, Johansson U, Orwar O, Eriksson PS (1999) Enriched environment increases neurogenesis in the adult rat dentate gyrus and improves. J Neurobiol 39(4):569–578

O'Connell A, Greene CM (2017) Not strange but not true: self-reported interest in a topic increases false memory. 25(8), 969–977. ISSN 0965-8211:1464-0686. https://doi.org/10.1080/09658211.2016.1237655. https://www.tandfonline.com/doi/full/10.1080/09658211.2016.1237655

O'Keefe J, Speakman A (1987) Single unit activity in the rat hippocampus during a spatial memory task. Exp Brain Res 68(1):1–27

Oliver KJ, Burnett GE Learning-oriented vehicle navigation systems: a preliminary investigation in a driving simulator. In: Proceedings of the 10th international conference on Human computer interaction with mobile devices and services. ACM, pp 119–126

Pangrazio L (2018) What's new about' fake news'?: critical digital literacies in an era of fake news, post-truth and clickbait. Páginas de educación 11(1):6–22

Parker A, Dagnall N (2009) Effects of retrieval practice on conceptual explicit and implicit consumer memory. Appl Cogn Psychol: Off J Soc Appl Res Mem Cogn 23(2):188–203

Parush A, Ahuvia S, Erev I (2007) Degradation in spatial knowledge acquisition when using automatic navigation systems. In: International conference on spatial information theory. Springer, pp 238–254

Pezdek K, Salim R (2011) Physiological, psychological and behavioral consequences of activating autobiographical memories. J Exp Soc Psychol 47(6):1214–1218

Pfeiffer M, Dünte T, Schneegass S, Alt F, Rohs M (2015) Cruise control for pedestrians: controlling walking direction using electrical muscle stimulation. In: Proceedings of the 33rd annual ACM conference on human factors in computing systems, CHI 15. Association for Computing Machinery, New York, NY, USA, pp 2505–2514. ISBN 9781450331456. https://doi.org/10.1145/2702123.2702190. https://doi.org/10.1145/2702123.2702190

Risko EF, Gilbert SJ (2016) Cognitive offloading. Trends Cogn Sci 20(9):676–688

Sacchi DL, Agnoli F, Loftus EF (2007) Changing history: doctored photographs affect memory for past public events. Appl Cogn Psychol: Off J Soc Appl Res Mem Cogn 21(8):1005–1022

Schlosser AE (2006) Learning through Virtual product experience: the role of imagery on true versus false memories. J Consum Res 33(3):377–383. ISSN 0093–5301:1537–5277. https://doi.org/10.1086/508522. https://academic.oup.com/jcr/article-lookup/doi/10.1086/508522

Schmidt A (2017) Augmenting human intellect and amplifying perception and cognition. IEEE Pervasive Comput 16(1):6–10

Sellen AJ, Whittaker S (2010) Beyond total capture: a constructive critique of lifelogging. Commun ACM 53(5):70–77

Sellen AJ, Fogg A, Aitken M, Hodges S, Rother C, Wood K (2007) Do life-logging technologies support memory for the past?: an experimental study using sensecam. In: Proceedings of the SIGCHI conference on Human factors in computing systems, CHI '19. ACM, pp 81–90

Shearer E, Matsa KE (2018) Pew research center: Journalism & media. https://www.journalism.org/2018/09/10/news-use-across-social-media-platforms-2018/

Silva A, Pinho M, Macedo L, Moulin C (2018) A critical review of the effects of wearable cameras on memory. Neuropsychol Rehabilitation 28(1):117–141

Silva AR, Pinho S, Macedo LM, Moulin CJ (2013) Benefits of SenseCam review on neuropsychological test performance. Am J Preven Med 44(3):302–307

Soares JS, Storm BC (2018) Forget in a flash: a further investigation of the photo-taking-impairment effect. J Appl Res Memory Cogn 7(1):154–160

Sparrow B, Liu J, Wegner DM (2011) Google effects on memory: cognitive consequences of having information at our fingertips. Science 333(6043):776–778. ISSN 0036–8075:1095–9203. 10.1126/science.1207745. http://www.sciencemag.org/cgi/doi/10.1126/science.1207745

Speake J (2015) 'I've got my Sat Nav, it's alright': Users' attitudes towards, and engagements with, technologies of navigation. The Cartograp J 52(4). ISSN 345–355(2015):0008–7041. 10.1080/00087041.2015.1108663. https://www.tandfonline.com/doi/full/10.1080/00087041.2015.1108663

Spinney L (2017) How Facebook, fake news and friends are warping your memory. Nature 543

Storm BC, Bjork EL, Bjork RA, Nestojko JF (2006) Is retrieval success a necessary condition for retrieval-induced forgetting? Psychonom Bull Rev 13(6):1023–1027

Storm BC, Stone SM, Benjamin AS (2017) Using the Internet to access information inflates future use of the Internet to access other information. Memory 25(6):717–723. ISSN 0965–8211:1464–1686. https://doi.org/10.1080/09658211.2016.1210171. https://www.tandfonline.com/doi/full/10.1080/09658211.2016.1210171

Strange D, Gerrie MP, Garry M (2005) A few seemingly harmless routes to a false memory. Cogn Process 6(4):237–242

Strange D, Garry M, Bernstein DM, Lindsay DS (2011) Photographs cause false memories for the news. Acta Psychol 136(1):90–94

Stroop JR (1935) Studies of interference in serial verbal reactions. J Exp Psychol 18(6):643

Tamir DI, Templeton EM, Ward AF, Zaki J (2018) Media usage diminishes memory for experiences. J Exp Soc Psychol 76:161–168. ISSN 00221031: 10.1016/j.jesp.2018.01.006. https://linkinghub.elsevier.com/retrieve/pii/S002210311730505X

Tannenbaum PH (1954) Effect of serial position on recall of radio news stories. J Quart 31(3):319–323

The Telegraph (2017) Driver ends up stranded on ski slope after relying on his sat-nav. https://www.telegraph.co.uk/travel/ski/news/driver-get-stuck-on-a-ski-slope-after-his-sat-nav-gets-him-lost/

Times and Star (2019) 'Don't just follow sat nav' warns driver whose car got stuck in a ditch high on a lakeland fell. https://www.timesandstar.co.uk/news/17832400.dont-just-follow-sat-nav-warns-driver-whose-car-got-stuck-ditch-high-lakeland-fell/

Toronto S (2016) Woman follows GPS; ends up in ontario lake. https://torontosun.com/2016/05/13/woman-follows-gps-ends-up-in-ontario-lake/wcm/fddda6d6-6b6e-41c7-88e8-aecc501faaa5

Tulving E, Madigan SA (1970) Memory and verbal learning. Annu Rev Psychol 21(1):437–484

Wade KA, Garry M (2005) Strategies for verifying false autobiographical memories. Am J Psychol 587–602

Wade KA, Garry M, Read JD, Lindsay DS (2002) A picture is worth a thousand lies: using false photographs to create false childhood memories. Psychonom Bull Rev 9(3):597–603

Wagenaar WA (1986) My memory: A study of autobiographical memory over six years. Cogn Psychol 18(2):225–252

Ward AF (2013) Supernormal: How the Internet Is Changing Our Memories and Our Minds. Psychol Inq 24(4):341–348. ISSN 1047-840X, 1532-7965. https://doi.org/10.1080/1047840X.2013.850148. http://www.tandfonline.com/doi/abs/10.1080/1047840X.2013.850148

Ward AF, Duke K, Gneezy A, Bos MW (2017) Brain drain: the mere presence of one's own smartphone reduces available cognitive capacity. J Assoc Consumer Res 2(2):140–154

Wegner DM, Ward AF (2013) How Google is changing your brain. Sci Am 309(6):58–61. ISSN 0036–8733. https://doi.org/10.1038/scientificamerican1213-58. http://www.nature.com/doifinder/10.1038/scientificamerican1213-58

Wegner DM, Giuliano T, Hertel PT (1985) Cognitive interdependence in close relationships. In: Ickes W (ed) Compatible and incompatible relationships. Springer, New York, NY, USA, pp 253–276. ISBN 978-1-4612-9538-9 978-1-4612-5044-9. https://doi.org/10.1007/978-1-4612-5044-9_12. http://link.springer.com/10.1007/978-1-4612-5044-9_12

Wen J, Deneka A, Helton W, Billinghurst M (2014) Really, it's for your own good... making augmented reality navigation tools harder to use. In: Proceedings of the extended abstracts of the 32nd annual ACM conference on human factors in computing systems. ACM, pp 1297–1302

Wigoder M (2001) History begins at home: photography and memory in the writings of Siegfried Kracauer and Roland Barthes. Hist Memory 13(1):19–59

Wilson A, Ross M (2003) The identity function of autobiographical memory: time is on our side. Memory 11(2):137–149

Wilson JC, Westerman DL (2018) Picture (im)perfect: illusions of recognition memory produced by photographs at test. Memory Cogn 46(7):1210–1221

Designing Task Resumption Cues for Interruptions in Mobile Learning Scenarios

Christina Schneegass and Fiona Draxler

Abstract Learning on a mobile device in everyday settings makes users particularly susceptible for interruptions. Guidance (memory) cues can be implemented to support users in resuming a learning task after a distraction. These cues can take a wide range of forms and designs and, to work effectively, need to be carefully adapted to the mobile learning use case. In this work, we present a structured in-depth literature review on task resumption support for mobile devices. In particular, we propose a design space based on 30 carefully chosen publications to highlight well-evaluated design ideas as well as currently underrepresented research directions. Furthermore, we evaluate the causes of interruptions in the domain of mobile learning and derive design ideas for task resumption support on mobile devices. To this end, we conducted two focus groups with HCI experts ($N = 4$) and users of mobile learning applications ($N = 3$). Based on the literature review, focus groups, and further related work, we discuss ideas and research gaps for task resumption cues in mobile learning. We derive six design guidelines to support researchers and designers of mobile learning applications and emphasize promising research directions and open questions.

1 Introduction

Smartphones may still be called "phones," but in addition to their initial purpose, mobile devices now offer games, activity trackers, and a multitude of other applications. They even contribute to the development of cognitive capabilities, as they have given rise to learning apps that enable users to learn whenever and wherever it suits them. For instance, smartphones facilitate the design of new (language) learning experiences such as micro-learning sessions (Heil et al. 2016) and learning on the go. Moreover, mobile devices include a variety of sensors that enable us to gather infor-

C. Schneegass (✉) · F. Draxler
LMU Munich, Munich, Germany
e-mail: christina.schneegass@ifi.lmu.de

F. Draxler
e-mail: fiona.draxler@ifi.lmu.de

© Springer Nature Switzerland AG 2021
T. Dingler and E. Niforatos (eds.), *Technology-Augmented Perception and Cognition*,
Human–Computer Interaction Series, https://doi.org/10.1007/978-3-030-30457-7_5

mation on the users and their situational characteristics through context and to adapt learning content and interface design accordingly (Economides 2008). Nevertheless, learning on the go makes users highly susceptible to distractions and interruptions that disturb the task flow (Leiva et al. 2012). For example, devices issue notifications for incoming messages, PA systems announce the next subway stop, and background noises in crowded and busy environments make it difficult to stay focused. Learners may also intentionally be interrupted by other people such as co-workers or waiters. Besides, due to an increased number of functionalities built into mobile devices as well as context-aware applications, the number of unwanted interruptions by the device itself has increased over the last years (Ho and Intille 2005).

Even short interruptions can have a severe adverse effect on the learning performance (Bailey and Konstan 2006). To reduce the impact of interruptions, research has explored several options, mainly (1) delaying notifications (e.g., Chen and Vertegaal 2004; Iqbal and Bailey 2005), (2) preparing the user for an upcoming interruption (e.g., Altmann and Trafton 2004; Hodgetts and Jones 2006a), or (3) supporting the resumption of the interrupted task (e.g., Cheng et al. 2018; Parnin and DeLine 2010; Toreini et al. 2018). When we evaluate these options in terms of their applicability in the context of mobile learning, options (1) and (2) have strong restrictions. The approaches are especially limited when the interruptions are unplanned, even though in public spaces, unpredictable interruptions are particularly likely. Therefore, this work will mainly focus on the design of task resumption strategies (3), notably the use of task resumption cues. In a general sense, a *cue* is "a stimulus, event, or object that serves to guide behavior [...]" (cf. American Psychological Association (APA) dictionary APA 2019b). If we consider this concept in light of our use case of task resumption support for learning, a cue can address a more specific purpose. In particular, it can help to retrieve a certain memory in response to a given stimulus (Niforatos et al. 2018) (e.g., showing the first two letters of a translation to remember the actual word), or to direct a user's attention (e.g., by highlighting the last sentence a user read before an interruption occurred as in Mariakakis et al. 2015). Thus, for this work, we define *Task Resumption Cues* as a specific design feature or signal of a digital system that is presented either before, during, or after an interruption to facilitate the resumption of a primary task content or status by aiding the user's memory and/or guiding their attention back toward the original task.

Task resumption cues have been designed for a variety of domains and application scenarios, such as reading, driving, office work tasks, or aircraft monitoring (Borojeni et al. 2016; González and Mark 2004; Mariakakis et al. 2015; Scott et al. 2006). Very little research has been done in the area of task resumption cues on mobile devices, even though interruptions during mobile use are particularly likely. The adaption of resumption cues designed for desktop settings to the application on mobile devices is possible. However, smartphones and tablets come with a set of unique limitations such as small display sizes and specific interaction techniques, which we need to consider. On the other hand, the integrated sensors and actuators open up new design possibilities.

More specifically, our research will take place in the domain of mobile learning as a typical application scenario. Mobile learning aims at integrating new information with prior knowledge as well as potential long-term storage of this information. Thus, interruptions during the learning process are particularly harmful, and learners could benefit from interruption support. In particular, we aim to augment mobile learning capabilities by helping learners quickly recover from interruptions or negative impacts in the first place. Therefore, the main research question of this work is *How can we design cues to effectively support task resumption during learning on a mobile device?*

We start approaching this question through automatically parsing existing literature based on keywords to generate an overview of the application of cues for task resumption across domains. We queried a broad set of publications from different online science libraries and applied several rounds of semi-automated filtering and weighting. Finally, we describe a resulting set of 30 papers ranging from 2002 to 2018, which, as their primary focus, present the design and partly also evaluation of a task resumption cue in a digital setting. We furthermore categorize these 30 publications along five dimensions to highlight individual design differences. We discuss the characteristics of those cues and their applicability in a mobile learning scenario.

In addition to this literature survey, we supplement our results with a focus group of experts and Mobile Learning Application (MLA) users to discuss the following: (1) potential causes of interruptions in typical mobile learning scenarios, and (2) novel and previously unexplored design ideas for task resumption support during mobile learning. We start this chapter by presenting the fundamental concepts of learning and memory processing. We introduce research on interruptions from a background of psychology and human–computer interaction and describe interruption characteristics and effects. Furthermore, we illustrate the use of task resumption support in existing applications before presenting the results of the two parts of our evaluation: the literature survey and focus groups. In conclusion, we combine the results of the two methodological parts to formulate a set of six design guidelines for task resumption specific to the context of mobile learning, in which we further draw on literature to discuss the central findings of our analysis. These guidelines are meant to support application designers as well as researchers in the creation and assessment of cues to support task resumption after interruptions in mobile learning scenarios.

2 Mobile Learning and Micro-Learning

As described in the introduction, this work aims to support mobile learning in interruption-prone environments by evaluating designs of task resumption cues in this context. To discuss potential distractions and derive strategies supporting task resumption, we have to understand the basic idea of mobile learning. In this section, we will define *Mobile Learning* from a psychological perspective and introduce the topic of *learning application design* from a technological standpoint. Besides everyday usage situations of mobile learning apps and, as a result, potential sources for interruptions, this section aims to outline features of the lesson and User Interface (UI) design that already facilitate learning in busy environments.

2.1 Mobile Learning

In a very general form, *learning* can be considered as "the acquisition of novel information, behaviors, or abilities [...]" (cf. American Psychological Association (APA) dictionary APA 2019c). Learning with a mobile device can, therefore, be understood as "any sort of learning that happens when the learner is not at a fixed, predetermined location, learning that happens when the learner takes advantage of the learning opportunities offered by mobile technologies" (O'Malley et al. 2005, p. 7). For our work, we consider mobile learning as learning with a mobile device and, therefore, learning that is flexible regarding time and location. However, "mobile learning" is not necessarily learning on the go or learning outside. It can also include learning in different settings of a home environment (e.g., when waiting for the tea water to boil or on the sofa while watching TV).

Because of their flexible usage, learning on mobile devices differs a lot from learning on stationary devices like desktop computers. For instance, learning applications which support both mobile and stationary usage such as Massive Open Online Courses (MOOCs) show a disparity in the usage behavior depending on the device a learner used. For example, in one project, learners spent more time on interactive material (e.g., watching videos) and less time on answering questions when they accessed platforms on a mobile device (Zhao et al. 2018).

With the increased ubiquity of smartphones and tablets, we can learn anywhere and anytime (Tatar et al. 2003). This pervasiveness does not only influence the learning material people prefer, but also the amount of information they can process, and their ways of interacting with the device. These restrictions gave rise to the nowadays popular micro-learning approach. This concept was designed to make learning in everyday environments more convenient and, thus, redefines learning sessions for mobile devices and emphasizes the importance of simple interaction techniques (Bruck et al. 2012). The following section will present the fundamental concepts of micro-learning in greater detail.

Micro-Learning The *micro-learning* approach is a specialized way of teaching contents on mobile devices. Based on psychological research that states the benefits of high repetition counts in contrast to long learning streaks (Cull 2000), this approach is often used, for example, in language learning. Micro-learning focuses on frequent repetitions while presenting micro-content units in micro-interactions to help users learn without information overload (Bruck et al. 2012). In the case of mobile language learning, micro-learning means that lessons are broken down into small information chunks. The user learns a set of consecutive words or phrases ordered by topics. New contents are unlocked gradually. Explicit grammar explanations are rare: Heil et al. (2016) evaluated 50 mobile learning applications and showed that they were only included in 20% of the applications. The absence of these explicit contents shows the emphasis on teaching simple and easily processable learning materials in MLAs. In its essence, the two central pillars of micro-learning are (1) *micro-content* and (2) *micro-interactions*, which we will further describe below.

Micro-Content When designing mobile learning applications, designers face many challenges related to the devices and their usage. For instance, typing text, as it might be necessary to learn new languages, can be cumbersome on mobile devices (Page 2013). Moreover, smartphones and tablets come with limited screen size, restricting the amount of content presented at once. Micro-learning, however, subdivides learning units into small chunks: micro-content items, which are more comfortable to deal with on mobile devices (Bruck et al. 2012).

Breaking the content into smaller units has several advantages. For instance, it is straightforward to design lessons such that they satisfy the aforementioned frequent repetitions instead of long streaks. This also increases the level of interaction and feedback for each action. Learning through smaller pieces of information is a universal principle rooted in cognitive psychology research (McLean and Gregg 1967; Miller 1956), since the number of chunks of information humans can keep in their short-term memory is limited and short learning units reduce the amount of information to be processed at once. We will go into details on memory requirements in Sect. 3.2. Short lessons are also useful when learners are in an environment that is known to cause interruptions and distractions, such as during a train commute. Furthermore, it has been shown that especially when on the go, people engage in short learning sessions, and research highlights the feasibility of micro-learning in idle moments such as waiting situations (Dingler et al. 2017).

One popular application which implements a micro-learning approach through micro-content is the application *Duolingo*.[1] The short interactive lessons make it a suitable option for the aforementioned idle moments.

Micro-Interactions and UI Design In addition to limiting the amount of content in a lesson, it is also very important to present this content in a short and easy manner. In particular, the limited screen size of mobile devices requires a careful interaction design. For example, Churchill and Hedberg (2008) propose one-step interactions with immediate feedback. All actions need to be centered around the learning task and have a short duration. Moreover, the design principles for multimedia learning by Mayer (2002) apply to mobile learning with some reservations. For example, implementing a lesson that is user-paced rather than continuous will be beneficial for mobile learning as well as using different presentation modalities such as text, graphical representations, and audio (Mayer 2002).

Aside from interaction techniques and the amount of learning content presented to the user, the design of the user interface can have a substantial effect on the quality of task resumption. Switching between tasks on the same device is highly limited by the display space. Task switching and task resumption work better if users can still see a part of the former task (e.g., Hodgetts and Jones 2006a; Iqbal and Horvitz

---

[1]Duolingo App: https://www.duolingo.com/, last access February 16, 2020.

2007a). On small screens, virtual desktops or workspaces can be created instead and can help structure tasks (Jeuris and Bardram 2016).

It needs to be noted that micro-learning is only one potential option to design MLAs. Although micro-learning is often applied in (language) learning applications, other designs are also possible. In our analysis, later on, we will primarily view the design ideas in the light of the benefits and constraints of micro-learning as it is the most common design approach. However, when it comes to the design of task resumption support, both learning content and interface design play a crucial role in any case. Depending on the content and its structure, a particular design for resumption support can be more or less suitable. In Sects. 5 and 6, we discuss various ideas to implement task resumption cues which are meant to support users when they are interrupted in a learning session.

To better understand the restrictions that mobile learning applications face in everyday usage scenarios and the necessity of simple interactions and content design, the following section will describe common usage situations of MLAs in greater detail.

2.2 Usage Situations of Mobile Learning Applications

Due to the constant availability of smartphones in users' daily lives, they provide the opportunity of learning at any time and at any place (Bruck et al. 2012). As a result, there is not just one common usage situation of mobile learning applications. Every usage context is different and creates different requirements. Moreover, every setting entails new potential interruptions that can distract the user from the learning task. In the following paragraphs, we describe possible and common usage situations based on prior user surveys by Demouy et al. (2016) as well as Schneegass et al. (2018).

The results of a survey by Demouy et al. (2016) show that learners, in particular, language learners, often engage in informal rather than planned learning sessions. Almost 60% of the survey participants stated to use the mobile device for learning when and where they had the opportunity to do so (Demouy et al. 2016). An advantage of mobile learning is that it can fulfill the learning demand during very time-limited periods of daily life such as commutes (Bruck et al. 2012). Users embed MLAs in daily routines or use them infrequently (Demouy et al. 2016). Learning situations can differ along with a variety of characteristics, including the location, time of the day, duration of the learning session, noise level, company, and others. Schneegass et al. (2018) clustered survey responses of 74 users of mobile language learning applications into five common, however, non-exhaustive, usage situations (Schneegass et al. 2018): (1) Many users started to learn at home in the evening several times a week while having company. Users interacted with the MLA spontaneously for around 15 min and experienced a mostly low-stress level. (2) In contrast, many users planned learning sessions in advance, which then took place at home when they were alone. At 30 min, the overall duration of these sessions was significantly higher than in situation (1). Cluster (3) describes learning at home without any company present, but is restricted almost entirely to the use of the smartphone as a preferred device. Usage situation (4) describes the use of MLAs in public transport. Users learn mostly in the morning, several times a week. The environment is noisy, and learning sessions are relatively short (around 15 min +-5). The last situation (5) describes an indoor, but public setting such as a university or library with a low noise level (Schneegass et al. 2018).

Depending on the respective scenario, there is a variety of interruptions that can occur. Only when we know the disruptive event and its characteristics (e.g., source, importance, duration, etc.), we can design the task resumption support accordingly. For example, resuming a task after receiving a simple notification on your phone might be easier than resuming a task after having switched trains. Section 4 provides further background on interruptions and their characteristics. Section 6, on the other hand, reports on experiences of MLA users and discusses potential types and sources of interruptions as they occur in daily life.

Before we take an in-depth look at interruptions, the following section provides a detailed background on the cognitive processes involved in interrupting situations. In particular, we will focus on the workings of attention and memory processes involved in learning.

3 Attention and Memory

As described in Sect. 2, learning can be described as the acquisition of new information (cf. APA 2019c). To enable this acquisition, we first need to understand the underlying mechanism of *Attention*. Attention makes us focus on a specific task, and an interrupting event can easily violate this focus. A person perceives every bit of information in their surrounding on an either conscious or subconscious level (APA 2019c). In the use case of learning, this perception can, for example, be reading a word or listening to a pronunciation. However, stimuli from the environment can attract our attention, for instance, loud noises or a touch. To explain why attention is essential for learning in busy and distracting environments, the following section provides an introduction to the filtering mechanisms of the brain.

3.1 Attention

Back in 1890, William James defined attention as a perception or thought which is "[...] taking possession of the mind, in clear and vivid form, of one out of what seems several simultaneously possible objects or trains of thought. Focalization, concentration of consciousness are of its essence. It implies a withdrawal from some things in order to deal effectively with others" (see James et al. 1890, p. 404). Thus, according to James, attention involves a person either voluntarily or involuntarily focusing on one object or thought, while neglecting everything else. Focus is necessary, since our cognitive resources to process information simultaneously are limited (Sweller et al. 1998), and we cannot attend to everything (APA 2019a). Since the ubiquity of today's smartphones enables learning anytime and anywhere (Tatar et al. 2003), they confront users of mobile learning applications with a multitude of stimuli competing for their attention. Even though a person focuses on the screen and tries to stay concentrated, a loud noise or a touch can lead to a shift of attention toward this external stimulus. The extent to which a person can stay focused on a specific task has been shown to depend on the task itself as well as the type of information load involved. If a person is engaged in difficult working memory processes (such as mobile learning), then the ability to sustain attention deteriorates (Lavie 2005, 2010).

In the context of learning, focused attention is essential. While learning can, in some situations, also take place subconsciously, it is more efficient when a learner is explicitly paying attention (Schmidt 1995). For example, in second language learning, Schmidt (2012) states that knowledge acquisition improves when learners are attentive. In conclusion, attention regulates the stream of incoming information. It is a brain's filtering process that decides which information reaches the working memory and which it processes voluntarily.

Consequently, the aim for every learning situation needs to be keeping the learner attentive to the task. As outlined in the introduction, learning on the go can be prone to interruptions and distractions. In such cases, the application needs to direct a user's focus of attention back to the exercise. However, this requires a robust and preferably automated mechanism to detect a person's current attention state.

When we achieve a state of focused attention on the learning content, we need to further process the information perceived. The following section introduces the mechanisms of integrating new information with already existing knowledge from a person's memory storage. For example, when school children want to learn the addition of two-digit numbers, they will call upon previously learned content on the addition of single-digit numbers from their long-term memory to align with the new information. Hence, we will give an overview of the concept of memory and explain which factors support the long-term storage of information.

3.2 Memory

As mentioned above, attention is the fundamental filtering process every chunk of information we perceive has to pass through. When information from the environment is actively perceived, it enters the memory storage. Memory is closely related to learning. In a definition by the American Psychology Association, learning is defined as "[...] the acquisition of skill or knowledge" (APA 2019d) and memory is defined as "[...] the expression of what you've acquired" (APA 2019d). Thus, the two concepts differ in the speed of knowledge acquisition, with learning being a more slow and cumbersome, and memory an instant process (APA 2019d). Below, we explain the cognitive processes of memory along with the *Multi-Store Model* by Atkinson and Shiffrin (1968) as depicted in Fig. 1. The model has been valued and

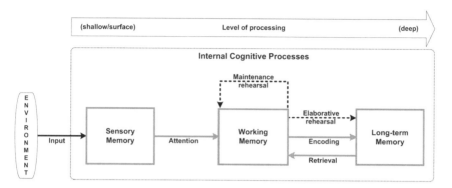

Fig. 1 The original multi-store model as proposed by Atkinson and Shiffrin differentiates between three stages of information processing in the human memory: (1) sensory memory, (2) short-term memory, and (3) long-term memory (see blue elements) (Atkinson and Shiffrin 1968). Khalil and Elkhider further highlight the different levels of processing and the two types of rehearsal (Khalil and Elkhider 2016)

criticized up until today. For example, Craik and Lockhart summarized a variety of critical issues (Craik and Lockhart 1972). Nonetheless, we consider this approach a good and easily understandable introduction to understanding memory processes and sufficient for our use case. Therefore, we will use this distinction of memory components in the course of this work.

The Multi-Store Model The model by Atkinson and Shiffrin postulates three types of memory: the Sensory Memory or sensory register (SM), the Short-Term Memory (STM) (or working memory), and the Long-Term Memory (LTM) (Atkinson and Shiffrin 1968). We can differentiate these three components by their capacity, duration, and ways of encoding of information. At first, every sensory stimulus from the environment is processed by the sensory memory (cf. Fig. 1, process from left to right). This first step can happen subconsciously and has a fast decay rate of less than one second. If the information passes the attention filter and is perceived consciously, it enters the short-term or working memory. Here, it resides for around 30 s until it decays, if not maintained by a rehearsal of given information (Atkinson and Shiffrin 1968). If an interruption occurs while the information is in the STM and not yet encoded into LTM storage, it is prone to decay if not rehearsed quickly. If the interruption disrupts the primary task longer than it takes the information to decay, it cannot be restored. Once encoded in the LTM, it is safe to interruptions (Oulasvirta and Saariluoma 2006). The long-term store is a (fairly) permanent information storage unit, which information gets transferred to from the short-term store (Atkinson and Shiffrin 1968). To retain information in the long-term memory, which is the goal of every learning process, we need to recall a memory from the LTM storage. If we rehearse the information, e.g., by repeating vocabulary over and over (as it is common with micro-learning), the likelihood of storing this information in the LTM increases. Khalil and Elkhider (2016) expand the Multi-Store Model by two different forms of *Rehearsal*, maintenance and elaborative rehearsal (cf. Fig. 1). Maintenance rehearsal describes a form of surface learning, where the user goes over the material many times to learn it without deeper knowledge processing. In contrast, elaborative rehearsal describes a process of understanding by organizing information with the help of previous knowledge (Khalil and Elkhider 2016). Both processes facilitate learning and are applied by current learning technologies.

In contrast to the long-term memory's unlimited capacities, the short-term memory is limited. Early research by Miller (1956) states that the magical number of items we can keep in the STM is seven (5+-2). However, Cowan (2010) and others re-evaluated the number of possible items during the last decades, and current research suggests that we can store between three and five meaningful items (for young adults). For example, we could store a set of newly learned vocabulary items or the digits of a phone number.

Although the Multi-Store Model implies that information can be stored in the LTM indefinitely, this is only partly true. Even memories in the LTM are prone to be forgotten if not retrieved and rehearsed once in a while. In his book "The seven sins of memory" (Schacter 1999), Schacter describes seven miscues of the human memory. *Transience*, the fading of memories over time, is one of them. Furthermore, Schacter describes six additional memory effects, namely absent-mindedness, blocking (memory interference), misattribution, suggestibility, bias, and persistence. All these effects show the complexity of human memory and how easy it is to interfere with them.

Besides the limitations stated above, the *Cognitive Load Theory* describes the restrictions of our cognitive capacities in regard to learning content and the design of learning instructions.

Cognitive Load Theory As explained above, two central components of the human memory system are long-term memory and working memory. The former is used for the permanent storage of information, whereas the latter processes incoming information from the perceptual system by connecting it to knowledge stored in the long-term memory (Baddeley 1997; Dillenbourg and Betrancourt 2006). The Cognitive Load Theory (CLT) now states that the resources of the human cognitive system (i.e., memory and processing resources) are physiologically restricted and derive recommendations for the design of learning instructions and materials (Sweller et al. 1998). In detail, the CLT considers three types of load during the processing of learning materials and instructions: (1) *Intrinsic Load* is created during the processing of the task itself. It is related to the learning content itself and refers to the number of elements which need to be held at the working memory at the same time. For example, Sweller describes vocabulary learning as a task with low element interactivity. In contrast, language syntax learning has high interactivity and, therefore, induces higher intrinsic load (Kirschner et al. 2009; Sweller et al. 1998). (2) *Extraneous Load* describes additional load that is caused by the format of the presented material and the instructions given. Good learning design aims to reduce the load of (1) and (2) to maximize the resources available for (3) *Germane Load* to take up in the cognitive process. Germane load fosters the construction of schema and, therefore, facilitates deep learning (Paas et al. 2004; Sweller et al. 1998). In conclusion, the goal of any learning application is to reduce the load induced by poor instructional design and increase the capacities for schema creation.

Despite the recommendations of the CLT, the human memory is limited in its ability and prone to miscues, which we will outline in more detail in the next section.

To overcome the limitations and miscues of the human memory, there are several (technology-based) methods that can support the users' memory performance. The following section will briefly outline general memory augmentation strategies from other domains before we focus on strategies to specifically support task resumption in the further course of this chapter.

3.3 Memory Augmentation Strategies

There are various techniques, with and without the application of technology, that can help to build and to recall memories. One common tool is the utilization of a memory *Cue*. A cue can be a certain stimulus, an object, or something completely unrelated, that is used to guide behavior (cf. APA 2019b). If a cue is applied to guide memory recall, it is called a *Retrieval Cue* (APA 2019g) and the concept of cue-supported memory enhancements is called *Cued Recall* (Buschke 1984). One example is the learning of word pairs as it is common practice when trying to remember second-language vocabulary. For example, presenting the English word "cat" and asking for the Spanish translation "gato" (and receiving feedback on it in the end) will increase the recall ability in a later testing situation.

A learning technique which makes use of retrieval cues is named *Mnemonic*, or Mnemonic Device. This technique forges an association between new and already encoded information, e.g., remembering one's password by connecting it to the birthday of a friend (cf. APA 2019e). A common example that is often already taught in elementary school is the planetary mnemonic; the names and order of the planets of our solar system are associated with a sentence where each word starts with the beginning letter of one planet. "**M**y **V**ery **E**ducated **M**other **J**ust **S**erved **U**s **N**achos"—Mars, Venus, Earth, Mercury, Jupiter, Saturn, Uranus, and Neptune, respectively. With the help of this mnemonic, it is easier to recall every planet and retain the correct order. Mnemonic strategies can occur in every shape, form, or modality. For example, the loci method makes use of a familiar location to facilitate recall (Roediger 1980), e.g., the walking path from home to work. New items to remember are converted or deposited at a specific location along the route (cf. Moè and De Beni 2005). To recall these items, one virtually walks the path and decodes the associations made with certain things or landmarks.

As noted earlier, technology can support memory recall. In particular, the domain of technology-enhanced life-logging evaluated several ways of memory augmentation to foster recall of past experiences. A study by Niforatos et al. (2016) applied a slide deck as a tool to support the recall of previous work meetings. Through the pictures and text on the slides, the participants had a 15% higher recall rate than in a free recall condition based on their memories (Niforatos et al. 2018). Moreover, Dingler et al. (2016) evaluated the use of multimedia memory cues for life-logging and highlighted the importance of generating effective cues. One constraint mentioned in this work is the difficulty of placing the memory cues into context. Due to the subjectivity of memory cues, their perception remains highly personal and depends on users' preferences (Dingler et al. 2016).

When we want to design technology to support the encoding and retrieval of information, we can imagine memory support in any modality. The usage of multimedia cues such as pictures or videos can transfer a large amount of information to help recall memories. Moreover, today's technology makes it relatively easy to capture such cues with the help of smartphone or life-logging cameras (Dingler et al. 2016).

Now that we have outlined the cognitive foundations as well as general related work of memory re-activation, the subsequent section will take an in-depth look at our use case of task interruptions.

4   Interruption Research

In today's world, multitasking is a common practice. The ubiquitous availability of technology makes it an enormous source for distractions and interruptions. In the context of using a mobile application, an interruption is an event or action that leads the user to shift the focus away from the application. Although some sources claim the positive effects of multitasking on cost-switching and attentional skills (e.g., Foehr 2006), the real-life implications of interruptions on task performance (in this case the learning task) are often negative (Carrier et al. 2015; Xiao and Wang 2017). In this section, we will explain the characteristics of interruptions, their consequences, and how negative effects can be mitigated. First though, we will explain the necessary terms and concepts of interruption research and the process of interruptions.

4.1   Process of Interruptions

The sequence of an interruption as depicted in Fig. 2 is defined by the task that is being interrupted—often referred to as the *primary task*—the interruption event or task—also called *secondary task*—and the return to the primary task (Trafton et al. 2003). The *interruption lag* is the time between the occurrence of an interrupting trigger or stimulus and the shift of attention toward the activity related to the source of the interruption. This phase can be exploited to prepare for an upcoming interruption and will be discussed in greater depth in Sect. 4.3. The *resumption lag*, on the other hand, is the time needed to return one's focus on the primary task after moving away from the secondary task (Trafton et al. 2003). Figure 2 illustrates the timeline of an interruption. In real-world scenarios, the distinction between primary and secondary task is often difficult, because series of tasks can be interleaved and convoluted.

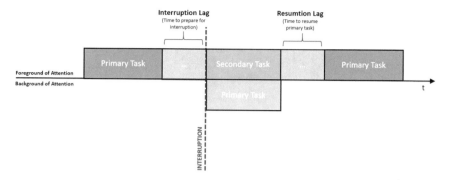

Fig. 2 A secondary task interrupting a primary task. The time preceding an interruption is called *Interruption Lag*, whereas the time following an interruption is called *Resumption Lag* (terminology cf. Trafton et al. 2003)

Nevertheless, we will use this differentiation to explain our use case, as the underlying principles remain the same.

Also, secondary tasks can have a different duration and are not all equally demanding. For example, learners can be interrupted because they have to switch trains on a commute. This can take several minutes and demand 100% of the user's attention. In another situation, the interruption occurs because the phone notifies learners about an upcoming appointment in 30 min. If learners are aware of this appointment, they might completely ignore this notification and can resume the primary task after just seconds. The next section will describe the characteristics of interruptions as well as their impact on task performance in greater detail.

4.2 Characteristics and Effects of Interruptions

Some interruptions might pass almost without notice while others significantly disrupt a primary task, i.e., they affect error rate and task completion time (Bailey and Konstan 2006; Katidioti et al. 2016; Kreifeldt and McCarthy 1981). Interruptions can also decrease the probability of information being stored in the LTM (Schacter 1999). Besides the nature of the interrupted activity, the disruptiveness of a task also depends on properties of the interruption. In regard to related work, we distinguish interruptions based on their source, duration, urgency, whether it was anticipated, and how the type of secondary task relates to the primary task in terms of modality and complexity (cf. Fig. 3). Below, we explain these characteristics in more detail and analyze the effects they have on interruptions.

Source Interruptions can have various sources, we differentiate *self-*, *device-internal*, and *external interruptions* (Katidioti et al. 2016; Miyata and Norman 1986). A self-interruption is internal to a person and thus self-initiated (Adler and Benbunan-Fich 2013). For instance, a person might decide to change to a different task because of

Source	Duration	Anticipation	Urgency	Modality	Complexity
self	short-term	planned	immediate	similar	similar
device-internal	long-term	unplanned	short delay	dissimilar	dissimilar
external			long delay		

Fig. 3 We characterize interruptions along the six dimensions of (1) source, (2) demand, (3) anticipation, (4) urgency, (5) modality, and (6) complexity

fatigue or boredom. In the literature, the term "internal interruption" is sometimes used interchangeably with "self-interruption," not to be confused with our definition of "device-internal." Device-internal interruptions refer to events on a user's device, such as incoming phone calls or app notifications. We consider this case separately from external—or environmental—interruptions, since there is a difference in the management capabilities: for example, device-internally, there is the option of tracking the user activity, and of scheduling or muting notifications accordingly. Examples of external interruptions are the arrival at a bus stop or a colleague addressing me at the office. The source of an interruption can have a significant effect on how much someone is disrupted: Katidioti et al. (2016) showed in their study that the overall completion time was lower for interruptions caused externally compared to self-interruptions. There was no difference in the duration of the resumption lag, the time needed to resume the primary task.

Duration Interruptions can vary in duration, we differentiate short- and long-term. Section 4.7 will outline the Memory-for-Goals theory, stating the need for priming. The theory encompasses the idea that over time, the presence of a goal fades in memory (Altmann and Trafton 2002). When a task is interrupted, its goal starts to decay. Shortly after an interruption, a goal will still be easy to recover. After a long interruption, the effort needed to restore the goal and resume the task becomes greater (Monk et al. 2008) and people need more time to recover from the interruption (Hodgetts and Jones 2006b). However, considering only the duration of an interruption is not sufficient to determine how disruptive it is (Gillie and Broadbent 1989).

Anticipation Anticipation indicates whether an interruption is planned and, therefore, is predictable or if it is unplanned. In general, unpredictable interruptions can induce stress and negatively affect the task performance (Cohen 1980). In the context of this article, anticipation will be most relevant from the stance of what is predictable from within an app. Hence, in the following, we will use the term *planned* or *anticipated* if the device or the app is potentially capable of sensing an upcoming interruption. Thus, a planned internal interruption could be an interruption caused by the system, for example, an integrated alarm clock.

Self-interruptions are generally not predictable by an application, and unless an attention-sensing mechanism is in place, they are also not identifiable. However, a self-interruption can result in a user action, e.g., the user leaving the app to browse social media or turning off the screen. Such actions or events can, of course, be tracked after they occur and indicate an internal interruption.

Finally, external interruptions can be classified into random and scheduled occurrences, depending on the application's scope of influence and its sensing capabilities.

Urgency Urgency is an important factor when deciding whether we need to deal with an interruption immediately, can delay it, or even ignore it (Ho et al. 2004). The immediacy of a secondary task has a great effect on how interrupting it will become. An unexpected phone call from one's boss, for example, can be more urgent than a social media notification—the receiver will more likely pick up the phone immediately instead of calling back later. Less critical events such as a social media notification or a system update notification do not require a quick response and might not even lead to an interruption. By estimating the interruptions' urgency, we can provide adequate task resumption support.

Modality The APA dictionary defines *modality* as "a medium of sensation, such as vision or hearing" (APA 2019f). The task modality, therefore, refers to the senses that a task activates. A reading task, for example, is visual, whereas listening to the radio is an auditory activity. Latorella (1998) suggested that the modality of the task and the interruption (either visual or auditory) has an impact on task performance later on. In particular, she reported that auditory interruptions are more disruptive than visual ones and hypothesized that the reason for this is the persistence of visually presented information. Furthermore, her results show the faster acknowledgment of interruptions in visual primary tasks compared to auditory tasks.

In addition to the modality, *similarity* of primary task and the secondary task has implications for how easy it is to switch to and execute the secondary task successfully (Anderson et al. 2018). In this context, two tasks are considered similar if they both use the same modality or cognitive resources. For instance, a reading task is similar to an interruption delivered as a text notification. Two homogeneous verbal modalities can generate conflicts in working memory resources. Also, interrupting a verbal auditory task with a verbal, graphical task can decrease performance (Stibler et al. 2005). Ledoux and Gordon (2006) also observed a similarity effect in reading. In their study, text comprehension rates were lower when an interrupting text was of the same style as the text in the primary task. However, they did not evaluate the thematic relationship between the two texts. Similarly, Czerwinski, Chrisman, and Schumacher (1991) showed in two experiments that operators were better at recalling the goals of a primary task when they were interrupted with a different task. A further study by Gillie and Broadbent (1989) indicates that users are slower when the primary task and an interrupting secondary task are similar. However, the results of two further experiments described in the same article remained ambiguous. There are also some mediating factors of this similarity effect. For example, when associative connections were established during the task, this can help overcome the detrimental effect of a similar interruption (Edwards and Gronlund 1998).

Complexity Furthermore, as with any task, an interruption may demand a high or low *cognitive load*, e.g., a complex arithmetic task versus a short audio signal that is only perceived peripherally. Complex interruption tasks increase the time it takes people to resume their primary task (Hodgetts and Jones 2006b; Monk et al. 2008). On the other hand, a study by Speier et al. (2003) suggests that—especially when the primary task is simple—interruptions can increase arousal and stress and thus, also improve the overall performance.

The demand in cognitive resources is also lower when it is easy to encode the problem state or when the secondary task does not require a problem state, that is, when no information needs to be kept in memory to perform the task (Borst et al. 2013). In this case, it is also easier to recover from an interruption. For instance, Kreifeldt and McCarthy (1981) found that interruptions caused users to perform slower on calculator tasks because they needed time to reorient after an interruption. Borst et al. (2013) suggest that the load on the problem state resource be reduced through external cues presented before an interruption.

Other Factors that Influence Disruption Besides general measures such as task completion time and error rate, interruptions can also influence the *affective state* of a user. Bailey and Konstan (2006) evaluated users' emotional reactions and found that interrupting tasks caused an increase of annoyance when presented during a primary task compared to when they were presented in between two tasks. Furthermore, the anxiety level in one session doubled when secondary tasks interrupted ongoing primary tasks.

If a primary task is interrupted by a secondary task, this can lead to an increased number of mistakes when resuming the primary task (Brumby et al. 2013). However, this does not always have to be the case, since the disruptive effect of interruptions depends on multiple factors. Nonetheless, regular disruptions can lead to users making about twice as many mistakes across tasks, both primary and secondary (Bailey and Konstan 2006). To counteract the adverse effect of an interruption, the interruption lag (the time between the occurrence of an interruption and the onset of the secondary task) can be manually increased to give time for reorganizing one's thoughts. A study conducted by Mark et al. (2008) evaluated *individual differences* of managing interruptions. They were able to show that personality traits such as openness to experience can predict the costs of an interruption that a person experiences.

Moreover, Rosen et al. (2011) specifically looked at interruptions during learning. They compared test results of students who received and wrote text messages during a lecture and found that the group that received a large number of texts scored significantly worse than those students who only received/sent a few messages or none at all. Delaying reading or sending messaging mitigated this effect, suggesting that students waited for more opportune moments to handle the interruptions.

A central component of the interruption process, which can mitigate the effects of interruptions, is the interruption lag. Therefore, the following section will consider this aspect more carefully.

4.3 Interruption Lag

The reaction to the interruption trigger can be immediate or delayed. Immediate interruptions occur, in particular, when a learner is not aware of the interruptions and cannot control them (external and internal, but unplanned). However, engaging with external and internal interruptions can sometimes be scheduled flexibly. For example, users can postpone notifications by setting their phone to flight mode, or by finding a quiet place for studying without distractions.

Being aware of an upcoming interruption furthermore provides the learner with the opportunity to prepare for it. In their study, Trafton et al. (2003) left it up to their participants how to use the time between the primary and secondary task. When given this opportunity, the majority of study participants used the time to prepare for the upcoming interruption. The effect of the preparation was an overall lower resumption time when proceeding with the primary task. Moreover, the interruption lag is suitable for goal encoding as we will describe in more detail in Sect. 4.7, (1) prospective ("What was I about to do?") and (2) retrospective ("What was I doing before?"), in accordance with the work of Trafton et al. (2003). In a study by Brumby et al. (2013), a ten-second interruption lag already reduced the number of mistakes made after resuming the primary task. In conclusion, if an interruption can be anticipated, delaying or managing an interruption can be a solution to mitigate the negative effects.

4.4 Interruption Management

Researchers have extensively evaluated the possibility of postponing or managing interruptions for mobile devices (Chen and Vertegaal 2004; Iqbal and Bailey 2005). One example is to delay notification delivery, such as in the bounded deferral strategy (Horvitz et al. 2005). Incoming notifications are not shown immediately but postponed until a more opportune moment occurs. Using these opportune moments to present potentially interrupting content, for example, delivering notifications in between two tasks, can have a less disruptive effect (Bailey and Konstan 2006). Nonetheless, it is not easy to find moments of inattentiveness during a day. A study by Dingler and Pielot (2015) evaluated users' attention on mobile devices during the day and concluded that intelligent notification delivery services would have to carefully make use of rare and quickly subsiding moments of inattentiveness. In this work, we will not go into more detail on the topic of interruption management, since many interruptions in our daily life cannot be postponed (like changing trains on a commute). However, we can support the user in resuming the task more easily after an interruption took place, in particular in mobile learning situations. For this purpose, we will now first present task resumption strategies that can already be found in existing apps and then continue with a more general, research- and theory-based analysis of resumption strategies.

Fig. 4 Duolingo uses daily
notifications to remind users
to continue with their
exercises

4.5   Task Resumption in Existing Applications

Developers and interaction designers started to integrate task resumption strategies
into apps long ago. The design may often have been the result of intuition rather than
a decision grounded on scientific reasons. Nevertheless, the strategies we identified
in common apps do tend to incorporate the principles we mentioned above. They
are frequently cue-based, use visual support, and aim to help users get right back to
where they left off. Some of them have already been integrated deeply into our daily
routines so that by now we are unlikely to even explicitly notice them as resumption
strategies.

Reminders Duolingo uses a reminder strategy: it issues notifications to remind users
that they should continue with their exercises (cf. Fig. 4). Similarly, the Facebook
messenger Android app[2] uses so-called "chat heads:" small bubbles that show conversation partners' profile pictures on top of any screen content and thus remind,
if not of conversation content, then at least of the people with whom the users had
ongoing conversations (cf. Fig. 5a).

Regaining Context Furthermore, we can find methods to regain context. Recent
app views on Android and iOS, but also Windows desktop systems, show the screen
content as recorded just before exiting an app (cf. Fig. 5b). Depending on the implementation of the app (and also depending on whether system memory or caches have
been cleared in the meantime), apps also return to this state when a user resumes it.
For instance, browsers typically return to or reload a previously viewed tab. Duolingo
returns the position in the skill list where you were before quitting. Netflix[3] includes
a "continue watching" option with a progress bar underneath previously viewed programs to indicate where a user stopped watching. Further apps provide a list of recent
documents (e.g., Dropbox[4] and Acrobat Reader.[5])

Repetition In addition to presenting the previous state, some programs also include
a recapitulation of past activities. Specifically, audio and video players such as the

---

[2]Facebook Messenger App: https://play.google.com/store/apps/details?id=com.facebook.orca&hl=en,
last access February 16, 2020.

[3]Netflix: https://www.netflix.com/, last access February 16, 2020.

[4]Dropbox: https://www.dropbox.com/, last access February 16, 2020.

[5]Acrobat Reader: https://get.adobe.com/de/reader/, last access February 16, 2020).

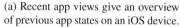

(a) Recent app views give an overview of previous app states on an iOS device.

(b) Chat Heads in the Facebook Messenger app on an Android device.

Fig. 5 Examples of existing task resumption cues on mobile devices

iOS app "Podcasts" provide the option of rewinding by a couple of seconds so that previous content can be repeated before playback continues.

However, there are also some apps where task resumption, especially after a long interruption, is explicitly not intended. News and map applications, for example, tend to update their interfaces to present new stories or to adjust to the user's current location. Another example is the Facebook app, which currently returns to the news feed upon opening. In these cases, the user experience design was not intended for task continuation, and showing up-to-date information is deemed more important than understanding what was done before.

4.6 Pedagogical Memory Re-Activation

In school teaching, a common approach to start a lesson is to re-activate the knowledge gathered in the previous learning session. Psychological and pedagogical research emphasizes the central role of including prior knowledge into the teaching process (Krause and Stark 2006). Re-activating prior knowledge in terms of human cognition and memory can be described as recalling information from the LTM and holding it in the STM or working memory for the integration of new infor-

mation (cf. Baddeley 2003). In pedagogy, the terms *open* and *specific* re-activation
are used to describe the integration of prior knowledge. Open re-activation describes
the general activation of a broad topic, e.g., by using visualizations like mind-maps
or brainstorming (Technische Universität Dresden 2014). In contrast, the specific
re-activation of knowledge targets a unique information chunk. Therefore, a common technique used for specific re-activation is asking questions (Krause and Stark
2006). Both strategies can be useful to re-activate a certain memory and can be more
appropriate depending on the use case (Technische Universität Dresden 2014).

4.7 Task Resumption Strategies

When users start to shift their attention back from an interruption task to the primary
task, they need time to reorient themselves. Task resumption strategies aim to keep
this time as short as possible and to help users regain full awareness of the task
context, to keep task completion time and error rate at a minimum. Oulasvirta and
Saariluoma (2006) stress the importance of interface organization for effortless task
resumption (Oulasvirta and Saariluoma 2006). For instance, they suggest to group
items based on higher level concepts that users can interpret. Thus, it is easier for
users to encode the workspace in memory, but most importantly also to recover this
knowledge when returning to the task: necessary controls are located more easily
and faster. A user interface which the user does not need to remember in detail also
decreases the amount of information to be stored in the problem state as defined
by Borst et al. (2013) (cf. Sect. 4.2). Cades et al. (2006) showed that dealing with
interruptions can be trained: participants' resumption lag decreased when they were
interrupted several times, even when they had had time to get used to the primary
task. Woelki et al. (2008) looked more closely at the effect of practice time. They
found that the disruptive effect of interruptions can be substantially decreased when
participants become used to executing a primary task. In Sect. 4.2, it was argued
that short interruptions are less disruptive. Therefore, reminding users to switch
back to their primary task is a valid strategy for minimizing the effort and cost of
task resumption: the decay of goals in memory will not have advanced far, and the
problem state will be easier to reconstruct.

Memory-for-Goals Theory In the Memory-for-Goals theory (Altmann and Trafton
2002), interruptions are viewed as a suspension of the primary task's goal. It states
that the user can only retrieve a suspended goal with the help of priming through
a memory cue. This cue needs to be presented a first time when the current goal is
suspended, for example, because of an interruption by a secondary task. The cues
are then presented a second time when the goal needs to be resumed to prime the
target (Altmann and Trafton 2002). Moreover, Trafton et al. (2003) differentiate
between two ways to encode a goal, namely (1) retrospective ("What was I doing
before?") and (2) prospective ("What was I about to do?"). Prospective memory cues
can be primed in the interruption lag, for example, by taking notes of what you were

about to do if the interruption had not happened and are recalled in the resumption lag. Retrospective cues can still be applied without the need of former priming.

Task Resumption Cues Finally, a major part of resumption strategies relies on cues that aid the user's memory or direct the focus of attention: they range from implicit stimuli such as barely noticeable highlights (e.g., McDaniel et al. 2004) to complex content cues that restore full task context (e.g., Sasangohar et al. 2014), and can be presented in very different ways and on various channels. For mobile scenarios, where interruptions are frequent, cannot necessarily be predicted, and vary significantly from one occurrence to the next, cues are particularly important. Well-designed cues provide a way of consistently dealing with the challenges that interruptions impose upon users. However, so far, there has been almost no research on mobile task resumption cues, in particular for mobile learning, a process that demands consistent attention and where disruptions greatly decrease performance. This lack of available solutions was the motivation for our systematic literature research and exploration of opportunities through a design space which we describe below.

5 Evaluation Part I: Literature Survey—Design Space on Task Resumption Cues

Priorly, we argued that cues have a high potential for supporting task resumption. In this section, we systematically analyze literature from various domains on task resumption cues. We extract and compare the characteristics of these cues based on five fundamental dimensions. We generate a design space, discussing all possible attributes in each dimension. We will point out well-evaluated cue designs, which have shown their potential for effective task resumption support. Additionally, we will highlight gaps in the design space that leave room for further evaluation and discuss our findings. We will begin this section by presenting the methodology of our literature review approach.

5.1 Methodology

We conducted a structured analysis of literature according to the methods used in Terzimehic et al. (2019), which we will outline in greater detail below. We started with a great number of publications representing a broad overview of the research field and narrowed down our selection in several steps. Once we had obtained a final set of papers, we evaluated the task settings and interruptions, extracted characteristics of task resumption cues, and analyzed findings of cue evaluations. This section outlines the procedure we applied for collecting the data points.

Selection of Literature Since Human–Computer Interaction (HCI) is an interdisciplinary domain and includes research from several domains (e.g., computer science, design, or psychology), the publications of HCI are distributed across several online publication libraries. We reviewed full, short, and work-in-progress papers from the ACM Digital Library[6] (ACM DL) as well as IEEE Xplore,[7] SpringerLink,[8] and ScienceDirect.[9] These libraries provide an extensive collection of documents from computer science, but also other disciplines such as medicine, where cues for task resumption are likely to be a relevant research topic. We searched these libraries for groups of terms related to (1) *interruption* and *resumption* and (2) *attention, task workflows*, and our focus areas *mobile* and *learning*. From the results of a first round of queries using those keywords, we extracted a third set of terms describing various types of *cues*. Our queries yielded 1207 (query 1) and 1936 (query 2) *unique* results in the ACM DL, 1187 and 548 in IEEE Xplore, a total of 9269 in SpringerLink, and 28052 in ScienceDirect across both queries.

The result items were pre-processed by removing duplicates and assigning ratings based on the occurrence of the search terms in title, abstract, or keywords. We weighted the query terms with scores in the range of 0–15 according to their significance. The total score of an article was defined as the sum of term scores. We added and reviewed abstracts to all articles with scores above 9 (ACM DL and IEEE Xplore) and 30 (SpringerLink and ScienceDirect), respectively,[10] and manually classified the best 217/380 results as *not relevant, marginally relevant*, and *relevant*. Since two raters performed the rating, we assessed our inter-rater reliability as proposed by Campbell et al. (2013) on approximately 10% of those 597 items and achieved a score of 91.6%. Disagreements on the rating were mostly due to uncertainties regarding the value of (sometimes vague) qualitative results and if to include those for further processing. We discussed these disagreements accordingly to reach a consensus. Thus, three results had to be eliminated upon closer inspection because they either did not include any evaluation of the strategies they proposed, because they only referred to cues defined elsewhere, or because the application area was too far from our context of use.

Finally, we performed additional forward and backward searches using Google Scholar and added a small number of publications referenced in our original selection. Thus, we obtained a final set of thirty articles describing 35 unique cues (two cues each are presented in Hudson et al. 2003; Lindblom and Gündert 2017; Parnin and DeLine 2010; Rule and Hollan 2016; Smith et al. 2009).

Creating the Design Space Once the selection was complete, we categorized the articles based on the task setting including the device setup, the interruption scenario, and the characteristics of the task resumption cues they present. For the classification

---

[6]ACM DL: https://dl.acm.org, last access February 16, 2020.

[7]IEEE Xplore: https://ieeexplore.ieee.org/Xplore/home.jsp, last access February 16, 2020.

[8]SpringerLink: https://link.springer.com, last access February 16, 2020.

[9]ScienceDirect: https://www.sciencedirect.com, last access February 16, 2020.

[10]Articles obtained from SpringerLink and ScienceDirect generally had higher scores because the result lists contained different types and amounts of meta-information.

of the cues, we used the dimensions modality, timing, and interactivity, and further attributes derived from the articles themselves. We defined these characteristics in an iterative process to generate a set of descriptive features that enabled us to clearly distinguish the unique cues from one another. Finally, we examined the evaluation state of the task resumption cues. We specifically noted reported findings regarding the effects of using cues on task performance and error rate. In complement to the categorization, we analyzed the articles' metadata, including the primary research area, year of publication, and journal or publication venue.

5.2 Results

In this section, we describe the literature sample by summarizing meta-information of the 30 publications and 35 cues in our literature set. We outline the setting (such as device and task) in which a task resumption cue is applied and the types of interruption. Moreover, we present our design space derived from the categorization of task resumption cues as well as details on the included resumption cues. Finally, we complement this with an overview of evaluation states and findings across all cues.

Meta-Analysis of Publications The year of publication ranges from 2002 until 2018 and comprises a set of eighteen full and short conference paper publications, nine journal articles, and four extended abstract submissions (cf. Fig. 6). The four articles that used mobile devices date from the years 2010, 2015, 2016, and 2018. These recent publications show that the state of technology is comparable to what is available nowadays. The leading publication venue is the *ACM Conference on Human Factors in Computing Systems (CHI)* with nine publications, followed by

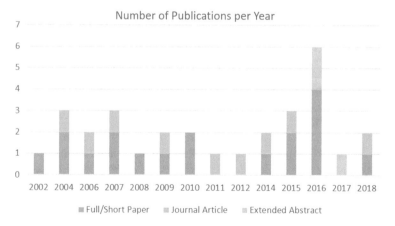

Fig. 6 The publications used to create the design space sorted by number per year and form of publication (i.e., full and short conference paper, journal article, or extended abstract submission)

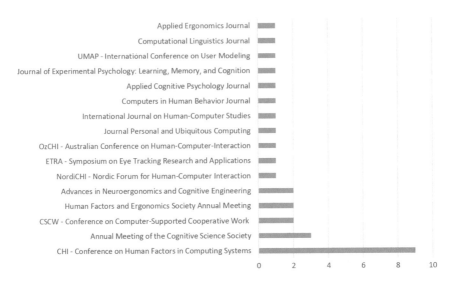

Fig. 7 Publication venues of all 30 articles presented in the design space and their occurrence frequency in our design space

the *Annual Meeting of the Cognitive Science Society* and the *ACM Conference on Computer-Supported Cooperative Work (CSCW)* with three publications each (see Fig. 7).

Task Setting and Interruptions Among the thirty different interruption situations described, 21 were using a desktop computer system, two scenarios used mobile devices (Mariakakis et al. 2015; Yeung and Li 2016), and two multi-device settings including both mobile and desktop devices (Cheng et al. 2018; Kern et al. 2010). Other studies evaluated contexts such as in-car interaction (Borojeni et al. 2016) or a smartboard scenario (Sasangohar et al. 2014).

Furthermore, the primary task setting varied strongly, including programming tasks (Parnin and DeLine 2010), reading tasks (Cane et al. 2012; Jo et al. 2015), resource allocation and military tasks (Clifford and Altmann 2004; Hodgetts et al. 2015; Scott et al. 2006), and various others. Secondary tasks used for the interruptions included phone calls (Borojeni et al. 2016; Yeung and Li 2016), noises (Mariakakis et al. 2015), video clips (Jo et al. 2015), search tasks (Scott et al. 2006), or similar. They varied in their degree of demand and urgency.

In fifteen cases, the interrupting event originated from the system or device itself and was hence classified as device-internal. In contrast, fourteen interruptions were caused by external triggers, and in only one case, the interruption was self-induced: when the participants did not understand a word in a reading task and had to look it up (Cheng et al. 2018). Across all scenarios, the majority of interruptions were unplanned, meaning that the participants did not expect the interruption to happen at a particular moment. In eight cases, however, the interruption was announced,

Table 1 Task setting: device, interruption source, and anticipation. There were no instances of unplanned self-interruptions

	External interruption		Device-Internal interruption		Self-Interruption
	Planned	Unplanned	Planned	Unplanned	Planned
Desktop PC	Jeuris and Bardramb (2016), Liu et al. (2014), Okundaye et al. (2017)	Franke et al. (2002), González and Mark (2004), Mancero et al. (2009), Rule and Hollan (2016), Scott et al. (2006), Toreini et al. (2018), Yang et al. (2011)	Clifford and Altmann (2004), González and Mark (2004), Liu et al. (2014), Parnin and DeLine (2010)	Altmann and Trafton (2004), Cane et al. (2012), Hodgetts and Jones (2006a), Hodgetts et al. (2015), Iqbal and Horvitz (2007a), Iqbal and Horvitz (2007b), Jo et al. (2015), McDaniel et al. (2004), Morris et al. (2008), Ratwani and Trafton (2008), Smith et al. (2009)	Liu et al. (2014)
Smartphone		Mariakakis et al. (2015)		Yeung and Li (2016)	
Other		González and Mark (2004), Lindblom and Gündert (2017), Sadeghian Borojeni et al. (2016), Sasangohar et al. (2014)	González and Mark (2004)		
Multi-Device Setting	Kern et al. (2010)			Cheng et al. (2018)	

leaving time for the participants to use the interruption lag for preparation and goal encoding. Table 1 gives an overview of task setting and interruptions.

Design Space: Facets and Dimensions In the following section, we will present the results of our literature review in the form of a design space shown in Table 2. This table includes all 30 publications, 35 cues, respectively, and classifies them along with a set of dimensions as explained below. On the horizontal axis, we aligned the different cue modalities presented in the literature along with their expressiveness in

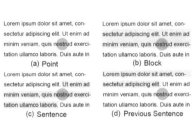

Lorem ipsum dolor sit amet, consectetur adipiscing elit. Ut enim ad minim veniam, quis nostrud exercitation ullamco laboris. Duis aute in
(a) Point

Lorem ipsum dolor sit amet, consectetur adipiscing elit. Ut enim ad minim veniam, quis nostrud exercitation ullamco laboris. Duis aute in
(b) Block

Lorem ipsum dolor sit amet, consectetur adipiscing elit. Ut enim ad minim veniam, quis nostrud exercitation ullamco laboris. Duis aute in
(c) Sentence

Lorem ipsum dolor sit amet, consectetur adipiscing elit. Ut enim ad minim veniam, quis nostrud exercitation ullamco laboris. Duis aute in
(d) Previous Sentence

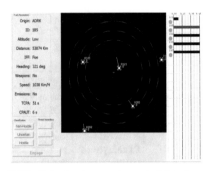

(a) Implicit visual cue: gaze markers by Jo et al. (2015)

(b) Explicit visual cue: primary task interface remains visible in Hodgetts et al. (2015)

Batch A			Batch B		
Task A1	Task A2	Task B1	Task B2	Task B3
☎: Greeting 1 †	☎: Greeting 2 † †	☎: Greeting 2 † †	☎: Greeting 2⁻ † †	☎: Greeting 2 † †
☺:"Yes"	☺: "I am (task label)."	☺: "I am (task label)."	☺:"I am (task label)"	☺:"I am (task label)"
☎: "What is it?"	☎: "Okay, here's your call."	☎: "Okay, here's your call."	☎: "Okay, you are (task label)."	☎: "Okay, you are (task label)."
☺:"I am (task label).	♦:(request)	♦:(request)	♦:(request)	♦:(request)
☎: "Okay, here's your call."	☺:(response)	☺:(response)	☺:(response)	☺:(response)
♦:(request)	♦:"Thanks. Bye."	♦:"Thanks. Bye."	♦:"Thanks. Bye."	♦:"Thanks. Bye."
☺:(response)		☎: "Continue your task."	☎: "Continue (task label)."	☎: "Continue your task."
♦:"Thanks. Bye."				

Legend: ☎::: synthesized voice; ☺: participant's human voice; ♦: experimenter's human voice
Greeting 1 †"Call from Peter, are you busy with something?"; Greeting 2 † †"Call from Peter, tell me if your busy with something, or say Nothing."

(c) Protocol of explicit auditory cue by Yeung & Li (2016)

(d) Tangible cue by Okundaye et al. (2016)

(e) User-defined workspace cues from Jeuris & Bardram (2016)

Fig. 8 Examples of different cues of different modalities and expressiveness

the case of visual and auditory cues. On the vertical axis, we ordered the publications along with four main categories: (1) the purpose of the cue, (2) the level of attention required for perceiving the cue, (3) the timing of cue presentation, and (4) the interactivity of the cue. The differentiation and all descriptions are based on the literature we derived within our analysis and are, therefore, not necessarily exhaustive in terms of what is imaginable with today's technology. In the following, we will describe each of these dimensions in greater detail and state examples for each characteristic included in the design space.

Modality and Expressiveness The modality refers to the signal through which a cue is represented and how it is perceived by the user. Modalities that we encountered

Table 2 Design space of task resumption cues

		Visual		Auditory		Haptic	Tangible	Other
		Implicit	Explicit	Implicit	Explicit			
Purpose	Retrospective	Cane et al. (2012), Clifford and Altmann (2004), Jo et al. (2015), Lindblom and Gündert (2016), Mancero et al. (2009), Mariakakis et al. (2015), Scott et al. (2006), Toreini et al. (2018)	Hodgetts et al. (2015), Lindblom and Gündert (2016), Parnin and DeLine (2010), Sasangohar et al. (2014)		Yang et al. (2011), Yeung and Li (2016)		Okundaye et al. (2017)	
	Reminder specific	Iqbal and Horvitz (2007a, b), Lindblom and Gündert (2016), Mancero et al. (2009), Sadeghian Borojeni et al. (2016)	Lindblom and Gündert (2016)					González and Mark (2004), Jeuris and Bardramb (2016), Rule and Hollan (2016)
	Reminder unclear	Liu et al. (2014), McDaniel et al. (2004)						
	Prospective	Clifford and Altmann (2004), Hodgetts and Jones (2006a)	Altmann and Trafton (2004), Lindblom and Gündert (2016)					González and Mark (2004)
	Spatial	Cane et al. (2012), Cheng et al. (2018), Jo et al. (2015), Kern et al. (2010), Mariakakis et al. (2015), Ratwani and Trafton (2008)						
	Other	Morris et al. (2008)	Parnin and DeLine (2010)	Smith et al. (2009)	Franke et al. (2002)	Smith et al. (2009)		Rule and Hollan (2016)
Attention	Full user attention	Cane et al. (2012), Clifford and Altmann (2004), Iqbal and Horvitz (2007b), Jo et al. (2015), Kern et al. (2010), Mancero et al. (2009), Mariakakis et al. (2015), Morris et al. (2008), Scott et al. (2006), Toreini et al. (2018)	Altmann and Trafton (2004), Parnin and DeLine (2010), Sasangohar et al. (2014)		Franke et al. (2002), Yang et al. (2011), Yeung and Li (2016)		Okundaye et al. (2017)	González and Mark (2004), Jeuris and Bardramb (2016)
	Peripheral	Cheng et al. (2018), Hodgetts and Jones (2006a), Iqbal and Horvitz (2007a), Lindblom and Gündert (2016), Liu et al. (2014), McDaniel et al. (2004), Ratwani and Trafton (2008), Sadeghian Borojeni et al. (2016)	Hodgetts et al. (2015), Lindblom and Gündert (2016)	Smith et al. (2009)		Smith et al. (2009)		Rule and Hollan (2016)

(continued)

Table 2 (continued)

		Visual		Auditory		Haptic	Tangible	Other
		Implicit	Explicit	Implicit	Explicit			
Timing	Before interruption	Clifford and Altmann (2004), Hodgetts and Jones (2006a), Lindblom and Gündert (2016), Morris et al. (2008), Sadeghian Borojeni et al. (2016)	Altmann and Trafton (2004), Hodgetts et al. (2015), Lindblom and Gündert (2016), Parmin and DeLine (2010)	Smith et al. (2009)	Yeung and Li (2016)	Smith et al. (2009)		González and Mark (2004)
	During interruption	Iqbal and Horvitz (2007a), Liu et al. (2014), Ratwani and Trafton (2008)						Jeuris and Bardramb (2016)
	After interruption	Cane et al. (2012), Cheng et al. (2018), Iqbal and Horvitz (2007b), Jo et al. (2015), Kern et al. (2010), Lindblom and Gündert (2016), Mancero et al. (2009), Mariakakis et al. (2015), McDaniel et al. (2004), Morris et al. (2008), Sadeghian Borojeni et al. (2016), Scott et al. (2006), Toreini et al. (2018)	Altmann and Trafton (2004), Hodgetts et al. (2015), Lindblom and Gündert (2016), Parmin and DeLine (2010), Sasangohar et al. (2014)	Smith et al. (2009)	Franke et al. (2002), Yang et al. (2011), Yeung and Li (2016)	Smith et al. (2009)	Okundaye et al. (2017)	González and Mark (2004), Jeuris and Bardramb (2016), Rule and Hollan (2016)
Interactivity	No user interaction	Cane et al. (2012), Cheng et al. (2018), Hodgetts and Jones (2006a), Iqbal and Horvitz (2007a), Jo et al. (2015), Kern et al. (2010), Liu et al. (2014), Mariakakis et al. (2015), McDaniel et al. (2004), Ratwani and Trafton (2008), Sadeghian Borojeni et al. (2016), Toreini et al. (2018)	Altmann and Trafton (2004), Parmin and DeLine (2010)					Rule and Hollan (2016)
	Simple user interaction	Iqbal and Horvitz (2007b), Lindblom and Gündert (2016), Mancero et al. (2009), Scott et al. (2006)	Hodgetts et al. (2015), Lindblom and Gündert (2016)	Smith et al. (2009)	Franke et al. (2002), Yang et al. (2011), Yeung and Li (2016)	Smith et al. (2009)		González and Mark (2004), Jeuris and Bardramb (2016)
	Complex user interaction	Clifford and Altmann (2004), Morris et al. (2008)	Sasangohar et al. (2014)				Okundaye et al. (2017)	

in our design space include visual (graphical), auditory, haptic or tactile, or tangible signals. In some scenarios, several modalities are combined as multi-modal cues. It is imaginable to design cues to be perceived by every human sense, including olfactory or thermal cues (i.e., creating a warm or cold sensation and associate a memory with it).

Expressiveness, on the other hand, depends on the amount of information a cue can convey. For example, textual cues can transfer a large amount of information on a small screen, whereas tactile cues (such as a vibration) are limited in their expressiveness. Keeping the expressiveness in mind is particularly important when generating cues that match the capabilities of mobile devices. In this work, we differentiate between *explicit* and *implicit* cue designs. *Explicit* cues present task- or content-related information, such as visual or spoken text. *Implicit* cues do not contain content information. They guide the user's attention through the use of highlights such as a sound or the cursor position. They support memory without explicitly presenting task-related information. Examples of cues with different modalities and expressiveness are shown in Fig. 8.

Visual cues can include any form of graphical display. They can consist of a small object, logo, icon, picture, or text and are intended to remind a user of a certain task or idea. In total, our literature review resulted in 24 visual cues. While text is very explicit and can convey a large amount of information, graphical visualizations such as icons or highlights are very implicit. These can take the form of colored frames around a window (Toreini et al. 2018), or an underlined sentence (Mariakakis et al. 2015). Even simpler, gaze points can visualize the last position of gaze fixation before an interruption occurred (Cheng et al. 2018). *Textual Cues*, or written cues, are a particular form of visual cues, which can include an almost unlimited amount of information. They can be divided into system- and user-generated cues. For example, a system can generate a summary of a previously read passage of a text before an interruption occurred. In contrast, the users can also generate these cues themselves in the form of electronic or handwritten notes (González and Mark 2004). They write these notes during the interruption lag and thus capture their thoughts about what they were doing before or what they were about to do. Note-taking is highly personal and can vary immensely in the level of detail and explicitness.

The same differentiation of explicitness can be applied to *auditory cues*. On the one hand, implicit auditory cues such as simple sounds can support task resumption (Smith et al. 2009), whereas, on the other hand, explicit *verbal cues* have a higher expressiveness and can transfer more information. Examples are verbal labels, e.g.,words characterizing the current task (Yeung and Li 2016), or complete sentences in discourse systems (Franke et al. 2002). Similarly to textual cues, verbal cues can be either self-recorded by the user or system-generated. Within our evaluation, four publications explore the application of auditory cues.

While *haptic* or *tactile cues* may lack the expressiveness of visual cues, they can still function as viable mechanisms to direct the focus of attention (Hopp et al. 2005). Smith et al. used directional and non-directional vibration cues to guide attention toward tasks (Smith et al. 2009). *Tangible cues* also rely on the sense of touch, but use tangible objects. In one example, Okundaye et al. (2017) proposed to use tangible RFID tag cards to store the current task content to support the switching between tasks (Okundaye et al. 2017). They state that the use of different artifacts is imaginable as well, either physical or digital. Both tangible and tactile cues are mentioned in one publication of our set each, and in both cases, the cues transmit implicit information on the task.

In four cases, we were not able to categorize the cue into one of the modalities, due to the implementation of multiple facets of one task resumption cue. For example, Rule and Hollan (2016) describe multiple cues, such as the emptiness of a specific input field, a pink marking, or a cursor location, all used in combination.

Both modality and expressiveness of a task resumption cue heavily depend on the nature of the interruption and the task which is to be resumed. For instance, visual or graphical cues are likely to be a suitable option when the primary task was a reading task (Jo et al. 2015). One reason for this is the importance of spatial orientation in reading, i.e., remembering the line and position of the last word read. Not all cue modalities are feasible in every situation. For example, in a noisy and busy environment, it might not be possible for the user to perceive a simple auditory cue. In contrast, a visually highly demanding task could benefit from a non-visual cue.

Purpose We define the purpose of a cue as the type of information that it is intended to convey to the user. Is it supposed to give a retrospective view on what happened before an interruption occurred? Should it bring the steps that are next to be performed back to mind, i.e., give a prospective view? Or should it remind users of the current task and its state, concretely or abstractly?

The task resumption cues in our literature set were designed for a variety of purposes, which we clustered into six categories. The first two align with the memory-for-goal theory (see Sect. 4.7), namely (1) *retrospective rehearsal* (indicating the last actions of a user) and (2) *prospective introspection* (showing the user's next steps). In addition, we derived three more categories based on the purposes mentioned in the specific publications: (3) *specific reminder* (a cue reminds the user of resuming a specific task or idea, e.g., Iqbal and Horvitz 2007a; Sadeghian Borojeni et al. 2014), (4) *open reminder* (reminds the user to resume something, e.g., Liu et al. 2017; McDaniel et al. 2004), (5) spatial awareness (guiding the visual focus on a screen, e.g., Cane et al. 2012; Cheng et al. 2018; Jo et al. 2015). We included the category *other* for all publications that specified a purpose of the task resumption cue that did not fit a category for various reasons or for cases where the purpose was left unspecified. Since a cue can have more than one purpose, we took the liberty of assigning more than one category to a single cue, which happened in seven cases. However, this differentiation, again, is based on the authors' descriptions and subjective categorizations. Therefore, it is possible to sort some of the cues into different or additional categories. Which purpose is appropriate in which context largely depends on the nature of a task: for example, in an assembly task, it is less important which steps were already executed, and in what order, but it is more essential to know which step to do next. In a learning setting, cues of many purposes could apply such as summarizing what content was presented before, making a retrospective cue potentially beneficial. Furthermore, reminders could encourage the repetition of content in short time intervals.

Attention Cues also differ in the level of attention they demand from a user. Some are perceived peripherally only, for example, when they are displayed on a secondary screen or are triggered on a device that is independent of the primary task. But the cue can also require full user attention, especially when the primary task and cue share the same presentation device or when user interaction is necessary.

In our literature set, 21 task resumption cues demand full user attention. Full attention means that a user has to proactively recognize, react to, or interact with the task resumption cue. For example, in the work of Kern et al. (2010), the system presents the users with a spotlight indicating their last point of view before switching between tasks. To resume the primary task, the users actively searched for the spotlight. In another example, the users have to actively recognize and trigger a playback of their last actions (Iqbal and Horvitz 2007b). Fourteen cues, however, occur in the periphery of the user's attention and might or might not be noticed. For example, in the work of Hodgetts and Jones (2006a), the interface of the primary task stays visible during the interaction with the secondary task. Furthermore, in the work of McDaniel et al. (2004), a small blue dot in the corner of the window reminds the user to resume the primary task. In this particular case, it is up to the user to notice the cue and react to it.

Timing The timing describes the moment of cue presentation during the interruption process (cf. Fig. 2 for the visualization of an interruption timeline). In the *pre-interruption* phase, the user is in the transition between the primary task and the secondary task, i.e., in the interruption lag. If the interruption is planned or announced, the interruption lag enables the user to prepare for the upcoming secondary task (Altmann and Trafton 2002). The *mid-interruption* phase describes the time during the secondary task when the user is not focusing on the primary task anymore, and all cognitive resources are on the secondary task. The *post-interruption* phase is the time when the user returns to the primary task after an interruption. During the resumption lag, the time the user needs for regaining context and continuing with the original task. A common method is to present cohesive cues during both interruption and resumption lag. Moreover, it is possible to combine more than one type of cue and present those at different points of time during the interruption process.

In the literature of this review, there were instances of all three possible presentation times. Hodgetts and Jones (2006a), for example, examined the use of cues to encode the state of a Tower of London problem before an interruption. In four publications, the cue was presented mid-interruption. In one example, the cue was a progress bar indicating the time spent on the secondary task and thus, motivating the user to resume the primary task (Liu et al. 2014). Another cue, which was presented mid-interruption, was to keep the window of the primary task visible during the secondary task (Iqbal and Horvitz 2007a; Ratwani et al. 2007). The window was supposed to be a reminder to resume the suspended task as quickly as possible. A major part of the resumption cues occurred after an interruption. Cues presented during the resumption lag are meant to facilitate context recovery (Rule and Hollan

2016) or restore visual focus (Mariakakis et al. 2015; Toreini et al. 2018). In other publications, cues are already primed during the interruption lag (pre-interruption) and then presented again in the resumption lag (post-interruption). For example, a content timeline of past actions shown before and after the interruption aims to support both retrospective and prospective goal encoding (Parnin and DeLine 2010), helping the users to think of their previous and next steps and remember those even after an interruption.

Interactivity Cues require different degrees of user interaction. Peripheral cues typically work without user interaction, as it cannot be ascertained whether they have even been noticed. Attention-demanding cues can just as well work on a presentation-only basis without interaction, but many also require simple or complex interaction. For example, when navigating through an activity log as in Scott et al. (2006), a user performs simple actions in the user interface. Interactivity is not easy to measure—also because the actual amount of interaction changes from one use case to the next—below we will, therefore, only differentiate the levels *no interaction*, *simple interaction*, and *complex interaction* for a typical scenario.

Cues that were only meant to be perceived and require no interaction were gaze markers (Kern et al. 2010), peripheral light cues (Borojeni et al. 2016), or the still visible primary task window during an interruption (Altmann and Trafton 2004; Hodgetts and Jones 2006a; Iqbal and Horvitz 2007a). Other cues required the user to perform a simple interaction, such as placing a tag (Mancero et al. 2009), or calling out audio labels (Yeung and Li 2016). In contrast to the number of cues which require simple or no interaction, the resumption cues rarely require more complex interactions. Only in three cases, the user is required to interact with the system in a more complex way: by taking mental or written notes (Clifford and Altmann 2004), interacting with an event timeline to find out more about past events (Sasangohar et al. 2014), and by choosing and exchanging RFID tag cards to regain task context (Okundaye et al. 2017). In general, the complexity of the required cue interaction increases with the complexity of the given tasks. If the user had to deal with a large amount of information at once, i.e., hold many information chunks in the working memory, the cue, as well as the possible interactions, would get more complex.

However, we subjectively assigned the differentiation between simple and complex user interaction in regard to the complexity of interaction shown in related work. Thus, it remains unclear how effortful users perceive the interaction with a specific cue.

Evaluations and Findings All thirty publications included in this design space were published under peer revision, either in conference proceedings or in a journal. They all presented exciting findings on the design of task resumption cues but the state of the evaluation and, therefore, the generalizability of these findings, varied greatly. Only sixteen of the thirty publications contain experimental results with $N > 15$. Three further papers present preliminary results with small sample sizes ($N \leq 15$). Seven publications report qualitative data based on interviews and questionnaires, while two papers do not evaluate the task resumption cue at all. Nonetheless, we

Table 3 Evaluation states and result tendencies of the publications references in the design space

	Negative results	Ambivalent results	Slightly positive results	Positive results
Quantitative experiments with $N > 15$	Hodgetts et al. (2015)		Jeuris and Bardramb (2016), Kern et al. (2010), Mariakakis et al. (2015)	Altmann and Trafton (2004), Cane et al. (2012), Clifford and Altmann (2004), Hodgetts and Jones (2006a), Iqbal and Horvitz (2007a), Iqbal and Horvitz (2007b), Liu et al. (2014), McDaniel et al. (2004), Ratwani and Trafton (2008), Borojeni et al. (2016), Sasangohar et al. (2014), Smith et al. (2009)
Quantitative experiments with $N \leq 15$ or extensive qualitative studies		Parnin and DeLine (2010)	Cheng et al. (2018), Jo et al. (2015), Morris et al. (2008), Okundaye et al. (2017), Parnin and DeLine (2010)	Scott et al. (2006)
Anecdotal evaluation or no evaluation		Franke et al. (2002), González and Mark (2004), Rule and Hollan (2016), Yang et al. (2011), Yeung and Li (2016)	Lindblom and Gündert (2017), Mancero et al. (2009), Toreini et al. (2018)	

included these publications since they reported interesting ideas based on literature reviews (for an overview of the evaluation states, see Table 3).

Among the articles that included an empirical study, the most commonly reported benefit of task resumption cues was that resumption times (and thus also task completion times) were shorter than without cues (Borojeni et al. 2016; Clifford and Altmann 2004; Hodgetts and Jones 2006a; Iqbal and Horvitz 2007a, b; Jeuris and Bardram 2016; Kern et al. 2010; Liu et al. 2014; Mariakakis et al. 2015; Ratwani et al. 2007; Sasangohar et al. 2014; Smith et al. 2009). Pilot studies in Jo et al. (2015) and Toreini et al. (2018) also showed that the resumption lag decreased. Similarly, Scott et al. (2006) found that in a complex scenario, the time to reach a decision was shorter with an assistive interface. In Parnin and DeLine's (2010) study, resumption lag was similar in all conditions. However, even in the condition where the interface provided no support, participants were allowed to take notes, and these probably served as an alternative cue. In the experiments described in various studies (cf. Borojeni et al. 2016; McDaniel et al. 2004; Sasangohar et al. 2014; Smith et al. 2009), cues were also found to reduce the error rate in the experiment tasks. For instance, Sasangohar et al. (2014) reported a "significant increase in the mission commander's decision accuracy for both simple and complex decisions". The positive effect could not be replicated in the evaluation of the cues designed by Hodgetts et al. (2015): the duration of the decision cycles was slower and the "defensive effectiveness" was lower in the cue conditions. However, the cues they used (two types of decision-support systems) were designed in a way that made the interface more complex and even when there was no interruption, performance was worse than in the no-support condition.

The qualitative feedback collected through questionnaires or interviews confirm benefits and reveal some additional aspects. For example, radio dispatchers reported that tagging incidents facilitated their search (Mancero et al. 2009) and echoing task labels after phone calls were considered a helpful reminder (Yeung and Li 2016). Using the interruption lag for labeling tasks before a phone call made participants feel prepared (Sadeghian Borojeni et al. 2014). Similarly, Morris et al.'s SearchBar (2008) eased retrieval of information in a second session, thus reducing the amount of redundant work. The RFID cards that Okundaye et al. (2017) used to recover work context were praised for their immediacy when re-accessing information.

The articles also mention a number of issues and challenges that need to be kept in mind when designing task resumption cues. For explicit cues, the choice of content is crucial. Parnin and DeLine (2010), for example, selected method names to visualize programmers' tasks, but the programmers did not consider this an effective means for triggering their memory. Especially when goals are implicit, suitable manifestations are difficult to design (Rule and Hollan 2016). In some cases, participants used their own strategies that possibly interfere with the system design: Mariakakis et al. (2015) noted that instead of using their gaze highlight, a participant marked her reading position through scrolling to a fixed positions and others memorized a key phrase as a "mental bookmark" (Mariakakis et al. 2015). Personal strategies were also observed by Jeuris and Bardram (2016): experts carefully adapted their work environment to their needs and introduced additional cues that supported task switching. González and Mark (2004) mentioned that on the other hand, participants did not always use tools available to them. They hypothesized that in their case, this was due to a lack of visibility of the tool and, therefore, stressed that artifacts need to be "visible and available." Furthermore, the interface design should not induce stress so that negative effects of long-term use are avoided (Liu et al. 2014). A noteworthy observation regarding the intensity of cues was that in Yang et al. (2011), participants stated that in a more disruptive context, stronger cues were used.

5.3   Discussion

Based on our extensive literature survey, we consider our design space a valuable first step toward an inclusive but comprehensible overview of task resumption cues. However, we are aware that the list of publications and, therefore, the design space does not present an exhaustive summary of the field. Thus, our categorization leaves potential for extension.

Selection of Publications Due to the variety of journals and conferences, we consider our choice of publications a valuable sample across several disciplines such as Human–Computer Interaction, Psychology, and Cognitive Science. Difficulties arose because there was not a fixed set of keywords that the authors used to categorize their work. To still cover a wide range of potentially relevant publications, we extended our list of query terms to include possible variations and followed up on promising references. However, it is possible that further work on task resumption cues is missing from our analysis due to a different terminology.

Research Gaps The distribution of publications in our design space shows that the predominant modality for resumption cues so far is visual: 24 out of the 30 articles presented only visual cues (cf. Table 2). The almost exclusive application of visual cues also means that there is potential for exploring other modalities. For instance, in mobile settings, tactile cues such as vibration patterns, could be developed further. They are easily noticeable by users themselves but provide privacy in the presence of bystanders and after some training, even patterns that encode an entire alphabet can be learned (Luzhnica et al. 2016). So far, little research has been done on the applications of tactile cues, especially in mobile scenarios. In the work of Smith et al. (2009), the authors emphasize the tactile cues potential for use in visually busy environments in which visual or auditory cues might be inappropriate, especially for short-term interruptions.

Moreover, both implicit and explicit cues were shown to have positive effects. Ideally, a cue would demand as little attention from a user as necessary to successfully resume a primary task, so the resumption lag is kept short and it is not necessary to further increase the load on the working memory. However, it remains an open question of how explicit a cue needs to be effective.

The feasibility of audio cues is strongly depending on the use case. The ability to perceive audio signals in a busy environment can only be ensured with the use of headphones. It is debatable if users consider audio cues an adequate alternative to visual cues. In the design space publications, audio cues are not exhaustively evaluated, e.g., in terms of different purposes or different levels of interactivity.

Promising Cue Designs Overall, clusters in the design space matrix and the evaluation results suggest that applying implicit as well as explicit visual cues can positively influence retrospective rehearsal. This goes in line with the findings of other domains such as supporting life-logging by showing contents of a prior meeting as described in Sect. 3.3. Respectively, presenting a summary of a certain subset of contents learned before an interruption could, therefore, lead to higher recall rates of all contents from this lesson. Additionally, the presentation of cues before and after the interruption has been extensively researched across several modalities with emphasis on visual presentation. If the cue is perceived implicitly, then the presentation of it can be either before *or* after the interruption. When designing explicit cues, showing them before *and* after the interruption has shown to be successful (Lindblom and Gündert 2017; Parnin and DeLine 2010). This technique supports the encoding of information during the interruption lag (cf. Sect. 4.3), which increases a memory's chance of being recalled regardless of the interruption's intensity or complexity (Oulasvirta 2005). However, presenting a stimulus before an interruption requires the recognition of upcoming interruptions and, therefore, has its limitations in the use case of mobile learning. Although the quality and robustness of attention sensing have improved over the years, the sensing mechanisms only cover a small niche of potential interruptions during mobile learning. And even if today's technology can sense boredom or disengagement (D'Mello et al. 2012), mind-wandering (Hutt et al. 2016), or transition phases between tasks (Okoshi et al. 2014), their ability to anticipate those interruptions in advance remains limited.

Regarding the task and device setting, we found that although interruptions are particularly frequent in mobile use cases, there has been almost no research in mobile interruption support. Our literature research revealed only four publications that considered interruptions on mobile devices (Cheng et al. 2018; Kern et al. 2010; Mariakakis et al. 2015; Yeung and Li 2016). Some ideas that were developed for desktop PCs can probably be translated to mobile scenarios (see Design Guideline 1 in Sect. 7). However, the affordance of devices and applications used on the move differs from static settings and, therefore, additional research is necessary. Besides, in public spaces, different types of interruptions are likely to occur. At the same time, there is also potential for completely different ideas to be explored.

In general, the empirical studies showed task resumption cues can decrease task completion time and increase task performance after an interruption. However, in many other cases, the described cues are concepts which are evaluated in preliminary studies with a small number of participants only. The effect of the task resumption cue was also not statistically proven in every case.

There is still room for improvement concerning the comparability of cues. In particular, no study empirically assessed more than two cues in the same task setting; instead, the settings varied significantly between studies. This variance was partly due to the cues serving very different purposes, but even when tasks were similar, the duration and type of interruption tasks differed. For future studies, it would be useful to revisit past publications before deciding on an interruption setting, and— if possible—include one that has previously been used in an evaluation to ensure comparability.

In conclusion, the literature survey performed in this section resulted in a variety of task resumption cue designs. The clustering of publications into a design space along with the cues' modality, purpose, attention, timing, and interactivity resulted in an interesting overview of the state of the art in this research domain. The design space highlighted frequently evaluated cue designs and yielded several gaps in research. Those hold potential for new designs of task resumption cues, but also call for further investigation. As described in the evaluation paragraph of this section, the publications cover a wide array of tasks and use cases, limiting the applicability of these task resumption cue ideas. To design cues that specifically target interruptions in mobile learning scenarios, the second part of this evaluation will present a more user-centered approach.

6 Evaluation Part II: Focus Group: Designing Task Resumption Cues for Mobile Learning

In the previous Sect. 5, we surveyed existing literature and related work regarding the design of task resumption cues to support recovery from interruptions in various domains and tasks. However, the applicability of those designs for a mobile learning scenario is limited. To supplement the literature-based findings and to explore the characteristics of interruptions in mobile learning scenarios, this section presents a supplementary creative design process of two focus groups of HCI experts and mobile learning app users. The following main research questions guide the focus groups: (1) What are the reasons for interruptions in mobile learning scenarios? (2) How can we design task resumption support for common interruptions? (3) What are out-of-the-box / creative ideas?

   We conducted the two focus groups with human–computer interaction and media informatics experts (having either a masters or doctorate degree in the respective field) and users to come up with novel and previously unexplored ideas for task resumption support. By asking experts' opinion, we aimed to get broad ideas, which would be discussed in the light of what could be realistically implementable. We did not intend to come up with entirely designed products, but with exciting ideas and design artifacts. This open process gives room for the imperfect, yet visionary ideas and creative thought processes. Besides, we asked users without a computer science or design background to come up with ideas which target their everyday problems with interruptions during learning.

6.1 Participants

For our focus group, we recruited four HCI and media informatics experts (3 female) with a mean age of $M = 29.4\,(SD = 1.0)$. All experts have formerly or are currently using learning applications on their smartphones. Moreover, we performed the same focus group procedure with three mobile learning app users with little to no background knowledge in human–computer interaction (2 female, 1 male) with a mean age of $M = 25.7\,(SD = 2.1)$. All users held at least a high school degree and have commonly used learning apps—such as *Duolingo, Phase 6,*[11] or *Mondly*[12]—on their mobile devices in the past or present.

6.2 Procedure

To foster creativity in the generation of new ideas, we aligned our procedure with earlier work of Koelle, Wolf, and Boll (2018), who applied the *Lotus flower method* (Michalko 2014, cited in Koelle et al. 2018) to derive design ideas for privacy notices for body-worn cameras. The Lotus Flower or Lotus Blossom Method (Tatsuno 1990, cited in Koelle et al. 2018) is a three-step design ideation procedure for group brainstorming sessions. With each step, the most interesting ideas are selected and will be the center of the next step to be developed further. This technique is considered structured, easy to use and explain, and useful to promote creative thinking (Higgins 1994, 1996; Smith 1998, cited in Koelle et al. 2018). The main goal of this technique is to generate a great variety of ideas and take a step back from obvious design solutions.

For the expert group, we formed two subgroups of two people each to facilitate a broader range of ideas in the brainstorming process. We voice recorded the focus group sessions and archived the sketches from the design phase. We transcribed the interviews and summarized the ratings of the sketches in an evaluation sheet.

The three-step process (cf. Fig. 9) was built bottom-up, starting with asking the participants to answer the following question: *What are causes of interruptions during mobile learning in everyday scenarios?* Each item is written on a sticky note, and similar reasons are grouped. When finished, the participants agreed on three causes of interruptions they felt are most relevant during mobile learning. Those causes became the center of the new brainstorming node in step 2 asking *How could we support the user to resume a learning task when being interrupted?* Again, the participants collected a set of task resumption strategies and picked the three most interesting and potentially helpful solutions to center step 3, the design phase. We asked the questions *How could the resumption support be designed/implemented in a learning application?* and let all participants draw sketches of as many ideas as they could come up with. Afterward, we evaluated the top three ideas of each group by the question *How well do you think does this idea support learners in resuming tasks after being interrupted?* on a 7-point Likert-Scale and an additional in-depth interview asking for details, advantages, and limitations of the chosen approaches. Next, we report our findings. For individual statements, we number our participants consecutively, labeling with an "E" for Expert and a "U" for User.

---

[11]Phase 6 App: https://itunes.apple.com/de/app/vokabeltrainer-phase6-classic/id441493173?mt=8, last access February 16, 2020.

[12]Mondly App: https://itunes.apple.com/de/app/mondly-33-sprachen-lernen/id987873536?mt=8, last access February 16, 2020.

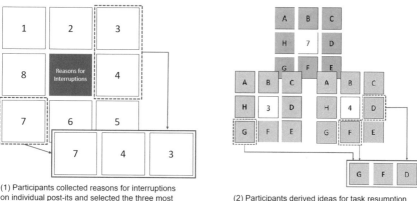

(1) Participants collected reasons for interruptions on individual post-its and selected the three most relevant reasons to become the node of the next design phase.

(2) Participants derived ideas for task resumption support for each of the three reasons selected in (1).

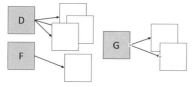

(3) For each idea from (2), the participants generated a set of design sketches to visualize their concept.

Fig. 9 The three steps of the design process applied in both focus groups (cf. Koelle et al. 2018)

6.3 Causes of Interruptions During Mobile Learning in Everyday Scenarios

This section presents the causes of interruptions the participants named during the focus groups. Since the usage situations of MLAs do not necessarily coincide with those of mobile devices in general, the interruptions potentially deviate, too. So especially for the user focus group, we asked the participants to imagine themselves during a learning activity and describe interruptions that are specific in this usage situation. By doing so, we hope to generate a list of interruptions that are specific to our use case of mobile learning. To characterize the different interruptions, we clustered them according to the schema presented in Sect. 4.2 (aligned with work of Katidioti et al. 2016; Miyata and Norman 1986) into self-interruptions, device-internal interruptions, and external interruptions. Furthermore, Table 4 presents an overview of all interruptions mentioned during both focus groups, which we aligned with our characterization of interruptions (cf. Sect. 4.2) based on detailed descriptions of the focus group participants.

Self-Interruptions The users of learning applications collected a set of 17 reasons for interruptions based on experience. Four of them concerned internal states, such as feeling tired (U2), hungry (U2+U3), cold (U2), or getting a headache (U2). Most

Table 4 Clustering of all interruption causes described by the focus group participants, aligned with the categories of interruptions as defined in Sect. 4.2. The column *Device-Internal—Planned* yielded no results and was thus removed

		Device-Internal	External		Self-Interruption	
		Unplanned	Planned	Unplanned	Planned	Unplanned
Short duration	Low demand	Sun shines on screen (U2)		Loud neighbor (U2)/ uneasy metro ride (U2, U3)		Sudden thoughts (E4)
	Medium/high demand	Instant message notifications (U3, E3, E4); missing network coverage (E3)	Listening to TV in the background (U1)	Approached by other person in room (U2); social interactions (E3, E4)	Hungry (U2, U3)	Hungry (U2, U3); mind-wandering (E4); cravings and needs (E4)
Long duration	Low demand	Advertisement video (U1)				cold (U2)
	Medium/high demand	Incoming phone calls (U3, E3, E4); updates and device failures (E1); low battery level (U1)	switching trains (U1); being called into doctors office (U1); daily chores (E3, E4); getting off train on a commute (E1, E2)	doorbell rings (U2, U3); walking the dog (U1, U3); social interactions (E3, E4)	end of learning time slot (E2, E4)	tired (U2); headache (U2)

of these interruptions are taking place when the participants are learning with their mobile device while sitting or lying on the sofa and disturb the concentration needed for the learning task. These interruption types can be either short or of longer duration and cannot easily be eliminated. The participants noted that these situations occur often and they would first target these internal problems (for example, by getting a blanket to get warm) and then resume the learning task. The experts listed mind-wandering (E4), cravings and needs (E4), sudden thoughts (E1)—such as the idea to look up something—and the end of a self-assigned time slot reserved for learning (E2, E4) as causes of self-interruptions.

Device-Internal Interruptions and Hardware Moreover, both experts and users noted down a set of interruptions caused by the mobile device and/or the learning application itself. This list included incoming instant messaging notifications (U3, E3+E4), incoming phone calls (U3, E3+E4), and distracting advertisements (U1) within the learning apps. Two participants furthermore mentioned hardware-related problems, such as updates and device failures (E1), a low battery level (U1), missing network coverage (E3), or the angle of the sunlight making it difficult to read on the smartphone screen (U2). The latter is described as a short-term interruption, which is likely to occur, for example, when learning outside or in a train or bus.

External (Environmental) Interruptions Especially when learning at home, the participants noted distractions caused by the environment. Exemplarily, they named the mailman ringing the doorbell (U2+U3), the neighbor being loud (U2), having to walk the dog (U1 + U3), other people in the room, e.g., the partner having a request (U2), or U1 stating that "the TV running in the background causes a distraction." One participant also mentioned that they learn outside the home and named distractions such as in general people approaching them (U2). More specifically, U1 mentioned that she is often learning while being in the waiting room of a doctor. Although she knows about the limitedness of the learning time in this situation, being called into the doctor's office usually interrupts her in the middle of a task. Additionally, an uneasy metro ride (U2+U3) can already distract users from the learning task, as well as having to switch trains (U1). The experts listed more general external causes such as social interruptions (E3+E4) and daily chores (E1+E2), but also getting off the train on a commute (E1+E2).

6.4 Design Ideas for Task Resumption Support

The variety of different causes for interruptions in mobile learning settings noted above shows the need for more fine-grained task resumption support as well as their evaluation in mobile scenarios. The ideas for task resumption support generated by participants of both focus groups are summarized in the following:

Design Idea 1: Increase Motivation for Task Resumption In one idea, the participants described a gamification approach to keep the learner aware of the disruptive effect of interruptions. In particular, for situations in which interruptions are avoidable (e.g., when the user receives a text message that could be reviewed later), increasing the motivation to keep learning can be helpful. The participants sketched a possible interface design, which includes a tree growing at the lower right corner of the screen (cf. Fig. 10). The growing of the tree indicates interruption-free learning time and will produce an increasing number of fruits, the longer a person resists an interruption.

If a distraction, e.g., a notification pop-up, occurs, the phone notifies users and if they are to react to this notification right away, the tree will shrink, resulting in a loss of fruits and points. This idea picks up the idea of a visual representation such as the one presented by Liu et al. (2014) or the ForestApp,[13] and combines it with a gamification approach. In the work of Liu et al. (2014), the user was presented in one condition with a blooming flower if they resisted giving in to distractions, or in a second condition, with a fading flower for staying in a distracting task, respectively. Similarly, common MLAs like Duolingo make use of simple gamification events such

---

[13]Forest App: https://www.forestapp.cc, last access February 16, 2020.

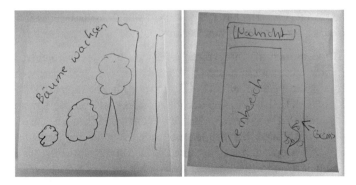

Fig. 10 Sketch from the focus group on increasing user motivation to support the changes of task resumption (Draxler et al. 2019)

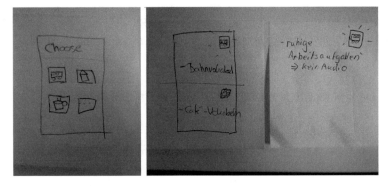

Fig. 11 Sketch from the focus group on different application modes which include different features of task resumption in regard to specific situations (Draxler et al. 2019)

as earning points for learning showing their feasibility for application in small-screen settings.

Another idea to target tiredness or feeling cold was to include more interactive learning tasks, such as having to take pictures of things for which one was supposed to learn translations (U2). After a short discussion and a readjustment of the initial task, the focus group members kept focusing on task resumption support after the interruption occurred.

Design Idea 2: Easier Comeback In case of longer and more demanding interruptions, the learning application could start with easier questions to get the user reacquainted with the topic. The participants propose to design the tasks in these situations in a short and easy manner and to include tasks which the user already answered correctly before the interruption occurred.

Design Idea 3: Adaptive Learning Modes The participants recommended implementing different learning modes within the application that would adapt the content, structure, presentation, and task resumption support (cf. Fig. 11). For example, a *home* learning mode adapts the MLA to a quiet environment in which the user can focus on the learning task. Thus, it would show the user tasks with high complexity and difficulty. However, a *commute* mode would expect interruptions and, therefore, rather focus on shorter units or repetitions of prior tasks. Within these modes, the learning content could furthermore be adapted to the environment (e.g., when learning a new language in the train, the app could ask for translations for "seat" and "stop"). Using this method, interruptions due to train-related issues such as the announcement of the next stop would cause less of a distraction from the learning environment and the content the user is learning. Differentiating between usage contexts should be a feasible technique due to increased quality of sensors built into mobile devices.

Design Idea 4: Reminder One member of the focus group suggested sending reminders to the learner to resume the learning task after an interruption. In particular, reminders can support users in situations where interruptions are unavoidable (e.g., changing trains). This reminder could be explicit, but also very subtle through a simple vibration to refresh the memory and remind of the ongoing learning task. Similar reminders have also been used by McDaniel et al. (2004) and Smith et al. (2009): simple visual, auditory, or tactile cues that keep users aware of backgrounded tasks they could or should return to. In an application domain, the Duolingo app issues daily notifications to get learners back on track if they do not continue their language practice.

Design Idea 5: Mnemonic Cues A solution proposed by E1 and E2 is to present the user an image at the moment of an interruption. This image would then be shown again as a mnemonic cue when the user continues learning. However, it is difficult to select an appropriate visual stimulus and if it has to be related to the learning content. Moreover, this does not work if the interruption lag is too short. Similarly, embedding the learning content in a storytelling frame would make it possible to use the method of loci for recovering context (Higbee 1979).

Design Idea 6: Summary—"What Happened so Far?" E1 and E2 suggested the presentation of automatically generated summaries, for example, in a textual form show immediately before an interruption (cf. Fig. 12b). In addition to facilitating task resumption, reading summaries can also improve recall and transfer performance of learning contents (Mayer et al. 1996). In addition, in the case of videos or photos, visual summaries have been shown to improve recall of events (Shekhar et al. 2017). In our everyday lives, we can encounter summaries when watching a TV series: episodes often feature a recap of relevant events in past episodes. However, generating meaningful summaries remains a challenge, as the relevancy of contents needs to be established or corresponding higher level concepts be identified. Summaries could also be presented as a set of questions for the user to answer upon task resumption as proposed by E3 and E4. Questions can help guide the learners back to the task and furthermore be a tool to adapt the following content according to user's performance on these questions. Asking questions is a common pedagogical method used in school to get students reacquainted with the content of the previous lesson (Krause and Stark 2006) and could be easily realized inside an MLA.

(a) Using images as mnemonic   (b) Presenting a summary of previous
cues on task resumption.

Fig. 12 Sketches from the focus groups (Draxler et al. 2019)

In addition to the function as a resumption cue, retrieval practice through testing has also been shown to improve long-term retention and improve knowledge transfer to new contexts (Roediger III and Butler 2011). In particular, testing is beneficial if some time has passed since an item was studied—for example, if the learning task was interrupted.

Design Idea 7: Regaining Focus The participants E3 and E4 proposed to include short meditation exercises to regain focus, for example, focused breathing. Although the exercise is not specifically related to the learning task, it can help users focus on the upcoming task again. Research has shown that mindfulness interventions can increase the attention level in subsequent tasks (Campillo et al. 2018) and decrease mind-wandering (Mrazek et al. 2012). Besides, short breathing exercises have been found to improve reading comprehension (Clinton et al. 2018). These findings suggest that integrating mindfulness components into the interruption recovery process of an MLA could indeed support task performance. Campillo et al. (2018) showed that visual and auditory mindfulness-based interventions improved subsequent auditory and visual memory and attention. Thus, this technique is particularly interesting to counteract self-interruptions such as mind-wandering, during which people's focus of attention shifts to internal thoughts. However, the duration of such interventions needs to be evaluated.

6.5   Discussion and Limitations

The participants of the focus groups engaged in interesting discussions around interruptions in the mobile learning context and often referred back to their own previous experiences. They quickly came up with a large number of situations where interruptions occur, which shows that there seem to be many sources of distractions. Causes of self-interruptions were mentioned frequently, suggesting that the physical needs and mental state of learners must be taken into account for a seamless learning experience. Self-interruptions were closely followed by device-internal or external social interruptions (e.g., messaging notifications)—situations, where interruptions are unplanned and task resumption cues are particularly promising.

During the design phase, the participants came up with ideas that build on different aspects of learning and mobile tasks: content-related strategies that sum up previous content or gradually change from prior topics to new content, but also content-independent concentration exercises. Most of the designs applied visual cues, but this was probably induced by the fact that we asked them to draw their ideas and this modality seemed the most obvious. Some of the concepts are similar to what has been used in research or existing applications, for example, the aforementioned summaries and reminders that motivate users to get back on track. Other ideas have not yet been examined in detail, especially in the context of mobile learning, and more in-depth research would be a valuable contribution. This includes situation-aware mnemonic cues, easing back in as in Design Idea 2, and the effect of concentration exercises. Further discussion of the participants' proposals can be found in Sect. 7, where we use them to extract a set of design guidelines.

Due to the composition of the focus group, the participants we selected reflect only a narrow sample of the overall population of MLA users and experts. The participants who took part in the focus groups are all between 20 and 30 years old and are mainly using language learning applications. However, we do believe that this sample represents a very important age group as they are from a generation that has grown up with technology, but already come to a point of maturity and developed daily routines. Nonetheless, additional focus groups with a larger and more diverse sample would definitely be a benefit for the design of useful task resumption cues.

To our surprise, the participants of the user focus group showed difficulties staying on topic during the session. Although we explained the use case of task resumption very thoroughly and confirmed their understanding, they often deviated from this original topic and discussed how interruptions could be avoided and managed. This is of course also a central process when dealing with interruptions, it is, however, not per se a tool to support the resumption of a task after an interruption. We consider this observation an indication that users either have difficulties understanding and imagining this specific situation or would rather prefer a tool to avoid interruptions rather than task resumption support.

Although we did explicitly not restrict the focus group participants to the capabilities of today's technology, the design ideas are of course influenced by technological limitations. Due to the rapid development of the computing power and sensing quality of mobile devices, the design ideas for task resumption support could become more complex in the future. However, until now many of the creative ideas participants came up with come with certain restrictions. In particular, sensing certain situations or interruptions is not yet possible. Furthermore, the process of sketching design ideas with pen and paper could have influenced participant's choice of cue design. It is obviously easier to sketch a visual design rather than, for example, an auditory cue. Nonetheless, we encouraged the participants to at least take notes on their ideas or, if possible, include other modalities such as sounds or vibrations, through abstractions (e.g., draw icons).[14]

7 Design Guidelines for Task Resumption Cues in Mobile Learning

So far, this chapter described a literature review in Sect. 5, which brought up several task resumption concepts in various disciplines. We clustered the results according to various design space categories and evaluated their potential for application in a mobile learning scenario. In addition, we also performed two focus groups to derive ideas and designs for task resumption cues as outlined in Sect. 6.

This section will now merge the results from the two approaches and evaluate the potential and limitations of individual features and functions for the application in a mobile learning scenario. We derive a set of six design guidelines for task resumption cues in mobile learning scenarios to support both researchers and designers.

Design Guideline 1:
Adapt to the Mobile Device's Qualities and Requirements
The task resumption cues proposed in the design space literature are almost exclusively designed for static desktop computer settings. On the other hand, some existing mobile apps include resumption support features but have not yet been evaluated from a research perspective (cf. Sect. 4.5). We strongly believe that many resumption strategies described in the design space could be translated to mobile settings, i.e., can be adapted to smaller screens and more simple interactions. If task resumption cues are adapted from stationary settings, it is important to simplify the interface to work with a small screen and to use input and output methods that smartphones provide. One further factor playing in the favor of mobile devices is the fact that resumption cues are often designed such that they require only a limited amount of interaction (cf. Table 2), which means they can more easily be integrated into a simple UI. For instance, timeline views, which present the user with a chronological overview of the past actions or created artifacts (as in Hodgetts et al. 2015, Morris et al. 2008, Parnin and DeLine 2010, Scott et al. 2006), could be adapted by simplifying the user interface to make sure it does not become too cluttered. Moreover, activity replay is also a

---

[14]Content of the section "Evaluation Part II: Focus Group: Designing Task Resumption Cues for Mobile Learning" has been published in a revised version in an extended abstract format in the adjunct proceedings of the MobileHCI 2019 conference (Draxler et al. 2019).

possible option—and has already been implemented in many media players—where users can repeat previously played content. In the particular case of mobile learning, the content to be repeated already exists and needs no or almost no modification for generating a replay. Replay in contexts where salient points need to be extracted first is more difficult to implement, but we deem the effort very promising from a task recovery point of view. To avoid overloading the user with too many information, a details-on-demand design can be implemented, where users can toggle the display of additional information as needed or desired.

Design Guideline 2:
Make use of the Interruption Lag
Interruptions on mobile devices are manifold. Some of them might be unpredictable such as external interruptions by other people or the environment. It is close to impossible to anticipate them. In contrast, some interruptions can be foreseen and/or delayed, such as internal notifications through the *Attelia* sensing system (Okoshi et al. 2014), which detects breakpoints of user's activities during smartphone usage without the use of any additional sensors. Task resumption cues that guide learners during the interruption lag and prepare for upcoming interruptions have shown a high potential for support. The time before an interruption can be used to encode the information to increase the chances of long-term-memory storage as well as for goal encoding ("What was I about to do next?") (Altmann and Trafton 2002). Briefly presenting a visual cue in the transitional period before an interruption can already foster mental note-taking and thus, task resumption (Clifford and Altmann 2004). More explicitly, the interruption lag could be used to present the user with the current state of the task to remember (Altmann and Trafton 2004) or to show a tree view of all lessen parts or a timeline of the learner's last actions (Parnin and DeLine 2010). Since the use of task resumption cues during the interruption lag has been shown to have a positive effect on task resumption, we can recommend to facilitate this time if an interruption can be anticipated (even if the anticipation time is short). However, there are contradicting findings regarding the length of the interruption lag, which need further evaluation (Altmann and Trafton 2004).

Design Guideline 3:
Leave App visible during Interruption
One of the most thoroughly evaluated types of task resumption cues is presented during the interruption. If a user is disrupted by a secondary task originating device-internally, such as an incoming notification, it will help to leave the task window at least somewhat visible. Multiple studies (cf. Hodgetts and Jones 2006b; Iqbal and Horvitz 2007a; Ratwani and Trafton 2008) have shown the positive effect of leaving part of the task screen visible on task resumption time after short interruptions. Showing a secondary task in a corner, or at least showing as much of the primary task as possible can ease task resumption (Iqbal and Horvitz 2007a). Implementing a split-screen mode to keep the learning task visible could, therefore, enhance resumption speed. Since the aforementioned user studies applied either a desktop or a multi-device setting, it has to be further evaluated to what extent the results are transferable to a mobile device. For example, the study of Iqbal and Horvitz (2007a) found longer

resumption times in windows that were less than 25% visible compared to windows that were more than 75% visible. However, on a smaller screen, these results might deviate. Further evaluation needs to investigate if even smaller hints such as icons or objects like the Facebook Messenger Chat Heads (cf. Sect. 4.5) can achieve similar results in reminding users to resume a learning task.

Design Guideline 4:
Cue Complexity should not exceed Task Complexity
In common learning applications, the design of a task creates a unique set of requirements for the user. Many common learning applications only address maintenance rehearsal processes (cf. Sect. 3.2). For example, language learning apps such as Duolingo only focus on numerous repetitions of vocabulary. These apps commonly neglect the explicit teaching of structures or grammar knowledge (Heil et al. 2016). The passive processes of maintenance rehearsal require less focused attention and less cognitive resources than deeper processing mechanisms. Other applications, e.g., for science learning or coding, might require more explicit processing mechanisms and, therefore, involve long-term memory encoding. In contrast to basic maintenance rehearsal, which takes place in the working memory, exercises like this would require deeper processing. So both app and learning content have an effect on the depth of processing required and, thus, influence the negative impact an interruption can have. In conclusion, maintenance rehearsal learning can be supported by simple cues such as summaries or further repetition tasks because learning contents are created to be short and simple (as common in micro-learning). In this situation, interacting with a complex task resumption cue could produce additional cognitive load through the task design, which can hinder central processes of learning such as schema construction (cf. Sect. 3.2). In general, many task resumption cues of very simplistic design such as visual highlighting (Mariakakis et al. 2015) or simple audio cues have shown their potential to support the user (Smith et al. 2009). However, participants of the focus group discussed to design cues with different levels of complexity and explicitness. For example, participants considered pictures (e.g., screenshots) as cues to be potentially more effective in helping one recall where a learning task was left off, as opposed to reading lengthy summaries. The efficiency of cues for task resumption with different levels of explicitness and complexity needs to be evaluated with regard to the strength and cognitive demand of interruptions. Especially when designing for complex learning tasks, the different degrees of cue complexity should be investigated.

Design Guideline 5:
Evaluate different Cue Modalities
Related work described in the design space (cf. Sect. 5) applies a variety of modalities for task resumption cues, including visual, textual, and auditory. The modality varied according to the interruption context. For example, the evaluation of auditory labels happened in a setting of an urgent and important interruption because user can quickly and easily generate and retrieve auditory cues (Yeung and Li 2016). The adaptation of modalities to different types of interruptions has not been evaluated in particular and has to be explored in future work.

Additionally, we want to highlight the potential of marginally researched modalities such as tangible or haptic cues. Complementary to the translation of cues from desktop settings, mobile devices open up new design opportunities. Input and output methods provide potential for a range of new designs such as haptic cues. Mobile devices are usually equipped with vibration motors and thus, are suitable for haptic cuing. Vibration signals are a popular method for notifications (Sahami et al. 2008) and are discreet. If the device is worn on the body, then vibrations can also be noticed in busy, noisy environments as well as when the phone is in the pocket or bag, in contrast to visual or auditory cues. Participants of the focus group suggested using simple vibrations for reminding users of suspended tasks (cf. Sect. 6.4). In theory, vibration patterns could convey a lot more information than they currently tend to do. However, it is important to assure a good learnability of new or complex cues (cf. Dingler et al. 2008) to assure that the users can recognize the encoded meanings if it exceeds simple reminders. Therefore, for task resumption, we recommend using haptic cues preferably for implicit cuing.

Moreover, the combination of multiple modalities as well as their use for a broader range of purposes need to be further explored. For the use in learning, it is, however, important to align the task and task resumption design with the multimedia principles defined by Mayer (2005). He states the importance of designing instructional messages during learning in the light of the workings of the human mind and claims that following these principles will lead more likely to meaningful learning. Even though Mayer supports multi-codality, meaning the use of different modalities (e.g., words and pictures), he also highlights the negative effect of superfluous or redundant materials for learning (Mayer 2002, 2005). Thus, when designing for learning tasks, the use of different modalities can foster the learning process as long as the usage of those is planned with care.

Design Guideline 6:
Evaluate the Cue in Different Situations
For the evaluation of any new cue design, it is important to consider a broad range of possible usage scenarios. As we described in Sect. 2.2, mobile learning can take place in a variety of situations and surroundings. These situations vary in their basic characteristics such as the time that can be spent on learning right now, or the noise of the environment. Many of the task resumption cues described in Sect. 5 only test their designs in a very narrow usage scenario and often perform very controlled laboratory evaluations. However, the effectiveness of task resumption cues strongly depends on the task and setting they presented in as well as the characteristics of the interrupting task itself. In the discussion with our focus group participants (cf. Sect. 6), we collected a variety of possible interruptions that can occur during learning with a mobile device. We recommend to evaluate task resumption cues in regard to these common interruptions.

8 Conclusion

This work contributes to the augmentation of cognitive capabilities by enabling learning anywhere and at any time in a constantly connected, but also constantly disrupting world. Specifically, this work investigates designs for task resumption to support users in handling distractions and interruptions in mobile learning scenarios. We explored different designs of task resumption support, in particular, memory cues, through a survey of existing literature from various domains. We clustered a set of 35 task resumption cues from 30 publications into a design space along the five dimensions (1) purpose, (2) required attention, (3) timing, (4) interactivity, and (5) modality of the cue. We furthermore described the individual characteristics of each dimension and discussed the evaluation of each cue in regard to the expressiveness and validity of the respective studies. Overall, a majority of quantitative studies showed slightly positive or positive impact of memory cues on task completion time and error rate after an interruption. Resumption cues can, therefore, be seen as a promising memory aid across different domains. Based on the design space, we can further say that a number of concepts and ideas such as visual task resumption cues have been thoroughly researched. On the other hand, we derived some research gaps like the exploration of different cue modalities such as haptic or tangible or identifying a suitable level of explicitness, where future work could investigate new cue designs. In addition to the literature review, we reported findings from two focus groups with HCI experts and users of mobile learning applications. These focus groups explored suitable cue designs for mobile learning tasks based on a set of common interruptions during mobile learning derived by the participants. Finally, we combined the findings of the literature survey and the focus group in the form of six design guidelines for task resumption cues. We discussed these guidelines in the light of their feasibility to be applied in mobile learning applications and highlighted potentially interesting starting points for future work. With our work, we provide an overview of various designs for task resumption cues to support researchers in navigating through the large amount of literature currently available on this topic. Additionally, we discuss the feasibility of different designs for the application in everyday settings on mobile devices and facilitate learning on the go.

References

APA Definition of Attention (2019a). https://dictionary.apa.org/attention. Accessed 11 Jan 2019
APA Definition of Cue (2019b). https://dictionary.apa.org/cue. Accessed 12 Jan 2019
APA definition of Learning (2019c). https://dictionary.apa.org/learning. Accessed 12 Jan 2019
APA Definition of Learning and Memory (2019d). https://www.apa.org/topics/learning/index.aspx. Accessed 05 Jan 2019
APA Definition of Mnemonic (2019e). https://dictionary.apa.org/mnemonic. Accessed 12 Jan 2019
APA Definition of Modality (2019f). https://dictionary.apa.org/modality. Accessed 15 Jan 2019
APA Definition of Retrieval Cue (2019g). https://dictionary.apa.org/retrieval-cue. Accessed 11 Jan 2019
Adler RF, Benbunan-Fich R (2013) Self-interruptions in discretionary multitasking. Comput Hum Behav 29(4):1441–1449
Altmann EM, Trafton JG (2002) Memory for goals: An activation-based model. Cognit Sci 26(1):39–83. https://doi.org/10.1207/s15516709cog2601_2
Altmann EM, Trafton JG (2004) Task interruption: resumption lag and the role of cues. Technical report, Michigan State University Eest Lansing Department of Psychology
Anderson C, Hübener I, Seipp A-K, Ohly S, David K, Pejovic V (2018) A survey of attention management systems in ubiquitous computing environments. arXiv:1806.06771
Atkinson RC, Shiffrin RM (1968) Human memory: a proposed system and its control processes1. In: Psychology of learning and motivation, vol 2. Elsevier, pp 89–195
Baddeley A (2003) Working memory: looking back and looking forward. Nat Rev Neurosci 4(10):829
Baddeley AD (1997) Human memory: theory and practice. Psychology Press
Bailey BP, Konstan JA (2006) On the need for attention-aware systems: Measuring effects of interruption on task performance, error rate, and affective state. Comput Hum Behav 22(4):685–708. https://doi.org/10.1016/j.chb.2005.12.009
Borojeni SS, Ali AE, Heuten W, Boll S (2016) Peripheral light cues for in-vehicle task resumption. In: Proceedings of the 9th Nordic conference on human-computer interaction. ACM, p 67
Borst JP, Buwalda TA, van Rijn H, Taatgen NA (2013) Avoiding the problem state bottleneck by strategic use of the environment. Acta Psychol 144(2):373–379
Bruck PA, Motiwalla L, Foerster F (2012) Mobile learning with micro-content: a framework and evaluation. In: Bled eConference, p 2
Brumby DP, Cox AL, Back J, Gould SJ (2013) Recovering from an interruption: Investigating speed- accuracy trade-offs in task resumption behavior. J Exp Psychol Appl 19(2):95
Buschke H (1984) Cued recall in amnesia. J Clin Exp Neuropsychol 6(4):433–440
Cades DM, Trafton JG, Boehm-Davis DA (2006) Mitigating disruptions: can resuming an interrupted task be trained? In: Proceedings of the human factors and ergonomics society annual meeting, vol 50. Sage Publications Sage CA, Los Angeles, CA, pp 368–371
Campbell JL, Quincy C, Osserman J, Pedersen OK (2013) Coding in-depth semistructured interviews: Problems of unitization and intercoder reliability and agreement. Sociolog Methods Res 42(3):294–320
Campillo E, Ricarte J, Ros L, Nieto M, Latorre J (2018) Effects of the visual and auditory components of a brief mindfulness intervention on mood state and on visual and auditory attention and memory task performance. Curr Psychol 37(1):357–365
Cane JE, Cauchard F, Weger UW (2012) The time-course of recovery from interruption during reading: Eye movement evidence for the role of interruption lag and spatial memory. Q J Exp Psychol 65(7):1397–1413
Carrier LM, Rosen LD, Cheever NA, Lim AF (2015) Causes, effects, and practicalities of everyday multitasking. Dev Rev 35:64–78
Chen D, Vertegaal R (2004) Using mental load for managing interruptions in physiologically attentive user interfaces. In: CHI'04 extended abstracts on human factors in computing systems. ACM, pp 1513–1516

Cheng S, Fan J, Dey AK (2018) Smooth gaze: a framework for recovering tasks across devices using eye tracking. Pers Ubiquitous Comput 22(3):489–501

Churchill D, Hedberg J (2008) Learning object design considerations for small-screen handheld devices. Comput Educ 50(3):881–893

Clifford JD, Altmann EM (2004) Managing multiple tasks: reducing the resumption time of the primary task. In: Proceedings of the annual meeting of the cognitive science society, vol 26

Clinton V, Swenseth M, Carlson SE (2018) Do mindful breathing exercises benefit reading comprehension? a brief report. J Cogn Enhanc 1–6

Cohen S (1980) Aftereffects of stress on human performance and social behavior: a review of research and theory. Psychol Bull 88(1):82

Cowan N (2010) The magical mystery four: How is working memory capacity limited, and why? Curr Dir Psychol Sci 19(1):51–57

Craik FI, Lockhart RS (1972) Levels of processing: A framework for memory research. J Verbal Learn Verbal Behav 11(6):671–684

Cull WL (2000) Untangling the benefits of multiple study opportunities and repeated testing for cued recall. Appl Cogn Psychol 14(3):215–235

Czerwinski M, Chrisman S, Schumacher B (1991) The effects of warnings and display similarity on interruption in multitasking environments. ACM SIGCHI Bull 23(4):38–39

Demouy V, Jones A, Kan Q, Kukulska-Hulme A, Eardley A (2016) Why and how do distance learners use mobile devices for language learning? EuroCALL Rev 24(1):10–24

Dillenbourg P, Betrancourt M (2006) Handling complexity in learning environments: theory and research, pp 141–165

Dingler T, Pielot M (2015) I'll be there for you: quantifying attentiveness towards mobile messaging. In: Proceedings of the 17th international conference on human-computer interaction with mobile devices and services. ACM, pp 1–5

Dingler T, Lindsay J, Walker BN (2008) Learnabiltiy of sound cues for environmental features: auditory icons, earcons, spearcons, and speech. International Community for Auditory Display

Dingler T, El Agroudy P, Le HV, Schmidt A, Niforatos E, Bexheti A, Langheinrich M (2016) Multimedia memory cues for augmenting human memory. IEEE MultiMedia 23(2):4–11

Dingler T, Weber D, Pielot M, Cooper J, Chang C-C, Henze N (2017) Language learning on-the-go: opportune moments and design of mobile microlearning sessions. In: Proceedings of the 19th international conference on human-computer interaction with mobile devices and services. ACM, p 28

D'Mello S, Olney A, Williams C, Hays P (2012) Gaze tutor: A gaze-reactive intelligent tutoring system. Int J Hum Comput Stud 70(5):377–398

Draxler F, Schneegass C, Niforatos E (2019) Designing for task resumption support in mobile learning. In: Adjunct proceedings of the 21st international conference on human-computer interaction with mobile devices and services, pp 1–6

Economides AA (2008) Context-aware mobile learning. World summit on knowledge society. Springer, Berlin, pp 213–220

Edwards MB, Gronlund SD (1998) Task interruption and its effects on memory. Memory 6(6):665–687

Foehr UG (2006) Media multitasking among american youth: Prevalence, predictors and pairings. Henry J Kaiser Family Foundation

Franke JL, Daniels JJ, McFarlane DC (2002) Recovering context after interruption. In: Proceedings of the annual meeting of the cognitive science society, vol 24

Gillie T, Broadbent D (1989) What makes interruptions disruptive? a study of length, similarity, and complexity. Psychol Res 50(4):243–250

González VM, Mark G (2004) Constant, constant, multi-tasking craziness: managing multiple working spheres. In: Proceedings of the SIGCHI conference on Human factors in computing systems. ACM, pp 113–120

Heil CR, Wu JS, Lee JJ, Schmidt T (2016) A review of mobile language learning applications: Trends, challenges, and opportunities. In: The EuroCALL review, vol 24. Universitat Politècnica de València, pp 32–50. https://doi.org/10.4995/eurocall.2016.6402

Higbee KL (1979) Recent research on visual mnemonics: Historical roots and educational fruits. Rev Educ Res 49(4):611–629

Higgins JM (1994) 101 creative problem solving techniques: the handbook of new ideas for business. New Management Publishing Company

Higgins JM (1996) Innovate or evaporate: creative techniques for strategists. Long Range Plann 29(3):370–380

Ho C-Y, Nikolic MI, Waters MJ, Sarter NB (2004) Not now! supporting interruption management by indicating the modality and urgency of pending tasks. Hum Factors 46(3):399–409

Ho J, Intille SS (2005) Using context-aware computing to reduce the perceived burden of interruptions from mobile devices. In: Proceedings of the SIGCHI conference on human factors in computing systems. ACM, pp 909–918

Hodgetts HM, Jones DM (2006a) Contextual cues aid recovery from interruption: the role of associative activation. J Exp Psychol Learn Memory Cogn 32(5):1120. https://doi.org/10.1037/0278-7393.32.5.1120

Hodgetts HM, Jones DM (2006b) Interruption of the tower of london task: support for a goalactivation approach. J Exp Psychol General 135(1):103. https://doi.org/10.1177n%2F154193120304700810

Hodgetts HM, Tremblay S, Vallières BR, Vachon F (2015) Decision support and vulnerability to interruption in a dynamic multitasking environment. Int J Hum Comput Stud 79:106–117

Hopp PJ, Smith C, Clegg BA, Heggestad ED (2005) Interruption management: the use of attention-directing tactile cues. Hum Factors 47(1):1–11

Horvitz E, Apacible J, Subramani M (2005) Balancing awareness and interruption: investigation of notification deferral policies. International conference on user modeling. Springer, Berlin, pp 433–437

Hudson S, Fogarty J, Atkeson C, Avrahami D, Forlizzi J, Kiesler S., Lee J, Yang J (2003) Predicting human interruptibility with sensors: a wizard of oz feasibility study. In: Proceedings of the SIGCHI conference on Human factors in computing systems, pp 257–264

Hutt S, Mills C, White S, Donnelly PJ, D'Mello SK (2016) The eyes have it: gaze-based detection of mind wandering during learning with an intelligent tutoring system. In: EDM, pp 86–93

Iqbal ST, Bailey BP (2005) Investigating the effectiveness of mental workload as a predictor of opportune moments for interruption. In CHI '05 extended abstracts on Human factors in computing systems-CHI'05, Portland, OR, USA. ACM Press, p 1489. ISBN 978-1-59593-002-6. https://doi.org/10.1145/1056808.1056948

Iqbal ST, Horvitz E (2007a) Conversations amidst computing: a study of interruptions and recovery of task activity. International conference on user modeling. Springer, Berlin, pp 350–354

Iqbal ST, Horvitz E (2007b) Disruption and recovery of computing tasks: field study, analysis, and directions. In: Proceedings of the SIGCHI conference on human factors in computing systems. ACM, pp 677–686. https://doi.org/10.1145/1240624.1240730

James W, Burkhardt F, Bowers F, Skrupskelis IK (1890) The principles of psychology, vol 1. Macmillan London

Jeuris S, Bardram JE (2016) Dedicated workspaces: Faster resumption times and reduced cognitive load in sequential multitasking. Comput Hum Behav 62:404–414

Jo J, Kim B, Seo J (2015) Eyebookmark: assisting recovery from interruption during reading. In: Proceedings of the 33rd annual ACM conference on human factors in computing systems. ACM, pp 2963–2966

Katidioti I, Borst JP, van Vugt MK, Taatgen NA (2016) Interrupt me: External interruptions are less disruptive than self-interruptions. Comput Hum Behav 63:906–915

Kern D, Marshall P, Schmidt A (2010) Gazemarks: gaze-based visual placeholders to ease attention switching. In: Proceedings of the SIGCHI conference on human factors in computing systems. ACM, pp 2093–2102

Khalil MK, Elkhider IA (2016) Applying learning theories and instructional design models for effective instruction. Adv Physiol Educ 40(2):147–156

Kirschner F, Paas F, Kirschner PA (2009) A cognitive load approach to collaborative learning: United brains for complex tasks. Educ Psychol Rev 21(1):31–42

Koelle M, Wolf K, Boll S (2018) Beyond led status lights-design requirements of privacy notices for body-worn cameras. In: Proceedings of the twelfth international conference on tangible, embedded, and embodied interaction. ACM, pp 177–187

Krause U-M, Stark R (2006) Vorwissen aktivieren. Handbuch Lernstrategien, pp 38–49

Kreifeldt JG, McCarthy M (1981) Interruption as a Test of the User-Computer Interface. In: Proceedings of the 17th Annual Conference on Manual Interaction, pp 655–667

Latorella KA (1998) Effects of modality on interrupted flight deck performance: implications for data link. In: Proceedings of the human factors and ergonomics society annual meeting, vol 42. SAGE Publications Sage CA, Los Angeles, CA, pp 87–91

Lavie N (2005) Distracted and confused?: Selective attention under load. Trends Cogn Sci 9(2):75–82

Lavie N (2010) Attention, distraction, and cognitive control under load. Curr Dir Psychol Sci 19(3):143–148

Ledoux K, Gordon PC (2006) Interruption-similarity effects during discourse processing. Memory 14(7):789–803

Leiva L, Böhmer M, Gehring S, Krüger A (2012) Back to the app: the costs of mobile application interruptions. In: Proceedings of the 14th international conference on human-computer interaction with mobile devices and services-MobileHCI'12, San Francisco, California, USA. ACM Press, p 291. ISBN 978-1-4503-1105-2. https://doi.org/10.1145/2371574.2371617

Lindblom J, Gündert J (2017) Managing mediated interruptions in manufacturing: selected strategies used for coping with cognitive load. Advances in neuroergonomics and cognitive engineering. Springer, Berlin, pp 389–403

Liu Y, Jia Y, Pan W, Pfaff MS (2014) Supporting task resumption using visual feedback. In: Proceedings of the 17th ACM conference on Computer supported cooperative work & social computing. ACM, pp 767–777

Liu X, Tan P-N, Liu L, Simske SJ (2017) Automated classification of eeg signals for predicting students' cognitive state during learning. In: Proceedings of the international conference on web intelligence. ACM, pp 442–450

Luzhnica G, Veas E, Pammer V (2016) Skin reading: encoding text in a 6-channel haptic display. In: Proceedings of the 2016 ACM international symposium on wearable computers, ISWC'16, New York, NY, USA. ACM, pp 148–155. ISBN 978-1-4503-4460-9. https://doi.org/10.1145/2971763.2971769

Mancero G, Wong B, Loomes M (2009) Radio dispatchers' interruption recovery strategies. In: Proceedings of the 21st annual conference of the Australian computer-human interaction special interest group: design: open 24/7. ACM, pp 113–120

Mariakakis A, Goel M, Aumi MTI, Patel SN, Wobbrock JO (2015) Switchback: using focus and saccade tracking to guide users' attention for mobile task resumption. In: Proceedings of the 33rd annual ACM conference on human factors in computing systems. ACM, pp 2953–2962. https://doi.org/10.1145/2702123.2702539

Mark G, Gudith D, Klocke U (2008) The cost of interrupted work: more speed and stress. In: Proceedings of the SIGCHI conference on human factors in computing systems. ACM, pp 107–110

Mayer RE (2002) Multimedia learning. In: Psychology of learning and motivation, vol 41. Elsevier, pp 85–139

Mayer RE (2005) Cognitive theory of multimedia learning. In: The Cambridge handbook of multimedia learning, vol 43

Mayer RE, Bove W, Bryman A, Mars R, Tapangco L (1996) When less is more: Meaningful learning from visual and verbal summaries of science textbook lessons. J Educ Psychol 88(1):64

McDaniel MA, Einstein GO, Graham T, Rall E (2004) Delaying execution of intentions: Overcoming the costs of interruptions. Appl Cogn Psychol Off J Soc Appl Res Mem Cogn 18(5):533–547

McLean R, Gregg L (1967) Effects of induced chunking on temporal aspects of serial recitation. J Exp Psychol 74(4p1):455

Michalko M (2014) Thinkpak: a brainstorming card deck; [a Creative-thinking Toolbox]. Ten Speed Press

Miller GA (1956) The magical number seven, plus or minus two: Some limits on our capacity for processing information. Psychol Rev 63(2):81

Miyata Y, Norman DA (1986) User centered system design: new perspectives on human-computer interaction, pp 265–284

Moè A, De Beni R (2005) Stressing the efficacy of the loci method: oral presentation and the subject-generation of the loci pathway with expository passages. Appl Cogn Psychol 19(1):95–106

Monk CA, Trafton JG, Boehm-Davis DA (2008) The effect of interruption duration and demand on resuming suspended goals. J Exp Psychol Appl 14(4):299

Morris D, Ringel Morris M, Venolia G (2008) Searchbar: a search-centric web history for task resumption and information re-finding. In: Proceedings of the SIGCHI conference on human factors in computing systems. ACM, pp 1207–1216

Mrazek MD, Smallwood J, Schooler JW (2012) Mindfulness and mind-wandering: Finding convergence through opposing constructs. Emotion 12(3), 442–448. ISSN 1931–1516:1528–3542. https://doi.org/10.1037/a0026678

Niforatos E, Laporte M, Bexheti A, Langheinrich M (2018) Augmenting memory recall in work meetings: establishing a quantifiable baseline. In: Proceedings of the 9th augmented human international conference. ACM, p 4

Okoshi T, Nakazawa J, Tokuda H (2014) Attelia: sensing user's attention status on smart phones. In: Proceedings of the 2014 ACM international joint conference on pervasive and ubiquitous computing: adjunct publication. ACM, pp 139–142

Okundaye O, Quek F, Sargunam SP, Suhail M, Das R (2017) Facilitating context switching through tangible artifacts. In: Proceedings of the 2017 CHI conference extended abstracts on human factors in computing systems. ACM, pp 1940–1946

O'Malley C, Vavoula G, Glew J, Taylor J, Sharples M, Lefrere P, Lonsdale P, Naismith L, Waycott J (2005) Guidelines for learning/teaching/tutoring in a mobile environment. Public deliverable from the MOBILearn project (D.4.1)

Oulasvirta A (2005) Interrupted cognition and design for non-disruptiveness: the skilled memory approach. In: CHI'05 extended abstracts on human factors in computing systems. ACM, pp 1124–1125

Oulasvirta A, Saariluoma P (2006) Surviving task interruptions: Investigating the implications of long-term working memory theory. Int J Hum Comput Stud 64(10), 941–961. ISSN 10715819. https://doi.org/10.1016/j.ijhcs.2006.04.006

Paas F, Renkl A, Sweller J (2004) Cognitive load theory: Instructional implications of the interaction between information structures and cognitive architecture. Instr Sci 32(1):1–8

Page T (2013) Usability of text input interfaces in smartphones. J Des Res 11(1):39–56

Parnin C, DeLine R (2010) Evaluating cues for resuming interrupted programming tasks. In: Proceedings of the SIGCHI conference on human factors in computing systems. ACM, pp 93–102

Ratwani RM, Trafton JG (2008) Spatial memory guides task resumption. Vis Cogn 16(8):1001–1010

Ratwani RM, Andrews AE, McCurry M, Trafton JG, Peterson MS (2007) Using peripheral processing and spatial memory to facilitate task resumption. In: Proceedings of the human factors and ergonomics society annual meeting, vol 51. Sage Publications Sage CA, Los Angeles, CA, pp 244–248

Roediger HL (1980) The effectiveness of four mnemonics in ordering recall. J Exp Psychol Hum Learn Mem 6(5):558

Roediger HL III, Butler AC (2011) The critical role of retrieval practice in long-term retention. Trends Cogn Sci 15(1):20–27

Rosen LD, Lim AF, Carrier LM, Cheever NA (2011) An empirical examination of the educational impact of text message-induced task switching in the classroom: Educational implications and strategies to enhance learning. Psicología Educativa 17(2):163–177

Rule A, Hollan J (2016) Thinking in 4d: preserving and sharing mental context across time. In: Proceedings of the 19th ACM conference on computer supported cooperative work and social computing companion. ACM, pp 389–392

Sadeghian Borojeni S, Löcken A, Müller H (2014) Using peripheral cues to support task resumption. In: Adjunct proceedings of the 6th international conference on automotive user interfaces and interactive vehicular applications. ACM, pp 1–4. https://doi.org/10.1145/2667239.2667290

Sahami A, Holleis P, Schmidt A, Häkkilä J (2008) Rich tactile output on mobile devices. European conference on ambient intelligence. Springer, Berlin, pp 210–221

Sasangohar F, Scott SD, Cummings ML (2014) Supervisory-level interruption recovery in time-critical control tasks. Appl Ergon 45(4):1148–1156

Schacter DL (1999) The seven sins of memory: Insights from psychology and cognitive neuroscience. Am Psychol 54(3):182

Schmidt R (1995) Consciousness and foreign language learning: A tutorial on the role of attention and awareness in learning. In: Attention and awareness in foreign language learning, vol 9, pp 1–63

Schmidt R (2012) Attention, awareness, and individual differences in language learning. In: Perspectives on individual characteristics and foreign language education, vol 6, p 27

Schneegass C, Terzimehic N, Nettah M, Schneegass S (2008) Informing the design of user-adaptive mobile language learning applications. In: Proceedings of the 17th international conference on mobile and ubiquitous multimedia. ACM, pp 233–238

Scott SD, Mercier S, Cummings M, Wang E (2006) Assisting interruption recovery in supervisory control of multiple uavs. In: Proceedings of the human factors and ergonomics society annual meeting, vol 50. SAGE Publications Sage CA, Los Angeles, CA, pp 699–703

Shekhar S, Singal D, Singh H, Kedia M, Shetty A (2017) Show and recall: learning what makes videos memorable. In: Proceedings of the IEEE conference on computer vision and pattern recognition, pp 2730–2739

Smith C, Clegg BA, Heggestad ED, Hopp-Levine PJ (2009) Interruption management: a comparison of auditory and tactile cues for both alerting and orienting. Int J Hum Comput Stud 67(9):777–786

Smith GF (1998) Idea-generation techniques: A formulary of active ingredients. J Creat Behav 32(2):107–134

Speier C, Vessey I, Valacich JS (2003) The effects of interruptions, task complexity, and information presentation on computer-supported decision-making performance. Decis Sci 34(4):771–797

Stibler KM, Craven PL, Barton J, Regli SH, Tremoulet PD (2005) Modality interactions in multitasking: Spatial and verbal resource priming vs. conflict. In: Proceedings of the Mini-Conference on Human Factors in Complex Sociotechnical Systems

Sweller J, Van Merrienboer JJ, Paas FG (1998) Cognitive architecture and instructional design. Educ Psychol Rev 10(3):251–296

Tatar D, Roschelle J, Vahey P, Penuel WR (2003) Handhelds go to school: Lessons learned. Computer (9):30–37

Tatsuno S (1990) Created in Japan: from imitators to world-class innovators. Ballinger Publishing Company

Technische Universität Dresden IHZ (2017) Toolbox "umgang mit vorwissen in der lehre". https://bildungsportal.sachsen.de/opal/auth/RepositoryEntry/6931742725/CourseNode/89718347352042/Texte_Toolbox.pdf. Accessed 06 Mar 2019

Terzimehic N, Häuselschmidt R, Schraefel M (2019) State or trait-process or goal? perspectives on mindfulness and opportunities for future research in hci. In: Proceedings of the SIGCHI conference on human factors in computing systems. ACM

Toreini P, Langner M, Maedche A (2018) Use of attentive information dashboards to support task resumption in working environments. In: Proceedings of the 2018 ACM symposium on eye tracking research & applications. ACM, p 92

Trafton JG, Altmann EM, Brock DP, Mintz FE (2003) Preparing to resume an interrupted task: Effects of prospective goal encoding and retrospective rehearsal. Int J Hum Comput Stud 58(5):583–603. https://doi.org/10.1016/S1071-5819(03)00023-5

Woelki D, Oulasvirta A, Kiefer J, Lischke R (2008) Practice effects on interruption tolerance in algebraic problem-solving. In: Proceedings of CogSci2008

Xiao X, Wang J (2017) Undertanding and detecting divided attention in mobile mooc learning. In: Proceedings of the 2017 CHI conference on human factors in computing systems. ACM, pp 2411–2415. https://doi.org/10.1145/3025453.3025552

Yang F, Heeman PA, Kun AL (2011) An investigation of interruptions and resumptions in multi-tasking dialogues. Comput Linguist 37(1):75–104

Yeung WL, Li SY (2016) Prototyping the machine-human dialogues in a smartphone voice call application with task resumption support. In: Proceedings of the 2016 CHI conference extended abstracts on human factors in computing systems. ACM, pp 1788–1793

Zhao Y, Robal T, Lofi C, Hauff C (2018) Stationary vs. non-stationary mobile learning in moocs. In: Adjunct publication of the 26th conference on user modeling, adaptation and personalization. ACM, pp 299–303. https://doi.org/10.1145/3213586.3225241

Christina Schneegass is a Ph.D. student in HCI at LMU Munich, Germany. She holds a B.Sc. and M.Sc. in Applied Cognition and Media Sciences from the University of Duisburg-Essen. Her research focusses on mobile learning in everyday scenarios, in particular, to provide learning support through implicit comprehension detection and interruption handling.

Fiona Draxler is a Ph.D. student in HCI at LMU Munich, Germany. She completed a Master's degree in Computer Science at TU Graz, Austria, and now focusses on Ubiquitous Learning. Specifically, she investigates the interplay between learners and their environment, and how learners can benefit from technology to increase their performance and motivation.

Sensory Enhancements

Insertables: Beyond Cyborgs and Augmentation to Convenience and Amenity

Kayla J. Heffernan, Frank Vetere, and Shanton Chang

Abstract Individuals are voluntarily inserting devices inside their bodies for non-medical purposes. As research into these insertable devices continues, and the practice gains traction, it is clear that earlier accounts of hobbyist makers and tinkerers reveal edge cases of use. While transhumanists still aim to augment their bodies past "human norms", they are no longer the only group interested in insertables. Beyond these innovators, early adopters of these devices are simply concerned with practical and convenience-based uses. The motivation of this chapter is threefold. The first is to present a background of insertable devices individuals are using for augmentation. The second is a more in-depth account of insertables use than previous research ($n = 115$). This allows us to answer, more accurately: 1. What devices are individuals putting in their bodies; 2. What do they use these devices for; 3. What are the motivations for modifying their bodies in this way; and 4. How do users of these devices identify themselves? The third, and final, contribution is a discussion of the motivations and self-identifications of individuals with these devices, and the implications of these. We show the progression from individuals using insertable devices to augment themselves to become "cyborgs". Now, "everyday" people are choosing to use insertables for the convenience and amenity-based purposes afforded by these devices. We contribute to the literature knowledge of these more commonplace uses, beyond augmentation. These are for access and authentication, and for storing and sharing information. Only a minority use them for augmentation purposes, which are now known to be edge cases. These are: extending senses; supporting human connections; acting as an alternative digital interface; and capturing biometric data. Motivations are evolving as device usage is moving from hobbyists and innovators to early adopters. Given they are less concerned with augmenting themselves, it log-

K. J. Heffernan (✉) · F. Vetere · S. Chang
University of Melbourne, Melbourne, Australia
e-mail: kheffernan@unimelb.edu.au

F. Vetere
e-mail: f.vetere@unimelb.edu.au

S. Chang
e-mail: shanton.chang@unimelb.edu.au

T. Dingler and E. Niforatos (eds.), *Technology-Augmented Perception and Cognition*,
Human–Computer Interaction Series, https://doi.org/10.1007/978-3-030-30457-7_6

ically follows that the majority also do not, or do not strongly, identify with any particular social movement. Users are no longer confined to the 'fringes'. Understanding this not only contributes updated findings, but also helps normalize the use of such devices.

1 Introduction

In 1998 Pentland observed that personal electronic devices were making a transition from luggable to wearable (Pentland 1998). In 2015 we expanded this to show the progression toward, and proposed a new category of, emerging devices within the body called insertables (Heffernan et al. 2015). Olarte-Pascual et al. (2015) also note this growing trend towards what they call "insideables". This progression began with medical devices becoming wearable and then implantable, for example, pacemakers. We, as a society, then became more comfortable with objects inside the body for convenience, illustrated by those used for menstrual and contraceptive purposes. This trajectory is explained in detail elsewhere (Heffernan et al. 2017). Individuals then began modifying their bodies with "subdermal or transdermal implants" (Graafstra et al. 2010). The difference with these latter devices, over implantable ones, is that they are no longer restorative nor medical in nature, but voluntarily inserted for non-medical uses. These are predominantly in the form of Radio Frequency Identification (RFID) and Near Field Communication (NFC) microchips.

Earlier research (Britton and Semaan 2017; Heffernan et al. 2016) explores small samples of individuals who fit Stebbins (1982) definition of hobbyist, in that they are "makers and tinkerers". Some of these have become professionals creating a "consumer market" for insertable devices (Britton and Semaan 2017; Stebbins 1982). In terms of Rogers' diffusion of innovations theory (Rogers and Shoemaker 1971) these are the "innovators". They have paved the way for, and their publicity has increased the knowledge of, insertable devices. This has engendered (very) early adopters to begin using them.

There are growing numbers of very early adopters beginning to use these devices, moving beyond only the first makers and hobbyists who pioneered the phenomenon. While there are thousands of individuals using these devices (Petersén 2018), percentagewise they still cannot be considered "mainstream". Due to this, it is too early to research adoption. Instead what is more appropriate is research into the users of the devices; what they are using and why, as well as their motivations and self-identity. This research looks at a larger sample than previous research ($n = 115$) which allows us to more accurately understand users of these nascent devices.

This chapter is organized as follows. First background material is presented to situate the research. Then the research design is explained, and results are presented. The discussion explores the growing use of insertable devices and the implications of the ways in which insertable-users refer to and understand themseleves. We end with calls for future research and summarize the contributions of this chapter.

2   Background

To situate the research, we provide a background of devices which are permanently, or for long periods of time, placed within the human body. We briefly explore a history of body modifications, medical devices, and insertables. To understand motivations, we also present an overview of why individuals use such devices, and how these users identify.

2.1   *What Goes in the Body and for What Purposes?*

Humans have been augmenting their bodies for millennia—from tattooing and scarification in 3000BCE ancient Egypt (Levy et al. 1979) to lip disks seen in African tribes from 8000 BCE (Keddie 1989) and body piercings since biblical times (Genesis 24:22). These ritualistic practices still continue today. A woman's worth, and how mature she is, is determined by how large her lip disk is (Seeger 1975). Body augmentation for aesthetic reasons is still present in modernity. Britton (2017) explores "a community of DIY cyborgs" and relies heavily on body modification literature to explain their use of insertables. The difference between insertables, and these more traditional body modifications, is that they do not just sit on the surface of the skin or pierce the flesh; they are completely inside the body. Another difference, over other body modifications, is that individuals are not merely making aesthetic changes. They are instead "remaking the human body through the aid of technology" (Munn et al. 2016).

Remaking oneself with objects inside the body is also not new: ancient Egyptians had dental implants (Irish 2004) and the first joint reconstruction occurred in 1821 (Gomez and Morcuende 2005). A plethora of restorative devices are placed inside the confines of the body: pacemakers and stents are lifesaving, while prostheses and cochlear implants restore individuals with "deficiencies" to a perceived "normal" state. These devices are now acceptable, as their restorative purposes are perceived to outweigh any unnaturalness. Yet, when these devices were first introduced, they were seen as an affront to what is "right" and natural. Even eyeglasses were "hotly debated in their time" (Pentland 1998) as they were unnaturally changing the "god given" body. Today there is no social stigma associated with spectacles. Indeed, we may even laugh at the notion that there ever was. Contact lenses and even Lasik laser eye surgery are now acceptable. The difference with insertables is that they are not medical nor restorative.

Objects, too, are already placed inside the body for non-restorative purposes; for example, cosmetic surgery in the form of various implants are not always restorative–dental, breast, buttocks, etc. While not everyone agrees with these procedures, nor would personally choose to undergo one, the practice itself is widely accepted at a societal level. Such procedures can be considered relatively common; in 2017 alone there were an estimated 170,000 breast implants and 36,000 buttocks implants globally (International Society of Aesthetic Plastic Surgery (ISAPS) 2015). Similarly, placing objects inside the body for convenience-based purposes, such as menstrual aids and contraception, are also accepted. Worldwide approximately 1% of women of reproductive age have a contraceptive implant (Alkema et al. 2013) and 14% have an intrauterine contraceptive device (Buhling 2014).

The uses of objects discussed in this section are clear; they are inserted into the body for lifesaving, restorative, cosmetic, or contraceptive purposes. We, as a society, have become more comfortable and accepting of devices being placed inside the body—first for restorative purposes, then for convenience based purposes. This has engendered the use of insertable devices. We have not discussed devices for sexual purposes, as they are only temporarily inside the body. The objects discussed in this section are inside the body permanently, or for extended periods of time. However, the availability of such sexual objects also illustrates the social-norm of devices inside the body as acceptable. With this comfort, some are now more permanently placing entirely non-medical devices inside their bodies.

2.2 Insertables for Augmented Perception and Cognition

This subsection provides examples of devices individuals are experimenting with to augment their senses, outside of medical and research settings. Neil Harbisson has an antenna in his head that allows him to "hear" color, including the infrared and UV spectrum (Harbisson 2012). Manel Muñoz has sensors implanted that allow him to feel changes in atmospheric pressure (OGGIONNI 2018). An image of Harbisson and Muñoz' augmentations is available in Fig. 1. Moon Ribas has implanted a "seismic sensor" that vibrates when there is an earthquake. This allows her to "feel" when they occur (Harrison et al. 2010). Harbisson, Muñoz and Ribas also work with the Transspecies Society to develop, what they call, "sensory organs". Their goal is not to make us transhuman, but to make us transspecies. They aim to achieve this by adding senses other species have, and which humans do not innately, through the use of implants (The Transspecies Society 2018). Examples of this include: giving humans magnetic senses akin to pigeons (Keeton et al. 1974), Harbisson's ability to perceive infrared and UV as bees can (Bradley-Munn and Gould 1979) and Muñoz's ability to detect atmospheric pressure like homing pigeons (Kreithen and Keeton 1974).

Tim Cannon implanted a large deck-of-card sized device in his forearm. This device could read his temperature and pulse and transmit these readings, via Bluetooth, to his smartphone. The device was equipped with an LED light to backlight his tattoo (see Fig. 2). This device, called Circadia, was a timeboxed proof-of-concept experiment to demonstrate the device could transmit data through the body.

Cannon's company, Grindhouse Wetware, went on to develop the North Star (shown in Fig. 3). The North Star Version 1 has LEDs, that turn on for a short period of time when a magnet is placed over the device. Magnets are also often inserted in the other hand to activate the lights more easily. This device contains a non-rechargeable

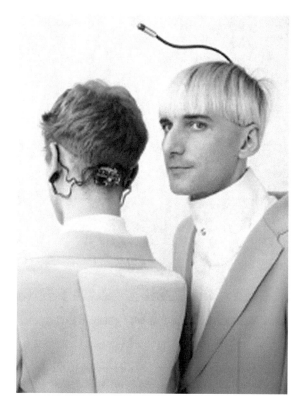

Fig. 1 Harbisson & Muñoz's Augmentations (Tse 2018)

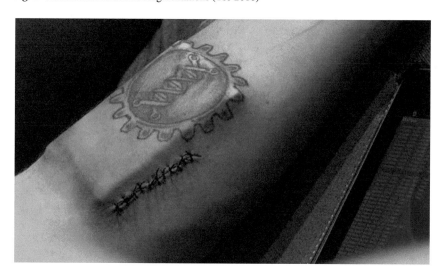

Fig. 2 Circadia implant (Photo Supplied)

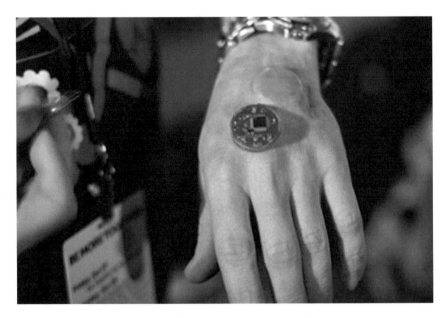

Fig. 3 North star show implanted and outside the body (Einhorn 2017)

battery, so eventually stops working. It was available to a small number of beta testers and had only an aesthetic use (Bradley-Munn and Michael 2016).

Rich Lee has attempted to implant "armor" in his legs in the form of a non-Newtonian fluid. This would harden when struck with force. He has since had this armor removed. Also with limited success, he has magnets in the tragus of his ear to use as "implanted headphones". Conceptually, sound from a worn coil would be transmitted to these magnets, which then function as "speakers" (Doerksen 2007).

None of the devices above is commercially available. Rather they are bespoke devices oft created avant-garde by the person who will have them inserted.

Despite news articles claiming so, insertables for memory or cognition do not exist. For example, research into stimulating long-term memory with electrodes, in rats, was extrapolated to name human memory implants as one of the 10 break-through technologies of 2013 (Cohen 2013). Neuralink's brain–machine interface is speculative research, and is intended for restorative purposes, not augmentation in healthy individuals (Musk et al. 2019).

Pelegrin-Borondo et al. (2017) present tenuous links from news articles as proof of insertables. Nonetheless, their research is still an important contribution which investigates the interest in, and acceptance of, insertables. The researchers do acknowledge that most of the insertables they research remain in the future. Their research gives insight into potential acceptance of future insertable devices that may, or may not, come to fruition. They specifically look at insertables that could enhance human capabilities—i.e., future devices—not extant insertables.

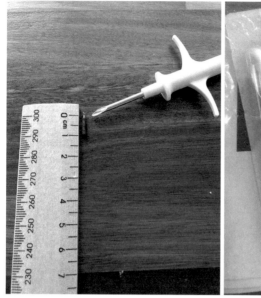

(a) NFC Microchip (Photo by Author)   (b) Magnet (Photo by Author)

Fig. 4   A NFC microchip and a magnet

Current commercially available insertables are RFID and NFC microchips (see Fig. 4a and magnets (see Fig. 4b). RFID and NFC use radio waves to communicate information wirelessly. The difference between them is that they each use a different frequency to do so. These technologies are used in many office access passes, public transport passes, passports, etc. The insertable versions of these microchips are passive, meaning they have no battery. They are powered only when they are placed in front of the correct reader. This gives them enough energy to transmit data back to the reader. To be inserted subdermally, they are much smaller than cards or passes and thus have much smaller antennas with cylindrical coiling. This results in these devices having very short read ranges—in the magnitude of centimeters.

In addition to individuals augmenting their bodies, described above, we documented 17 individuals in Heffernan et al. (2016) using RFID microchips and NFC microchips ($n = 12$) and magnets ($n = 11$). This research found microchips were used for practical purposes. These were

- Access and authentication to buildings (homes and offices), vehicles (cars and motorcycles), and devices (phones and laptops);
- Storing information for self-recall or sharing with others, and;
- Temperature readings (Heffernan et al. 2016).

Microchips only provide augmentation in the sense that they allow individuals to do things that others cannot. They do not augment the user's perception or cognition. Magnets, on the other hand, were found to provide sensorial expansion as they

- "Vibrate when they come into contact with electromagnetic fields" allowing users to "feel" such fields;
- Enhance human connection, and;
- Support alternative digital interactions (Heffernan et al. 2016).

These magnets are used to augment human perception by allowing them to feel an extra dimension of the world (electromagnetic fields) that we humans otherwise cannot.

2.3 Why Do People Use Devices Inside the Body?

The trajectory toward devices inside the body, in the medical field, has "increased the perception that bodies can be modified and, thus, expanded the very concept of what it means to be human" (Lai 2012). This has been a catalyst for other non-medical insertable devices to become acceptable. Indeed, we have already seen this with the rise of elective surgeries, whereby people modify their bodies. When something in the body is not working as expected, or desired, we can improve or augment ourselves back to a perceived "normal".

The motivations for individuals placing traditional objects within the body are relatively straight forward–lifesaving or restorative (i.e., medical devices), convenience (e.g., contraception) or aesthetic (e.g., silicone implants, piercings or contacts). There is also an argument to be made that objects are an extension of the self (Csikszentmihalyi 1993). This is of particular interest when these objects are voluntarily placed within the body. The body can become an evolving, ongoing project (Shilling 2004) (p. 305) with the use of devices shaping "our interactions and agency" (Vaisutis et al. 2014a).

With regard to inserting the nascent devices this research is concerned with, public discourse around the purpose of these often focuses on biohackers wanting to be "cyborgs" (Petersén 2018). In academic literature, human enhancement is mentioned as a motivator by some individuals (Britton and Semaan 2017; Heffernan et al. 2016) who see insertable devices as the next stage of human evolution. These individuals want to enhance themselves to extend human capabilities. Others speak of motivations of identification, convenience, or control (Graafstra et al. 2010; Michael 2010). Graafstra et al. (2010) claim "hundreds of people have embarked on a mission to interact with their mobile phones, their cars, and their house via a chip implant, providing personalized settings for their own ultimate convenience." The former manager of the Baja Beach Club Barcelona speaks of their VIP Microchip program; microchips have "unrivaled convenience" due to not needing to "carry cash or credit on oneself or a physical purse" (Michael and Michael 2010). He speaks of the VIP members experiences' saying, "this was perceived to be of greater benefit to females, whose apparel generally is not fitted with secure deep pockets" and "I would feel very relieved as a consumer if all this would happen. I just want to be free of the extras that are a nuisance" (Michael and Michael 2010).

Indeed, users want "faster, more natural and convenient means... to transmit information to a computer" (Jacob 1996). They are looking for natural user interfaces that allow for input without "explicitly drawing user's attention" (Hettiarachchi et al. 2014). Such ubiquitous devices must be "small and unobtrusive" and "comfortable to an extent its existence could be forgotten" (Kao et al. 2015). Mann (1997) also notes that users should look as "normal" as possible while wearing and using them. Further, Lupton (2014) quotes designer Jennifer Darmour saying, "objects need to be designed more carefully so that they may be "seamlessly" integrated into the "fabric of our lives." A way to meet these design constraints is by having no devices at all through the "integration of functions into objects that we do not feel clutter us, which are part of our life" (Wallace 2003) or as part of the two things that are always with us: clothing and our actual bodies (Michael and Michael 2006). Similarly, Holz et al. (2012) identify that only interfaces under the skin are truly always available.

2.4   Identity of Users of Insertable Devices

Individuals are inserting passive RFID and NFC microchips into their bodies (Heffernan et al. 2016; Katina Michael and Michael 2005). These devices do not have battery or sensors, nor do they integrate with the body (they are simply placed inside it). Yet these cause the media and social commentators to claim the rise of cyborgs and an eminent dystopian demise of society as we know it (Cheer 2020; Ledford 2010; Ungerleider 2012); Witze 2013). The media portrays these individuals as "wetware hackers," "citizen science hobby biologists," or "biohackers" (Cheer 2020; Ledford 2010; Petersén 2018; Ungerleider 2012; Witze 2013). Ip et al. (2008) refer to them as an "underground" movement "ignoring criticism from various conservative groups to implement and practice the new body art of RFID implanting." Graafstra et al. (2010) describes insertable users as "technically-savvy citizens... predominantly interested in novel convenience-oriented solutions." DIY implantees, techno-hobbyists, transhumanists, cyber-punks, do-it-yourselfers, hobbyists, midnight engineers, grinders, bio-punks (Bahney 2006; Britton and Semaan 2017; Foster and Jaeger 2007; Graafstra et al. 2010)—the list of names for these users go on. These names are imposed from the outside, regardless of whether the actual individuals using these devices agree with the term. We include more literature in the results, where it is pertinent to help understand the terms individuals are using.

2.5   Research Gap

Thus far in this chapter, we have presented a history of objects and devices that go inside the body permanently, or for long periods of time. We have discussed nascent insertable devices. We have also presented current knowledge as to why people choose to use such devices and how they identify. This previous research presented is either using small samples (Britton and Semaan 2017; Graafstra et al. 2010; Heffernan et al. 2016; Michael 2010; Michael and Michael 2010) or is speculative regarding prototypes (Holz et al. 2012).

What this practice looks like now, beyond the early innovators, is not yet documented in academic literature. This research looks at currently extant devices, which are commercially available, and explores reasons for using them. It uses a larger sample than previous research, as the number of individuals using these devices has grown. We will answer, more accurately and representative of the (very) early adopters:

1. What devices are individuals putting in their bodies;
2. What do they use these devices for;
3. What are the motivations for modifying their bodies in this way, and;
4. How do users of these devices identify themselves?

We will explore the self-identity of these users, rather than labeling them from the outside. Certainly, as more people get inserted with these devices, they can no longer all be on the fringes. As a means of comparison, tattoos and piercings are no longer just for "punks" but businessmen alike–getting a tattoo does not a punk make. Insertables may no longer just be confined to a fringe movement or group. Is augmentation, or convenience, the motivator for these emergent users? This research is important as it will more accurately document the practice. It also contributes to normalizing the use of insertable devices if they are no longer seen as extremists on the fringes.

2.5.1   Research Scope and Significance

This research is only concerned with insertable devices that go in, through and underneath the skin defined as per Heffernan et al. (2017). All other devices are out of scope. Even contraceptives that can be inserted by a user (e.g., diaphragms, female condoms, vaginal rings) still have a quasi-medical use, so are excluded from this research. We also exclude piercings without a digital component.

With the number of devices that can be inserted increasing, the number of people receiving them has thusly increased significantly (Harrison 2015; Reinares-Lara et al. 2016). This research is motivated to understand uses, motivations, and identity with the growing users of these devices. While the use is still niche, there are thousands of users and this is growing everyday. Understanding the current applications, and the perceived benefits to users, contributes a representative understanding of the practice now, as opposed to older research earlier in the adoption cycle. Additionally, this may aid additional growth of users, and applications.

3 Research Design

Two data collection techniques were employed—interviews and a survey. First, interviews were utilized to understand, in-depth, participant's experiences and perceptions. Interviews allowed us to understand the landscape of insertables use, in participants terms, for rich context. Interviews do not impose assumed categorizations which may limit data yielded. After 23 interviews were conducted, it became increasingly difficult to recruit. This is likely due to the limited number of people with insertable devices and geographic, time-zone, and language barriers making interviews difficult. A survey was devised to gather a depth of data in a more palatable way for more participants. 92 valid responses were received to the survey. This also gives a quantitative orientation to the qualitative interview data. The data were analyzed thematically in an inductive approach to draw themes from qualitative comments. The methodology of each is described in this section, and participant demographics presented.

3.1 Interview Methodology

The interviews were conducted by the first author with 23 individuals known to have, or previously have had, insertable devices. Interviews began in March 2015 and have been ongoing; however, the majority were conducted in 2015. Recruitment was via advertisements on special interest forums (biohack me), Facebook groups (RFID Implantees, RFID implantees—Australia/ New Zealand, Magnetic Implants), tweeted on Twitter using relevant hashtags, and organized through direct contact with individuals known to have insertable devices. The interviews were semi-structured and conversational in nature, with a general outline of the questions to be asked followed where appropriate, but flexibly changed based on responses given. The interviews were recorded and later transcribed by the first author. Any additional notes taken during the course of the interviews were added as memos. For example, demonstrations of using the insertable devices, any difficulties encountered (e.g., slow reading of microchips), and descriptions of device locations which were pointed out non-verbally during interviews.

3.2 Survey Methodology

The survey questions were formulated based on the face-to-face interviews. The survey was opened for a trial period of 7 days and shared with colleagues to validate the logic and to remove ambiguities. Minor changes were made based on this feedback. The survey was opened for just over a month (May to June 2016) to any participant with the survey link. This link was sent in direct emails to individuals with whom interviews had fallen through. It was also advertised on forums, Facebook, and Twitter as described in the interview methodology above. Participants were also recruited from snowballing, whereby participants shared the survey with other individuals known to have insertables, or on their own social media channels.

The response data were scrubbed. The data scrubbing process involved:

- Checking for internal consistencies within the responses. One participant had indicated that they did not have insertables, but answers indicated that they did; this was manually corrected. One participant indicated that they did not have any magnets, but later answers revealed they did; this was also manually corrected.
- Removing participants who had not provided consent (1).
- Removing duplicate responses, identified by email address (4).
- Removing participants who had abandoned the survey before answering any questions (14) or had not answered enough questions to be deemed useful (10).
- Removing participants who did not have insertables (e.g., had implantable medical devices or had purchased insertable devices but not yet inserted them (18)). This included one participant with a contraceptive implant: while we can argue this is an insertable, and they held the belief it was, they are not included in the scope of this research. It is interesting that these participants discovered the survey and opted in to responding to it—do they identify as "insertable users"?

3.3 Participant Demographics

Table 1 shows the demographic breakdown of all participants. Demographic data is incomplete as some participants answered in-depth about their first insertable device and then abandoned the survey. They were therefore not presented demographic questions. Due to this, no results have been presented by demographic data.

The majority of participants were male, in line with Heffernan et al. (2016) which also saw more male respondents using insertables than females. Both the age, and gender, demographics are similar between each cohort, showing that the samples are complementary to each other. The mode age was 35 across both cohorts, and the average age of both was within just 1.5 years of each other.

Location data is incomplete as 22% of respondents did not specify one. For the interview cohort, fewer countries were represented, likely due to the location of the researcher causing time-zone barriers. Language requirements (English) may have also skewed the geographic breakdown. A survey is easier to respond to in one's non-native language and can be done at their convenience. The survey cohort still showed a majority of participants in North America and Oceania. This may be due to the groups the survey was shared with, and the fact that the survey was in English. Recruiting via these forums may also skew toward people who identify in a certain way, as they voluntarily joined these special interest groups. There is known to be a large population of insertables users in Sweden (Petersén 2018), so it is interesting they are not represented in the survey respondents.

Table 1 Demographic summary of participants

Demographic	Interview $n = 23$ (%)	Survey $n = 92$ (%)	Total $n = 115$ (%)
Gender	87 male	60 male	65 male
	13 female	15 female	15 female
		5 non-binary	3 non-binary
		20 not specified	17 not specified
Age	Mean ± SD	Mean ± SD	Mean ± SD
	32.5 ± 2.98	31.4 ± 1.82	31.6 ± 1.57
	35 (mode)	35 (mode)	35 (mode)
	18 (min)	17 (min)	17 (min)
	47 (max)	51 (max)	51 (max)
Location	48 North America	38 North America	41 North America
	47 Oceania	11 Oceania	18 Oceania
	4 UK	15 UK	13 UK
	1 other	12 Europe	9 Europe
	2 other	2 other	
	22 not specified	17 not specified	

Given the similarities between the two groups, the majority of findings in this chapter are presented combined. Where it is notable to break down the results by cohort, this is clearly stated.

4 Results

We begin by presenting findings of the establishments where participants purchased and inserted their devices. This illustrates the growing nature of insertables use. Next, we present the types of devices people are inserting into their bodies. We report on those inserting multiple devices—both more than one of the same device type and different device types. Third, we detail the uses of said devices. Fourth, we record the motivations reported for inserting these devices. Fifth, we describe the self-identification reported by participants. We briefly explore the limitations of these devices. Lastly, we document the future intentions of participants.

4.1 Purchasing and Inserting Devices

This section presents findings regarding purchasing and inserting devices. This includes where the devices were purchased and inserted. We also report on where in the body the devices are. The findings here are broken down by cohort, where appropriate, and clearly identified. This demonstrates the growing nature of insertables used to situate the need for this research.

4.1.1 Purchasing Insertable Devices

Table 2 presents from where participants purchased their insertable devices. This finding is broken down by cohort.

The interview cohort mainly purchased devices from leading online retailer Dangerous Things (www.dangerousthings.com) or directly from the body modification studio where they were getting the device inserted. For the survey cohort, conducted later, these remained the top sources of insertables. However, many more online retailers were mentioned. 16% used other online sources including Chip my life, Digiwell, Freevision Corp, Trossen Robotics, Sleep all day (now defunct), and Star Security Technologies. This shows the growing popularity of these devices. More suppliers are being created as demand, and interest, grows.

4.1.2 Insertion Setting

Table 3 shows which provider participants used to have their devices placed into their bodies. This finding is also shown broken down by cohort.

For the interview cohort, the majority had their devices inserted at body modification or tattoo studios—see Fig. 5. However, the survey cohort was much more likely to self-insert, with over double taking this option (21%). The survey cohort was also

Table 2 Purchasing location of insertables

Purchase location	Interview ($n = 23$) (%)	Survey ($n = 92$) (%)
DangerousThings.com	46	42
Other online retailer	1	16
Body modification studio	26	31
Directly from the manufacture	9	10
Not specified	18	1

Table 3 Insertion setting

Insertion setting	Interview ($n = 23$) (%)	Survey ($n = 92$) (%)
Body modification studio	61	55
Friend	12	16
Doctor/GP	6	5
Self-inserted	10	21
Not specified	11	3

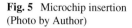

Fig. 5 Microchip insertion
(Photo by Author)

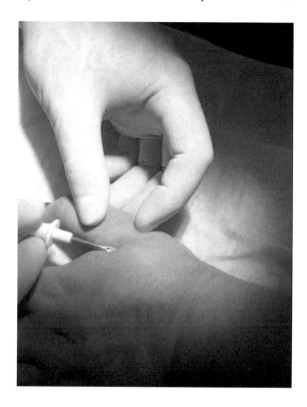

slightly more likely to get a friend to insert. "Friends" included those with no medical, or body modification, training (8%), a person with some medical training, e.g.,
as an EMT or nurse (5%) and someone with previous experience inserting but not
accredited, e.g., the founder of insertable companies who have had much practice
(3%). This shows that with the growing number of online suppliers, and availability
of devices, consumers may be more likely to self-insert.

With this growing number of suppliers, it follows that more people are inserted
every year. The survey data collection was completed midway through 2016, and
21 respondents had inserted that year. The mode year ($n = 24$) was 2014, with the
earliest reported insertion date as 2005. Additional devices were inserted as early as
2010, with the average again 2014.

4.1.3 Body Part Affected by Insertion

The webbing of the hand (see Fig. 6) remains the most popular location for microchips
(70%) as per Heffernan et al. (2016), with over half of these in the left hand. Similarly,
for magnets the fingertip was still the most common placement with the left being
most common. This is likely due to the piercer/body modification artist suggesting

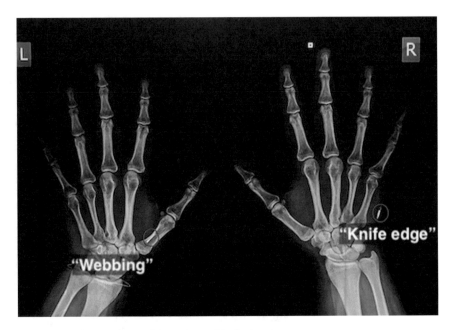

Fig. 6 Standard microchip position (X-ray of Author)

the non-dominant hand. They do this to ensure better healing due to less impact. Given the majority of people are right handed, the left is most common for insertion.

Non-standard placements for devices included are as follows:

- 2 microchips in the fingers;
- 1 magnet in the tragus of the ear;
- 1 RFID in the shoulder;
- 1 microchip (not specified) in the back;
- 1 RFID in the forearm;
- 1 magnet in the big toe;
- 1 bio-therm microchip (for temperature reading) in the armpit, and;
- 1 RFID microchip in the earlobe through a piercing (see Fig. 7).

It is not clear why respondents choose these non-standard locations. For microchips, the hand affords flexibility to place the device in front of a reader. For magnets, they must be inserted near nerve endings, making finger tips ideal.

This increased availability of online companies to purchase from, resulted in the survey cohort being more likely to self-insert. There were, however, no differences regarding insertion procedure, rejection, or body part chosen, showing the standard positions of the webbing of the hand for microchips and fingertips for magnets is now established and remains static.

Fig. 7 Microchip through piercing (Photo Supplied by Participant)

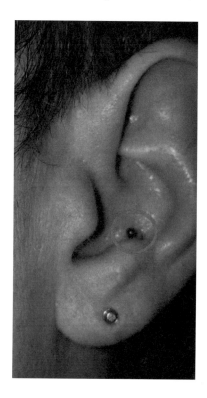

5 Insertable Devices

Above we have shown that participants are purchasing and inserting devices into their bodies. This section presents findings regarding the type of devices that they are inserting. This helps us understand question 1—what devices individuals are placing inside their bodies. We also present findings of those who have multiple devices inserted.

5.1 Insertable Device Types

Here we will present what devices participants had inserted into their bodies. We also provide a description of the capabilities of each device, to aid understanding.

As shown in Table 4 NFC Microchips are the most popular form of insertables among participants. NFC microchips are able to be read by Android, and newer iOS, devices. It follows that they are the most common and given they are the most accessible to read and write. Off the shelf NFC solutions also exist for physical

Table 4 Device type inserted

Device	Percentage of participants (%)	Count
Magnet	57	54
NFC microchip	64	74
RFID microchip	50	57
Other	8	9

and logical access, further increasing their appeal. RFID microchips, the next most common, tend to also represent access. A user can replace an existing pass with an insertable. They use this for RFID building access systems.

57% had magnets in situ. This is of interest as while the microchips have practical uses (access and authentication or to launch items) the magnets, for the majority, do not offer a tangible use. Magnets augment human perception by allowing the users to "feel" electricity. A minority of participants do use this sensation in their day-to-day jobs; for picking up small metallic objects or to check whether cables are "live" with electricity. However, the majority use them purely for augmented perception.

Only 8% of the sample had other devices. These include

- 1 large bespoke device for body temperature;
- 2 North Star implants, as described in Insertables for Augmented Perception and Cognition (see Fig. 8a);
- 1 "Firefly tattoo" implant—an inserted capsule, of similar size as the microchips, containing the radioactive element Tritium which glows in the dark (see Fig. 8b);
- Diamonds (presumably as dental implants, however not specified), and;
- The Nexplanon birth control implant.

Two respondents had devices inside their bodies for medical purposes: one subdermal contraceptive implant (a minimally invasive procedure akin to the process for inserting microchips), and one a pacemaker. These are arguably very different devices—the individual choosing the Nexplanon contraceptive likely did so for convenience, while the respondent with a pacemaker had little choice in the matter. On the continuum of devices proposed in Heffernan et al. (2017), recreated in Fig. 9, the contraceptive device is an interesting case blurring the lines between implantable and insertable. It is removable, voluntary and often convenience-based, unlike the pacemaker. However, it is also prescribed, must be inserted by a medical professional and has a medical interaction. Both these participants were interested in getting digital insertables. The participant with the pacemaker had already purchased an insertable device (not specified) but was still waiting to have it inserted as they had not found someone to do so. Similarly, two additional respondents had purchased devices but not yet inserted, even though they were planning to. The data from these four were excluded from analysis.

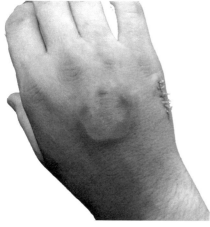
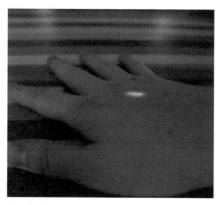

(a) North Star (Photo by Author)   (b) Firefly 'Tattoo' Long exposure photo
                                          from participant

Fig. 8 North star and firefly "Tattoo"

Fig. 9 Continuum of
devices within the body
(Heffernan et al. 2017)

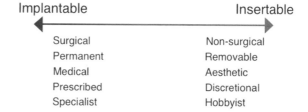

Implantable	Insertable
Surgical	Non-surgical
Permanent	Removable
Medical	Aesthetic
Prescribed	Discretional
Specialist	Hobbyist

5.1.1 Multiple Devices Inserted

This section presents participants who have more than one device inserted. It looks at the number of participants who have each type of device. We also present those who have each combination of device—i.e., not the actual number of devices themselves. For example, 18 have magnets only, but some of these have more than one magnet.

A visualization of this is presented in Fig. 10. The numbers do not add up to 115 ($n = 112$) as three participants had only other devices. Similarly, the sum of figures of each type of device is greater than the total number of participants, as participants have multiple devices. The average number of devices in a participant was 2.4. There were 269 discrete devices inside the 115 participants.

Participants who have two kinds of microchips do so as NFC and RFID have differing frequencies which can be used for access to different systems. What is of interest is the 36 participants who have a microchip (of either type) with a magnet—as for the majority magnets have no practical use. These participants are likely more interested in augmentation. This will be explored in the discussion.

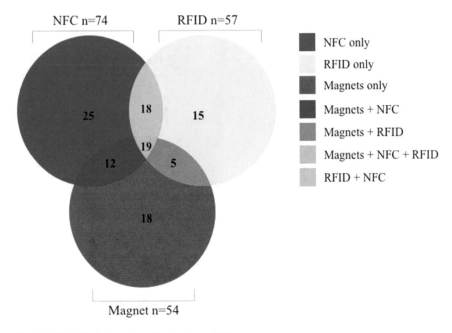

Fig. 10 Multiple devices visualization ($n = 112$)

Table 5 Multiples of the same device type

Device type	Percentage (%)	Count ($n = 115$)
>1 Magnet	49	28
>1 NFC microchip	15	12
>1 RFID microchip	32	19
>1 Other	0	0

What is also of interest is the participants who have more than one of the same devices inserted—see Table 5. Participants who have multiple different devices do so as each device offers a different function. For example, an RFID microchip may be used for access to one existing security system and an NFC microchip for access to another (e.g., work and home). NFC-based systems are also cheaper and easier to purchase and install for home access. As for multiple devices of the same type of microchip—it is probable this is due to the systems which they are using the devices to access. Each microchip can only hold one unique ID (UID). If the users do not have access to add their UID to a security system as a valid token, then they may need another microchip. This would have the UID of the security system cloned onto it to be accepted as a valid token.

Multiple magnets are reported to make electromagnetic fields "feel" different, and to allow the user to feel the "shape" of the electricity.

5.2   Insertables Usage

Now that we understand what devices participants are putting into their bodies, we can explore the uses of these. This section answers question 2 What do people use insertable devices for. See Table 6 for these uses. An initial understanding of what insertable devices were used for was discovered in the earlier interviews, reported in Heffernan et al. (2016). Here the survey has added a quantitative edge to the most common uses. The survey data allows us to report the more common uses of insertable devices. These are: access and authentication ($n = 92$); storing and sharing information ($n = 91$); and extending senses ($n = 15$). The smaller interview cohort surfaced what are now known to be edge uses of insertables to: support human connections ($n = 2$); act as an alternative digital interface ($n = 2$); and to capture biometric data in the form of body temperature ($n = 3$).

Four participants reported that they used their RFID to share information. It is important to note that traditionally RFID can only store an ID. These participants have either answered incorrectly or have a microchip with both RFID and NFC components (for example, the Dangerous Things' NExT).

Overall, we can group these reported uses into two broad categories: convenience and amenity, and sensory augmentation.

5.2.1   Convenience and Amenity

We classify access and authentication and storing and sharing information as amenity-based uses. This section describes what specific uses fall under these broad categories. We also explore other practical uses reported by participants.

Access and Authentication

The majority (76%) of respondents use their devices for access, including

- Home access (66%);
- Office access (44%);

Table 6   Insertable device usages

Usage	RFID	NFC	Magnet
Home access	19	22	N/A
Office access	16	6	N/A
Phone access	7	37	N/A
Computer access	13	18	N/A
Vehicle access	14	18	N/A
Share information	4	41	N/A
Launch items	2	26	N/A
Other	2	4	28

Fig. 11 Using a microchip
for access (Photo by Author)

- Phone access–NFC only (70%);
- Computer access (62%), and;
- Vehicle access (38%).

These participants are exclusively using NFC or RFID microchips, depending on the type of system, lock or peripheral they have. Only NFC can be used to unlock phones, as RFID is not available in these devices; even then NFC is only in some compatible smartphones. A peripheral device is currently needed to be able to unlock computers, as this function is not built in to available devices either. Modifications are required to enable vehicle access, as cars also do not have NFC locks as standard (Fig. 11).

Storing and Sharing Information
70% of respondents use their device to store and share information. 48% use it to launch items on Smartphones, either for their own use or to share with someone. Once again, this is only available to those using microchips. What was not asked was how often they actually do, or can, share information with others in practice. We did not ask participants this as self-reported data estimating how many times they shared a contact, sometimes over a decade, is not reliable data. Being able to share information requires the intended recipient to have a compatible device with NFC switched on. For RFID microchips, a compatible reader is not built into any mainstream devices; therefore, an external reader is needed to scan them.

Some launch items on their own phones, for personal use, such as apps or websites (e.g., Pokémon Go, 2-factor authentication, Facebook, Google, SMS app with a template message ready to send, Email, calculator, etc.). These are apps participants use often. They do not want to have to search through screens of apps to find it.

Fig. 12 Sharing information
with an NFC microchip
(Photo by Jesper Hede)

Instead they simply scan their microchip and the item launches, saving time and effort. Some participants have their devices connected to microcontrollers to control custom projects, including one art installation. One participant had configured their device to launch different tasks based on the time of day and their location. It is important to note that the logic for this is all stored on the phone; all the microchips do launch the task to start.

> Sometimes I'll write useful information onto the chip, so I always have it 'on hand'.–Survey Response 79

Some participants have information stored on their microchip for sharing with other people. This includes opening things "to prove you have it" (e.g., a funny message, a YouTube Rick Roll, etc.). Others use it as a way to share useful content (e.g., LinkedIn profile, contact details for networking, Instagram pages or other websites, etc.). One participant stores their BTC (bitcoin) address, another cryptographic material, while another stores medical information for their own consumption and reference (Fig. 12).

Other Practical Uses

46% of participants selected "other" when asked what they used their device for. Only 6 of these (17%) were for practical uses.

One participant had cloned a festival wristband onto their microchip. This allowed them to use this instead, to scan themselves into stages.

A minority of magnet users have found practical uses for these. This includes "feeling" whether items are working. This was noted by some participants as occasionally being useful. For three participants, who were electricians, this was seen as always useful. Other practical uses included being able to pick up items with the magnet, such as small screws, which can help participants find them easier if they are dropped. The screens on modern laptops are placed in sleep mode when they are closed. The mechanics behind this are based on magnets; when the screen magnet comes into contact with the keyboard magnet (to the left of the caps lock key) the screen turns off. Participants with magnets can achieve this by placing their finger in this spot. This occasionally has a practical use for them, to hide what they are looking at if required.

> When a desk lamp wasn't working anymore, I was troubleshooting whether it was just the lightbulb or whether the lamp itself was defective. I was able to feel the electromagnetic field from the base of the lamp, so I concluded that the lamp itself was fine, but the lightbulb needed to be replaced.–Survey Response 75

> When I'm working with hardware (computers, soldering, etc.), I can pick up the severed component leads and tiny screws easily.–Survey Response 25

> I wanted to be able to sense magnetic fields. I am an electronic engineer, so I deal with electrical fields all the time. Sensing these fields all the time has allowed me to troubleshoot high power electronics faster than someone who cannot sense fields.– Survey Response 16

The firefly tattoo is used as a "built in torch", however in practice this is only used aesthetically to backlight tattoos. The light is not strong enough to provide a practical purpose. This is illustrated by the fact that participants could not, as an example, use it to find a keyhole in the dark. Three participants were experimenting with building external devices that could be used with their magnets to feel other signals, e.g., vibrate with a proximity sensor, or to be used as "implanted headphones".

> The one in my tragus is really cool because we did some stuff with Arduino and an inductor and I was able to hear tones, it was really a cool thing because it sounds like it's coming from inside your head rather than through your ears like it does with headphones, so that was pretty cool."–Interview Participant 16

5.2.2 Sensory Augmentation

It could be argued that being able to perform the above practical uses from insertables can be considered human augmentation. Individuals without these devices cannot perform these actions without peripherals or other objects. 24% (16 participants) with magnets did use the devices for sensory augmentation in a more traditional sense—to expand what they are able to feel. They have increased their perception to include an extra sense, from within their body, that others do not have.

> "Basically, I got it to feel fields, that's what was most interesting to me. It's not really a practical skill it's more 'look at what we can do, science is great' kind of thing.–Interview Participant 6

The majority of uses of magnets are for sensory augmentation enabling them to sense electromagnetic fields. Another use is to perform "bar tricks" without a practical use (see Fig. 13).

Fig. 13 Lifting a hair clip
with an inserted magnet
(Photo by Author)

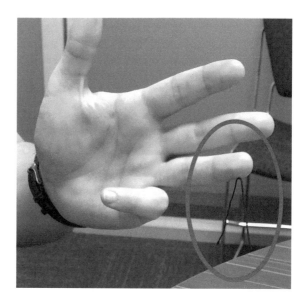

5.3 Motivations for Using Insertables

What participants use these devices for, as above, could be used to infer their motivations. However, as we endeavor to avoid wrongly stating these, participants were asked why they chose an insertable. This helps us answer question 3—what are the motivations for using insertable devices. In the survey, this question was a free text response for respondents to explain their motivations. Free text was chosen as to not impose categorizations which may not reflect participants' true motivations. Some participants mentioned multiple reasons, which were then coded into multiple themes. Resultant themes, along with the rationale for each, are shown in Table 7. These reasons fall into the overarching themes of convenience and amenity, cyborgs and augmentation, and other.

5.3.1 Convenience and Amenity

The number one response given for using insertables is that they are permanent (47%). That is, until they are explicitly removed. In Heffernan et al. (2016) we refer to this as "permanent impermanence"—the devices can be removed but they are also always available until such a time. 6% explicitly stated they like that these devices are hidden.

Table 7 Reasons for choosing an insertable

Coded theme	Theme description	Count	Percentage (%)
Convenience and amenity			
Permanence and convenience	Devices cannot be lost, stolen or forgotten. Devices are always available and therefore more convenient. Devices become' a part of me'	60	53
Amenity	An example of a practical use was given, e.g., "for office access". Wanting to test and learn	38	33
Experimentation and education	Wanting to experiment with different uses	29	25
Wearable wouldn't work or doesn't exist	Expressing the belief that a wearable would not work, or doesn't exist, for their desired purpose—mostly regarding magnetic sense	14	12
Wearables uncomfortable/too many	Expressing that they are "over" too many wearables, wearables aren't comfortable, and they need to be remembered	7	6
Hidden	Explicitly mentioning they are hidden, clandestine, or can't be seen by others	7	6
Cyborgs and augmentation			
Extend human senses	Expressing a desire to have a new sense or extend the human body	31	27
Cyborg	Using the exact word "cyborg"	12	10
Next stage of evolution	Expressing the belief that having devices inside the body is the next stage of human evolution	7	6
Bio-hacking	Specifically mentioned being interested in bio-hacking, distinct from body modifications in that it is not aesthetic	4	3
Other			
Early adopter	Using the exact phrase "early adopter"	23	20
Cool	Expressing that a wearable would not be as "cool"	11	10
Other	Reasons included for "fun," "why not," mentioning they wanted to express themselves or doing it for publicity	6	5
Body modification	Mentioned explicitly looking for a body modification when they discovered insertables	6	5
Not specified	Did not answer this question	9	8

That [a wearable] would be a half measure. So, I wanted to just basically dive right in and just have it on me all the time... then it wouldn't be waterproof, so you could use it in less circumstances. I just figured this was a fair bit more interesting and since it's only damaging to my skin and I have enough scars as it is, it doesn't matter.–Interview Participant 5

Wearables can be lost or misplaced. An insertable device is much more convenient.–Survey Response 78

I had recently lost my wallet; I had known about the procedure for quite some time and this motivated me to experiment with a data source that couldn't be lost or misplaced. The complicated process of what is basically being issued new numbers for accounts and ID led me to imagine a different way of authentication in regard to credentials and financial accounts. I felt that actually inserting the chip would prove to be a more valuable experience because of the psychological certainty that I had an object and that data that it contained that could not be lost.–Survey Response 85

The second most common reason (33%) was having a practical use for a specific task to perform.

Unlocking my Android smartphone by scanning the xNT NFC compatible tag implant instead of entering a pattern or code which isn't safe, because anyone can look over your shoulder while you enter it.–Survey Response 75

I'm only really interested in the practical stuff, not the aesthetic type body mods.–Interview Participant 1

5.3.2   Cyborgs and Augmentation

While permanence falls under convenience, participants also spoke about having devices which became a part of them. This is opposed to a wearable which is external. Insertables allow them to more permanently augment their bodies with technology.

The difference is about that permanence and having that more a part of you.–Interview Participant 10

27% were interested in extending, or augmenting, their senses and abilities. Using insertables allows them to do so permanently. 10% explicitly mentioned wanting to become a "cyborg" while 6% felt extending oneself with insertable devices is the next stage of human evolution.

5.3.3   Other Reasons

Others were interested in insertables because they wanted to experiment and learn more about these devices and what they could do (25%). Some identified themselves as early adopters who want to shape this technology as it emerges (20%).

There aren't many 'insertables' that are actually useful; most are more like 'gimmicks.'–Survey Response 109

To test, learn and provide input back to the community about the devices and show others that this is not as bad as they think.–Survey Response 81

The future is not quite here yet, so I wanted to see what is possible and push the boundaries.–Interview Participant 19

I don't believe that this is about functionality. It's about testing the limits, it's about making a statement, it's about finding out in your own self what you pick to do. Rather than about it being really functional.–Interview Participant 2

Additional reasons stated were that wearables were uncomfortable or too much maintenance (6%). Others expressed a desire to experiment with bio-hacking (3%).

Wearables get lost, damaged, don't fit sometimes, just look kinda... tacky. It's not my aesthetic.–Survey Participant 8

5.4 Limitations of Insertables

The motivations outlined in the previous section relate to perceived, or perhaps wishful, utility of the devices. Some participants expressed that they are still trying to understand how to use their device. They feel there is a need for devices to become more mainstream to be more useful. 30 participants spoke of problems and limitation with the existing devices. These are shown in Table 8. They acknowledge that for more people to adopt and insert devices, these problems need to be addressed.

The majority (53, 46%) of participants had Android phones, with 29 (25%) having iPhones (of these, 14 had both an Android and iOS device). The 25% with iPhones are not able to program their microchips with their phone as those with Android devices can. This contributes to the ecosystem and programming difficulties reported.

The RFID and NFC implants are interesting but they kind of lack an ecosystem of devices that work with it.–Interview Participant 3

[I'm] Still working out solutions to read / write, and program the NFC device easily.–Survey Response 42

More people should get them. Then there will be more usage options for them.–Survey Response 13

It's becoming normal to use. The breakthrough will be when VISA or MC make paying cards implantable–Survey Response 81

The small counts in these results are attributed to the fact that limitations were extracted as themes from transcribed conversations and free text responses in other questions. They were not explicitly asked in the survey. There is a gap for future research to further explore this. Participants are also early adopters who are likely more forgiving of issues.

Table 8 Reported limitations with insertables

Coded limitation	Description	Count
Ecosystem	A lack of an ecosystem of NFC and RFID reading devices in available products. Requiring extensive knowledge to program or build bespoke solutions (e.g., to unlock cars)	8
Programming	Difficulty in programming a device to do what they want it to do. This includes those who do not have access to an Android device to program the microchip, and getting their microchip accepted as a valid token in security systems	7
NFC availability	Lack of NFC capabilities in iPhones to program or be read by others readily. Also, few people having NFC switched on	5
Speed	Taking too long to scan. At times, it is possibly quicker to performed desired action with a physical pass or typing in information manually	4
Scalability	Not being able to use the same microchip for multiple things, e.g., home access and work access	3
Difficult to scan	Difficulty finding the reader location on smartphones, or the correct location for a reader to scan the smaller, cylindrical microchip which these readers were not designed to scan	2

5.5 Future Intentions

Survey participants ($n = 92$) were asked whether or not they intended to insert more devices—see Table 9. 98% either wanted to get more insertable devices or had not yet made up their minds. Only 2% did not want any more devices. These two participants each had microchips, presumably meeting their needs. They did not feel the need to insert more devices. As participants are open to modifying their bodies in this way again, we can infer that they do not regret doing so. Once again, this may be skewed by the sampling universe of groups regarding implants—those who regretted insertion would be unlikely to join such groups.

Table 9 Future intentions to insert

Do you intend to get more insertable devices?	Counts	Percent of participants (%)
Yes	59	64
No	2	2
Not sure	31	34

Table 10 Desired future intentions to insert

Category	Count	%
Amenity		
More practical uses	47	41
Access	23	20
Payment	21	18
Identification	11	10
Quantified self	11	10
Transit systems	6	5
Storage	6	5
Security	5	4
Smartphone capabilities	5	4
GPS	3	3
Augmentation		
Extend human senses	24	21
Neural interfacing	3	3
Information receipt	5	4
BCI	2	2
Behavior change	1	1
Other		
LED inserts or cosmetic uses	6	5
Pleasure	2	2

All participants were also asked what they wish they could do with their devices—see Table 10. Participant responses once again fell into two overarching categories: more practical uses (amenity) and extending human senses (augmentation).

5.5.1 Amenity

41% wanted the ability to use these devices for more practical uses such as access (20%), payments (18%) identification (10%) or for use on transit systems (5%). More storage (5%) was also mentioned as something participants wanted.

> On the one hand I would love to be able to use them for small contactless payments, but only if it is secure.–Survey Response 70

Others (10) wanted to be able to use an insertable device for quantified-self tracking–to collect statistics on their fitness (steps, heart rate, etc.) and sleep, to monitor their health. These are technologically unfounded desirers, currently not possible with battery and size limitations.

Health monitoring would be very useful.–Survey Response 71

I like the quantified-self kind of stuff; I would love to do one that's telling me if I have a vitamin deficiency or low blood platelets or anything of that nature. I'm a distance runner; already when I run, I monitor my heart rate, wear a watch and count all my steps, GPS data logging all my runs. I have Bluetooth on the phone and watch and headphones. I would love to have more stuff that was integrated even further that was being logged. I'd love to see where my blood oxygen level is as I run. I'm very anxious to take it further and there's almost nothing on the market.–Interview Participant 9

I have a FitBit and don't get me wrong the second I can implant it I'm not going to wear it anymore. It's annoying to have to remember it, it's annoying to have to take it off, it's annoying to have to do all those things. Wearables are going to have their day and eventually they'll start to kind of come in to, hopefully, a general generic communication protocol, at which point we can start integrating the implantables in to that personal area network. Which is this wireless layer that's surrounding you and conveying your data to all the appropriate places; kind of almost like your wireless data circulatory system. Interview Participant 16

Interestingly, three mentioned wanting GPS capabilities. This is a common fear (and misconception) of the public—that these devices will be used for tracking. These were all survey participants and they did not elaborate on the rationale behind wanting devices with GPS capabilities, nor what they would use it for.

5.5.2 Augmentation

24% want to extend human senses, either beyond normal ranges or by adding an additional sense that humans do not innately have. Senses that participants wanted to improve included vision, hearing, an innate sense of direction and being able to receive information eyes free. No one mentioned memory or cognition explicitly; however, neural interfacing and BCI may include some augmentation in this manner.

I love the idea of augmented vision... it would be interesting to imagine that. These are fun, imaginary things that augment things you see. But I don't imagine they're in the near future. But I certainly would love if there was an easy way to integrate more, I guess visual data, into your body.–Interview Participant 10

I'd be very interested in developing technology in improving capacity for sight. Improving vision, night vision, potentially being able to interpret data from eyes independently, anything like that. I'm interested in developments that would augment capacity to hear or really, opportunities to augment any of the senses.–Interview Participant 12

A minority wanted to be able to use the devices for more extreme uses of neural interfacing and BCI. These participants are at the fringes of this fringe practice. The majority are not interested in pursuing this path. Once again, these are wishful uses. When it comes to the realities of brain surgery to control a computer, it's not clear how willing even the most extreme users would be. That is, if any medical professional or body modification artist, would even be willing to perform such a procedure. Questions remain whether or not it would be ethical to augment the body in this way. Some augmentations (e.g., cosmetic) are accepted, as is the use of stimulants (e.g., caffeine) to improve performance. Are technologies for augmentation really that different? Do they give their users that much more of an advantage over others as to be unfair?

> The most infamous one, the thing that I have been closest on is basically a vibrator that can be recharged with haptic charging and it is basically just inserted at the pubic bone above the penis. It would conduct vibration through the penis.–Interview Participant 14

> BCIs are like the end game–brain computing interface is where it's at.–Interview Participant 18

> Neural interfacing with computers–Survey Response 3

5.6   How Do Users Identify?

To answer the fourth, and final, question, how do users of these devices identify, participants were asked if they identified with any movements, or if they had a name for the practice of what they were doing. Asking participants this avoids projecting categorizations onto them, from the outside, in ways that they do not actually identify. These are shown in Table 11. Again, this question was a free text response where some participants mentioned multiple identities, that were then coded in to multiple categories. As before, these identities broadly align with convenience and amenity and augmentation-oriented responses.

Table 11 Self-identification of Participants

Identity	Count	% who mentioned
Convenience and amenity		
No movement	25	22
Early adopter/technologist/STEAM related	13	11
Augmentation oriented		
Biohacker/hacker/body hacker	31	27
Transhumanism	23	20
Grinder	14	12
Cyborg	1	1
Other identity		
Body moder	6	5
Not specified	53	46

5.6.1   Convenience and Amenity

Many (22%) did not identify with any social movement, as they were using insertables for amenity and convenience. A further 9% named a social movement, however, used qualifying statements, for example, they "have" to be part of the movement because they have inserted devices. This shows they have weak ties with these social movements.

> Yeah. I kind of have to [gestures to implants]. You'd have to be interested in how it works and extending it.–Interview Participant 1

I feel like I kind of have to.–Interview Participant 13

> No, primarily. Like, I guess if someone said, "are you a bio-hacker" I'd be like "Yeah, I guess so" but it's not something I kind of present myself as.–Interview Participant 8

> I feel like I kind of have to. I'm kind of an outsider in it, you know. It would be like being gay or being straight or being racial wise African-American or something that like. I guess I fall in to a category, but I don't like to label a lot. I don't consider myself to be one of the front-runners, I don't consider myself along those lines.–Interview Participant 13

11% provided rationale for why they were using these devices, that are not actually social movements such as "early adopter", "technologist" or naming other STEAM-related fields. This shows that they do not identify with a social movement but are instead using these devices for amenity-based purposes.

Given the majority of participants are using their devices for amenity, it follows logically that the majority also do not identify with a movement. They choose insertables for these purposes as they cannot be lost, forgotten, or stolen. They are simply moving access from luggable keys, or wearable passes, to a small device inside the body—from pants pocket to skin pocket.

5.6.2   Cyborgs and Augmentation

27% self-identified as "hackers", either specifically or using terms like "bio-hacker" or "body hacker". 20% identified with the transhumanism movement, or stated they were transhumanists and 12% mentioned the term grinder. The hacker ethos can be described as using technical skills to solve a problem using novel solutions (Gehring 2004). The terms bio-hacker and body-hacker, used interchangeably, refer to individuals who apply this hacker ethic to improve their bodies. This is an umbrella term which can include such sub-genres as nootropics, nutri-genomics, and DIY biology. Nootropics refer to using smart drugs, or micro-dosing with drugs such as LSD, to enhance cognitive function (Wong 2017). Nutri-genomics refers to using nutrition in an attempt to effect gene expressions for enhancements and longevity. One example of such, is individuals using Vitamin A1 to attempt to gain "night vision" (Licina and Tibbetts 2015). Some individuals refer to themselves as "biohackers" when they modify their diet, for example, with Bullet-proof coffee (Asprey 2017), or when they take drugs like metformin off label to increase their body's sensitivity to insulin, in hopes of extending longevity. DIY biology is where individuals experiment, at low cost and without regulation, with bio-augmentations including bioinformatics to understand biological data and genetic engineering using techniques such as CRISPR. DIY biology is not about self-experimentation and editing one's own genes; it is citizen science. Implications of DIY biology are for artistic expressions, education or to democratize access to medicine such as the Open Insulin Project (Schulz 2016). None of the above subcategories of biohackers directly involve the use of devices within the body. This shows participants either to identify with multiple movements or are just not sure of what definition their activity falls under. Some participants feel like these sub-movements are "stealing their term" when they're really just:

> dieting and using your body like you're meant too. That's not biohacking, quit stealing our term–Interview Participant 16.

12% mentioned the term grinder. The grinder movement can also be considered as a type of bio-hacking, where the hacker ethos is employed to solve a problem using devices inside the body, such as insertables.

> I think a lot of people have given it a lot of names. I mean human beings like labels, right? There are cyborgs. I don't really approve of that. My definition of cyborg... the extended word is cybernetic organism meaning your biology and technology work together in some functional way. So in that respect, just the RFID transponders, I wasn't living up to that definition. The transponder just sat in my body. When you talk about cochlear implants that's really a truly cybernetic design and a person became a cybernetic organism at that point. But in reality, the new label the people are coming up with is bio-hacking or bio-hacker and then a subset of that would be grinder which is really kind of ugh I don't like it at all but it's the label they slap on us.–Interview Participant 3

20% identified with the transhumanism movement. They want to accelerate "the evolution of intelligent life beyond its currently human form and human limitations by means of science and technology, guided by life-promoting principles and values" (Stephan et al. 2012). The end goal is to move beyond the "limitations of our minds and physical bodies" (Kline 2015) and replace the need for fallible human parts. Microchips and magnets are all that is technologically possible at the moment.

"Cyborg" is often a term used by the media to describe these individuals. Only one person said they identified as such. This is despite the fact that 12 respondents attributed using insertables, over wearables, to "wanting to be a cyborg." There is a difference between joking about being a cyborg because one has a device inside their body, and actually identifying as such.

5.6.3   Other Identities

A minority (5) identified as "body-moders." While 44% of the total sample have piercings and 47% have tattoos, this is not their motivation for getting insertable devices. Only 4% attributed their rationale for enjoying body modifications. Some were explicitly against getting piercings (17%) or tattoos (20%) themselves. Yet they are willing to modify their bodies with insertable devices. This shows that, while there is a very small overlap with the body modification subculture, it is a weak tie. The insertables have amenity while body modifications do not.

6 Discussion

The practice of individuals voluntarily choosing to use insertable devices is growing. We have shown that more individuals are inserting devices, most of whom inserted in more recent years. Devices are purchased from a growing availability of retailers. As more individuals are becoming aware of these devices, and more places are available to purchase them, more are adopting insertables. This rise in suppliers shows that hobbyists are indeed becoming professionals as speculated in Heffernan et al. (2016), following Stebbins (1982). This is in line with Harrison (2015) who notes, of magnets, "this increase in uptake coincides with an increase in the range and type of available devices as well as literature on the subject." The innovators, along with researchers, are increasing the awareness of these devices thereby increasing uptake.

6.1 Motivated by Convenience and Amenity Not Cyborg Dreams

The addition of the survey cohort showed the more common uses of insertable devices, as opposed to our previous research. Heffernan et al. (2016) showed uses which are now known to be more extreme, and infrequent, edge cases.

Participants used insertable devices because they had a specific use case in mind. Individuals are choosing insertables because these devices, once inserted, cannot be forgotten, lost or easily stolen; participants wanted access options that are always available. Some participants felt that these devices were more secure, or were more convenient than PINs, keys, or wearables. Given that participants had a practical, convenience based, use in mind it makes sense that they were likely to have more than one microchip—to provide access to more than one system and add additional functionality. Furthermore, the majority of future uses participants expressed would be of interest, were practical examples—showing that amenity is a strong motivator for insertables use. Over double the number of participants wanted a more practical use, rather than to be able to augment or extend their senses.

Despite claims of "cyborgs" augmenting their bodies, we have shown this does not apply to the majority of insertable users. Convenience is paramount. Many do not identify with movements and are not interested in experimenting to augment their bodies. It remains to be seen if insertable devices which can augment perception become commercially available, rather than needing to be designed and developed be-spoke by makers and tinkerers, will individuals adopt these? Is there a need, or a want, from the market for these? Given that we have shown the majority of participants are using devices for convenience-based amenity and do not, or do not strongly, identify with a movement is the use of insertable devices even a "movement" or is it just individuals using a technology?

6.2 Not a Movement, Simply Early Adopters

Previous research, and media broadcasts, often refer to individuals using insertables as "cyborgs", "biohackers" or "transhumanists". This may be a case of correlation and causation becoming conflated. While some of these individuals identify as such, they certainly do not all. The act of using an insertable device does not mean one attributes themselves to such a movement. They also use common technologies, such as smartphones, but that does not mean that smartphone users are transhumanists. We have seen a similar trajectory from the earlier quantified-self (QS) movement of individuals tracking health metrics, to millions of consumers purchasing Smartwatches and activity trackers. The QS movement still exists, but a majority of those using these now mainstream devices, while still interested in health, are not necessarily part of this QS movement.

According to Fine and Kleinman (1979) a social movement, or what they refer to as a subculture, must have self-identification. We have shown that the majority of insertable users do not. Certainly, the media is giving sensationalist attention to this group, referred to as "community response" in Fine and Kleinman (1979). Has this led to the lack of self-identification with a group? Or is it simply a case of the natural progression as insertables use moves from innovators to early adopters?

Given the main reasons stated for use is a practical need, or convenience, it is logical that a lack of strong affiliation follows. Users have extended out of "fringes" and therefore a majority also do not identify with any particular movement regarding this practice. As the sampling universe was grouped regarding insertables it is even more interesting that a majority had no, or no strong, affiliation; yet they are still motivated to join these online forums. There are likely more individuals using insertables, who also do not identify with a movement, and therefore do not join these groups. Insertables users likely join these groups for help with configuring their devices, given the current usability limitations.

Hudson, Alcock and Chilana (2016) define individuals who have no prior experience with fabrication and 3D printing as "casual makers." These are individuals who are motivated to use 3D printing as a means to an end—they have a particular object they want to (re)create for practical purposes. These are a distinct group from the makers, who belong to makerspaces and are driven by a desire to experiment. This is reflective of our findings—many using insertables are casual users who have a practical based need (e.g., access to a building in a way they cannot forget or lose). They are not part of a broader movement. Some had weak ties, feeling like they must be part of a movement because they have these devices inserted. Of course, some are more serious makers, which will remain, while early adopters begin to adopt some parts of these technologies.

6.3 Augmentation at the Fringes

While this research revealed the more common reasons participants are choosing insertable devices are not for augmentation, a minority are still interested in extending human senses. These participants are more likely to identify with a movement, or as part of a subculture.

This transhumanist subset of insertables users, however, acknowledge the technology does not currently provide such uses. They are experimenting with what is possible. These individuals are more concerned with how they are performing these tasks (from a device within their body) than the usefulness of the task itself. They are early adopters, pioneering this movement to gain a critical mass, for the uses to increase and improvements to occur. Eventually, they see these devices becoming ones that do extend senses. Still, these individuals do not meet the typical definition of a "cyborg" meaning a cybernetic organism (yet?), Does placing tools within the body make us "cyborgs"?

Fernandes (2016) states "they do not truly augment the human body; they just provide augmented access." Similarly, and also reflecting the results in this chapter, insertables pioneer Amal Graafstra states: "what I have done is simply move an RFID tag from my pants pocket to a skin pocket. There is no biological interaction, and to me that interaction is what defines a cyborg" (Graafstra et al. 2010). The currently used insertables are passive "standalone units with no coupling to the user's biological system," as were Holz et al. (2012) implanted user interfaces. These devices are not making us cybernetic organisms, yet they arguably augment us by extending abilities, thereby allowing the users to do things others cannot. It could even be argued that we are all already cyborgs due to our reliance on technology to replace functions (e.g., memory) and those devices are an extension of ourselves (Kline 2015).

Katina Michael and Michael (2006) describe devices, which fall under the category of insertables, as aiming to "add new 'functionality' to native human capabilities, either through extensions or additions" (Michael and Michael 2006). We have shown, for many, that new capability is really just a convenience-based single function.

Magnets are the only commercially available insertable used for sensory augmentation. Some wanted to experience a new bodily sense, in the case of magnets. Participants with magnets spoke about choosing a device to extend their senses persistently, as opposed to a wearable which they would have to explicitly put on. Many expressed this also wouldn't enable the same sensations to be felt. Harrison's work supports the beliefs of these participants, as in his study a group implanted with magnets "required significantly less force" than a group "wearing" magnets "in order to perceive the stimulus" (Harrison 2015).

Murata et al. (2017) conducted a survey demonstrating a relatively low resistance to using wearables and insertables to improve human physical ability and intellectual power. Olarte-Pascual et al. (2015) asked participants to score, out of 10, their interest in 5 different types of theoretical implants (those to: increase strength; increase physical speed; increase speed of thought and computational speed; delay ageing; allow a user to remote control machines). They found all these insertables were "considered to be of interest" as each scored over 5 out of 10 on this scale. While these devices were considered "interesting," the participants still did not intend to use them, even if they had access to them. It would be interesting to understand if people would intend to use such devices if they were wearable.

Augmenting senses impermanently, via an external wearable device, is likely more palatable and acceptable to society on a whole. We come to this conclusion given the societal pressures toward insertables. Size and battery power needed for augmentation would also increase the invasiveness of having such technologies within the body, therefore, further reducing the acceptability.

6.4   Continued Adoption of Insertable Devices

Insertable devices appear to instill fear and anxiety in the general public (Lai 2012) and generate fears of dehumanization. While others embrace the technology stating that "reasonable people" would enhance themselves with such technology if available (Schermer 2009). Others go as far as to claim this is "inevitable" (Bhattacharyya 2012). This chapter has shown that "normal" individuals are using passive devices for access, authentication and storing and sharing information. They are using devices, no more invasive than a piercing, for mundane uses. Contributing this to the literature will, hopefully, help normalize the practice, which may help with continued adoption of these devices.

We have not discussed perceived ethical issues, as our participants are users of these devices, they do not believe such issues exist. Perceived ethical issues will likely be a factor for other individuals to adopt, or reject, these devices. Olarte-Pascual et al. (2015) found that emotions (positive, negative, and apprehension) explained 71.53% of the variance in participants intention to use insertable devices.

Still, Olarte-Pascual et al. (2015) concluded that "part of society is ready to accept technological implants to increase innate capacities." They, however, have reservations regarding the ethical implications of launching such devices which "could lead to the coexistence of people with implants–and, thus, superior capacities–alongside people without, thereby widening the digital and social divide" (Olarte-Pascual et al. 2015). Murata et al. (2017) respondents also raised questions regarding the morality of these devices when they are inside the body. Will we be creating sub-classes of humans as some fear? Ethical implications of augmenting the body, particularly with insertable devices, is an arena that needs to be explored in future research.

We have not discussed any risks involved with using insertables, as no participants experienced any such issues. Of course, with any object going into the body, there is a risk of infection. Particularly if safe insertion practices are not followed.

Insertable devices are similar to discrete wearable technologies such as the Smartwig (Tobita et al. 2012), in that they look "natural, because the devices are hidden and invisible." They are undetectable to an observer (Vega et al. 2015b). The difference between wearables and insertables is in some cases quite small (a few millimeters of skin). Yet the latter instill fear, while the former are accepted as useful. This is despite the fact that insertables currently have fewer uses than wearables. There is a gap to understand the public reactions toward, and discourse around, acceptability of insertables, as social norms impact adoption. This exploration should explore the relationship of humans with technology and what this technology says about human values:

- How does the idea that technology is value laden impact on the way that individuals feel about, and use, insertable technologies?
- Why are these devices, with limited capabilities, more worrisome than luggable or wearable devices? Is it because they go inside the body?
- Would attitudes to these technologies, and propensity to insert, change if people understood the technologies better?
- Given some participants already had implantable medical devices, this leads us to ask: does already having something inside the body increase propensity to use an insertable device?
- The overlap between magnets and microchips represents participants who have both types of devices—sensorial and convenience based. Are individuals, who already have one device inside their body, more open to explore using additional devices?

For use of insertable devices to continue to move from early adopters, to possibly an early majority, these questions need to be explored. Usability and limitations of these devices will also need to be more thoroughly understood in targeted research. Some participants also did not have the technological capabilities to configure their device for their intended purposes. These issues will need to be addressed for these devices to continue to move along the innovation diffusion model, toward adoption (Rogers and Shoemaker 1971). What insertable devices are being developed by the new professionals, and how individuals will accept these, are also an arena for future research. Do people want to augment their bodies, but devices are not yet available? Will devices that do so be small enough to be palatable to the market, or be considered too invasive to be viable in an early majority?

7 Conclusions

Individuals are voluntarily inserting devices inside their bodies for non-medical purposes. We have illustrated the recent growing nature of this practice. By taking into account the (very) early adopters, not just the bespoke experiments of a few, we can understand what the use now looks like. We have more accurately answered: what devices are individuals putting in their bodies; what do they use these devices for; what are their motivations, and; how do they identify themselves? We have contributed to the literature an account of the more commonplace convenience-based and amenity uses of insertables. The growing popularity of these devices has resulted in more suppliers being created as demand grows, and the commercially available devices are largely for these convenience and amenity purposes.

These findings allow for a discussion of the motivations and self-identifications of participants. By exploring their self-identity, rather than labelling them from the outside, we have shown it is no longer only individuals augmenting themselves to become "cyborgs" using these devices. As more people are choosing to be inserted with these devices, they can no longer all be on the fringes. Motivations are evolving as device usage is moving from hobbyists and innovators to early adopters. Users are less concerned with augmenting themselves and are instead interested in the amenity afforded by these devices. It logically follows that the majority also do not, or do not strongly, identify with any particular social movement regarding this practice. This research documents the current uses, motivations, and identities of insertable users. This normalizes the use of insertable devices by showing they are no longer confined to fringe movements. Beyond the innovators, the early adopters are less likely to identify with a social movement. Rather, they are inserting devices for practical and convenience-based purposes; everyday people use these devices. This is common as innovations move from innovators, to early adopters, to ubiquitous. As an example, 20 years ago those with multiple body piercings could be considered "punks", whereas now the growing popularity of piercings has seen the democratization of individuals who have them. Microchips are no longer just for "cyber-punks" and "transhumanists", but individuals who see a convenience-based benefit, which is worth the small amount of pain of a needle for them. These are devices with amenity that are beginning to be used by more individuals. As the amenity continues to grow, so too will the number of individuals using these devices, outside of a social movement.

References

Alkema L, Kantorova V, Menozzi C, Biddlecom A (2013) National, regional, and global rates and trends in contraceptive prevalence and unmet need for family planning between 1990 and 2015: a systematic and comprehensive analysis. The Lancet 381(9878):1642–1652

Asprey D (2017) Head strong: the bulletproof plan to activate untapped brain energy to work smarter and think faster-in just two weeks, vol 3. HarperCollins

Bahney A (2006) High tech, under the skin. New York Times 2

Bhattacharyya A, Kedzior R (2012) Consuming the cyborg. ACR North Am Adv

Bradley-Munn SR, Michael K (2016) Whose Body Is It?: The body as physical capital in a techno-society. IEEE Consum Electron Mag 5(3):107–114

Brines ML, Gould JL (1979) Bees have rules. Science 206(4418):571–573. American Association for the Advancement of Science

Britton LM, Semaan B (2017) Manifesting the cyborg through techno-body modification: from human-computer interaction to integration. In: Proceedings of the 2017 CHI conference on human factors in computing systems, pp 2499–2510

Buhling KJ, Zite NB, Lotke P, Black K et al (2014) Worldwide use of intrauterine contraception: a review. Contraception 89(3):162–173. Elsevier

Cheer L (2014) Australian man who's had a microchip inserted into his hand so that he can do more with the iphone 6...maybe. https://www.dailymail.co.uk/news/article-2746648/Australian-man-microchip-inserted-hand-use-iPhone-6.html. Accessed 31 May 2020

Cohen J (2013) 10 breakthrough technologies. https://www.technologyreview.com/10-breakthrough-technologies/2013/. Accessed 31 May 2020

Csikszentmihalyi M (1993) Why we need things? History from things: essays on material culture, pp 20–29. Smithsonian Institution Press Washington, DC

Doerksen MD (2017) Electromagnetism and the N th sense: Augmenting senses in the grinder subculture. Sens Soc 12(3):344–349. Taylor & Francis

Einhorn F (2017) Bodyhacking: Designing for New Senses. https://www.frogdesign.com/designmind/bodyhacking-designing-for-new-senses. Accessed 31 May 2020

Fernandes T (2016) Human augmentation: beyond wearables. Interactions 23(5):66–68. ACM New York, NY, USA

Fine GA, Kleinman S (1979) Rethinking subculture: An interactionist analysis. Am J Soc 85(1):1–20

Foster KR, Jaeger J (2007) RFID inside. Spectrum IEEE 44(3):24–29

Gehring VV (2004) The Internet in public life

Gomez PF, Morcuende JA (2005) Early attempts at hip arthroplasty: 1700s to 1950s. Iowa Orthop J 25:25. University of Iowa

Graafstra A, Michael K, Michael M (2010) Social-technical issues facing the humancentric rfid implantee sub-culture through the eyes of amal graafstra. In: 2010 IEEE international symposium on technology and society. IEEE, pp 498–516

Harbisson N (2012) I listen to color. https://www.ted.com/talks/neil_harbisson_i_listen_to_color. Accessed 31 May 2020

Harrison C, Tan D, Morris D (2010) Skinput: appropriating the body as an input surface. In: Proceedings of the SIGCHI conference on human factors in computing systems, pp 453–462

Harrison I (2015) Sensory enhancement, a pilot perceptual study of subdermal magnetic implants. PhD thesis, University of Reading

Heffernan KJ, Vetere F, Chang S (2015) Insertables: I've got it under my skin. Interactions 23(1):52–56. ACM New York, NY, USA

Heffernan KJ, Vetere F, Chang S (2016) You put what, where? hobbyist use of insertable devices. In Proceedings of the 2016 CHI conference on human factors in computing systems, pp 1798–1809

Heffernan KJ, Vetere F, Chang S (2017) Towards insertables: Devices inside the human body. First Monday 22(3)

Hettiarachchi A, Premalal A, Dias D, Nanayakkara S (2014) Toward context-aware just-in-time information: micro-activity recognition of everyday objects. In Proceedings of the 26th Australian computer-human interaction conference on designing futures: the future of design, pp 422–425

Holz C, Grossman T, Fitzmaurice G, Agur A (2012) Implanted user interfaces. In Proceedings of the SIGCHI conference on human factors in computing systems, pp 503–512

Hudson N, Alcock C, Chilana PK (2016) Understanding newcomers to 3d printing: motivations, workflows, and barriers of casual makers. In Proceedings of the 2016 CHI conference on human factors in computing systems, pp 384–396

International society of Aesthetic Platic Surgery (ISAPS) (2015) ISAPS international survey on aesthetic/cosmetic: procedures performed in 2014

Ip R, Michael K, Michael M (2008) Amal Graafstra-The Do-It-Yourselfer RFID Implantee: The culture, values and ethics of hobbyist implantees: a case study

Irish JD (2004) A 5,500-Year-Old Artificial Human Tooth from Egypt: A Historical Note. Int J Oral Maxillofac Implant 19(5)

Jacob RJ (1996) The future of input devices. ACM Comput Surv (CSUR) 28(4es):138-es. ACM New York, NY, USA

Kao H-LC, Dementyev A, Paradiso JA, Schmandt C (2015) NailO: Fingernails as an input surface. In: Paper presented at the Proceedings of the 33rd Annual ACM Conference on Human Factors in Computing Systems

Keddie G (1989) Symbolism and context: the world history of the labret and cultural diffusion on the pacific rim. In: Circum-Pacific conference, session, vol 8

Keeton WT, Larkin TS, Windsor DM (1974) Normal fluctuations in the earth's magnetic field influence pigeon orientation. J Comput Phys 95(2):95–103

Kline RR (2015) The cybernetics moment: Or why we call our age the information age. JHU Press

Kreithen ML, Keeton WT (1974) Detection of changes in atmospheric pressure by the homing pigeon, Columba livia. J Comput Phys 89(1):73–82. Springer

Lai A-L (2012) Cyborg as commodity: Exploring conceptions of self-identity, body and citizenship within the context of emerging transplant technologies. ACR North Am Adv

Ledford H (2010) Life hackers. Nature 467(7316):650. Nature Publishing Group

Levy J, Sewell M, Goldstein N (1979) II. A short history of tattooing. Dermatol Surg 5(11):851–856. LWW

Licina G, Tibbetts J (2015) A Review on Night Enhancement Eyedrops Using Chlorin e6. Sci Mass

Lupton D (2014) Self-tracking cultures: towards a sociology of personal informatics. In: Proceedings of the 26th Australian Computer-Human Interaction Conference on Designing Futures: the Future of Design. ACM, pp 77–86

Mann S (1997) Eudaemonic computing ('underwearables'). In: Digest of papers. First international symposium on wearable computers. IEEE, pp 177–178

Michael K (2010) RFID implantable devices for humans and the risk versus reward. In PerAda workshop on security, trust and privacy. Universita di Roma IJLa Sapienza$i$, Rome, Italy

Michael K, Michael MG (2005) Microchipping people: The rise of the electrophorus

Michael K, Michael MG (2006) Towards chipification: The multifunctional body art of the net generation

Michael K, Michael M (2010) The diffusion of rfid implants for access control and epayments: a case study on baja beach club in barcelona. In 2010 IEEE international symposium on technology and society. IEEE, pp 242–252

Munn SRB, Michael K, Michael M (2016) The social phenomenon of body-modifying in a world of technological change: past, present, future. In: 2016 IEEE conference on norbert wiener in the 21st century (21CW). IEEE, pp 1–6

Murata K, Adams AA, Fukuta Y, Orito Y, Arias-Oliva M, Pelegrin-Borondo J (2017) From a science fiction to reality: Cyborg ethics in Japan. ACM SIGCAS Comput Soc 47(3):72–85. ACM New York, NY, USA

Musk E et al (2019) An integrated brain-machine interface platform with thousands of channels. J Med Int Res 21(10):e16194. JMIR Publications Inc., Toronto, Canada

Oggionni M (2018) Be pleasurable, be innovative. The emotional side of design thinking. Italy

Olarte-Pascual C, Pelegrin-Borondo J, Reinares-Lara E (2015) Implants to increase innate capacities: integrated vs. apocalyptic attitudes. Is there a new market? Univ Bus Rev (48):102–117

Pelegrin-Borondo J, Reinares-Lara E, Olarte-Pascual C (2017) Assessing the acceptance of technological implants (the cyborg): Evidences and challenges. Comput Hum Behav 70:104–112. Elsevier

Pentland AP (1998) Wearable intelligence. Scientific American, Incorporated

Petersén M (2018) Thousands of Swedes are inserting microchips into themselves – here's why. In: The Conversation. https://theconversation.com/thousands-of-swedes-are-inserting-microchips-into-themselves-heres-why-97741. Accessed 31 May 2020

Reinares-Lara E, Olarte-Pascual C, Pelegrin-Borondo J, Pino G (2016) Nanoimplants that enhance human capabilities: A cognitive-affective approach to assess individuals acceptance of this controversial technology. Psychol Mark 33(9):704–712. Wiley Online Library

Rogers EM, Shoemaker FF (1971) Communication of Innovations; A Cross-Cultural Approach. ERIC

Schermer M (2009) The mind and the machine. On the conceptual and moral implications of brain-machine interaction. Nanoethics 3(3):217. Springer

Schulz C (2016) The Role of Hackers in the Open Innovation Process of the Pharmaceutical Industry

Seeger A (1975) The meaning of body ornaments: a Suya example. Ethnology 14(3):211–224 (1975). JSTOR

Shilling C (2004) The body in culture, technology and society. Sage

Stebbins RA (1982) Serious leisure: A conceptual statement. Pacif Soc Rev 25(2):251–272 (1982). Sage Publications Sage CA, Los Angeles, CA

Stephan KD, Michael K, Michael M, Jacob L, Anesta EP (2012) Social implications of technology: The past, the present, and the future. Proce IEEE 100(Special Centennial Issue):1752–1781. IEEE

Tobita H, Kuzi T (2012) Smartwig: wig-based wearable computing device for communication and entertainment. In: Proceedings of the international working conference on advanced visual interfaces, pp 299–302

Tse WL (2018) Unamed photograph. In https://dazedimg-dazedgroup.netdna-ssl.com/525/azure/dazed-prod/1240/9/1249650.jpeg

Ungerleider N (2012) Biohackers and Diy Cyborgs Clone Silicon Valley Innovation. Fast Comp

Vaisutis K, Brereton M, Robertson T, Vetere F, Durick J, Nansen B, Buys L (2014) Invisible connections: investigating older people's emotions and social relations around objects. In: Proceedings of the SIGCHI conference on human factors in computing systems, pp 1937–1940

Vega K, Cunha M, Fuks H (2015) Hairware: the conscious use of unconscious auto-contact behaviors. In: Proceedings of the 20th international conference on intelligent user interfaces, pp 78–86

Wallace J (2003) Craft knowledge for the digital age: how the jeweller can contribute to designing wearable digital communication devices. In: Proceedings of sixth asian design conference. Citeseer

Witze A (2013) People: The science life: Contest brings out the biohackers. Sci News 183(1):32–32 (2013). Wiley Online Library

Wong S (2017) Leading the high life. Elsevier

Augmented Senses: Evaluating Sensory Enhancement Applications

Francisco Kiss and Romina Poguntke

Abstract Humans are dependent on their sensory perception being built upon their classical senses. Accordingly, researchers have been envisioning for decades to augment and enhance the existing spectrum of human senses by technological means. In this chapter, we will give an overview of scientific work that has been occupied with augmenting human senses to facilitate or enhance our capabilities. Further, we will present three exemplary applications extending the powers of the visual, auditory, and tactile senses following a threefold evaluation concept.

1 Introduction

In the previous chapter, Heffernan et al. discussed *insertables*, devices inserted into the human body to achieve augmentation. The authors approach this phenomenon from a social and technical perspective, exploring the motivation and behavior of users who participate in this practice. In this chapter, we shift the focus from the users of augmentation to the goal of augmentation and provide an encompassing overview of the aim of sensory augmentation: enhance human perception beyond its natural limits.

The Human pursuit of amplification and enhancement of perception dates to ancient times, with the use of lenses to see in the distance (Sines and Sakellarakis 1987). Classical approaches to this area of work have long strived to both extend perception beyond what is natural, and restore perception when below the typical thresholds. These trends can be seen in present technologies, particularly in products widely available to consumers: amplification tools, such as digital microscopes, and accessibility technologies, such as hearing aids. However, Schmidt suggests to capitalize on emerging technologies and rethink how we go about enhancing human

F. Kiss (✉) · R. Poguntke
University of Stuttgart, Stuttgart, Germany
e-mail: francisco@franciskokiss.eu; franciskokiss@gmail.com

R. Poguntke
e-mail: romina.poguntke@vis.uni-stuttgart.de

© Springer Nature Switzerland AG 2021
T. Dingler and E. Niforatos (eds.), *Technology-Augmented Perception and Cognition*,
Human–Computer Interaction Series, https://doi.org/10.1007/978-3-030-30457-7_7

capabilities, moving beyond tools and aids, and into the realm of sensory augmentation (Schmidt 2017).

Multiple examples illustrate this vision of augmented perception. For instance, in a clear attempt to transcend tools and empower natural sensing, Ekuni et al. designed a system capable of adjusting magnification and focus of a head-mounted telescope (Ekuni et al. 2016). Explicit user control and actuation, typically characteristic in tool usage, are removed from the interaction. Instead, the intention of the user is detected, based on ocular and muscular movements, and thus the system is controlled, resembling the way senses work naturally. On a different note, Gronvall et al. enabled humans to perceive wireless communications taking place in their vicinity (Grönvall et al. 2016). By mapping radio wave signals to visual and auditory stimuli, the authors managed to make perceivable a phenomenon that is not natural within human sensory capacities. Other work focuses on interpersonal and social aspects of sensation and perception. For example, Kasahara et al. (2016), built a system for head-mounted displays and incorporated eye-tracking, enabling the viewer to see other's from a first-person perspective parallel to their own perspective.

At this point, it is meaningful to distinguish between different terms describing the augmentation of senses. While some researchers refer to this topic as "sensory enhancement", we will use both expressions as synonyms for describing the scientific attempt to add an additional functionality to an existing sense. Hereby, the human's perspective is widened by enabling or facilitating to perform certain feats aiming to provide a greater perception of reality. Another term which is frequently used when dealing with this topic is the "amplification of senses". In contrast to the augmentation or enhancement, amplifying a sense neglects the possibility to add another dimension to the human perception or range of action, but rather relies on heightening, strengthening or refining what the sensory system naturally detects. This process can be understood as the increment in what we perceive having different natures: we can perceive through a particular sense to a greater degree (sensory amplification), or we can perceive through a sense, information that is unavailable within this sense's natural domain (sensory substitution).

Often, but not exclusively, people with reduced or missing senses benefit from technological advancements that substitute or complete the sensory information they cannot obtain naturally. This particular field, accessibility, has a strong impact on the quality of life of numerous people and is, therefore, highly relevant. However, accessibility aims to help users reach the naturally optimal perception for a given sense, while our research attempts to enable users to perceive further beyond what is naturally possible.

With sensory augmentation, we aim to extend human perception. This usually consists of building an additional functionality on top of one (or many) of the natural human's senses. This additional functionality provides more control on the information perceived through that sense, or an increment in its quantity or quality, or information about reality totally alien to that sense. The achievement of this goal makes necessary the incorporation of technology to develop applications capable of supporting the desired augmentation.

In this chapter, we provide three examples of sensory augmentation based on technological means. The three projects described in this chapter differ in nature and strive for different goals, but they all share in common a general approach and research framework. Our intent is to aid researchers in their efforts on future applications and explorations of sensory augmentation.

Each of the chosen projects emphasizes the importance of one of the three steps in the evaluation of a design: validating a concept, evaluating a prototype and testing the design in the real world, with real people. The first project we chose explores the use of thermal feedback to create a new sense, in particular, the ability to sense the likelihood of precipitation. The second project investigates enabling directional hearing, thus allowing a person to focus audition into a specific sound source. In the third project, we used minimalist visual stimuli to improve the sense of orientation for swimmers, and thus compensated the lack of visual cues in open waters.

All these research projects resulted in physical prototypes, which were evaluated in user studies. Beyond the individual contribution of each project, we believe that they generated useful knowledge at a higher level of abstraction, gained through experience and through the intermediate steps and design iterations, which are rarely reflected in publications. We present the sum of these insights, as well as the new questions that arise from the gained knowledge and findings.

2   Background

To understand the field of sensory augmentation, it is first necessary to review some fundamental concepts. In this section, we first summarize the main characteristics of the five classical senses, followed by their non-classical siblings. Through these summaries, we will attempt to provide a fundamental understanding of both the physiological and cognitive aspects of perception, for each sense. We conclude this section by presenting representative previous work from the field of Human-Computer Interaction (HCI), illustrating some examples of sensory augmentation.

2.1   Five Classical Senses

We call senses the physiological mechanisms that enable organisms to obtain data from reality. This data is generated by *observable* physical phenomena, which interacts with the sensory organs. Sensory organs are sensible to variations in some aspect of the physical world, producing the physiological signals that (in the case of higher vertebrates) are decoded during cognition. Since sensory organs are sensitive to particular aspects of reality, they can capture a delimited type of information. This classification of senses has been traditionally circumscribed to the commonly called *five senses*[1]: audition, taste, smell, touch, and sight.

The physiology and cognitive mechanism behind each sense define not only the aspects of reality each sense can perceive, but also its natural limitations. These limitations suggest challenges to be overcome, while the closed domains of perception define frontiers to be explored. Thus, alone the definition of each individual sense suggests a starting point for its enhancement.

2.1.1 Auditory Sense

Hearing is perceiving sound. Physical phenomena producing vibrations generate waves that propagate through a medium, which in the case of human perception is typically air. When these waves reach the ears, mechanoreceptors within them translate vibrations into electrical signals that neurons carry to the brain. Having two ears enable humans to perceive two separate flows of information (signals) describing the same phenomenon. The human brain can obtain additional information about phenomena, such as relative position and distance of the sound source, based on the differences between the two signals (Jeffress 1948).

Human hearing presents some limitations in its perception capabilities. Humans can normally hear sounds within a spectrum of 20–20.000 Hz. Compared to other higher mammals (e.g., dogs), the human sense of hearing is not very sensitive to sounds of low intensity. Despite these limitations, the sense of hearing is a versatile source of information about reality, and also a fundamental part of human communication.

2.1.2 Gustatory Sense

Humans perceive taste through gustatory *calyculi* (or taste buds), which are concentrated on the upper side of the tongue (Chiras 2013). Through chemical reactions, gustations enable us to detect particular and limited properties of matter we put in our mouths. This sense helps organisms, in general, to identify beneficial nutrients and detect poisons, and in humans pervades the social and even emotional spheres of life (Verbeek and van Campen 2013).

The fundamental limitation of the human sense of gustation is the reduced amount of properties we can detect. These have been useful along human development, helping us identify food. However, plenty of substances cannot be detected by our taste. Additionally, the need of introducing matter into the mouth to detect its properties is potentially dangerous, given the existence of many substances that are lethal even at very low concentrations, as well as others being corrosive or reactive.

---

[1]Even if sometimes the five classical senses are called Aristotelian senses, Aristotle defined in *De Sensu et Sensibilibus* only four senses, describing the taste as a form of touch. However, by the eleventh century, multiple sources started counting the senses as five (Anderson 2003).

2.1.3 Olfactory Sense

Similarly to the sense of taste, smell occurs through a chemical reaction. Olfaction occurs in humans in a small surface of tissue inside the nose, which is populated by cells specialized in perceiving smells. The sense of smell enables us to recognize the presence of chemical compounds in the air (Chiras 2013). The practical uses of this information range from primal tasks, such as assessing the quality of food or detecting predators, to complex social interactions, such as infants recognizing the presence of their mothers (Russell 1976; Schaal 1988).

Despite the versatility of human olfactory sense and the large variety of scents we can recognize, our sense of smell is limited in sensitivity and accuracy when compared with other high vertebrates', both prey and predators. Additionally, smell can easily trigger emotional responses and memories (Verbeek and van Campen 2013). This is both a limitation (given its potential negative effects) and a potential for creating interfaces.

2.1.4 Tactile Sense

The sense of touch resides in the skin, the hairs and some inner surfaces of the body (such as the tongue and throat). Pressure receptors tightly packed over these areas are able to detect different kinds and intensities of pressure, as well as their variations (Heller 2013). This enables us to perceive a wide range of individual phenomena, such as the tickling caused by an insect moving on our skin, the pressure of the ground on the soles of our feet, or even the direction, speed, and intensity of a caress. We can also perceive vibrations through touch, a sensation used with growing popularity in HCI applications (e.g., phone vibration notifications).

The sense of touch provides information about our immediate surrounding, to the point of enabling us moving around in a dark room. It also has a social significance, due to its implications for social distance and intimacy.

Some of its limitations are the difference in resolution and sensitivity between different areas of the body, as well as the need for contact with an object to perceive it.

2.1.5 Visual Sense

The sense of sight is arguably the one we depend on the most. Photons emitted from light sources interact with matter and are reflected, dispersed and diffracted, and some of them end up being captured by photoreceptors within our eyes. Two different kinds of photoreceptors enable us to distinguish shapes and colors, and thus we are able to see our surroundings. We can perceive numerous characteristics of objects and phenomena, in some cases from vast distances. Vision is a fundamental component of most human activities and plays a large role in social interaction, work, and leisure. Binocularity, namely having two eyes, allows us to perceive distances and spaces, adding the so-called third-dimension to our perception of reality.

However, the vision has many limitations. We are sensitive only to a narrow range of light frequencies and are capable of perceiving a limited dimensional granularity for both space and time (Kaufman 1974). Objects and phenomena can be easily hidden from us by interposing objects in the line of sight. Additionally, even if the focusing mechanisms of the human eye are versatile and capable of perceiving both minuscule objects at close distance and larger ones from far away, the limits of our vision are easily noticeable in both cases.

2.2 The Other Senses

Our perception is not limited to the five classical senses: we can perceive pain, time, temperature, and balance. We can also sense states and variations within our bodies, such as hunger, pulmonary stretch, blushing or sexual arousal. Some of these aspects of reality are related to specific organs that detect concrete physical phenomena, but others, such as the sense of direction, are constructions made at a cognitive level from information gathered by diverse physiological sensors (Goldstein 2010).

All these non-classical senses play integral roles in our perception of reality. While the classical senses mostly serve us to perceive the extern world, the non-classical senses are how we perceive ourselves *internally* (see Fig. 1). They are vital and help regulate our life functions, as well as strongly determine how we experience life.

Their individual limitations are harder to overcome than those of the five classical senses, particular for senses where both the subject and mechanism of perception exist inside our bodies, often in a decentralized manner.

Fig. 1 Humans perceive external reality through the classical senses, while the non-classical senses provide information about internal states

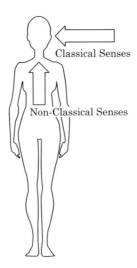

2.3 Human Senses in Human–Computer Interaction

It is possible to argue that most HCI applications engage one or more human senses: there is no other way to interact with humans! Historically, computer interfaces have relied mainly on the visual sense. This trend is true even today, with numerous electronic consumer products presenting information to users with screens or LEDs. This does not mean that other interaction modalities have been ignored by research; plenty of technologies use sound or vibrations to convey information. Some applications even investigate the usage of smell and taste as interaction interfaces. However, the extension of the senses using digital technology remains vastly unexplored in a methodical manner. Hence, in this section, we review some works that probe into this young research area, even if in some cases it does not directly address sensory augmentation as its central research focus.

Following the general trend of visual interfaces, the augmentation of vision has gained popularity faster than for other senses. Most AR and VR technologies and products rely primarily on vision as interaction modality (e.g., Google Lens, HoloLens, Vibe, Oculus). It is tempting to assume that typical AR applications and VR environments are augmented vision, but this is not the case; while AR and VR *augment* subjects of human perception by means of visual elements and symbols, visual sensory augmentation affects everything perceived by a user. Some examples of the latter are already gaining in ubiquity. Such is the case for infrared (IR) and thermal vision, both technologies now available in the consumer grade products. Using these two technologies, Abdelrahman et al. proposed an enhancement to natural human vision, enriching normal view with the thermal spectrum and depth maps created with IR cameras (Abdelrahman et al. 2018). In an evaluation of the system, while performing daily tasks, participants found the extended vision useful and convenient, highlighting the potential benefits of perceiving temperature through sight.

Fan et al. created a visual sensory augmentation that made *electrosmog* visible to users (Fan et al. 2016). Using a Head-Mounted Display (HMD), the researchers made the presence and intensity of electromagnetic fields visible by blurring the view of users, as if they were inside a cloud.

More recently, Li et al. presented a biomimetic soft lens controlled by electrooculographic signals (Li et al. 2019). In other words, a technology that can be used to create contact lenses with zooming functionality. Further, the focusing of the lens is controlled by detecting the eye movements, resulting in a truly implicit interface, resembling the control mechanism of natural senses.

Another example of sensory augmentation is work from Niforatos et al. in "Augmenting skiers' peripheral perception" (Niforatos et al. 2017). The authors created a system that made the user aware of other skiers behind her. The system detected other skiers using a laser scanner and provided information about their presence and position using LEDs positioned within the field of view of the user. Also enhancing the environmental awareness, Schoop et al. used sonification instead of LEDs to inform cyclists of the presence and behavior of vehicles outside their field of view (Schoop et al. 2018).

Generally speaking, most sensory augmentations can be classified in one of the two categories: either apply a specific technology (e.g., thermal vision) to certain scenarios, or attempt to address concrete practical problems (e.g., risks in sports). The abstract approach of extending the dimensions and characteristics of human senses has not yet been studied, but we argue it can potentially benefit both researchers and users.

3 Concept

Augmenting the human senses implies increasing the part of reality humans perceive. By definition, this expands our potential awareness and enriches our experience of reality. Perceiving more can also come at a cost, since our attention is a finite, limited resource; having more information to process can possibly overload our cognitive mechanisms (Bray 2008). However, as commonly demonstrated by people wearing glasses, an increment in the quality, level of detail and granularity of the perceived information is not detrimental, but beneficial and desirable.

To investigate the potential of sensory augmentation, we first needed to define the concept: sensory augmentation (SA) is the extension or increment of the perception of a particular aspect of reality, beyond the natural human capacity, and by means of technology. It is important to note that this definition includes only a subset of AR, and excludes accessibility technologies (see Fig. 2). However, while the goal of accessibility technologies is different from SA, its user-centered approach is fundamental for SA: humans have developed multiple tools to enhance and amplify our perception, such as telescopes and microscopes, but these serve very specific purposes in very delimited use cases and situations, always depending explicit intent, volition and attention. On the other hand, accessibility technologies (e.g., contact lenses or hearing aids) do not require extra attention or effort to be used, but are continuously incorporated in our daily lives, becoming part of what we are and how we

Fig. 2 Sensory Augmentation is a subset of Augmented Reality and not an Accessibility technology

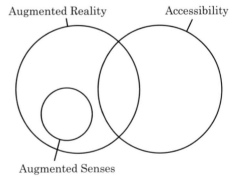

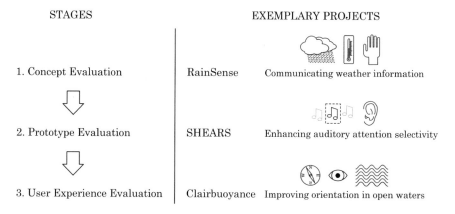

STAGES   EXEMPLARY PROJECTS

1. Concept Evaluation   RainSense   Communicating weather information

2. Prototype Evaluation   SHEARS   Enhancing auditory attention selectivity

3. User Experience Evaluation Clairbuoyance Improving orientation in open waters

Fig. 3 Depicting the three evaluation stages and the projects selected to illustrate each stage. All these projects aim to augment human sensing capabilities by technological means

experience reality. We envision SA as a combination of the user-centered approach of accessibility technologies with the functionality of tools. During our research efforts, we strived to accomplish these ideals, gaining valuable practical knowledge, which we exemplify with three projects. Each of these examples is focused on a different stage of evaluation (see Fig. 3).

The first project, *RainSense*, is about conveying weather forecast information. Here we focus on the evaluation of the concept as such. The second stage emphasizes the evaluation of the prototype. For this, we present *SHEARS*, a design to enhance selective hearing in noisy environments. Finally, the last stage addresses usability and user experience, from a user-centered design approach. We illustrate this by presenting the evaluation of *Clairbuoyance*, a wearable augmentation that facilitates orientation under water, in low visibility conditions.

Along these three exemplary applications, we present the development process of augmenting existing sensory capabilities, starting with the exploration phase of an underlying concept in form of

a. investigating the practical requirements for association cues when communicating weather information through thermal stimuli (*RainSense*).

Next, we assess the technical implementation and thus the feasibility of an already validated concept. For this,

b. allowing a fine-grained control of isolating auditory cues using a physical prototype (*SHEARS*)

needed to be transferred into practices and evaluated. As a final stage, the user experience and usability is crucial in the design process. In practice, the user study on

c. compensating lack of visual cues to enhance orientation under water (*Clairbuoyance*)

was conducted in a swimming pool to simulate a realistic yet controlled environment. By providing such conditions, we could assess authentic user experience data.

In the following sections, these three projects are described in detail, followed by a general discussion on lessons learned and design recommendations.

4   Examples of Applications on Sensory Augmentation

Starting with *RainSense*, we show an exploratory approach to creating a new sense using an existing one. Hereby, we used thermal feedback to convey information about the weather. Building upon this, classical conditioning learning is aimed to be used for establishing a *sense for weather*, or in particular, we provide information on precipitation. With *SHEARS*, we describe a concrete enhancement for auditory perception, giving humans an increased ability for selective hearing attention. Finally, *Clairbuoyance* visually enhances the sense of direction of swimmers, particularly in situations of low visibility.

4.1   RainSense—Enhancing the Tactile Sense for Weather Communication

Our idea of establishing a *sense of precipitation* comprises of two parts. First, exploring the suitability of thermal stimuli exploiting the advantages of temperature feedback, such as unobtrusiveness and low time effort and complexity for decoding. Secondly, to use the theory of classical conditioning, often also referred to as Pavlovian conditioning named after its originator Pavlov and Gantt (Pavlov and Gantt 1941). Hence, applying the principles of this learning theory, we envision to use our tactile perception to associate thermal input with weather information and consequently develop a *sense of precipitation*.

4.1.1   Design

Temperature is an integral part of weather and variations of temperature are closely related to precipitation. Thus, the use of thermal feedback to convey weather information, particularly about precipitation likelihood, reflects and builds upon a commonplace association between stimuli and observable natural phenomena. The choice to use thermal feedback was further supported by previous work showing that temperatures are associated with emotions (Wilson et al. 2016), and are prone to subjective interpretations (Wilson et al. 2015), in contrast to pressure, for example. Exploiting its advantage as an unobtrusive but salient channel for providing feedback, we derived from related work that thermal feedback could be applied using mobile devices (Wilson et al. 2011).

For designing the temperature stimulus in combination with weather information, we used the work of Lee and Lim (2010) as inspiration, which suggests that context is necessary for experiencing a meaningful sensation of a thermal stimulus. With respect to the optimal location for presenting the thermal stimuli, prior work suggested the thenar eminence to be perfect, saying that non-glabrous locations are also convenient (Wilson et al. 2011). With the aim of placing the device in a way that minimizes discomfort and obtrusiveness, we chose a spot between the radial and the ulnar artery. This presents the additional benefit of the skin thickness being lower, increasing sensitivity to thermal stimuli (Whitton and Everall 1973). Following design recommendations by Wilson et al. (2011), we here found a suitable location without hair. Thus, we evaluated different stimuli rates informed by the other recommendations to test both, warm and cold stimuli and to vary their intensity (Wilson et al. 2011), investigating their suitability for being associated with weather information.

4.1.2   Evaluation

In our study, we addressed the first part of our concept (Poguntke et al. 2018), namely whether thermal feedback is suitable for communicating weather information. We further investigated how such feedback optimally looks like. Accordingly, we conducted an experiment asking 16 participants ($M = 22.9$, $SD = 1.63$ years) consisting of six females and ten males, to wear a thermal feedback presenting wearable prototype.

Our physical hardware prototype (see Fig. 4), provided thermal feedback to users by heating or cooling the surface of a Peltier element connected to an Arduino Pro Mini. A Bluetooth connection enabled controlling the feedback direction (i.e., cold or heat), the intensity of the stimuli, and their duration through the commands from our Android application.

This Android application logged weather information provided by the Weather Underground API. Using this API and the device's current GPS location, the application received information on upcoming precipitation likelihood. As soon as a forecast containing that the precipitation probability exceeded a threshold of 49% was received, the application triggered a thermal stimuli. For evaluating the concept in the lab, before deploying the system in the wild, we replaced weather-based triggering with a direct control, to allow the experimenter to activate the feedback instantly.

In total, we tested 16 stimuli, eight presenting warm and eight presenting cold cues, being delivered for 10 10 s. Each participant was asked to rate his or her subjective level of pleasantness on a 5-point Likert item scale. In complement to the quantitative assessment, we collected qualitative feedback on the general concept of communicating weather information through thermal stimuli. Hence, we asked

Fig. 4 Hardware prototype providing thermal stimulus whenever the weather forecast predicts precipitation within the upcoming 60 min

each participant two questions: *'Do you think that the perceived cold/warm feedback would be recognized in your daily routine?'* and *'Which weather condition could be forecasted when cold/warm feedback is transmitted?'*.

From the results (cf. Poguntke et al. 2018), we found that cold stimuli with a variation of 7 Celsius degrees to room temperature and being presented at the interior side of the wrist had been perceived as most pleasant. In our qualitative data, we found that cold stimuli have been associated with precipitation and thus conveyed a feeling of unpleasant weather changes. Participants agreed that implicit feedback about the weather seemed beneficial to them.

On a more general level, we found that thermal stimuli can potentially convey weather information, fulfilling the conceptual requirements for sensory augmentation. Having successfully accomplished, this evaluation stage enables to, in subsequent work (beyond the scope of this section), evaluate the feasibility and user experience of such system.

4.2 SHEARS—A Selective HEARing System to Enhance Auditory Attention

Humans are naturally good at locating the source of sounds in space and use this skill frequently. This enables to associate visual and sound cues in early stages of our cognitive development, and effectively navigate reality during all our lives. However, we are not able to focus hearing at will into a single sound source and disregard the rest of the soundscape, such as we would do we sight. Even if we can concentrate our attention into particular sounds to some extent, this requires effort, particularly in loud, noisy environments.

The "cocktail party phenomenon", as named by Moray in 1959, describes the effect of people being able to perceive their name in background noise while focusing on a different particular sound signal (Moray 1959). This phenomenon is not present in everyone, but in roughly one-third of human beings (Wood and Cowan 1995). Conway et al. found a correlation between this effect and a low working memory capacity in individuals presenting it, directly related to the ability to selectively focus attention (Conway et al. 2001).

In a more general context, urban life and a constantly rising competence for attention between notifications, advertising, media, and communication pose a challenge to human cognitive capabilities and in some cases, lead to stress and cognitive exhaustion (Bawden and Robinson 2009). In this context, the ability to focus our attention on chosen signals has a huge potential benefit (Bray 2008). Commercially available products, such as Bose's headphones,[2] aim to enhance hearing attention in delimited use case scenarios, such as conversations with a single interlocutor. However, an all-encompassing approach, that enables users to control the focus and spread of hearing attention selectivity is yet to be developed.

To explore how to enable this ability in humans, we designed *SHEARS*, a Selective HEARing System capable of tailoring what the user hears in a given direction. As its name indicates, the system enables users to single out individual sound signals and perceive them without the detrimental surrounding noise.

4.2.1 Design

The main challenge of providing this sensory enhancement is not the technical implementation, but the way the auditory information flow is controlled. This consists of two main aspects: selecting the portion of space where hearing is to be focused, and switching this sensory enhancement on and off, since making it permanent would hinder drastically the users' perception of the surrounding soundscape.

We based the mechanism for selecting sound sources in the way we use visual attention. Thus, users of *SHEARS* control where they focus their hearing by pointing their head toward the desired sound source. This comes natural to humans, as when we turn our heads automatically toward the direction of a sudden sound or look to people who talk to us.

We proposed a method for toggling the sensory enhancement based on the findings from two sessions of a *future technologies* workshop (Vavoula and Sharples 2007), each one with six participants. The collected feedback suggested a preference for gesture-based controls, with a particular emphasis on the common mimic of cupping a hand next to the ear.

---

[2]https://www.bose.com/en_us/products/wellness/conversation_enhancing_headphones/hearphones.html.

4.2.2 Evaluation

We implemented a prototype in order to evaluate the proposed design. A directional microphone was attached to a hard cap and its signal amplified with a mobile phone. The user could listen to the amplified signal using in-ear headphones. An infrared proximity sensor was attached to the side of the cap over the user's ear, and sents a signal to the smartphone via Bluetooth when detecting something in its proximity. Thus, the user was able to toggle *SHEARS* by performing the suggested mimic and to control the focus of the sound selection by pointing with the head.

Using a circular array of speakers, we created a system capable of simulating spatial soundscapes, able to reproduce sound coming from all direction for a participant positioned in the center of the array. In the first experimental evaluation, we created two tasks based on different soundscapes. The first task aimed to evaluate the feasibility of the system and consisted of a different series of numbers being reproduced on each of the speakers simultaneously and participants were asked to identify a particular series. The second task simulated a real-life scenario: the speakers played audio tracks simulating the announcements of a train station. To add realism and increase the difficulty of the task, we added recordings of ambient noise from a local train station. The task of the participants was to retrieve the departure time and platform of a train headed to a specific destination.

The results of this first evaluation showed the system capable of delivering the information and manifested the shortcomings of our first prototype. Participants found the gestural control method impractical and confusing and suggested that a physical button would be more convenient. Some participants also complained about the latency in the audio signal caused by the amplification over the smartphone.

Based on these findings, we improved our prototype by replacing the smartphone with a custom made amplifier based on the LM386 operational amplifier, and the gesture-based control was derogated in favor of a simple physical button connected to the system by a long cable. Thus, the user was able to activate the enhanced hearing while pressing the button. Additionally, we replaced the in-ear headphones for active noise-canceling headphones to improve the SNR while *SHEARS* were being used. The final version of the prototype is shown in Fig. 5.

This second iteration of the prototype was evaluated in a controlled experiment consisting of three tasks. The tasks are abstractions of general features of human hearing: retrieving information from a sound source in space, locating the spatial location of a particular sound signal, and a combination of both while performing a demanding cognitive task. Most common auditory scenarios can be represented by these proposed tasks. When compared to the control condition (not using *SHEARS*), the enhanced directional hearing provided a significant performance increment in errors on all tasks, in terms of error made.

The results of the evaluation suggest that enabling focused directional hearing is not only feasible, but also can improve understanding in noisy environments. These findings open up a new dimension in the augmented senses design space, namely a physical control of auditory perception. In that context, further exploration of the control methods are necessary, since the use of buttons proved to work good enough

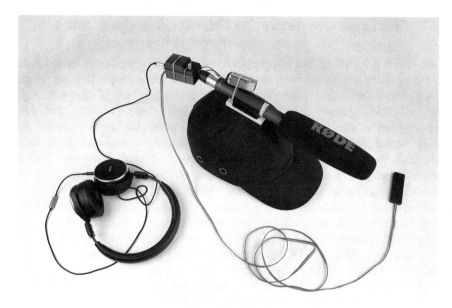

Fig. 5 Improved audio amplifier and controller

but it is still far from a satisfactory control methodology for enhanced senses. From the observed behavior of the experiment participants, and the collected feedback from interviews, we gathered that pointing with the head was for some participants not completely intuitive, since people tend to point with one of the ears toward sound sources when trying to improve hearing. Even if this phenomenon did not produce noticeable effects for most users, this should be investigated in more depth.

On a more general level, we learned that the design elements proposed by potential users during workshops might be a good start but not necessarily the ultimate solution to define interaction designs. Some problems in the interaction were impossible to predict during the early ideation and concept evaluation phases and appeared first when giving the potential users a physical prototype. Testing the design during controlled experiments also allowed us to observe strategies developed by users to face particular challenges, suggesting improvements or alternatives to the implementation of a design, or to the design itself. The importance of physical prototypes is even clearer when augmenting the human senses, since it is hard for most people to imagine what they cannot normally perceive nor have not seen before. This intuitive idea was supported by the observed evolution of the design and its reception by potential users during this research project.

Finally, this evaluation stage, namely the evaluation of feasibility, and particularly based on physical prototypes, proved to be critical. In this study case, the evaluation of the concept provided a valid general understanding, but some very valuable insights could be first made when having users interact with a prototype.

4.3   Clairbuoyance—Improving Orientation in Open Waters

Orientation is a combination of perceptual and cognitive components, in which the sense of vision usually plays an important role. Excluding people who experience visual impairments (and thus rely on different orientation strategies), we strongly depend on visual cues to navigate our environment effectively. The lack of cues does not only has an effect on avoiding obstacles, but hinders the creation of cognitive maps, which give us a general spatial understanding of our surroundings. In these situations, we depend on other senses to orient ourselves but there are some situations where directional cues are insufficient or completely absent. Open waters are an example of this environment: below water, swimmers cannot see, touch, or hear any environmental features that provide any sense of direction. This results in the inability to swim in a straight line, resulting in longer paths and times, and additional exertion (Novak 1983). Above the surface, the situation might be better, since coastal features, such as trees, buildings, or markings intended for this very purpose can be used as a rough reference. Still, this forces swimmers to periodically stop swimming, raise the head above the surface, and look around. Swimmers must then make a compromise between maintaining their stroke rhythm and keeping a straight line toward their desired goal. Current technological tools that attempt to improve the orientation of swimmers, such as compasses and GPS navigation devices, present similar problem, since they are either attached to the wrist of swimmers, or hanging from a belt, forcing users to stop swimming to assess their headings.

To tackle this situation, we created *Clairbuoyance*, a system capable of enhancing the sense of direction of swimmers in open waters. Our design consists of augmented swimming goggles, that provide visual signals to provide directional cues to the user.

4.3.1   Design

Our choice of feedback modality was based on design suggestions from previous work. In a meta-analysis of over 40 studies, Burke et al. showed the convenience of visual-auditory feedback over visual-tactile for single tasks related to conveying direction in terms of error-rates and reaction times (Burke et al. 2006). Förster, Bächlin and Tröster observed that visual and haptic feedback are more appropriate than audio for wearable systems for swimmers (Bächlin et al. 2009; Förster et al. 2009). Thus, we decided to use visual feedback in our design, since it performed better than other modalities in both aspects: providing navigational cues and swimming.

The decision of using visual feedback as a modality leads to the medium to provide it. Augmented glasses have been used successfully by several authors above water in similar tasks (Firouzian et al. 2017; Poppinga et al. 2012; Tseng et al. 2015a, b; van Veen et al. 2017). Along with the swimsuit, swimming goggles are the most ubiquitous gear used by swimmers, making them a convenient support for our design. This also proved to be an advantage in the dimensions of usability, portability, social acceptance, and comfort.

Clairbuoyance provides information about the current orientation of the swimmer. Based on the design for ActiveBelt by Tsukada et al., we differentiated between two general scenarios: feedback relative to the direction toward a goal, and absolute feedback for having a general sense of direction (Tsukada and Yasumura 2004). In our particular use case scenario, the users move only on the plane of the water surface and thus the information about orientation can be represented with a single dimension, namely an angle respect North.

Absolute orientation describes a general awareness of directions, in a similar way to what we experience in familiar environments: even without being aware of precise cardinal directions, we have a notion of in which direction things are and are able to navigate accordingly. In this case, all directions around the user are potentially important, there is no preferred direction and thus the feedback can be described in the form of a continuous signal. We named this mode as Absolute Continuous Feedback (ACF).

Relative orientation depends on a particular direction, and since the relevant orientation information is projected on the horizontal plane, there are only three possible discrete values that the feedback can present: the current hearing is correct, the desired heading is to the right, and the desired heading is to the left. We named this mode as Relative Discrete Feedback (RDF).

Once the basic concept was established and an early prototype achieved a basic functionality, we presented the design informally to the public in events (such as demos in different venues) and the local swimming pool. This way, we were able to gather insights and collect impressions on the reception of such a device by potential users. This resulted in an iterative design process, where potential users were involved in shaping the interaction.

4.3.2 Evaluation

This project entailed the three discussed stages of evaluation: a concept evaluation, based on qualitative data gathered during interviews and public demonstrations of early prototypes; a feasibility evaluation, based on quantitative data collected in functionality tests using multiple prototype iterations; and a user study, assessing user experience and performance. In this section, we focus on the third evaluation stage of the project, namely the experiment aimed at assessing user experience.

We implemented both feedback modes (RDF and ACF) into physical prototypes to conduct a study. The prototypes were based on standard swimming goggles, each device augmented with a magnetometer, accelerometer, and gyroscope to calculate the heading independently of the movements and posture of the swimmer (see Fig. 6). The feedback was provided by means of LEDs positioned on the outer area of the user's field of view. RDF was provided by actuating an LED on the direction the user should turn, or by providing no feedback when the user was in the correct course (see Fig. 7). For ACF, the LEDs constantly displayed a color matching each direction

Fig. 6 Final version of the prototype

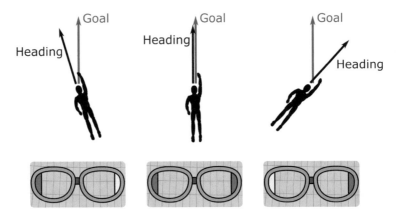

Fig. 7 Relative discrete feedback mode: a light indicates toward which side to turn

(see Fig. 8), providing unambiguous information about the user's absolute heading. The prototypes were waterproof, wireless, and lightweight, enabling to conduct an experiment with swimmers in water.

We evaluated *Clairbuoyance* in an Olympic-sized swimming pool, since the risks of running an experiment in open waters were too high. We ensured the safety of participants by closing the pool to the public and having a professional lifeguard on duty during the whole experiment. Additionally, only one participant was allowed into the pool at a time. We evaluated three conditions: the two feedback methods, and

Fig. 8 Mapping of cardinal directions to the RGB color spectrum for absolute continuous directional feedback

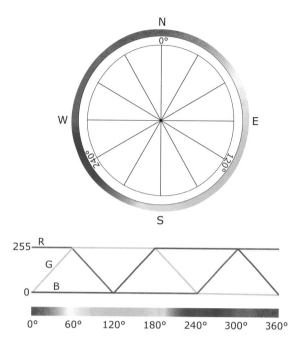

a control condition where participants had no feedback at all. For all three conditions, participants were asked not to look ahead or raise the head above the water surface.

The evaluation consisted of the participants swimming toward a series of targets on each side of the pool, following one of three equivalent patterns for each condition. The assignment of patterns to conditions, as well as the order of conditions, was counterbalanced across participants. The patterns were designed in a way that minimized the possibility of participants using the lines at the bottom of the pool as a reference to orient themselves toward the goal (see Fig. 9). We recorded the time that participants needed to complete each segment and the distance by which they missed the target. Participants filled NASA-TLX for each mode and SUS for each condition, as well as provided further qualitative feedback during semi-structured interviews.

A total of 24 participants (16 male, 8 female) took part in the study, half of them recreational swimmers, the other half advanced swimmers, who trained on a regular basis. The age of participants ranged from 18 to 62 years old, with a mean of 26.54 years ($SD = 10.93$).

From the collected quantitative and qualitative data, we gathered that the design process resulted in a concept well received by the participants of the experiment, with mean System Usability Scores of 70.72 for RDF and 71.57 for ACF. This scores can be interpreted as "good" (Bangor et al. 2008). Additionally, most advanced swimmers (11 out of 12) indicated a high preference for RDF over ACF, adducing the lack of feedback when their heading was correct minimzed distractions and helped them stayed focused. Eight out of twelve amateur swimmers preferred the RDF over ACF,

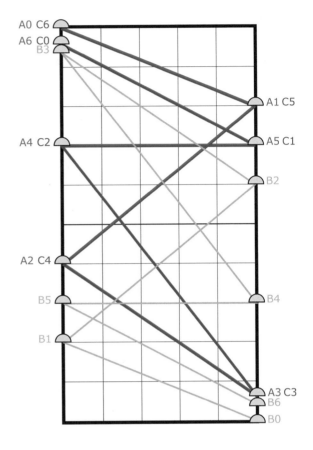

Fig. 9 Path A (red), Path B (green), and Path C (blue) were assigned in a counterbalanced fashion to the three conditions (base, ACF, and RDF). Path targets were ordered increasingly, starting at 0. The dimensions of an Olympic swimming pool are 25 m by 50 m, thus each path had a length of approximately 175 m

stating it offered stronger feedback with constant confirmation status. These results align with previous observations from Knaving et al. (2015), and from Tholander et al. (2015), confirming both the expected difference in requirements between novice and advanced users for sports technology, and that the latter prefer more fine-tuned controls. The use of the device, when compared to the base condition, did not show an increment in accuracy (on the contrary, RDF performed significantly worse), but it resulted in shorter task completion times. Combined with the participants' statements from the interviews, this suggests that swimmers felt reassured by the feedback and swim faster, which resonates with the correlation between trust and performance (especially speed) observed by Psychountaki and Zervas in their work (Psychountaki and Zervas 2000). The unexpected higher performance of the control condition regards the accuracy of participants while swimming toward the goal can be likely explained by a behavior we observed in most participants: without visual feedback to orient themselves, swimmers usually "cheated" by disobeying the instructions of not peeking, and raising their heads every now and then to orient themselves.

On a meta-level, this project highlighted the importance of evaluating sensory augmentations in use case scenarios that are as close as possible to real-life situations. Conducting the experiment in a real open-water situation would have probably resulted in a different outcome for the accuracy of swimmers, since cheating would have been impossible. Despite this limitation, recreating a scenario as realistic as possible (without endangering the participants) produced a series of insights that reached beyond the original goals of the experiment. Having representative demographics (with participants of different degrees of proficiency), and an environment close to the real-life situation, allowed to observe unexpected behaviors, such as the preference of a feedback method according to the expertise of the participant, or a variation in speed according to how sure felt the participants about their orientation. Even if is it intuitive to assume that experiment designs should resemble the concrete application scenarios as close as possible, controlled experiments usually require closed systems and evaluation frameworks to minimize the effects of external factors. Our experience in this project emphasized the necessity of going out of the lab when designing sensory augmentations, since these are intended to be used in the real world.

Finally, the above insights discussed highlight the importance of user experience in sensory augmentation design. Having the concept and its feasibility evaluated and validated resulted in a system capable of providing functionality, but the real value of this project was produced arguably through the interaction of users with the prototypes in a realistic usage scenario. The individual perspective of users, depending on their particular backgrounds, needs and capabilities, produces unique opportunities to gain a deeper understanding of the effects, benefits, and shortcomings of interaction design in general, and particularly sensory augmentation.

5 Discussion and Lessons Learned

In this chapter, we have presented three exemplary applications of technologies to augment human senses. Beyond the individual contributions of each research project, we gained practical knowledge about designing applications to enhance and augment sensation and perception through technology. Each of the projects emphasized one of the three fundamental stages of user-centered design, namely (i) validating a concept, (ii) testing a prototypical implementation of the concept in a controlled environment, and (iii) evaluating the concept outside of the lab, with the target users in a realistic usage scenario. These three projects explore different sensory domains and modalities, but share a common trait: the philosophy of augmenting reality *through augmenting the user*, instead of augmenting objects perceived by the user. This approach reinforces the idea that computers act merely as mediators between users and reality (or other humans), and thus their presence in interactions will be increasingly reduced as our technology and design techniques are refined. This idea is reflected in our projects through the use of minimalist interventions, aiming to produce unobtrusive feedback and reduce user interfaces to the bare minimum.

Based on the results of the three projects' evaluations, as well as insights gained along the evaluation process itself, we derived some general observations. In the following we will present these, phrasing them as *lessons learned*.

1. *Combine imagination and reality*—When exploring the feasibility of a concept, we often rely on the imagination skills of our participants. However, we gather from our evaluations that it is crucial to paint a mental picture of the idea that should be conveyed. For this, lively explanations and the creation of a setting in the participants' minds must be secured for evaluating concepts of augmenting technologies.

2. *Identify the object of study*—Sometimes developing a concept may involve many aspects, each of them being an innovation challenge in its own right. Particularly when creating a novel, ground-breaking prototypes, we experienced that not every aspect can be implemented as perfectly as it would be for a product-mature design. For an efficient use of available resources, it is, therefore, critical to identify the precise focus of the evaluation before taking steps toward implementation, investing effort only in the relevant aspects to be evaluated. For example, if the control mechanism of the prototype is not in the focus of the study, this part could be solved using the Wizard-of-Oz approach.

3. *Identify modality opportunities*—When dealing with limiting factors, such as cognitive load, it is important to identify where the augmentation or enhancement will have the least negative impact. Specific application scenarios might offer clear opportunities, such as the case of open waters, where visual stimuli are mostly naught and using visual feedback results in negligible cognitive demand. Identifying and profiting from these situations is crucial to ensure unobtrusive applications.

4. *Use simple solutions*—When dealing with complex technology to explore future concepts, several iterations are often required before a prototype achieves a sufficient degree of functionality. Our experience in prototype development suggests that simple solutions are preferable over refined and complex designs. In particular, we have learned that users, when confronted with physical devices and real tasks, prefer simple controls and simple feedback over sophisticated systems, even if these result in additional effort or take more time to use.

5. *Put the user first*—Adding to the previous lesson, even if simple solutions are often favorable, the simplicity of a solution can be a matter of perspective. For example, a simple implementation of a simple concept might still result in a complex interaction. Hence, it is necessary to emphasize simplicity *from the point of view of the user*. We are designing technology primarily for the user and thus, we need to pay attention that the user is not being left behind. The user experience should always be assessed when testing a device, if not even integrated into the design process before implementing prototypes.

5.1 *Future Work*

Although we have presented only a small insight into what can be achieved through combining technology with human sensing capabilities, there is much more to explore in the area of augmenting senses. As Schmidt et al. (2017), pointed out, there are some key questions that haven't been answered yet. In practice, we have only limited understanding of how the enhancement of existing sense affects the user himself. Does the combination of certain capabilities increase or decrease the performance of the pure capability on its own? Can we facilitate learning when we use different sensing modalities? Is there a limit to the magnitude in which we can enhance a given aspect of sensation? Further topics of interest are matters of ethics in the field of sensory augmentation. Giving users supernatural sensory capacities creates an asymmetry in social interaction that enables abuse and misuse, prompting to consider the need for regulation.

With the discussed challenges in mind, there are several tasks future work could focus on. Besides the technical advancements that imply improved and smaller hardware leading to better performance and higher portability, there are ethical considerations that need to be put into practices. When enhancing existing capabilities, future research will need to find ways to preserve the individual's privacy and to avoid misuse of technological achievements. Hereby, integrating and adapting approaches from the domain of usable security could help, as well as further research in the user acceptance of sense augmentation. For now, we are not sure yet in how far novel sense creations or capability enhancing hardware will enter the mass market in order to provide benefit for the average user. Hence, thorough investigations of usefulness and also the perception of end-users are necessary when attempting to adapt the technology for the masses.

6 Summary

In this chapter, we have presented three applications which illustrate a threefold design process. In particular, we started with the concept evaluation of the *RainSense* project exploring what kind of thermal stimuli would be needed to appropriately communicate weather information. This was followed by the prototype evaluation of the implementation of *Solo*: a wearable directional microphone facilitating to isolate sound sources. The last stage of our design process focused on the assessment of user experience data which was collected in a semi-controlled setting when evaluating *Clairbuoyance*, an augmented swimming goggles prototype. Finally, we discussed possible pitfalls and future challenges when augmenting the human senses. Alongside these considerations, we provided *lessons learned* based upon our own research providing valuable insights for future research.

References

Abdelrahman Y, Wozniak P, Knierim P, Henze N, Schmidt A (2018) Exploration of alternative vision modes using depth and thermal cameras. In: Proceedings of the 17th international conference on mobile and ubiquitous multimedia, MUM 2018. ACM, New York, NY, USA, pp 245–252. ISBN 978-1-4503-6594-9. https://doi.org/10.1145/3282894.3282920

Anderson ER (2003)

Bächlin M, Förster K, Tröster G (2009) Swimmaster: a wearable assistant for swimmer. In: Proceedings of the 11th international conference on ubiquitous computing, UbiComp'09. ACM, New York, NY, USA, pp 215–224. ISBN 978-1-60558-431-7. https://doi.org/10.1145/1620545. 1620578

Bangor A, Kortum PT, Miller JT (2008) 24(6):574–594. doi: 10.1080/10447310802205776

Bawden D, Robinson L (2009) J Inf Sci 35(2):180–191. ISSN 0165-5515. https://doi.org/10.1177/0165551508095781

Bray DA (2008) Information pollution, knowledge overload, limited attention spans, and our responsibilities as is professionals. In: Global Information Technology Management Association (GITMA) World Conference-June

Burke JL, Prewett MS, Gray AA, Yang L, Stilson FRB, Coovert MD, Elliot LR, Redden E (2006) Comparing the effects of visual-auditory and visual-tactile feedback on user performance: a meta-analysis. In: Proceedings of the 8th international conference on multimodal interfaces, ICMI'06. ACM, New York, NY, USA, pp 108–117. ISBN 1-59593-541-X. https://doi.org/10. 1145/1180995.1181017

Chiras DD (2013) Human biology. Jones and Bartlett Publishers

Conway AR, Cowan N, Bunting MF (2001) Psychon Bull Rev 8(2), 331–335

Ekuni S, Murata K, Asakura Y, Uehara A (2016). Bionic scope: wearable system for visual extension triggered by bioelectrical signal. In: ACM SIGGRAPH 2016 Posters, SIGGRAPH'16. ACM, New York, NY, USA, pp 41:1–41:1. ISBN 978-1-4503-4371-8. https://doi.org/10.1145/2945078. 2945119

Fan K, Seigneur J-M, Nanayakkara S, Inami M (2016) Electrosmog visualization through augmented blurry vision. In: Proceedings of the 7th augmented human international conference 2016, AH'16. ACM, New York, NY, USA, pp 35:1–35:2. ISBN 978-1-4503-3680-2. https://doi. org/10.1145/2875194.2875203

Firouzian A, Kashimoto Y, Asghar Z, Keranen N, Yamamoto G, Pulli P (2017). Twinkle megane: Near-eye led indicators on glasses for simple and smart navigation in daily life. In: Giokas K, Bokor L, Hopfgartner F, (eds) eHealth 360. Springer International Publishing, pp 17–22. ISBN 978-3-319-49655-9

Förster K, Bächlin M, Tröster G (2009) Non-interrupting user interfaces for electronic body-worn swim devices. In: Proceedings of the 2nd international conference on pervasive technologies related to assistive environments, PETRA'09. ACM, New York, NY, USA, pp 38:1–38:4. ISBN 978-1-60558-409-6. https://doi.org/10.1145/1579114.1579152

Goldstein EB (2010) Sensation and perception, 8th edn. Thomson Wadsworth. ISBN 978-0-495-60149-4

Grönvall E, Fritsch J, Vallgårda A (2016) Feltradio: sensing and making sense of wireless traffic. In: Proceedings of the 2016 ACM conference on designing interactive systems, DIS'16. ACM, New York, NY, USA, pp 829–840. ISBN 978-1-4503-4031-1. https://doi.org/10.1145/2901790. 2901818

Heller MA (2013) The psychology of touch. Psychology Press

Jeffress LA (1948) 41(1):35

Kasahara S, Ando M, Suganuma K, Rekimoto J (2016) Parallel eyes: exploring human capability and behaviors with paralleled first person view sharing. In: Proceedings of the 2016 CHI conference on human factors in computing systems, CHI'16. ACM, New York, NY, USA, pp 1561–1572. ISBN 978-1-4503-3362-7. https://doi.org/10.1145/2858036.2858495

Kaufman L (1974) Sight and mind: an introduction to visual perception. Oxford University Press

Knaving K, Wozniak P, Fjeld M, Björk S (2015) Flow is not enough: understanding the needs of advanced amateur runners to design motivation technology. In: Proceedings of the 33rd annual ACM conference on human factors in computing systems, CHI'15. ACM, New York, NY, USA, pp 1561–1562. ISBN 978-1-4503-3145-6. https://doi.org/10.1145/2702123.2702542

Lee W, Lim Y-K (2010) Thermo-message: exploring the potential of heat as a modality of peripheral expression. In: CHI'10 extended abstracts on human factors in computing systems, CHI EA'10. ACM, New York, NY, USA, pp 4231–4236. ISBN 978-1-60558-930-5. https://doi.org/10.1145/1753846.1754131

Li J, Wang Y, Liu L, Xu S, Liu Y, Leng J, Cai S (2019) 0(0):1903762. https://doi.org/10.1002/adfm.201903762

Moray N (1959) Q J Exp Psychol 11(1), 56–60

Niforatos E, Fedosov A, Elhart I, Langheinrich M (2017) Augmenting skiers' peripheral perception. In: Proceedings of the 2017 ACM international symposium on wearable computers, ISWC'17. ACM, New York, NY, USA, pp 114–121. ISBN 978-1-4503-5188-1. https://doi.org/10.1145/3123021.3123052

Novak J (1983) pp 345–349

Pavlov IP, Gantt WH (1941) Conditioned reflexes and psychiatry, vol 2. International Publishers, New York

Poguntke R, Kiss F, Kaplan A, Schmidt A, Schneegass S (2018) Rainsense: exploring the concept of a sense for weather awareness. In: Proceedings of the 20th international conference on human-computer interaction with mobile devices and services adjunct, MobileHCI'18. ACM, New York, NY, USA, pp 9–15. ISBN 978-1-4503-5941-2. https://doi.org/10.1145/3236112.3236114.

Poppinga B, Henze N, Fortmann J, Heuten W, Boll S (2012)

Psychountaki M, Zervas Y (2000) 91(1):87–94. https://doi.org/10.2466/pms.2000.91.1.87 PMID:11011876

Russell MJ (1976) 260(5551):520

Schaal B (1988) 13(2):145–190

Schmidt A (2017) 16(01):6–10. ISSN 1536-1268. https://doi.org/10.1109/MPRV.2017.8

Schmidt A, Schneegass S, Kunze K, Rekimoto J, Woo W (2017) Workshop on amplification and augmentation of human perception. In: Proceedings of the 2017 CHI conference extended abstracts on human factors in computing systems, CHI EA'17. ACM, New York, NY, USA, pp 668–673. ISBN 978-1-4503-4656-6. https://doi.org/10.1145/3027063.3027088

Schoop E, Smith J, Hartmann B (2018) Hindsight: enhancing spatial awareness by sonifying detected objects in real-time 360-degree video. In: Proceedings of the 2018 CHI conference on human factors in computing systems, CHI'18. ACM, New York, NY, USA, pp 143:1–143:12. ISBN 978-1-4503-5620-6. https://doi.org/10.1145/3173574.3173717

Sines G, Sakellarakis YA (1987) 91(2):191–196. ISSN 00029114, 1939828X. http://www.jstor.org/stable/505216

Tholander J, Nylander S (2015) Snot, sweat, pain, mud, and snow: performance and experience in the use of sports watches. In: Proceedings of the 33rd annual ACM conference on human factors in computing systems. ACM, pp 2913–2922

Tseng H-Y, Liang R-H, Chan L, Chen B-Y (2015a) Lead: utilizing light movement as peripheral visual guidance for scooter navigation. In: Proceedings of the 17th international conference on human-computer interaction with mobile devices and services, MobileHCI'15. ACM, New York, NY, USA, pp 323–326. ISBN 978-1-4503-3652-9. https://doi.org/10.1145/2785830.2785831

Tseng H-Y, Liang R-H, Chan L, Chen B-Y (2015b) Using point-light movement as peripheral visual guidance for scooter navigation. In Proceedings of the 6th augmented human international conference, AH'15. ACM, New York, NY, USA, pp 177–178. ISBN 978-1-4503-3349-8. https://doi.org/10.1145/2735711.2735800

Tsukada K, Yasumura M (2004) Activebelt: Belt-type wearable tactile display for directional navigation. In: International conference on ubiquitous computing. Springer, pp 384–399

van Veen T, Karjanto J, Terken J (2017) Situation awareness in automated vehicles through proximal peripheral light signals. In: Proceedings of the 9th international conference on automotive user interfaces and interactive vehicular applications, AutomotiveUI'17. ACM, New York, NY, USA, pp 287–292. ISBN 978-1-4503-5150-8. https://doi.org/10.1145/3122986.3122993.

Vavoula GN, Sharples M (2007) 2(4):393–419. ISSN 1556-1615. https://doi.org/10.1007/s11412-007-9026-0

Verbeek C, van Campen C (2013) 8(2):133–148

Whitton JT, Everall J (1973) British J Dermatol 89(5), 467–476

Wilson G, Halvey M, Brewster SA, Hughes SA (2011) Some like it hot: thermal feedback for mobile devices. In: Proceedings of the SIGCHI conference on human factors in computing systems, CHI'11. ACM, New York, NY, USA, pp 2555–2564. ISBN 978-1-4503-0228-9. https://doi.org/10.1145/1978942.1979316

Wilson G, Davidson G, Brewster SA (2015) In the heat of the moment: subjective interpretations of thermal feedback during interaction. In Proceedings of the 33rd annual ACM conference on human factors in computing systems, CHI'15. ACM, New York, NY, USA, pp 2063–2072. ISBN 978-1-4503-3145-6. https://doi.org/10.1145/2702123.2702219

Wilson G, Dobrev D, Brewster SA (2016) Hot under the collar: mapping thermal feedback to dimensional models of emotion. In: Proceedings of the 2016 CHI conference on human factors in computing systems, CHI'16. ACM, New York, NY, USA, pp 4838–4849. ISBN 978-1-4503-3362-7. https://doi.org/10.1145/2858036.2858205.

Wood N, Cowan N (1995) J Exp Psychol Learn Mem Cogn 21(1):255

Reflections

Privacy and Security in Augmentation Technologies

Mohamed Khamis and Florian Alt

Abstract In this chapter, we present a privacy and security framework for designers of technologies that augment humans' cognitive and perceptive capabilities. The framework consists of several groups of questions, meant to guide designers during the different stages of the design process. The objective of our work is to support the need for considering implications of novel technologies with regard to privacy and security early in the design process rather than post-hoc. The framework is based on a thorough review of the technologies presented earlier on in this book as well as of prior research in the field of technology augmentation. From this review, we derived several themes that are not only valuable pointers for future work but also serve as a basis for the subsequent framework. We point out the need to focus on the following aspects: data handling, awareness, user consent, and the design of the user interface.

1 Introduction

Novel technologies enter the market at a rapidly accelerating pace. A fundamental challenge is that designers of such technology usually need to think about the benefits it provides to the users first with the ultimate goal of developing a product that generates revenue. At the same time, this usually leads to that security and privacy are only a secondary design goal and are not considered but at a later stage of the design and development process, if at all.

Integrating security and privacy measures post-hoc is difficult for many reasons. This can even impact the success of augmentation technologies. For example, privacy concerns were among the main reasons Google Glass is no longer available as a consumer product. There are even several documented cases where users of

M. Khamis (✉)
University of Glasgow, Glasgow, UK
e-mail: mohamed.khamis@glasgow.ac.uk

F. Alt
Bundeswehr University, Neubiberg, Germany
e-mail: florian.alt@unibw.de

T. Dingler and E. Niforatos (eds.), *Technology-Augmented Perception and Cognition*,
Human–Computer Interaction Series, https://doi.org/10.1007/978-3-030-30457-7_8

257

Google Glass were assaulted due to privacy concerns of bystanders (Wolf et al. 2014). Another example is head-mounted displays (HMDs). By being able to track users' moves, for example, it is possible to find out if users are slow to react to information displayed on HMDs. This is sensitive information a user might not want in the hand of third parties. At the same time, Mixed Reality companies such as Oculus deliberately decided not to focus on security measures such as data encryption (Ng 2018), because in their view this would lead to unnecessary complexity, which would negatively influence the experience in the first place. An attack that causes the leakage of the user's sensitive data might have significant privacy implications. For example, the fact that data on OpenSim[1] is unencrypted enables attackers to steal or manipulate content and to impersonate users (Korolov 2016).

The aforementioned examples demonstrate the need to more carefully think about possible security and privacy implications as we design novel technologies early on in the design process. The objective of this chapter is to provide an overview of possible implications on security and privacy as we are designing technologies with the goal of augmenting human perception and cognition. In particular, we critically review state of the art with the ideas presented in the previous chapters in consideration and discuss how applications might put users' security and privacy at risk. Ultimately, we derive a framework meant to help designers of such novel technologies to consider privacy and security early on in the design process. Our chapter is complemented by a discussion of future research directions, including both challenges and opportunities, resulting from the aforementioned technologies becoming available.

2   Background

The following section introduces basic terms and concepts from privacy and security. In particular, we focus on the properties of secure systems, attack and threat modeling, and briefly motivate the need for user-centered security.

2.1   Properties of Secure Systems

The objective of security mechanisms is to preserve three properties of a system against misuse and interference: confidentiality, integrity, and availability (Andress 2014).

Regarding *confidentiality*, two concepts can be distinguished: (1) *data confidentiality* refers to the need of preventing data to become available to unauthorized entities; (2) *privacy* means an individual's data should be used, disclosed, and exchanged according to a set of rules that the user has consented to. An example of a confiden-

---

[1]OpenSim is an open-source platform for hosting virtual worlds. It was used for many years by Second Life and forms the basis of the US Military MOSES project.

tiality breach would be private user data (e.g., blood pressure readings) leaking from a server or an on-body sensor and being made accessible to an unauthorized entity, such as an insurance company.

Maintaining a system's *integrity* refers to ensuring that systems are consistently performing their function without intended or unintended unauthorized manipulation. A further aspect concerns the integrity of data, meaning that data should be altered only by authorized entities. An example of an integrity breach is when a malicious program (e.g., malware) manipulates the readings from a sensor or user data stored in a database.

Finally, *availability* refers to ensuring that systems and data are promptly usable. Denial of service (DoS) attacks are among the most common ways to disrupt the availability of systems. Other examples include preventing users from making emergency calls.

2.2 Attack Modeling

The aforementioned properties of security systems may be compromised as results of an attack. For example, attackers try to exploit vulnerabilities to disclose data and, hence, breach confidentiality, alter data to breach integrity, or deny services or access to data to breach availability. In order to protect these properties—confidentiality, integrity and availability—a common approach is to model potential attacks. Subsequently, potential threats can be better understood and, ultimately, countermeasures be designed.

Firstly, it is necessary to understand the *causes of an attack*. Attacks can be a result of software and hardware vulnerabilities (e.g., backdoor, or network vulnerability); also, attackers often address humans as the weak link in secure systems (e.g., via social engineering attacks, such as phishing or deep fakes); or attackers often exploit unintended characteristics of a system, so-called side channels. In the latter form of attack, adversaries exploit information gained from a system's implementation rather than from a weakness of a system. Examples of such attacks include exploiting power consumption or network traffic to infer which type of data is being transmitted or exploiting smudge (Schneegass et al. 2014) and heat traces (Abdelrahman et al. 2017a) on interfaces to infer user input.

Secondly, two different *types of attacks* can be distinguished: active and passive attacks. During active attacks, adversaries try to actively alter system resources. In contrast, the goal of passive attacks is to learn about vulnerabilities of a system or to get access to confidential information without affecting system resources. As a result, the latter type of attacks is much more difficult to detect. An attempt to reset someone's account credentials is considered an active attack. Observing a user as they authenticate in public (i.e., shoulder surfing) is considered a passive attack.

Thirdly, designers need to be aware of *attackers' motivations*. This is not only useful to determine the likeliness of an attack but also the potential effort an attacker is willing to spend. Some attackers aim for profit (e.g., credit card fraud, ransomware, stealing, and/or selling resources). Others aim at disrupting certain processes (e.g., hacking a political party's website), often with the intention to make a statement. Some individuals enjoy the challenge and perform attacks for "fun". Finally, so-called white-hat hackers perform attacks to test systems (e.g., network security analyst performing penetration tests).

The fourth aspect to consider is the *resources and capabilities of the attacker.* On one hand, attacks can be performed by so-called script kiddies. On the other hand, adversaries may be well-organized cyber-terrorists or nation-sponsored hackers, having significant resources in terms of money and computing power.

2.3   Threat Modeling

An understanding of the attackers, their capabilities, their motivations, and their resources helps identifying the threats that a system can be exposed to. Subsequently, designers or system providers can decide, how to protect against possible attacks. It is important to realize that protecting against all possible attacks is usually unfeasible, since it requires considerable effort and resources. Hence, a more promising strategy is to prioritize which threats to protect against. For example, if an attack can be performed by adversaries with little to no technical background (e.g., most user-centered attacks, such as guessing or shoulder-surfing credentials), then defending against these potentially common attacks should be prioritized. Another common approach is to understand the potential consequences of an attack. For example, protecting against attacks that have mild consequences (e.g., embarrassment) can sometimes be prioritized over attacks that could impact health or lead to bankruptcy.

The following questions may guide designers and providers when designing appropriate security measures: Who are the most likely attackers? What are the capabilities of attackers? What are potential consequences of attacks? What is the weakest link in the system that attackers will likely exploit?

2.4   Human-Centered Security

The final part of this section is dedicated to human-centered security. After a brief motivation we summarize approaches to achieve human-centered security.[2]

Researchers have long discussed the role of humans in secure systems. It has been argued that humans are often the weakest link in secure systems. At the same time, this is often a result of systems not being designed for the way in which people interact with computing systems. Take, for example, authentication mechanisms. To make people create strong passwords, policies today require users to choose passwords consisting of eight or more characters, containing uppercase letters, lowercase letters,

---

[2]"Usable Privacy and Security" is another term that describes this field.

symbols, and digits. At the same time, users are required to create such passwords for an average of 100 different accounts. The obvious consequence is that humans will reuse passwords or write them down. This, however, is less a result of the user's inability to remember such passwords, but of the poor design of this security mechanism for its use case. Text-based passwords emerged in the 1960s where people had on average access to one computer and authenticated a few times per day. Today, however, we interact fundamentally different with computers. Mobile, networked devices allow us to access sensitive information, every time and everywhere. For example, we access the smartphone more than 80 times per day (Harbach et al. 2014), leading both to a significant overhead in authentication time and to the need to use more passwords that can be remembered. As a result, users will optimize for convenience especially because security is never their primary task but something that gets in their way as they are trying to do other things.

This has been recognized by the research community. The National Cyber Security Center in the UK has a team dedicated to "people-centered Security", whose lead argues that "security must work for people. If security doesn't work for people, it doesn't work" (W 2017). Similarly, researchers have acknowledged that "users are not the enemy" (Adams and Sasse 1999) and identified the need to design secure systems that are usable by the average human.

In response to this, researchers came up with approaches to design such systems. Whitten and Tygar argue that "security software is usable if the people who are expected to use it are reliably made aware of the security tasks they need to perform; are able to figure out how to successfully perform those tasks; don't make dangerous errors; and are sufficiently comfortable with the interface to continue using it" (Whitten and Tygar 1999). Ka-Ping Yee suggests guidelines for usable and secure authorization (Yee 2005). For example, he suggests that the most straightforward way for users to perform tasks should be matched with the most secure option (e.g., default options are the most secure ones) and that users must maintain accurate awareness of their own authority to access resources, as well as being aware of and able to reduce others' authority to access own resources. Many of these recommendations correspond to Jakob Nielsen's usability heuristics for user interface design (Nielsen 1994). This similarity implies that there are many usability concepts that, when applied, would result in improved use of the security system, which in turn results in higher security.

Therefore, we conclude that the main aim of human-centered security is to make privacy and security an integrated, natural, unburdened part of human-computer interaction. According to Cranor and her colleagues, the following are the core challenges of designing usable and human-centered security systems:

Security concepts are complicated for the average user.   For the average user, understanding concepts such as encryption, HTTPS, etc. is hard and hence might result in poor security behavior (Whitten and Tygar 1999).

Security is a secondary task.   Humans never use a system with the aim to authenticate or download security updates. Hence, their motivation for secure behavior can be generally considered rather low (West 2008).

Human capabilities are limited.   For example, the average user has about 90 web accounts but not the cognitive abilities to memorize 90 unique passwords that abide to commonly used password policies (Adams and Sasse 1999).

Misaligned priorities.   An organization's interest in protecting its data might lead them to requiring employees to use complicated security mechanisms. At the same time employees want to get their work done as fast as possible. As a result, they may find workarounds to make security less cumbersome (Adams and Sasse 1999).

Habituation.   People are used to dismissing warnings (e.g., clicking "next") which increases the likelihood the user will perform an insecure action (Sunshine et al. 2009).

2.5   Security and Privacy Implications of Human Augmentation

The proliferation of novel technologies always comes with new implications. This applies to any form of innovation—from the industrial revolution to AI-generated videos and content. In the last two decades, security and privacy implications were among the most discussed concerns of advances in computation as technology is becoming ubiquitous at an ever-increasing pace. This led to researchers investigating frameworks for designing privacy-aware ubiquitous systems (Langheinrich 2001). Researchers have recently started investigating the privacy implications of particular augmentation technologies, such as eye tracking (Katsini et al. 2020; Steil et al. 2019a), thermal imaging (Abdelrahman et al. 2017a), and life logging (Elagroudy 2019; Steil et al. 2019b). Similarly, recent work investigated the possibly malicious use of human augmentation technologies and proposed countermeasures to address them. For example, researchers explored how to protect against thermal attacks that aim for retrieving passwords from heat traces left on touch surfaces (Abdelrahman et al. 2017a), how to hide sensitive content that could be recorded by life loggers (Korayem et al. 2016), and how to prevent the identification of a user through their eye tracking data (Steil et al. 2019a).

While efforts to tackle privacy and security issues of individual technologies are a step in the right direction, we argue that there is a need for a high-level framework that would allow researchers and practitioners to address privacy and security issues from the beginning of the user-centered design process of human augmentation technologies. In other words, we need to address the issues proactively before they arise, rather than patching them up after the release of products. Without doing that, we risk that (a) augmentation technologies are never picked up due to security or privacy concerns, and (b) augmentation technologies are used maliciously.

3   Methodology

After introducing human-centered security and highlighting the importance of understanding the implications on user privacy, security, and safety, now we explain our methodology in identifying said implications in the context of augmentation technologies.

To help designers of technology that augments our perception and cognition mitigate potential privacy and security issues, we set out by obtaining an *understanding of potential privacy and security concerns*. Therefore, we carefully reviewed both the technology presented in the previous chapters alongside prior work in this field. Selected projects considered for our analysis are listed in Table 1. For each project we (1) extract the core concept, (2) identify which data is collected and the consequences of storing and sharing this data, (3) discuss which information could be derived if somebody had access to the collected data, (4) discuss new attack channels that are now feasible due to the use of this concept, (5) discuss how the technology can be used maliciously, and (6) derive possible implications on users' security and privacy with a focus on data manipulation and physical harm. This part primarily evolves around implications on the user of a technology, implications from the surroundings of the user of a technology (e.g., new attack vectors), implications of third parties on the user (e.g., implementation of privacy and data confidentiality by a company), and implications on those people around the user.

In a second step, these implications were used as a basis to *identify themes that require further research*. To do this, we performed a data walkthrough and discussed what it would take to address the concerns revealed in the first step.

Third, we derived a *framework* that provides designers a structured approach of considering potential security and privacy implications during the design process. In particular, the framework evolves around questions regarding data collection, data storage, user control over the data, and the user interface design.

Although unanticipated, our review identified not only potential security and privacy concerns (Sect. 4), but also opportunities for novel security mechanisms (Sect. 5). More specifically, we discuss how perception and cognition enhancing technologies can be leveraged to build novel authentication mechanisms that are both secure and usable. With this discussion, we hope to provide fertile ground for future research between people working in the field of technology augmentation and usable security and privacy.

4   Privacy, Security, and Safety Implications of Technology-Augmented Perception and Cognition

The past chapters have provided forward-looking concepts and systems that demonstrate a great potential of augmenting the perception and cognition of humans. Without doubt, these developments will bring tangible benefits to users. However, similar

Table 1 Selected projects related to human augmentation

Chapter	Project	Description
Chapter "7"	RainSense	A system supporting users to develop a sense of precipitation through thermal output; the system receives weather information via Bluetooth and subsequently provides thermal feedback by means of a Peltier element
Chapter "7"	Solo	A system enabling users to focus on sounds in a given direction by means of pointing at a sound source. It filters out surrounding noise, enabling users to perceive individual sound signals
Chapter "7"	Clairbuoyant	A system enhancing the sense of direction of open water swimmers. It uses augmented swimming goggles for providing visual directional cues
Chapter "6"	Insertables for non-medical purposes	A survey with 115 participants to understand what devices they are putting in their body, what they use these devices for, their motivations for doing so, and how they identify themselves

to any technological innovation, there are downsides that, if not accounted for, could have significant negative impacts on humans' lives.

In the following, we will highlight a number of issues related to privacy, security, and safety that researchers and practitioners should account for when designing systems to augment human perception and cognition.

4.1 Understanding Consequences of Data Sharing

The abundance of sensors users will be carrying in the future allows myriads of personal information to be collected, almost anytime and anywhere. This information can be used for many applications, providing benefits for the user. At the same time, the collected data are usually transferred to servers for analysis. This potentially affects users' privacy: non-trusted companies that manage the collected data could potentially sell the data to third parties.

For example, chapter 6 demonstrated how biometric data collected through insertables can be transmitted to external devices or even remote servers for analysis. Interviews reveal that early adopters of insertables hope to see them used to read their internal blood oxygen level and interpret data from their eyes. At the same time, there could be severe privacy implications in case such data is shared with third parties. For example, insurance companies could use the data about a user's biometrics to decide whether or not to insure them.

Another example is the work on task resumption in chapter 4 where the idea is to help users recover from being interrupted during tasks, as it has been shown that such interruptions strongly influence productivity. At the same time, information on interruptions is sensitive, for example, such interruptions may be caused by a colleague to have a private chat. As a result, knowledge on the type of interruption might influence on personal evaluation of even payment if known to employers. For example, if an employer learns that an employee is being interrupted a lot by matters that are not related to their work (e.g., personal messaging notifications), they might use this information against them.

The particular challenge we see here is that it is often difficult to infer which consequences it might have if data is available to third parties. Designers and developers need to exercise great care and develop an understanding of what it means to collect, store, and process certain types of data.

4.2   Loss of Data Control

The increasing number, ubiquity, and capability of sensors makes it significantly harder for the user to control what information is being collected and shared with other parties. This could make informed consent of data collection and sharing almost impossible. The reason is that the amount of data that is collected is so massive that humans are cognitively incapable of keeping up with it and are left alone understanding, or even realizing, that data is being collected. In the following we discuss different forms of loss of control over data.

For example, chapter 6 describes a trend to insert RFID and NFC tags into people's bodies. These chips carry information that could potentially be sensitive (e.g., credentials to access a building). At the same time, users do not have full control on when this data can be accessed. If an attacker approaches one of those users with an NFC reader, they can extract the information without the user's consent. Similarly, an attacker could read off information on a user's inserted RFID if the user is unconscious, sleeping, or inattentive.

Insertables (chapter 6) introduce a further threat: communicating biometric data to surrounding devices or to remote servers may introduce a new attach channel: if data is sent in an unencrypted way, man-in-the-middle attacks can result in attackers intercepting sensitive information about the user as they are transferred wirelessly. This can happen without the user's control.

In contrast to an attacker actively extracting data, the user could disclose private data through unexpected means when using augmenting technologies. For example, in chapter 7, Poguntke and Kiss introduced a technology amplifying a users' sense of hearing where users could perform a mid-air gesture to specify a direction for which they want to increase their sense of hearing, for example, a group of people in close vicinity. The design of this gesture in itself might be problematic, since it reveals a user's interest.

Another challenge arises in situations where information can be inferred from data. For example, the data collected to support task resumption strategies discussed in chapter 5 does not only reveal which content the user accessed and interacted with, but it could also reveal when the user worked on what. While a user might have consciously consented to sharing data on the content they accessed, they might not be aware of additional information it allows to be derived nor what it could be used for.

In summary, it is unrealistic to expect that users are aware of the consequences as novel technologies take away control over their data. Designers need to carefully think how to enable control over users' data. Furthermore, as users are asked to provide consent, it needs to be clearly communicated to the user what potential consequences are.

4.3   Novel Attack Channels

Many technologies we reviewed add novel output channels and, hence, enable novel attacks via these channels. A particular challenge stems from the fact that many of these channels might initially not have been designed to convey sensitive data and designers thus need to think about novel ways to protect these channels.

For example, chapter 4 presented how visual, auditory, haptic, and tangible output modalities can be leveraged to provide cues for task resumption. This includes, for example, large screens able to convey personal information. Traditionally, large screens were not meant to convey this type of information. In particular, if used in shared workspaces or public, there is a need to develop means for protecting users' privacy.

Similarly, the technologies presented in chapter 7 offer novel means to present information. Examples of output channels that have recently become mainstream include head-mounted displays (HMDs) and smartwatches. The visual feedback provided through their screens makes them subject to shoulder surfing (Eiband et al. 2017). Note, that not only visual output is subject to eavesdropping. For example, Solo (chapter 77) allows for listening to conversations at a distance and these conversations could as well be eavesdropped by bystanders of a person wearing the Solo system.

From this we learn that designers need to carefully consider the output channel used for technologies augmenting human senses. Of particular interest here is the context of use. If such a technology is used in a public or shared space, means need to be provided to secure the technology against attacks from bystanders.

4.4   The Cyborg Stalker

An interesting aspect is that technologies augmenting users' perception and cognition could be exploited by the augmented users themselves in malicious ways. This means that designers should not only think of how to protect their users' privacy, but also try to understand how users can misuse their innovations.

For example, an attacker could use the Solo system (chapter 7) to eavesdrop on conversations of people in public. Lifelogging cameras are known to cause privacy issues when bystanders are in the field of view (Li et al. 2017; Thomaz et al. 2013) or screens that are showing sensitive content (e.g., desktop screen showing emails) (Korayem et al. 2016). Some HMDs are now augmented with thermal cameras (Abdelrahman et al. 2018), which could be used to infer the emotions of surrounding bystanders (Abdelrahman et al. 2017b), or even to perform thermal attacks to extract users' inputs (e.g., passwords) on screens and keyboards (Abdelrahman et al. 2017a).

This points at interesting directions for future work. To mitigate malicious use, technologies could consider their current context and accordingly enable or disable certain features. For example, a lifelogging camera can automatically blur people's faces and black out recorded screens.

4.5   Impact of Data Manipulation

As we become more dependent on the technologies we use, their impact on our lives increases. Consequently, any manipulation of system variables, configurations, or any other aspects impacting system integrity can likewise influence us.

One particular challenge we foresee as augmentation technologies are becoming ubiquitous is fake data. For example, RainSense (see chapter 7) is meant to make users aware of weather conditions and potentially notify them about that it might rain during the day. Access to the data on which the prediction for rain is based, adversaries could misuse the system to trigger the prediction of rain and ultimately make the user purchase accessories (such as an umbrella) or clothes even though they do not need them.

This is just one example highlighting the need to carefully think about how data can be collected, transmitted, and be stored in a secure manner, such that adversaries cannot simply temper with data.

4.6   Physical Harm

We identified a number of ways in which augmentation technologies could have severe consequences and physically harm the user, if not carefully designed. In the following we sketch cases in which this can happen directly or indirectly.

Examples, where the system could indirectly lead to physical harm is the wrong display of information. For example, Poguntke and Kiss proposed using visual feedback to convey a swimmer's orientation to herself. Any potential tampering with the shown orientation could result in misleading the user. This might not only have social and economic implications (e.g., losing a competition), but in extreme cases it could even have safety implications (e.g., leading the swimmer to a dangerous area in open water).

Another example of indirect harm could be the increased value of human body parts as augmentation technology, for example, in the form of insertables, is added. As humans start to use expensive insertables, a new type of crime could arise from illegally harvesting insertables from their users. Or, a human with an insertable used for authentication (e.g., unlock a security door) could be physically harmed to gain access to their authentication token. Note that similar attacks occur in the context of biometric features (finger, iris, etc.).

This amplifies the need to ensure that these technological advancements are safe and do not subject users to hazardous situations. The previous section highlighted how manipulating the data that is perceived by the user could have fatal consequences. Indeed, an HMD that is communicating with other servers could be prone to man-in-the-middle attacks, in which an attacker can overlay a virtual bridge over a real cliff, hence subjecting the user's life to danger (Mathis and Khamis 2019). Designers should keep similar issues in mind when designing such technologies.

4.7   Summary

To summarize, while technology augmentations can bring many benefits to users, there is a number of privacy, security, and safety issues that should be considered and further investigated: (1) the augmentation itself could become the very reason behind the leakage of private data; (2) obtaining informed consent before data is exchanged or used is becoming increasingly challenging; (3) adversaries will come up with novel attacks for each new, exposed channel; (4) designers should keep in mind that the augmentations can be potentially exploited by its users (e.g., to spy on others); and (5) designers should be aware of the amplified impact of data manipulation which could lead to physical harm.

5 Directions for Future Research

Our review of related work revealed a need for further research in different areas. Particular areas we identified are supporting informed consent, understanding and mitigating the effects of data manipulation, and exploring the influence of augmentation on malicious use.

Of particular interest in this context is the European Union's General Data Protection Regulation (GDPR)[3]. One of the core principles is the need for a lawful basis for processing data. In particular, explicit informed consent from users is required in case data is made publicly available. One specific challenge here is also that it needs to be possible to revoke this consent at any time. Furthermore, there is a need to inform users about the extent of data collection and provide them an overview of which data is stored and how it is being processed upon request. Finally, providers need to ensure that data can be erased within 30 days. While not being specific to augmenting technologies, these requirements are nevertheless highly relevant, since they strongly influence the way in which technologies, underlying architectures, and user interfaces need to be built.

5.1 Informed Consent

Achieving informed consent is becoming increasingly challenging in the ubiquitous computing age. Augmentation technologies raise similar concerns. Some of the augmentations, such as Insertables (chapter 6), require collecting data. There are two main aspects where it is becoming increasingly challenging to ensure the user gives full, informed consent in the context of augmentation technologies:

5.1.1 Informed Consent in Data Usage

More and more data are being collected about the user. At the same time, the amount of information that can be inferred from this data is not only increasing but also becoming more complex and less obvious for the regular user. For example, it is not immediately clear to users that their eye movements can reveal their mental states (Majaranta and Bulling 2014) or even their political temperament (Dodd et al. 2011).

Currently, consent for collecting, using, and sharing the user's data is obtained by asking users to read and accept long and complicated terms and conditions that lay out the privacy policies. This presents a research opportunity: we should move away from the use of text-based privacy policies that suffer from low usability to novel approaches that are more understandable and support informed consent. For

---

[3]https://ec.europa.eu/commission/priorities/justice-and-fundamental-rights/data-protection/
2018-reform-eu-data-protection-rules/eu-data-protection-rules_en.

example, Kelly et al. (2009) proposed designing a "Nutrition label" for privacy. In their work, they suggest standardizing privacy-related facts by presenting them in a concise form similar to how food products are labeled with nutrition facts that summarize the amount of calories, vitamins, fats, etc. in a product. In their proposal, they suggest emphasizing "what" information is collected, "how" it can be used, and "who" may the user's information be shared with. Another example is how many tech companies are starting to use alternatives to text-based privacy policies. Apple, Google, and Facebook use videos to illustrate which data is collected, how it is used, and with whom it is shared. The privacy policy pages are structured in a more intuitive way compared to the traditional text-based privacy policies.

While these improvements are all in the right direction, augmentation technologies require us to design ways to communicate an unprecedented amount of information to ensure informed consent. Therefore, there is a need to design methods to effectively and efficiently communicate privacy-related information when using augmentation technologies. This presents another research opportunity: a promising starting point is to explore different mediums (e.g., videos, virtual reality, narrated stories, games) to communicate privacy policies of augmentation technologies to the users. As for example in Solo, augmentation technologies may also create an increasing number of situations, in which data of people who are not the main users of a technology are collected willingly or unwillingly. This creates another opportunity for future research, i.e., how can consent be obtained from non-users?

5.1.2 Informed Consent in User Actions

There is a growing trend to build systems that work in the background without the user's explicit input. Examples include systems that respond to the user's behavior (e.g., gaze behavior, body movements, etc.) or systems that respond to implanted RFIDs (e.g., see chapter 6), the user's face, or fingerprint. While these technologies make interactive systems seamlessly integrated around us and reduce the cognitive load required to control them, they present new challenges.

As interaction becomes more passive rather than active, it becomes more likely that users perform unintended, or even unauthorized, inputs. This has negative implications on security. For example, contact-free bank cards have become more common recently as they are more usable. They are faster because they do not require the user to enter a PIN as long as the payment is below a certain threshold. This usability improvement also means that payments can be done without the user's permission if the card is stolen. Similarly, there have been reported cases where a smartphone's fingerprint sensor unlocks a user's phone upon sensing their fingerprint, even if the user did that unconsciously (e.g., while asleep (TheGuardian 2017)) or forcibly (e.g., police unlocking a dead person's phone (BBC 2018)). A similar issue that is heavily studied is the Midas touch problem in gaze interfaces (Drewes 2019; Jacob 1990; Khamis et al. 2018), in which systems interpret regular eye movements as gaze input and result in unintended input. While fingerprint unlock without consent and

Midas touch are two distinct problems, they are both forms of unintentional input, which suggests that some of the solutions proposed to address one of them might be promising for the other.

This presents a research opportunity: Future work in augmentation technologies should strive balance between high usability of systems based on implicit interaction and a high level of security. One approach is to detect intention during implicit interactions. Similar to how gaze interfaces require users to perform special gaze movements (Vidal et al. 2013) or to dwell at targets before selecting them (Jacob 1990), implicit systems such as fingerprint sensors and readable insertables should similarly adopt measures to confirm the user's intention. For example, fingerprint sensors can be augmented with other sensors to estimate if the user is intending to authenticate (e.g., by exploiting gaze direction). Systems that read input from insertables should rely on more than just the presence of the insertable in close proximity and instead involve a user action to make it less likely that user's input is interpreted unintentionally (e.g., contracting certain body muscles).

Therefore, important questions that will drive future research are: How can we make sure that the user's implicit action is intended? How can we ensure consent without greatly compromising usability and responsiveness of systems?

5.2 When Users Are Evil—Augmentations Can Be Used Maliciously

In the past, using a technology maliciously required resources (e.g., expensive equipment) and special skills (e.g., programming knowledge). As hardware becomes cheaper, people with limited technical knowledge can use technologies maliciously to spy or cause harm to others. A recent example is the work of Abdelrahman et al. (2017a), which showed that thermal cameras can be used to infer passwords entered on mobile devices. Although they used an algorithm to map the thermal images to PIN and pattern entries, many of the thermal images reveal the user's password through visual inspection by a non-expert attacker. Similarly, the ubiquity of mobile devices means that users are accessing sensitive information in public areas, which in turn means that attackers can potentially gain access to sensitive information by merely shoulder-surfing others (Eiband et al. 2017). This is another attack that does not require any technical expertise.

Human augmentation raises similar concerns. Augmented users will carry cameras and sensors that may allow them to spy on others (e.g., listening to distant conversations as highlighted in chapter 7), infer sensitive information about them without their consent (e.g., revealing their PINs using thermal imaging (Abdelrahman et al. 2017a)), or even harm others (e.g., robotic limbs (Al-Sada et al. 2019) could unintentionally hit bystanders).

An interesting direction for future research is investigating applications of augmentation technologies that are potentially malicious with the goal of identifying privacy and security issues before a technology becomes ubiquitous.

Table 2 Framework for privacy and security assessment of augmentation technologies. The right column describes how the framework could be applied by designers and developers who are aiming to make a commercial product out of the Solo prototype

Part I: Data Handling	Example: Solo
What data is collected?	Audio data, head pose/visual attention
How is data collected?	Microphone/eye tracker or camera to detect head pose
How is data being transmitted?	Over a (secure/insecure) network
Where is data being processed?	In the cloud/on the device
Where is data being stored?	In the cloud/on the device
Part II: Awareness and Consent	
How to communicate to stakeholders that data is being collected?	Visual/audio feedback can be provided to the user and other stakeholders whose privacy and security are impacted
How to communicate to stakeholders that data is being shared?	Visual/audio feedback can be used to communicating this information to the user and stakeholders
Do stakeholders understand what happens to their data?	Investigate how to make the functionality of the system clear to stakeholders
How to obtain informed consent from stakeholders?	While obtaining informed consent from the user can be straightforward, obtaining it from stakeholders, such as bystanders, is more difficult. One way is to make stakeholders aware by, for example, broadcasting notifications to nearby smartphones and smartwatches
Part III: Control Over The Data	
Which types of control do stakeholders have over their data?	Investigate how to allow both the augmented user and stakeholders to access and be able to request deletion of the data that was recorded
How can users request their data being deleted?	The augmented user should be provided with a mechanism (e.g., an app) that allows deletion of collected data. One way to ensure the same for stakeholders is to provide each of them with a link from which they can review, and if desired, delete their data that was collected by the device

6 Towards a Security and Privacy Framework for Technology Augmentation

We complement our exploration of security and privacy implications in the context of human augmentation with presenting a framework. This framework is meant to make the designers of such technologies think of suitable approaches that mitigate issues related to privacy and security.

We envision the framework to be used in the following way. Questions are grouped based on different phases of the design process. In particular, questions relate to how data is being handled (this is relevant as designers create a system architecture), user consent, and control over data (these aspects mainly relate to the user interface). Designers can now answer each question in the context of their design and reflect on whether or not it has been addressed meaningfully.

In the following, we present the questions, alongside a brief explanation for why we think this is relevant. Table 2 summarizes the questions of the framework and demonstrates how it could be applied by designers and developers who aim to make a commercial product out of one of the concepts presented in this book. Note, that in the context of the framework we not only refer to users but more generally to *stakeholders*, since our exploration revealed that also other groups of people, such as bystanders, are affected by augmentation technologies.

6.1 Data Handling

What data is collected?   The purpose of this question is to make designer reflect on the need to collect certain types of data. Whereas some data might be essential for the functionality of the technology, others might serve secondary purposes, such as identifying potential usability issues or help improve a technology or service.

How is data collected?   One important question is how data is collected. While some services might collect data from accessing sensors, other data might be collected from third party services. This is relevant, since it ultimately means that others might have access to sensitive data as well.

How is data being transmitted?   With modeling and machine learning becoming increasingly important and powerful tools, the processing power of devices is often not sufficient. As a result there is a need to transmit data to a server that then executes performance-heavy tasks. At the same time, this poses the risk of data leaking during transmission. Hence, designers need to ensure that data is transferred in a secure manner and neither be intercepted nor manipulated (e.g., by encrypting them).

Where is data being processed?   Closely related to the question above, one question is where data is being processed. From a user perspective it is clearly desireable to process data on their personal device. As this is not possible (e.g., due to limitations in computing power), designers need to think careful where data is being processed and by whom.

Where is data stored?   Data storage is another important aspect. In particular in cases where lots of data is being collected, storage on the device itself might not be possible (think about fine-grained behavioral data or image/video data). In this case, a designer needs to think carefully, where data is being stored and who can access it.

6.2 *Awareness and Consent*

In response to the Lederer's pitfalls in designing for privacy, the following part of the framework postulates that designers carefully think about how users can be made aware of what happens to their data and how consent can be obtained.

How to communicate to stakeholders that data is being collected?   Most fundamentally, stakeholders should be made aware at any point in time, which data
   is collected about them.
How to communicate to stakeholders that data is being shared?   In particular in
   cases where data is shared with third parties, e.g., for processing, there is a need
   to communicate this to stakeholders.
Do stakeholders understand what happens to their data?   One fundamental aspect
   of protecting stakeholders' privacy is comprehension. In particular, designer need
   to make sure that stakeholders are fully aware of what happens to their data.
   Important questions to ask here are whether the stakeholder understands what
   kind of information is shared, with whom it is shared, through which medium it
   is conveyed, where and how it is processed and where it is being stored.
How to obtain informed consent from stakeholders?   According to the GDPR,
   informed consent must be obtained from people once data is made available to
   third parties. Here, designers must make sure to provide suitable means for (a)
   obtaining informed consent and (b) enabling stakeholders to revoke this consent
   at any time.

6.3 *Control over Data*

Finally, designers need to take into consideration how users could be provided control over their data. Means of control need to be realized as part of the user interface of a technology.

Which types of control do stakeholders have over their data?   Beyond requesting
   mere deletion of their data, designers might want to think about providing stakeholders an opportunity to only delete parts of the data. This might be useful specifically for data that are not essential for the functionality of a technology. Enabling
   stakeholders to do so might also be beneficial for the providers of technology,
   since rather than completely opting out of a service or technology, stakeholders
   might only disable the collection of or delete parts of the data stored about them.
How can stakeholders request their data being deleted?   A core principle in GDPR
   is the opportunity to have their data be deleted within 30 d. Designers need to think
   about a way how stakeholders can make this request (in particular, if they are not
   the users) and how the system architecture can be designed in a way to do this
   with minimal effort.

7   Discussion

In the following sections we reflect on the framework, in particular discussing aspects that require further investigation.

7.1   Required Expertise

Our framework is generally targeted at the *designers* of systems augmenting humans. At the same time, employing the framework is likely to require different types of expertise, in particular such that is not available in traditional design processes. For example, to properly design secure transmission or storage of data, experts in network or data security may be required. This need has been recognized by the community (Alt and von Zezschwitz 2019) and is also backed by prior work, showing that software developer often either do not have the required expertise for building secure systems or do not see the need for it Naiakshina et al. (2019).

Another example that becomes particularly apparent with the GDPR is the need for experts, overseeing that data is handled in a privacy-preserving way, e.g., data-protection officers or even lawyers.

7.2   Interplay with Commercial Interest

Another aspect that would be interesting to explore is how our framework interplays with commercial interests. This is particularly important in times, where data is an important currency. Many business models today are based on access and control over user data. As an ever-increasing amount of sensitive data is being used, companies may need to rethink their business models in such a way that these comply with the suggestions put forth by this framework. For example, companies may want to return to traditional pay-per-use or subscription-based business models.

7.3   Need for End User Involvement

Many of the aspects identified in our framework can be addressed by experts, e.g., implementing encryption to ensure secure data transmission. At the same time, there are several aspects that may require the design of novel approaches and, subsequently, the involvement of end users to test these approaches. This is particularly true for aspects that concern the user interface of human augmentation technologies. For example, there is no standard way of communicating to people that data about them is being collected. This strongly depends on the technology and its output modalities.

If the device has a display, it could be used to design an appropriate visualization to communicate to users that data is being collected. In other cases, this need might even require adding additional output technologies, such as an LED, that were previously not part of the product. In order to find out how to best design such novel approaches, designers may need to involve end users and conduct user studies to find out how to optimally design for a certain aspect.

7.4   Influence Beyond the Design Phase

Considering our framework may have consequence beyond the design process. For example, the way in which a company decides to implement ways for users to have control over their data or to request their data being deleted, may require thinking about a support infrastructure or even create the need to hire people that deal with such requests. This might ultimately influence also the business model.

8   Conclusion

In this chapter, we introduced a framework for privacy and security, meant to guides the design of technologies augmenting humans' perception and cognition. The framework was derived from work presented in the chapters of the book.

We first identified the implication of novel technologies on privacy, security, and safety. We found the understanding of consequences of data sharing, control of the data, novel attack channels, the opportunity to leverage such technologies for malicious purposes, data manipulation, and safety to be critical aspects.

The analysis also revealed a need for more research. In particular, future work needs to obtain a better understanding of what can be learned from the stakeholders' data obtained from technologies meant to augment humans' perception and cognition; researchers need to think about how informed consent could be obtained from the stakeholders, both regarding the use of their data as well as regarding user actions; and researchers could focus on understanding how augmentations could be used maliciously and how to mitigate such cases.

Finally, our framework provides three sets of questions that guide the design of secure and privacy-preserving designs of novelx augmentation technologies. Specifically, designers need to carefully consider how they handle data (collecting, processing, storing, sharing), how stakeholders could be made aware of the implications of using the technology, how they could provide consent, and how they can be provided control over their data.

For the future we intend to evaluate the framework with researchers working on augmentation technologies. In particular, we plan to interview them on how the framework helped them in creating concepts, developing a system architecture, and designing their user interfaces.

References

Abdelrahman Y, Khamis M, Schneegass S, Alt F (2017a) Stay cool! Understanding thermal attacks on mobile-based user authentication. In: Proceedings of the 35th annual ACM conference on human factors in computing systems, CHI '17. ACM, New York, NY, USA. https://doi.org/10.1145/3025453.3025461

Abdelrahman Y, Velloso E, Dingler T, Schmidt A, Vetere F (2017b) Proc ACM Interact Mob Wearable Ubiquitous Technol 1(3):33:1–33:20. ISSN 2474–9567: https://doi.org/10.1145/3130898

Abdelrahman Y, Wozniak P, Knierim P, Henze N, Schmidt A (2018) Exploration of alternative vision modes using depth and thermal cameras. In: Proceedings of the 17th international conference on mobile and ubiquitous multimedia, MUM 2018. ACM, New York, NY, USA, pp 245–252. ISBN 978-1-4503-6594-9. https://doi.org/10.1145/3282894.3282920. http://doi.acm.org/10.1145/3282894.3282920

Adams A, Sasse MA (1999) Commun ACM 42(12), 40–46. ISSN 0001–0782. https://doi.org/10.1145/322796.322806

Al-Sada M, Höglund T, Khamis M, Urbani J, Nakajima T (2019) Orochi: investigating requirements and expectations for multipurpose daily used supernumerary robotic limbs. In: Proceedings of the 10th augmented human international conference 2019, AH 2019. ACM, New York, NY, USA, pp 37:1–37:9. ISBN 978-1-4503-6547-5. https://doi.org/10.1145/3311823.3311850

Alt F, von Zezschwitz E (2019) J Interact Med (icom) 18(3). ISSN 1618-162X. https://doi.org/10.1515/icom-2019-0019, http://www.florian-alt.com/?org/unibw/wp-content/publications/alt2019icom.pdf

Andress J (2014) The basics of information security: understanding the fundamentals of InfoSec in theory and practice. Syngress

BBC (2018) Police 'visit funeral home to unlock dead man's phone'. https://www.bbc.co.uk/news/technology-43865109. Accessed 19 Apr 2019

Dodd MD, Hibbing JR, Smith KB (2011) Atten Percept Psychophys 73(1). ISSN 24–29(2011):1943–393X. https://doi.org/10.3758/s13414-010-0001-x

Drewes H, Khamis M, Alt F (2019) Dialplates: enabling pursuits-based user interfaces with large target numbers. In: Proceedings of the 18th international conference on mobile and ubiquitous multimedia, MUM '19, New York, NY, USA. ACM. https://doi.org/10.1145/3365610.3365626

Eiband M, Khamis M, von Zezschwitz E, Hussmann H, Alt F (2017) Understanding shoulder surfing in the wild: stories from users and observers. In: Proceedings of the 35th annual ACM conference on human factors in computing systems, CHI '17. ACM, New York, NY, USA. https://doi.org/10.1145/3025453.3025636

Elagroudy P, Khamis M, Mathis F, Irmscher D, Bulling, A, Schmidt A (2019) Can privacy-aware lifelogs alter our memories? In: Extended abstracts of the 2019 CHI conference on human factors in computing systems, CHI EA '19. ACM, New York, NY, USA, pp LBW0244:1–LBW0244:6. ISBN 978-1-4503-5971-9. https://doi.org/10.1145/3290607.3313052

Harbach M, Von Zezschwitz E, Fichtner A, De Luca A, Smith M (2014) It's a hard lock life: a field study of smartphone (un)locking behavior and risk perception. In: Proceedings of the tenth USENIX conference on usable privacy and security, SOUPS '14. USENIX Association, Berkeley, CA, USA, pp 213–230. ISBN 978-1-931971-13-3. http://dl.acm.org/citation.cfm?id=3235838.3235857

Jacob RJK (1990) What you look at is what you get: eye movement-based interaction techniques. In: Proceedings of the SIGCHI conference on human factors in computing systems, CHI '90. ACM, New York, NY, USA, pp 11–18. ISBN 0-201-50932-6. https://doi.org/10.1145/97243.97246

Katsini C, Abdrabou Y, Raptis G, Khamis M, Alt F (2020) The role of eye gaze in security and privacy applications: survey and future hci research directions. In: Proceedings of the 38th annual ACM conference on human factors in computing systems, CHI '20. ACM, New York, NY, USA. https://doi.org/10.1145/3313831.3376840

Kelley PG, Bresee J, Cranor LF, Reeder RWA (2009) "nutrition label" for privacy. In: Proceedings of the 5th symposium on usable privacy and security, SOUPS '09. ACM, New York, NY, USA, pp 4:1–4:12. ISBN 978-1-60558-736-3. https://doi.org/10.1145/1572532.1572538

Khamis M, Oechsner C, Alt F, Bulling A (2018) Vrpursuits: interaction in virtual reality using smooth pursuit eye movements. In: Proceedings of the 2018 international conference on advanced visual interfaces, AVI '18. ACM, New York, NY, USA. https://doi.org/10.1145/3206505.3206522

Korayem M, Templeman R, Chen D, Crandall D, Kapadia A (2016) Enhancing lifelogging privacy by detecting screens. In: Proceedings of the 2016 CHI conference on human factors in computing systems, CHI '16. ACM, New York, NY, USA, pp 4309–4314. ISBN 978-1-4503-3362-7. https://doi.org/10.1145/2858036.2858417

Korolov M (2016) Army reveals OpenSim's top security risks. https://www.hypergridbusiness.com/2016/10/army-reveals-opensims-top-security-risks/. Accessed 29 Apr 2019

Langheinrich M (2001) Privacy by design-principles of privacy-aware ubiquitous systems. In: Proceedings of the 3rd international conference on ubiquitous computing, UbiComp '01. Springer, Berlin, Heidelberg, pp 273–291. ISBN 3-540-42614-0. http://dl.acm.org/citation.cfm?id=647987.741336

Li Y, Vishwamitra N, Knijnenburg BP, Hu H, Caine K (2017) Proc ACM Hum-Comput Interact, 1(CSCW). 67:1–67:24. ISSN 2573-0142. https://doi.org/10.1145/3134702

Majaranta P, Bulling A (2014) Eye tracking and eye-based human-computer interaction. Springer London, London, pp 39–65. ISBN 978-1-4471-6392-3. https://doi.org/10.1007/978-1-4471-6392-3_3

Mathis F, Khamis M (2019) Privacy, security and safety concerns of using HMDs in public and semi-public spaces. In: Proceedings of the CHI 2019 workshop on challenges using head-mounted displays in shared and social spaces, SHMD '19

Naiakshina A, Danilova A, Gerlitz E, von Zezschwitz E, Smith M (2019) "If you want, i can store the encrypted password": a password-storage field study with freelance developers. In: Proceedings of the CHI conference on human factors in computing systems, CHI '19. Association for Computing Machinery, New York, NY, USA. ISBN 9781450359702. https://doi.org/10.1145/3290605.3300370

Ng A (2018) VR systems Oculus Rift, HTC Vive may be vulnerable to hacks. https://www.cnet.com/news/hack-a-vr-system-lead-a-player-astray-yes-say-researchers/. Accessed 29 Apr 2019

Nielsen J (1994) Enhancing the explanatory power of usability heuristics. In: Proceedings of the SIGCHI conference on human factors in computing systems, CHI '94. ACM, New York, NY, USA, pp 152–158. ISBN 0-89791-650-6. https://doi.org/10.1145/191666.191729

Schneegass S, Steimle F, Bulling A, Alt F, Schmidt A (2014) Smudgesafe: geometric image transformations for smudge-resistant user authentication. In: Proceedings of the 2014 ACM international joint conference on pervasive and ubiquitous computing, UbiComp '14. ACM, New York, NY, USA, pp 775–786. ISBN 978-1-4503-2968-2. https://doi.org/10.1145/2632048.2636090, http://www.florian-alt.org/unibw/wp-content/publications/schneegass2014ubicomp.pdf.schneegass2014ubicomp

Steil J, Hagestedt I, Huang MX, Bulling A (2019a) Privacy-aware eye tracking using differential privacy. In: Proceedings of the 11th ACM symposium on eye tracking research & applications, ETRA '19. ACM, New York, NY, USA, pp 27:1–27:9. ISBN 978-1-4503-6709-7. https://doi.org/10.1145/3314111.3319915

Steil J, Koelle M, Heuten W, Boll S, Bulling A (2019b) Privaceye: privacy-preserving head-mounted eye tracking using egocentric scene image and eye movement features. In: Proceedings of the 11th ACM symposium on eye tracking research & applications, ETRA '19. ACM, New York, NY, USA, pp 26:1–26:10. ISBN 978-1-4503-6709-7. https://doi.org/10.1145/3314111.3319913

Sunshine J, Egelman S, Almuhimedi H, Atri N, Cranor LF (2009) Crying wolf: an empirical study of ssl warning effectiveness. In: Proceedings of the 18th conference on USENIX Security symposium, SSYM '09. USENIX Association, USA, pp 399–416

TheGuardian (2017) Qatar airways plane forced to land after wife discovers husband's affair midflight. https://www.theguardian.com/world/2017/nov/08/qatar-airways-plane-forced-to-land-after-wife-discovers-husbands-affair-midflight. Accessed 19 Apr 2019

Thomaz E, Parnami A, Bidwell J, Essa I, Abowd GD (2013) Technological approaches for addressing privacy concerns when recognizing eating behaviors with wearable cameras. In: Proceedings of the 2013 ACM international joint conference on pervasive and ubiquitous computing, Ubi-Comp '13. ACM, New York, NY, USA, pp 739–748. ISBN 978-1-4503-1770-2. https://doi.org/10.1145/2493432.2493509

Vidal M, Bulling A, Gellersen H (2013) Pursuits: spontaneous interaction with displays based on smooth pursuit eye movement and moving targets. In: Proceedings of the 2013 ACM international joint conference on pervasive and ubiquitous computing, UbiComp '13. ACM, New York, NY, USA, pp 439–448. ISBN 978-1-4503-1770-2. https://doi.org/10.1145/2493432.2493477

W, E. CyberUK (2017) People-the strongest link. https://www.ncsc.gov.uk/blog-post/cyberuk-2017-people-strongest-link. Accessed 25 Apr 2019

West R (2008) Commun ACM 51(4), 34–40. ISSN 0001-0782: https://doi.org/10.1145/1330311.1330320

Whitten A, Tygar JD (1999) Why johnny can't encrypt: a usability evaluation of pgp 5.0. In: Proceedings of the 8th conference on USENIX security symposium, SSYM '99, vol 8. USENIX Association, Berkeley, CA, USA, p 14. http://dl.acm.org/citation.cfm?id=1251421.1251435

Wolf K, Schmidt A, Bexheti A, Langheinrich M (2014) IEEE Pervasive Computing 13(3):8–12. ISSN 1536-1268. https://doi.org/10.1109/MPRV.2014.53

Yee K-P (2005) Guidelines and strategies for secure interaction design. In: Garfinkel S, Cranor L (eds) Security and usability: designing secure systems that people can use, chapter 13. O'Reilly Media, Champaign, IL, USA, pp 253–280

Mohamed Khamis is a Lecturer (Assistant Professor) of Human-centered Security at the School of Computing Science of the University of Glasgow, UK. He received his PhD from Ludwig Maximilian University of Munich. His research focuses on understanding the privacy implications of ubiquitous technologies and on designing usable systems for security and privacy protection.

Florian Alt is a professor of Usable Security and Privacy at the Research Institute CODE of the Bundeswehr University, Munich. His research focuses on the role of humans in security critical systems. He is an active member of the HCI community (SC Chair of CHI 2020 and 2021, TPC Chair of Mensch und Computer 2020). Florian holds a PhD in computer science from the University of Stuttgart.

Summary and Outlook

Evangelos Niforatos and Tilman Dingler

Abstract Evolution has always been the main driving force of change for both the human body and brain. Presently, in the Information era, our cognitive and perceptual capacities cannot merely rely on natural evolution to keep up with the immense advancements in modern technologies. But systems we use daily (e.g. computers, smartphones, etc.) remain mostly unaware about our current state, causing what has been described as the "cognitive gap"—the inability of systems to adapt to the current cognitive and circadian state of the user (Niforatos et al. 2017). In this edited volume, authors contribute ideas and investigations into bridging this gap by bringing the machine (system) closer to the human (user). From improving our working memory, our ability to retain and learn new information to extending our perceptual and executive capabilities with wearable or implantable hardware, modern technologies bear an unprecedented potential to seize the role of natural evolution for humans. One should tread lightly in this "Brave New World" of Human Augmentation, however. In this final chapter, we summarize the key contributions of each chapter in this book, assume a philosophical standpoint over augmentation technologies and share our vision on their future outlook.

1 Memory and Learning

Virtual reality (VR) has been utilized for bolstering neurofeedback: a technique used broadly in electroencephalography (EEG) for teaching self-regulation of brain functions. In chapter The Effect of Neurofeedback Training in CAVE-VR for Enhancing Working Memory, Accoto et al. employed a cave automatic virtual environment (CAVE-VR) during neurofeedback learning for improving the performance of work-

E. Niforatos (✉)
Delft University of Technology, Delft, the Netherlands
e-mail: e.niforatos@tudelft.nl

T. Dingler
University of Melbourne, Melbourne, Australia
e-mail: tilman.dingler@unimelb.edu.au

© Springer Nature Switzerland AG 2021   281
T. Dingler and E. Niforatos (eds.), *Technology-Augmented Perception and Cognition*,
Human–Computer Interaction Series, https://doi.org/10.1007/978-3-030-30457-7_9

ing memory. In particular, they investigated how different levels of vividness may influence working memory performance in a CAVE-VR environment. Results from trials with 21 participants showed that high vividness during neurofeedback training increases neurofeedback performance while bearing positive effects on participants' motivation and concentration levels. Accoto et al. reached the conclusion that further research is necessary for unveiling any long-term effects of prolonged neurofeedback training.

In the era of smartphones and wearable devices, people easily capture information such as pictures and videos on a daily basis, which can help to evoke memories for reminiscing about or remembering a past experience. In chapter Memory Augmentation Through Lifelogging: Opportunities and Challenges, Dingler et al. elaborated on the concept of lifelogging as the practice of documenting life experiences with the use of technology, and in the form of "lifelogs." The authors described several lifelogging technologies from the perspective of capturing and reviewing towards a consolidated memory prosthesis. They described how capturing a Lifelog does not need to be all-encompassing, but works if it combines explicit and implicit recording techniques to support memory. The authors also shared their concerns on data privacy and security as well as on the use of lifelogging cameras in public settings. Finally, they remain optimistic about lifelogging applications and its variants becoming steadily more mainstream to fulfil the human desire for a perfect memory.

As we have seen in chapter Memory Augmentation Through Lifelogging: Opportunities and Challenges, technology has always had a direct impact on what humans remember. However, the increasing reliance on modern technologies and tools may also hinder our innate ability to remember. In chapter Technology-Mediated Memory Impairment, Clinch et al. elaborated on two distinct forms of cognitive risks associated with current and emerging technologies: memory inhibition and memory distortion. In particular, they discussed specific examples of memory inhibition, such as the Google effect, the photo-taking impairment and alteration in spatial memory due to the use of navigation technologies (e.g. GPS). Clinch and her colleagues also considered the likelihood of technology to distort what one remembers, including doctored-evidence effects, the creation of false memories for current or historical affairs ("fake news") and retrieval-induced forgetting. They also reported results from a study of 48 participants, where retrieval-induced forgetting and false memory creations were tested for a real-world experience. The results showed that the participants had limited awareness of manipulations made during the retrieval practice schedule, suggesting that technology could not only alter one's memories but could do so without one becoming aware. From a cyber-security perspective, the authors conclude that it is only a matter of time before parties will exploit the cognitive vulnerabilities of human memory.

Despite the fact that modern technologies bear significant ethical implications and cognitive risks, they have substantially contributed to moving learning outside of the traditional classroom. In chapter Designing Task Resumption Cues for Interruptions in Mobile Learning Scenarios, Schneegass and Draxler introduced the concept of task resumption cues during learning on mobile devices in the wild. The authors described how these cues could come in a wide range of forms and designs with the aim to support users in resuming a mobile learning task. First, through an in-depth literature review, the authors suggested a design space by drawing on 30 publications on task resumption support. In particular, they defined five dimensions: (1) purpose, (2) required attention, (3) timing, (4) interactivity and (5) modality. Next, the authors reported on two focus groups which they organized with HCI experts and users of mobile learning applications, with the aim to identify causes of interruptions and generate design ideas. By combining the two approaches, the authors elicited six design guidelines for supporting researchers and designers in creating effective mobile learning applications.

2   Sensory Enhancements

Apart from our cognitive faculties, technology has started to disrupt how we perceive the world around us by extending our sensing capacities or what is possible with our bodies. Individuals are voluntarily inserting devices into their bodies for non-medical purposes, such as for unlocking a door without using a key. In chapter Insertables: Beyond Cyborgs and Augmentation to Convenience and Amenity, Heffernan et al. introduced the term "insertables" for describing the practice of augmenting one's body beyond "human norms," initially taken up by hobbyists, makers and tinkerers. Gradually, an increasing number of early adopters are interested in the use of insertables from a utilitarian perspective. Heffernan et al. presented a comprehensive summary of the devices utilized as insertables for grasping which use cases are supported, the motivation for using insertables in the first place and how insertable users view themselves. By sharing personal accounts of insertable users, the authors unveiled the progression from individuals using insertable devices for simply augmenting themselves, to gradually becoming "cyborgs." However, the majority of users opt-in for insertables for the convenience and amenity-based purposes provided by these devices. These purposes are for access and authentication, and for storing and sharing information. Only a minority use them for augmentation purposes, which are now known to be edge cases. These are extending senses, supporting human connections, acting as an alternative digital interface and capturing biometric data. Heffernan et al. also explained that as insertables become more mainstream, moving from hobbyists and innovators to early adopters, so does the motivation behind their use. This emerging utilitarian approach to using insertables gradually attenuates any connection to any particular social movement. In turn, this is viewed as a strong indication that augmenting our bodily capacities with hardware is gradually becoming more socially acceptable.

The idea of augmenting our bodies with insertable hardware may be a relatively new one, but humans have been pursuing the amplification and enhancement of perception since the prehistoric era. In chapter Augmented Senses: Evaluating Sensory Enhancement Applications, Kiss and Poguntke provided an overview of scientific work about augmenting the human senses by technological means. They showcased three prototypes that extend the visual, auditory and tactile senses: (1) RainSense–a system that enhances the tactile sense for weather communication, (2) SHEARS–a selective hearing system for enhancing auditory attention and (3) Clairbuoyance–a system for improving orientation in the open sea. The authors shared early insights both from the design and the preliminary evaluation of the three prototypes. They concluded that investigating the perceived usefulness of end-users thoroughly is paramount when designing augmentative technology for mainstream adoption.

3 Reflections

As technology weaves itself deeper into the fabric of our lives, the notion of ownership of the collected data becomes harder to pinpoint. Thus, granting users control over their data becomes increasingly relevant, especially as we are now entering the era of "Augmented Human." In chapter Privacy and Security in Augmentation Technologies, Khamis and Alt proposed a privacy framework that supports designers in conceptualizing augmentation technologies that respect privacy. The framework was created by drawing on the rest of the chapters of this edited volume, and it consists of several groups of questions, intended to guide designers during the different stages of designing novel technologies. The authors focused on the following aspects: data handling, awareness, user consent and the design of the user interface. *Data handling* in particular, is one of the primary pillars of the framework, focusing on the data types collected, how data is collected and transmitted and finally, how data is processed and where. The authors highlighted the importance of understanding the consequences of data sharing, data control and data manipulation. They concluded that novel technologies might yield exciting use cases, but also create novel opportunities for malicious attempts.

4 Philosophical Perspectives

Human history has known three major revolutions: (1) the agricultural one ∼10,000 BC, (2) the industrial one 1760–1840 and (3) the digital one 1950–today. Admittedly, each revolution drastically altered all aspects of human life, impacting our lives from societal structure to life expectancy. It is also remarkable that humanity needed ∼12,000 years to transition from the agricultural to the industrial age, whereas only a century for entering the digital era. The common denominator in all three revolutions seems to have been the introduction of a groundbreaking technological intervention. Thus, technological advancement has an immense and ever-accelerating impact on humanity. It is theorized that the next revolution will lie in biotechnology: changing the very make-up that is the basis of our biological existence. Much has been written in the science fiction literature about genetic enhancements, with ethical debates fluctuating between a mere simmering and outrage (e.g. He Jiankui (Normile 2018)). Modifications will provide advantages for personal extravagance (e.g. insertable piercings), professional advancement (e.g. a boost in intelligence or flippers between the toes) or become necessary enhancements (e.g. from flu shots to adjusting to increasingly toxic air qualities). In fact, Max Tegmark coined the next stage of human existence as "Life 3.0" (Tegmark 2017) with

- Life 1.0 describing our biological origins and progress through evolution.
- Life 2.0 comprising the cultural developments of humanity.
- Life 3.0 as the technological age we find ourselves in now, a stage where we are able to learn and even redesign our own hardware and internal structure (genomics).

The performance artist Stelarc,[1] whose work focuses on extending the capabilities of the human body, puts it this way; *"In this age of body hacking, gene mapping, prosthetic augmentation, organ swapping, face transplants, synthetic skin, what it means to be a body, what it means to be human and what generates aliveness and agency becomes problematic. In the spaces of proliferating Prosthetic Bodies, Partial Life & Artificial Life, the body has become obsolete."* "*What it means to be human is perhaps not to remain human at all. Being human means being curious, experimenting. Not accepting the biological status quo.*"

Bodily augmentations may still require some time before they become mainstream. Digital technologies, however, already extend our cognitive and perceptual capabilities. The immense logging capacities of modern digital technologies generate sheer volumes of data about the entire spectrum of human life. All aspects of human activity may be recorded, processed, monitored and adjusted; logging body movements, financial transactions, health indicators, eating habits, consumption of products, information and media. Ubiquitous data, the term used to describe this highly diverse, readily available and life-descriptive information bears significant implications as we have seen. The potential of ubiquitous data to support our cognitive processes (e.g. memory recall) should not go unnoticed. In fact, Hölderlin's assuring quote may describe this potential accurately: *"But where the danger is, also grows the saving power."*

Often, when developing tools for augmenting cognitive processes, the question comes up whether technology enhances our cognitive aptitude or helps to build and improve innate skills. The difference between these two notions becomes apparent when the tool is removed. Does the skill persist? Clark and Chalmers (1998) coined the term *active externalism* describing the active role our environment plays for our cognitive processes. They argue that cognition is not limited to the physical boundaries of our skull. External objects play a crucial role in cognitive processes, such as memory retrieval, linguistic processes or skill acquisition. For example, we use our fingers to augment our working memory in calculations or use pen and paper to perform multiplications. While the brain is performing operations, it delegates some of its workload to its external environment. Kirsh and Maglio (1994) demonstrated how performing actions in the world could lead to quicker solutions of certain cognitive and perceptual problems than performing them mentally. They showed how physically rotating a shape by 90°, for example, could be done in about 100 ms, plus 200 ms required to press a respective button. In contrast, mentally rotating the

---

[1] http://stelarc.org/projects.php.

shape took about 1000 ms. They distinguished *pragmatic actions*—where the world is altered because some physical change is desirable for its own sake—from *epistemic actions*, in which the world is altered to aid and augment cognitive processes, such as recognition or search, i.e., to understand the world. In the rotating shape example that would mean a person gains knowledge about the world (does the shape fit an appropriate slot?) by pragmatic action (physically rotating the shape) quicker than through epistemic action (rotating the shape in the head). Hence, tools and technologies augment our cognitive processes and our understanding of the world. Obviously, such knowledge gain remains even if the tool is removed. In other tasks, such as performing a tricky calculation, a calculator becomes coupled with the person as a tool. According to Clark and Chalmers (1998) such coupling is considered an externally augmented cognitive process, which is sufficient if the tools (the relevant capacities) are generally available when they are needed: "*In effect, they are part of the basic package of cognitive resources that I bring to bear on the everyday world. These systems cannot be impugned simply on the basis of the danger of discrete damage, loss, or malfunction, or because of any occasional decoupling: the biological brain is in similar danger, and occasionally loses capacities temporarily in episodes of sleep intoxication*" (Clark and Chalmers 1998). Hence, augmented cognition is considered to be a core cognitive process, not an add-on extra.

The increasing spread of ubiquitous computing devices supports this notion. Devices are portable and increasingly wearable, ingrained in our everyday life and therefore near-constantly available. Hence, the functions and support they provide become part of our everyday cognitive processes, including looking up information, jotting down notes and sharing them. The notion of augmented cognition is taken to the next level by some of the ideas and prototypes presented in this edited volume. Cognition-aware (Dingler 2016) and pervasive memory augmentation systems (Niforatos 2018) support the user in-situ according to current abilities and aptitudes. Proactive display of (memory) cues may enhance a memory of the past or invite the user to continue a learning task, and therefore facilitate learning and memory recall. Seamless cognitive support will be ingrained in our everyday life and the cognitive boost we receive through such systems may become so self-evident that it will only be noticed when the system errs or fails.

5 Outlook

At this point, one may ask what is more to come? What would be the work and social context that we would point to or speculate about? At first, wearable devices will be equipped with a wide range of sensors that provide additional information on our cognitive and perceptual processes (Vourvopoulos et al. 2019). Gradually, novel sensors will find their way into our body and brain, where they will augment our cognitive and perceptual processes by mitigating shortcomings, substituting what is missing and extending what is needed. The conglomerate of human senses and skills may well grow to become an app economy in which we can add and update sensors and augmentations at will, targeted to our societal roles and professional requirements. Devices will be fully cognition-aware and adjust to our fitness, alertness, tasks, moods and emotions. In essence, technology will always be there with us when needed and imperceptible when not-truly materializing the vision of ubiquitous and pervasive computing. Health services will be highly proactive and personalized. We will have in-depth insights into our metabolism and follow individualized diets targeted at improving our health state and productivity levels. Ultimately, Brain–Computer Interfaces may become the standard way we interact with computer systems. A merger between human and machine will be made possible by accelerating the human–machine communication throughput. The resulting symbiosis will allow us to reap benefits far beyond our innate perceptual and cognitive abilities, which rather than a nice-to-have may very well become a necessity for basic participation in work and social life.

References

Clark A, Chalmers D (1998) Analysis 58(1):7–19

Cognition-aware systems to support information intake and learning. PhD thesis, University of Stuttgart

Kirsh D, Maglio P (1994) Cognit Sci 18(4):513–549

Niforatos E (2018) The role of context in human memory augmentation. PhD thesis, Università della Svizzera Italiana

Niforatos E, Vourvopoulos A, Langheinrich M (2017) Amplifying human cognition: bridging the cognitive gap between human and machine. In: Proceedings of the 2017 ACM international joint conference on pervasive and ubiquitous computing and proceedings of the 2017 ACM international symposium on wearable computers, pp 673–680

Normile D (2018) For China, a CRISPR first goes too far

Tegmark M (2017) Life 3.0: being human in the age of artificial intelligence. Knopf

Vourvopoulos A, Niforatos E, Giannakos M (2019) Eeglass: an eeg-eyeware prototype for ubiquitous brain-computer interaction. In: Adjunct Proceedings of the 2019 ACM international joint conference on pervasive and ubiquitous computing and proceedings of the 2019 ACM international symposium on wearable computers, pp 647–652

Evangelos Niforatos is an Assistant Professor in Human-AI Interaction at the Faculty of Industrial Design Engineering (IDE), TU Delft, the Netherlands. He received a PhD in Informatics from Universitá della Svizzera italiana (USI), Switzerland in April 2018. He then joined North Inc. (now Google) in Canada as an HCI Research Scientist and Project Lead in the Advanced R&D department. At North Inc., he was part of the team that designed, developed, and successfully launched Focals, the first socially acceptable smart glasses that closely resemble a typical pair of glasses. As a postdoctoral researcher at NTNU in Norway, his research focused on designing and developing "neuroadaptive systems"—systems that augment human perception and cognition. Ultimately, he is interested in building technologies that extend the human capacities.

Tilman Dingler is a Lecturer in the School of Computing and Information Systems at the University of Melbourne. He studied Media Computer Science in Munich, Web Science in San Francisco, and received a PhD in Computer Science from the University of Stuttgart, Germany, in 2016. Tilman is an Associate Editor for the PACM on Interactive, Mobile, Wearable and Ubiquitous Technologies (IMWUT) and serves as Associate Chair for CHI among others. He is co-founder of the SIGCHI Melbourne Local Chapter. Tilman's research focuses on cognition-aware systems and technologies that support users' information processing capabilities.

Printed in the United States
by Baker & Taylor Publisher Services